The Development of the Infant and Young Child

OTHER BOOKS BY THE AUTHOR

The Normal Child: Some Problems of the Early Years and their Treatment, 9th edn.
1987 Edinburgh, *Churchill Livingstone*. Translated into Japanese, Greek, Farsi, Spanish, French, Italian

The Normal School Child: His Problems Physical and Emotional
1964 London, *Heinemann*

Common Symptoms of Disease in Children, 9th edn.
1987 Oxford, *Blackwell Scientific Publications*. Translated into Greek, Spanish, Italian, Japanese, Portuguese and German

Treatment of the Child at Home: A Guide for Family Doctors
1971 Oxford, *Blackwell Scientific Publications*. Translated into Greek

Basic Development Screening — 0–2 years, 3rd edn.
1982 Oxford, *Blackwell Scientific Publications*. Translated into Italian, Greek, Spanish and Japanese

Babies and Young Children: Feeding, Management and Care, 7th edn.
(with C. M. Illingworth)
1983 Edinburgh, *Churchill Livingstone*. Translated into Polish

Lessons from Childhood: Some Aspects of the Early Life of Unusual Men and Women
(With C. M. Illingworth)
1966 Edinburgh, *Churchill Livingstone*. Translated into Japanese

The Child at School: A Paediatrician's Manual for Teachers
1974 Oxford, *Blackwell Scientific Publications*. Translated into Italian

Your Child's Development in the First Five Years (Patient Handbook)
1981 Edinburgh, *Churchill Livingstone*

Infections — and immunisation of your child (Patient Handbook)
1981 Edinburgh, *Churchill Livingstone*

The Development of the Infant and Young Child

NORMAL AND ABNORMAL

R. S. Illingworth

MD FRCP DPH DCH
Hon MD Sheffield, Hon DSc Baghdad, Hon DSc Leeds
Emeritus Professor of Child Health, The University of Sheffield;
Formerly Paediatrician, The Children's Hospital, Sheffield and
the Jessop Hospital for Women, Sheffield

NINTH EDITION

CHURCHILL LIVINGSTONE
EDINBURGH LONDON MELBOURNE AND NEW YORK 1987

CHURCHILL LIVINGSTONE
Medical Division of Longman Group UK Limited

Distributed in the United States of America by
Churchill Livingstone Inc., 1560 Broadway, New
York, N.Y. 10036, and by associated companies,
branches and representatives throughout the world.

First Edition   1960
Second edition   1963
Third edition   1966
  Japanese edition   1968
Fourth edition   1970
Fifth edition   1972
Sixth edition   1975
  French edition   1978
  Polish edition   1978
  Japanese edition   1979
Seventh edition   1979
  Spanish edition   1983
Eighth edition   1983
  Italian edition   1986
Ninth edition   1987
  Reprinted   1990

ISBN 0 443 038406

British Library Cataloguing in Publication Data
Illingworth, Ronald S.
    The development of the infant and young child —
    9th ed.
    1. Children — Growing
    I. Title
    612'.652   RJ131

Library of Congress Cataloging in Publication Data
Illingworth, Ronald Stanley, 1909–
    The development of the infant and young child.
    Includes index.
    1. Child development. 2. Child development
    deviations. 3. Child development — Testing. I. Title.
    [DNLM: 1. Child development. 2. Growth. WS 103
    129d]
    RJ131.175   1987 612'.65   83–1945

Produced by Longman Singapore Publishers (Pte) Ltd.
Printed in Singapore

Preface to the Ninth Edition

In preparing this new edition I have repeatedly read every word of the previous one. I have made a more rational arrangement of chapters. Many sections have been completely rewritten, including the value and importance of developmental assessment, the different approaches of psychologist and clinician to the method of assessment, the essential principles of developmental diagnosis, the range of normality, the fallacies in norms of development, prenatal factors, the prognosis of very low birth weight infants, the prediction of mental superiority, and the problems of learning disorders and brain damage. Summaries have been added to several chapters. Great care has been taken to make the index comprehensive.

I have throughout tried to include useful and helpful references, deleting some old ones, and adding over 130 new ones, though trying to keep the number down to a mimimum for reasons of space.

Once more reviewers have criticised me for not including the pathology of disease, physical development, laboratory investigation and treatment of disease. But it was never my intention to include those: it would involve very considerable lengthening of the book, making it run into two or three volumes. The whole purpose of this book has always been to try to help in the understanding and basis of normal development, the reasons for variations, the methods of establishing developmental diagnosis, and the avoidance of pitfalls in diagnosis and prediction. This has been based on many years of experience since I was taught the rudiments by Arnold Gesell and Catherine Amatruda, who enabled me to continue to learn in subsequent decades.

I have throughout tried to make this a practical book on the method of developmental diagnosis.

Sheffield, 1987   R.S.I.

Preface to the First Edition

A thorough knowledge and understanding of the normal development of the infant and young child is just as fundamental to anyone concerned with the care of children, especially paediatricians, as is anatomy to the surgeon. Family doctors, paediatricians and others must know the normal, and the variations from the normal, before they attempt to diagnose the abnormal. I doubt whether a paediatrician will complete any out-patient clinic without having had to make at least one developmental assessment. Without such an assessment he is unable to make a proper diagnosis, to arrange proper treatment, and to help the parents or family doctor or school medical officer as much as he should.

The doctor inevitably has to assess the development of every baby which he sees in a well baby clinic, for otherwise he is not doing his job properly; he could not hope to diagnose the abnormal, to detect the early signs of cerebral palsy or of mental subnormality, or a hearing or visual defect, of subluxation of the hip, or of hydrocephalus, unless he were first conversant with the normal and then looked for the variations from the normal. In the hospital ward one does not carry out a developmental examination on an ill child with bronchopneumonia, and in a private house one does not assess the development of every young child with asthma; but in both places there are innumerable circumstances in which a developmental examination is essential, and without it the examination is seriously incomplete.

It is because I regard developmental assessment as an essential part of everyday practice that I wrote this book, in order to describe just what can be learnt about a child's development with a minimum of equipment in an ordinary mixed clinic, and not in a special room, at a special time, or with special complicated equipment. Everyone dealing with children needs this knowledge. It is not just the province of an expert who does nothing else.

Because I am convinced that the best assessment must be based on a full consideration of prenatal, perinatal and environmental factors which affect development, and on a careful developmental history, I have written separate chapters on these matters. I have placed particular emphasis on the normal variations which occur in all fields of development, and on the reasons for these variations. I have repeatedly emphasised the difficulties in developmental assessment, and the reasons why assessments in infancy can never have a high correlation with intelligence tests in older children, and still less with success in later life. I have discussed in detail the reasons for the limitations in developmental testing. Perhaps the most important chapter is the last one — on the pitfalls in developmental assessment.

The limitations and fallacies must be known and understood. There is a rapidly increasing interest in the physiology and pathology of pregnancy in relation to the fetus, and attempts to correlate events in pregnancy with the development of the infant are liable to give entirely fallacious results unless the difficulties of developmental testing, its possibilities and its limitations, are fully understood. As in other kinds of research, one must avoid the mistake of making accurate analyses of inaccurate data.

This book does not attempt to discuss the normal physical and emotional development of the child. I have confined the book to the study of the infant and preschool child.

I wish to express my gratitude to Arnold Gesell and Catherine Amatruda, above all others, for giving me the privilege to work under them and for teaching me the fundamentals of child development, so that I could then continue to learn for the rest of my working life.

R.S.I.

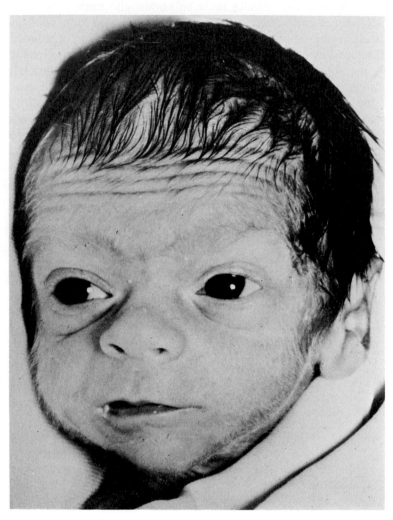

'What does the future hold?' (A normal preterm baby.)

CONTENTS

1

Developmental testing: an overview

The development of mental testing

I propose to give a brief outline of the development of mental testing. For a more complete account the reader should refer to textbooks of Psychology.

Studies of individual children

According to Goodenough, Tiedemann in Germany (1787) was the first to publish a detailed record of the development of one child, but it was not until Charles Darwin[8] in 1877 published a detailed account of the development of one of his own 10 children that interest was aroused. Charles Darwin wrote: 'My first child was born on December 27th, 1839, and I at once commenced to make notes on the first dawn of the various experiences which he exhibited, for I felt convinced, even at this early period, that the most complex and fine shades of expression must all have had a gradual and natural origin.' He described the rooting reflex, hearing in the newborn period, the absence of tears in the first few weeks except when his coat sleeve accidentally caught his child's eye, the first coordinated movements of the hands at 6 weeks, the cephalocaudal sequence of development, the reciprocal kick, hand regard at 4 months, the first sign of anger (at 10 weeks), of humour (at 3 months), of fear, imitation and of enjoyment of the sound of the piano (at 4 months). He described the first association of a person with her name (at 7 months), the first signs of jealousy, love, curiosity, association of ideas, deceit, moral sense, inhibitions, laughter, shyness, sympathy and handedness. He had already published his famous and fascinating book *The Expression of the Emotions in Man and Animals*,[7] which incorporated some of these and many other observations on crying, sobbing, laughter and other emotions.

In 1893 Shinn published one of the most complete records of a young baby's development. In 1931 Shirley wrote an extremely full account of 25 children in their first 2 years.

Developmental tests — historical aspects

According to Bayley[1], Binet's original aim was to identify children who were unlikely to benefit from regular school instruction. Binet emphasised that test scores did not imply that all 'intelligence' is inherited, or that a low score merely indicates poor innate endowment, or that environmental factors were irrelevant. In 1912 Stern and Kuhlman suggested that a child's relative status could be indicated by a ratio between his mental age and his chronological age — the intelligence quotient.

In the early part of this century Arnold Gesell, while studying mentally defective children, began to think about the early signs of mental deficiency and so set about the study of the normal infant. In 1925 he established 'norms' on a small series of children, seen at monthly intervals: later he revised the norms on a large number of children. A large series of books followed, of which I consider the most valuable today are *Developmental Diagnosis*,[23] and *Biographies of Child Development*. These established 'norms' of development, describing the development of infants and children from just after the newborn period to the age of 5 years. The philosophy of development, the technique of developmental testing and the interpretation of results are all discussed in detail in his books. Knobloch and Pasamanick[23] and Knobloch and colleagues[24] brought Gessell and Amatruda's book up to date. In 1933 Bayley[1] established 'norms' on a large number of children. In 1954 Ruth Griffiths[15] tested 571 children aged 14 days to 24 months — up to 31 children in each monthly period. In 1967 the Denver study[11,12] was published, based on a sample of over 1000 children, a sample, however, which was 'selected' and not representative of the country as a whole. A revised and abbreviated Denver screening test, taking 5–7 minutes, was later described.[13]

In Scandinavia the Boel tests have proved popular, and have been used in Denmark, Holland and Italy.[21] The word Boel is an acronym for the Swedish 'blicken orienterar efter ljud' — 'look orients after sound' — and is a test for the visual, auditory and tactile sense, intended for infants aged 7–9 months. A red object is used to attract visual attention, and four bells attached to the tester's fingers attract auditory attention.

The Brazelton and Dubowitz tests for the screening of the newborn are discussed in Chapter 11.

The importance of knowledge of normal development

A thorough knowledge of the normal should be just as much the basis of the study of children as is physiology and anatomy for medicine in general. It is an essential basis for the study of the abnormal and of disease. I believe that all concerned with the care and management of children should not only know the normal, but should be thoroughly conversant with the very common normal variations, which do not amount to disease, and, just as important, should try to understand the reasons for those variations. In this book I have tried to discuss these matters in detail.

The value of developmental assessment

Every parent wants to know whether his child is developing normally, especially if in a previous pregnancy there had been a miscarriage or still-birth, or if the child had proved to be mentally or physically handicapped. If there was an infection, toxaemia or other illness in pregnancy, or diffi-culty delivery, it would be natural for parents to be anxious to know whether their new baby is developing normally. A family history of mental subnormality, cerebral palsy or other handicap would heighten their anxiety. An elderly mother, with no other children, who has lost her husband or is separated from him, is likely to be unduly concerned about her child's development.

Developmental assessments of infants provide important information to the obstetrician with regard to the safety of special investigations, treatment and management in pregnancy or labour. The safety of in vitro fertilisation, chorionic villi sampling, amniocentesis and ultrasound, the safety of older drugs, such as anticoagulants, and of newer drugs in pregnancy, the management of infections, illnesses, hypertension and toxaemia, the advis-ability of preterm induction of labour and the risks of postmaturity, the assessment of newer methods of fetal monitoring and of problems arising in labour, all depend largely on the effect on the fetus and his development after birth.

Developmental assessments provide vital information for the neonatol-ogist, who has to face difficult ethical problems with regard to the resusci-tation of very low birthweight babies or of the infant thought to have suffered serious perinatal brain damage. He has to assess the risks of methods of management and treatment in the intensive care unit. A neo-natologist must be more than a skilful technician: he must follow up and assess the product of his handiwork.

The surgeon may need a developmental assessment when faced with the ethical problem of deciding whether he is justified in embarking on exten-sive or risky surgery for some major congenital anomaly when he suspects that a baby is seriously mentally subnormal. He may also need to obtain follow-up findings on mental development after specialised surgery for such conditions as craniostenosis, subdural effusion, or the use of hypothermia in surgery for congenital heart disease.

The paediatrician needs to be able to assess a baby's mental development when faced with sucking and swallowing problems in the newborn, back-wardness in any field of development, or with a child of unusual appearance or behaviour. He may well be the first to recognise malnutrition, emotional deprivation, or child abuse — and later he will need to assess the results of such problems — so that he can determine how much of the damage is reversible.

By his full developmental examination he is able to make an early diagnosis of defects of vision or hearing, of subluxation of the hip or other handicaps which are treatable, and for which early diagnosis is important. In the older infant or preschool child he should detect features such as clumsiness, or features of learning disorders, whose recognition is important for the school teacher.

The paediatrician needs developmental assessment to observe the effect of treatment of metabolic disorders, exposure to toxic substances, convulsions, meningitis and many conditions which may cause brain damage. By his developmental and physical examination he makes an early diagnosis of handicap, not only for treatment, but for the purpose of counselling the parents. Later he will need his knowledge of development for the purpose of assessing educational needs and choice of school.

In order to make a decision about suitability for adoption, developmental assessment is essential: but it must be made by an expert, and not by a doctor inexperienced in the field. It is a tragic disaster if an infant is labelled as unsuitable for adoption, when he is normal (Ch. 17); and it is tragic for parents if an infant is said to be normal, when he is seriously handicapped. Any diagnosis of mental subnormality should be made only by an expert. Though parents usually like to be informed as soon as possible if a child is handicapped, it is a mistake even to air one's suspicion to the parents unless one is sure, for it would cause untold anxiety. (But for telling adopting parents, see Chapter 17.) Not only do errors in developmental assessment cause great anxiety and unhappiness, but they may lead to unnecessary investigation and treatment.

Developmental assessment is frequently of great importance for medico-legal purposes. Numerous claims are made against doctors or hospitals, on the grounds that a child's mental or physical handicap was caused by brain damage arising from negligence when he is found to be mentally subnormal or to have cerebral palsy; a plaintiff may blame the obstetrician for causing it during labour or delivery. The paediatrician needs to know the relevant prenatal factors which tell a different story. A carefully written contemporaneous record of prenatal conditions, of proper management in pregnancy, of fetal monitoring in labour, and of skilled management after birth, may go a long way to the disposal of an unjustified claim. A plaintiff may ascribe a child's handicap, epilepsy or other disability, to vaccine damage, improper management of meningitis or hydrocephalus or other condition. Of even greater importance is the written evidence that before the vaccine or other assumed cause of the handicap, there were already firm indications of mental subnormality or other neurological deficit. For instance, a head circumference at birth, unusually small in relation to weight, or subsequent developmental lag or defective growth of head size, before the vaccine was given, would indicate a pre-existing mental abnormality. Well-kept notes by the obstetrician, neonatologist, paediatrician, clinic doctor or health visitor may provide vital evidence in the law court.

Screening or specialist assessment?

I have no doubt that the developmental assessment by an expert is of great value; but the expert is likely only to see those children who are referred to him by another person, because there is some doubt about a child's normality. I believe that very rough developmental screening should be part of the examination of any infant and young child (except when he is ill, as with an acute infection). In Chapter 5 I have tried to summarise a few of the most important milestones and the ages at which they are usually passed; if they are not, the child should be referred for an expert opinion. Elsewhere I have summarised the minimal but essential items for screening.[18] It is doubtful[4] whether more detailed universal screening of all infants by purely objective tests is useful.

I have repeatedly found that reasonably intelligent parents, when they have become anxious about some aspect of their child's development, often have a good idea of how far the child has developed as compared with the average. Several papers reached the same conclusion.[6,22] I am doubtful whether it is wise to give parents a questionnaire about their child's development, to be filled in by them,[14] because of the danger that they would misinterpret the development, and experience unnecessary worry as a result. I have tried to avoid this danger by explaining for parents the essentials of development and the normal variations which are so common.[17,19]

PSYCHOLOGIST OR CLINICIAN? DIFFERENT ATTITUDES

Psychologists and clinicians have a different approach to developmental diagnosis. The psychologist (and often the clinician), wants a unitary figure or score for his assessment. The psychologist seeks scientific accuracy, and therefore purely objective tests irrespective of the history (for example, of preterm delivery), and irrespective of the physical examination. He eschews diagnosis by clinical impression, which is so liable to be wrong. He can only use scorable items of behaviour. He pays little attention to the complexities of human development, and the multitude of factors, other than innate intelligence, scoring them on a pass or fail basis. All items of development are likely to be rated as of equal importance. Ruth Griffiths, for instance, in her popular development testing scheme, scored each of five fields of development, added them, and divided by five, to obtain a final score, which is then compared with the age to give the intelligence quotient (IQ). As Knobloch and Pasamanik wrote in their discussion[23] this IQ score is likely to be based largely on verbal and problem tests. They comment that it leads to the fallacy of regarding intelligence as a global entity, which does not differentiate the various types of intelligence, giftedness or disability.

The clinician bases his diagnosis on the history, the physical and developmental examination, special investigations where relevant, and on his interpretation of the result. He needs all this because there are numerous factors, prenatal, perinatal and postnatal, which profoundly affect development, and are unrelated to the mental endowment with which he was born.

In order to try to understand development, one must know the innumerable factors which affect it. Hence in Chapter 2 I have outlined the many prenatal or perinatal factors which are highly relevant to a developmental diagnosis; and in Chapter 3 I have outlined the many environmental and other postnatal factors which are essential to understanding. For instance, one needs to know about various aspects of the home environment. If a mother keeps her baby off his feet (in the mistaken idea that if he bears weight on the legs, he may develop rickets, knock knee or bow legs), then on examination one would find that his weight-bearing is unusually poor in relation to his age: but it does not reflect the baby's intellectual potential.

The clinician will try to assess, from the mother's story, the rate of development — because he wants to know if it is steady, slowing down or accelerating — and he wants to know various other aspects of development which she has observed, so that he can check his own objective findings against the mother's observations. He needs to know about genetic factors, preterm delivery, illnesses in pregnancy or illnesses experienced by the child, drug-taking in pregnancy or drugs taken by the child, the amount of stimulation which she gives the child — and numerous other important factors. In Chapter 8 I have discussed the details of history-taking.

The clinician will conduct a full physical examination of the child in order to determine whether there are conditions such as a visual or auditory defect, cerebral palsy or hypotonia, which will greatly affect development, but which is not directly related to his inborn intellectual endowment. The physical examination will include the measurement of the maximum head circumference in relation to his weight (Ch. 9). This is of vital importance in many developmental assessments.

The clinician will perform a full detailed developmental examination in all fields. Chapter 4 discusses the normal features of the newborn, and Chapter 5 the normal features after the newborn period.

Apart from his need for a detailed knowledge of normal development, he must understand the normal variations which are so common (Chs 6 and 7). In Chapter 12 I have discussed the method of developmental testing in the older infant and child.

In Chapter 13 I have discussed the interpretation of the results of all the above findings — the history, physical and developmental examination, and any tests which were done. The clinician will pay far more attention to some fields of development (e.g. responsiveness, alertness, concentration) than to others (especially gross motor development). He will then be in a position to determine how far the child has developed in relation to the average for his age, and so will arrive at the developmental quotient (DQ) — not necessarily in overall development, but often in separate fields of development. He knows, in arriving at such a score or scores, that the DQ is not static, but that it will be profoundly affected in the future by innumerable environmental factors, health, nutrition, the quality of the home, friends and school.

PREDICTIVE VALUE

Many psychologists insist that developmental assessment in infancy is of little or no value. Many studies have shown that there is only a slight correlation between tests in infancy and early childhood and later IQ scores. Yang,[26] for instance, reviewing the Gesell, Cattell, Bayley and Piaget tests, concluded that 'they have proved to be systematically poor predictors of later performance'. It has been suggested that the IQ of the parents is a better measure of a child's potential than tests in infancy.

I have indicated my view as to the reasons for these negative findings. Nearly all the studies were based on purely objective scorable tests which are of much less importance than other aspects of development which are difficult to score. Many of the items used have been inadequately defined (e.g. 'walks well'): most of the studies have excluded all children who are the most likely to have a mental handicap — the very ones in which developmental assessment is the easiest, and in which there is likely to be a high correlation between scores in infancy and later IQ tests: and the studies have ignored highly relevant factors, such as preterm delivery, environmental factors, physical and sensory handicaps, head size in relation to weight, and risk factors, such as the presence of other congenital anomalies. Clarke[5] wrote that 'the rather poor long term predictions of normal development (except extreme, e.g. autism) are not inadequacies in our methods of assessment, but in development itself'.

I believe that one of the reasons for the low correlation between test results in infancy and subsequent findings is exclusion of numerous categories of children in the establishment of norms.[20] I have never understood the logic of establishing norms on a highly selected group of children — and in the process excluding the very children in whom prediction of future potential is so important, and in which prediction is so much easier than in the average child.

Arnold Gesell's norms were based only on Caucasian children from an apparently homogeneous group of parents of similar socioeconomic class. Children with a history of birth injury or other disease, or those who on follow-up were found to be abnormal, were excluded. The Denver Group[12] excluded preterm or breech-born infants or children with a physical defect. Bayley[1] chose for her norms a highly selected group of children from

University parents: the mean IQ of the children at 9 years was 129. Beintema[2] excluded all with low birthweight, preterm or otherwise, non-
Caucasian children, all with physical abnormalities or serious noeonatal
disease. Brazelton[3] was even more rigorous in exclusions. He did not
include non-Caucasian children, preterm infants, those weighing 3175 g or
less at birth, children born to mothers who had been given barbiturates,
or had had possible intrauterine problems, children who needed special care
in the newborn period or who had experienced some hypoxia. The Kansas
Group[16] excluded all with marked delay in one developmental area as
compared with other areas. Others excluded twins. It follows that the
norms were based on a specially selected group of children who were not
representative of the population as a whole. It is not clear to me how those
excluded could then be assessed. If one were to conduct a survey of
haemoglobin levels in preschool children, it would seem irrational to
exclude all children at risk of anaemia — those born preterm, all coloured
children, and all with malnutrition and all from social class five.

Others workers, especially those who have taken other relevant factors
into account, have found that developmental tests in infancy are of value.
Siegel, for instance,[25] in a study of 80 preterm infants and 68 full-term
infants, found significant correlation between Bayley tests at 4, 8, 12 and
18 months with cognitive and language development at 2 years: he wrote
that 'infant tests, in conjunction with assessment of the child's environment, appear to be useful in predicting developmental functioning and
delay at two years'.

I have summarised elsewhere the rationale of Arnold Gesell's philosophy
of development. I wrote: 'It would seem reasonable to suppose that if
careful detailed observation were made of the course of development of a
sufficiently large number of babies, record being made of the age at which
various skills were learned, it should be possible to establish some relationship between records so obtained and their subsequent progress through
childhood. Though it is impossible to say what is 'normal', there is no
difficulty in defining the 'average', and it should be easy to determine the
sequence and rate of growth of the average child and to note the frequency
with which deviations from the usual growth pattern occur as a result of
known or unknown factors. Having determined the developmental pattern
of average children, it should be possible to determine whether an individual child has developed as far as the average one of his age, taking into
account all factors which might have affected his development. By making
further examinations at intervals in order to assess his rate of development,
and by taking into account all possible factors in the child and his environment which might affect the future course of his development, one ought
to be able to make a reasonable prediction of his future progress provided
that one knows the frequency of abnormal growth patterns. Arnold Gesell
and his staff at the Yale Clinic of Child Development made much studies
for 40 years or more, and they were convinced that such prediction is in

fact possible.' By 1930 Gesell estimated that he and his staff had examined more than 10 000 infants at numerous age periods. He wrote that 'attained growth is an indicator of past growth processes and a foreteller of growth yet to be achieved'. He emphasised the 'lawfulness of growth', and said that 'where there is lawfulness there is potential prediction'. He constantly called for caution in attempting to predict a child's future development, because of all the variables concerned. To use his words: 'Diagnostic prudence is required at every turn', and 'so utterly unforeseen are the vicissitudes of life that common sense will deter one from attempting to forecast too precisely the development career of any child.'

I cannot agree that it is is only the severe cases of mental subnormality which can be diagnosed in infancy. In a study at Sheffield we followed up 135 children who were considered at any time in the first 2 years of life to be mentally retarded, however slightly. Cases of Down's syndrome, hypothyroidism, hydrocephalus and anencephaly were excluded. In 10 of the children the mental retardation was of postnatal origin, and in the others it was of prenatal or natal origin. Apart from these exclusions, the cases were in no way selected, in that we included all children thought by me or my staff to be retarded — even though one or two very shortly after the initial assessment were subsequently thought to have reverted to normal. The initial diagnosis was based on a clinical assessment in the out-patient department, using some of the Gesell tests, with full consideration of the developmental history and other data. All but two of the survivors were traced and re-examined, using for the most part Terman and Merrill tests at the age of 5 years or later. All but five of them were retarded. In 77 the initial diagnosis was made in the first year, and in 59 it was made in the second year. A total of 34 had died. In all 10 on whom autopsies were performed, gross anomalies of the brain were present.

Of the 101 survivors who were traced, 59 on follow-up examination were seriously subnormal (IQ score below, 50), 25 had an IQ score of 50 to 75, 13 had an IQ score of 76 to 94, and four had an IQ score of 100 or more. I have referred to those in Chapters 6 and 7. Of 67 who were thought to be severely subnormal in infancy, 55 on follow-up examination were found to be seriously subnormal (ESN.S.) Of 20 who were regarded as only slightly retarded in infancy, only two on follow-up examination were found to be seriously subnormal.

The figures indicate that mental subnormality can be confidently diagnosed in the first 2 years, apart from the obvious forms such as Down's syndrome. For practical purposes this is the most important function of developmental tests. It does not matter much whether a baby has a developmental quotient of 110 or 130: but it matters a great deal for purposes of adoption if his developmental quotient, being 70 or less, suggests that the child is going to be mentally subnormal in later years.

At the Children's Hospital, Sheffield, infants were examined every week for the purpose of assessment for suitability for adoption. They were seen by me personally in their first year, at the age of 6 weeks or 6 months. On the basis of tests described in this book they were graded as follows:

Grade 1   Possibly above average
      2   Average
      3   Possibly below average
      4   Inferior

When they reached school age they were examined by psychologists or School Medical Officers (who knew nothing of my grading), IQ test scores being made on the basis of Terman and Merrill and other methods. The following were the mean IQ scores at school for each of the grades allotted in infancy. The total number of children followed up and tested at school age was 230. Five additional babies could not be followed up because of emigration or because they could not be traced: otherwise the series was complete. Table 1 shows the grades allotted in infancy and the mean IQ at age 5 to 8 years.

Table 1   Grading in infancy in relation to IQ at school age

Grading allotted in infancy	Total	Mean IQ at 5–8 years
1	69	111.5
2	92	108.0
3	54	94.9
4	15	76.0

Table 2 shows the scores allotted in infancy to children who proved later to have a high or low IQ score.

Table 2   Grading in infancy in relation to IQ at school age

Grade in first year	1 Total 69	2 Total 92	3–4 Total 69
IQ at school			
Below 80	1 (1.5%)	1 (1.1%)	
Over 120		1 (1.5%)	

Only one child placed in Grade 1 and one in Grade 2 subsequently had an IQ below 80 (actually 79 and 69 respectively). One child in Grade 3 had an IQ of 132. The differences between Grades 2 and 3, and 3 and 4 were significant at the 0.1% level.

It should be noted that in the earlier part of this investigation the assessment was rendered more difficult by the fact that the infants had been in an institution for the first 6 months of their life, and came direct from it, so that there was the factor of emotional deprivation which would have retarded their development. It was not possible to decide how much retardation had been caused by this factor and how much of it would be reversible. The institution was subsequently closed, the infants being placed in foster homes at the age of 9 or 10 days. The figures support the contention that mental inferiority can be diagnosed more easily than mental superiority. One is more likely to underestimate potential than to overestimate it.

Others have made similar observations. A Johns Hopkins study[10] indicated that a trained pediatrician can accurately diagnose developmental disabilities before the age of 12 months: there was a good correlation between the early diagnosis of cerebral palsy and mental subnormality in the first year with subsequent findings. There were very few false diagnoses. Others[9] showed that CNS signs in the first year correlate with learning problems at school at 7 years of age.

I have little statistical evidence from my own work that mental superiority can be diagnosed with reasonable confidence in infancy. Some of the workers quoted have adduced evidence to that effect. But the fact that mental retardation can be diagnosed in infancy indicates that developmental tests, in this important practical matter at least, do have a definite predictive value.

Knobloch rightly pointed out that the principal function of developmental tests in infancy is the detection of abnormal neurological conditions and of subnormal developmental potential. She added that these tests are not intended to detect mental superiority or precise IQ scores later. Although a small percentage may be considered superior, the question of whether they remain so depends on their later experiences. She added that: 'As clinicians we would feel that an examination which would allow us to make the following statement is an eminently acceptable and useful tool. This infant has no neurologic impairment, and his potential is within the healthy range: depending on what his life experiences are between now and 6 years of age, he will at that time have a Stanford-Binet IQ above 90, unless qualitative changes in the central nervous system are caused by noxious agests, or gross changes in milieu alter major variables of function', and: 'The studies that we have done indicate that when care is taken to eliminate bias and the infant examination is used as a clinical neurological tool by a physician adequately trained in its use, good correlations are obtained. These studies have not been challenged by the critics of infant evaluation: they have merely been ignored.'

Developmental prediction. What we can and cannot do

Everyone who attempts to assess the development of babies should be fully conversant with the limitations of developmental prediction. Below I have summarised what we can hope to do, and what we must not expect to be able to do.

What we can do (but not necessarily in the earliest weeks), is as follows:

1. We can say how far a baby has developed in relation to his age, and we can therefore compare him with the average performance of others at

that age; and we can say something about his rate of development. By so doing we can say something about his developmental potential.

2. We can diagnose moderate or severe mental subnormality.

3. We can diagnose moderate or severe cerebral palsy.

4. We can assess muscle tone.

5. We can diagnose moderate or severe deafness.

6. We can diagnose moderate or severe visual defects.

7. We can diagnose subluxation or dislocation of the hip.

8. We can diagnose neurological defects in infancy.

9. As a result of our developmental and neurological examination, we are in a better position to give genetic counselling.

What we cannot do is as follows:

1. We cannot draw a dividing line between normal and abnormal. All that we can say is that the further away from the average the child is in anything, the more likely he is to be abnormal.

2. We cannot make accurate predictions of his future intelligence and achievements, because these will be profoundly affected by environmental and other factors in the future. There never will be a high correlation between developmental assessment in infancy and subsequent intellectual achievement.

3. We cannot eliminate the possibility that he will undergo mental deterioration in future months or years.

4. If he has suffered severe emotional deprivation before we assess him, we cannot assess at one examination the extent of the damage which he has suffered, or its reversibility.

5. If he is retarded and has no microcephaly, we cannot be sure that he is not a slow starter (delayed maturation).

6. If he was a low birthweight baby, and we do not know the duration of gestation, we cannot tell after the newborn period whether we should allow for prematurity or not — though the motor nerve conduction time will guide us in this.

7. We cannot make a sensible prediction for a full-term baby at birth or in the first 4 weeks unless there are grossly abnormal signs; and still less can we made a valid assessment of a prematurely born baby until after due correction for prematurity he has reached at least 4–6 weeks of age. For instance, if he were born 8 weeks prematurely, it would be unwise to assess him until at least 12 to 14 weeks after delivery.

8. We cannot rely on diagnosing mild cerebral palsy or mild mental subnormality in the early weeks.

9. If we find abnormal neurological signs in the first few weeks we cannot be sure unless they are gross that they will not disappear; and if they disappear, we cannot be sure that when he is older, at school age, the finer tests of coordination and spatial appreciation then available will not show that there are in fact some residual signs, such as clumsiness. The older the

infant, the less likely it is that abnormal signs will disappear, and after the first year it is unlikely that they will be anything but permanent.

10. We cannot eliminate in infancy the possibility that he child will subsequently display specific learning disorders, or difficulties of spatial appreciation.

11. We cannot translate into figures Gesell's 'insurance factors' — the baby's alertness, interest in his surroundings, social responsiveness, determination and powers of concentration — features which are of much more predictive value than the readily scorable items, such as gross motor development or sphincter control. Without special equipment we cannot score the quality of his vocalisations — and they are important.

12. We cannot say what he will do with his talents or with what we have termed his developmental potential. (See Ch. 13).

13. We cannot prove, in any but exceptional cases, that a child's mental or neurological deficits are due to birth injury rather than to prenatal causes.

14. We cannot normally predict mental superiority.

Finally, it must be remembered that there are many aspects of ability; they include verbal, numerical, spatial, perceptual, memorising, reasoning, mechanical and imaginative qualities. It would hardly be likely that tests in infancy would detect these with a high degree of reliability.

Dangers of developmental assessment

I wrote elsewhere that many people are now assessing babies without knowing why they are doing it, how to do it, or what to do when they have done it. I would now add that many do not realise what harm they can do by developmental assessment.

One obvious danger is a wrong diagnosis — consisting either of passing a baby as normal when he is not, or incorrectly saying that he is abnormal. If a baby is passed as normal for adoption, so that he is adopted without the adopting couple knowing that he is handicapped, it is a tragedy for the adopting couple and it may be a tragedy for the child, for it may lead to rejection. It is major tragedy for a child who is prevented from being adopted on the grounds that he is abnormal, when in fact there is nothing wrong with him (Ch. 17).

I have heard of health visitors in two cities 'failing' 40% of babies in the 6-month assessment, and telling the mothers that the babies had failed. I have seen mothers upset when a nurse has said 'Isn't he sitting yet?' 'Her head is small.' 'Hasn't he got a big head?' I have heard of babies in an 8-month assessment being referred to a psychiatrist because of supposed backwardness!

A 5-month-old baby who was brought to a paediatrician for assessment for adoption was said to have a spastic arm. As a result the foster mother began to imagine that the arm-was spastic, postponed adoption and then decided not to adopt. The child was normal and had nothing wrong with him. It was not until he was 4 years old that after great difficulty adoption was arranged: in the meantime this bright normal child had suffered the psychological trauma of repeated changes of mother.

I have seen many children wrongly said to be spastic, mentally subnormal or hydrocephalic, when there was nothing wrong with them: the wrong diagnosis had caused inestimable suffering. One mother was told by a doctor 'Your child may be a spastic, but don't worry.' Fortunately I was immediately asked to see the intensely worried mother, and examining the baby on the next day found a mentally superior normal baby with no trace of spasticity.

Mothers want to know and have a right to know as soon as possible if their child is handicapped, but there are many occasions when one is doubtful whether the young infant has an abnormality or not. Unless there is an available treatment (as for hypothyroidism, or subluxation of a hip) one should say nothing until certain. If treatment is available, and special investigation is required, then the mother must be told. A couple wishing to adopt a child must be told if there is doubt about the baby; they may have to delay adoption so that one can see the child again for reassessment before the adoption is clinched. Otherwise if there is no necessary treatment available, nothing should be said until a firm decision has been made. The doctor must use his ingenuity in arranging so see the child again without causing distress. If it is thought that there are doubtful signs of cerebral palsy, then no harm will be done by waiting to re-examine the child before telling the parents: if it is so mild that one cannot be sure, no treatment will make any difference and no harm can be done by waiting. I have repeatedly seen much distress by a doctor's or nurse's unwise expression of doubts about a baby.

The mere name of the 'assessment clinic' may alarm mothers. I believe that developmental assessment is just part of the routine examination of a baby anywhere — in a child health clinic, hospital or home, and that the only place for the so-called assessment clinic is for the overall assessment of a handicapped child by all the relevant specialists.

Summary

For many reasons, developmental assessment is an essential part of paediatric practice.

The basic essentials for it are a thorough knowledge of the normal, of the normal variations, and the reasons for those variations.

All clinical diagnoses should be based on the history, the examination and the interpretation of the history and findings on examination.

The history must include all prenatal, perinatal and postnatal factors which profoundly affect development, most of which are not directly related to the child's mental endowment. Of particular importance is preterm delivery, for it is essential to allow for prematurity when assessing development.

The examination will include full physical examination, including the head circumference in relation to weight, the assessment of vision and hearing, and other physicial factors which affect development.

Purely objective tests, without attention to the history and full physical examination, inevitably omit factors of the greatest importance for assessment.

All persons carrying out developmental assessment should understand its great value, its predictive importance, and its limitations which are largely due to the many variables which alter the course of development.

Unwise comments to parents about a child's development will cause great anxiety.

REFERENCES

1. Bayley, N. Mental growth during the first three years. Genet. Psychol. Monogr. 1933.14.1.
2. Beintema, D. J. A neurological study of newborn infants. Clinics in developmental medicine No. 28. London. Heinemann. 1968.
3. Brazelton, T. B. Neonatal behavioral assessment scale. Clinics in developmental medicine No. 50. London. Heinemann. 1964.
4. Carmichael, A., Williams, H. E. Developmental screening in infancy — a critical appraisal of its value. Australian Paediatr. J. 1981.17.20.
5. Clarke, A. D. B. Predicting human development. Problems, evidence, implications. Bull. Br Psychol. Soc. 1978.31.249.
6. Coplan, A. Parental estimate of child's developmental level in a high risk population. Am. J. Dis. Child. 1982.136.101.
7. Darwin, C. The expression of the emotions in man and animals. London. Murray 1872.
8. Darwin, C. A biographical sketch of an infant. Mind. 2.285. (See Dev. Med. Child. Neurol. Supplement 24.1944.)
9. Denhoff, E., Hainsworth, P., Hainsworth, M. The child at risk for learning disorder. Clin. Pediatr. (Phila). 1972.11.164.
10. Farber, J. M., Shapiro, B. K., Palmer, F. B., Capute, A. J. The diagnostic value of the neurodevelopmental examination. Clin. Pediatr. (Phila). 1985.24.367.
11. Frankenburg, W. K., Camp, B. W., van Natta, P. A., Demers-Seman, J. A., Voorhees, S. F. Validity of the Denver developmental screening test. Child Development. 1971.42.475.
12. Frankenburg, W. K., Dodds, J. B. The Denver developmental screening test. J. Pediatr. 1967.71.181.
13. Frankenburg, W. K., Fandal A. W., Sciarillo, W., Burgess, D. The newly abbreviated and revised Denver developmental screening test. J. Pediatr. 1981.99.995.
14. Frankenburg, W. K., Van Doorninck, W. J., Liddell, T. N., Dick, N. The Denver prescreening developmental questionnarie (PDQ). Pediatrics. 1976.57.744.
15. Griffiths, R. The abilities of babies. London. University of London Press. 1954.
16. Holmes, G. E., Hassanein, R. S. The kid's chart. Am. J. Dis. Child., 1982.136.997.
17. Illingworth, R. S. Your child's development in the first five years. London. Churchill Livingstone. 1981.
18. Illingworth, R. S. Basic developmental screening. Oxford. Blackwell. 3rd Edn. 1982.
19. Illingworth, R. S., Illingworth, C. M. Babies and young children. London. Churchill Livingstone. 7th Edn. 1983.
20. Illingworth, R. S. Norms for development. Dev. Med. Child Neurol. 1986.28.122.

21. Junker, K. S., Barr, B., Maliniemi, S., Wasz-Höckert, O. BOEL — a screening program to enlarge the concept of infant health. Paediatrician. 1982.11.85.
22. Keshavan, M. S., Narayanan, H. S. Parental estimation of child's developmental level. Am. J. Dis. Child. 1983.137.87.
23. Knobloch, H., Pasamanick, B. Gesell and Amatruda's developmental diagnosis. Hagerstown. Harper and Row. 3rd edn. 1974.
24. Knobloch, H., Stevens, F., Malone, A. Manual of child development. Hagerstown. Harper and Row. 1980
25. Siegel, L. S. Infant tests as predictors of cognitive and language development at two years. Child Dev. 1981.52.545.
26. Yang, R. K. Early infant assessment, an overview. In: Osofsky, J. D. (Ed.) Handbook of infant development. New York. Wiley Interscience Publications. 1979.

2

Prenatal and perinatal factors relevant to developmental assessment and diagnosis

A child's developmental level is the end result of a wide variety of factors, prenatal, perinatal and postnatal.

In establishing a developmental diagnosis one must be thoroughly conversant with these factors.

In this chapter I shall attempt to summarise those prenatal and perinatal factors which I think are particularly relevant. The literature on the subject is vast. With regard to prenatal factors alone I have had to select from over 2000 papers seen by me.

Preconception: genetics

Prenatal factors operating before conception include the intelligence, personality, education and attitudes of the parents, and the way in which they were brought up. As for intelligence, it has even been suggested that because it was found that the coefficient of correlation of intelligence tests of husbands and wives was as high as that of brothers and sisters, the IQ of parents may be a better guide to a child's intelligence than developmental tests in infancy.

Sir Francis Galton in 1869 was one of the first to study the genetics of intelligence. He made the observation that 977 eminent men had 535 eminent relatives, as against a total of four eminent relatives among 977 ordinary men. Terman and Oden followed up 1528 children with an intelligence quotient of 140 or more. Three hundred and forty-eight of their children had a mean IQ of 127.7. The number with an IQ of 150 or more was 28 times that of unselected persons.

The genetic factor of intelligence — 'intelligence A', as distinct from 'intelligence B', which is intelligence A modified by environmental factors — has been studied by comparing the intelligence of children placed in foster homes with that of their real and adopting parents. There was no correlation between the child's IQ and that of the true mother at first, but there was increasing correlation with advancing age, presumably because of genetic factors. It has been said that the correlation of IQ between biological children and their parents was twice as high as it was between adopted children and adopting parents, whether or not the biological parents raised them.[110] The genetic aspect of intelligence has also been investigated by the method of studying identical twins reared apart, though an obvious fallacy of such studies lies in the possibility that similar foster parents might be chosen for identical twins. The IQ of identical twins reared apart is more correlated than that of fraternal twins reared in the same home; but the environmental factor determines the extent to which the genetic potential is realised.

It is strange that retinoblastoma, myopia, asthma and high serum uric acid levels are associated with a high IQ. In the case of myopia, it is said that children show a higher than average IQ before the myopia develops.[14] A Swiss paper[132] studied 23 patients with congenital adrenal hyperplasia due to 21-hydroxylase deficiency, comparing them with 27 unaffected siblings and 48 parents. The patients and siblings had a significantly higher IQ score than average, but the parents did not.

The genetic aspect of mental subnormality is of great importance when one is assessing infants with regard to suitability for adoption. Severe mental subnormality occurs equally in the social classes, but mild mental subnormality is more common among the children of the poor than the well-to-do; to put it another way, the intelligence of a mildly retarded child is more likely to approximate to that of the parents than that of a severely retarded one.

Before one can give genetic advice in a case of mental subnormality full investigation is essential in order that one can detect metabolic and other forms of mental subnormality with a known genetic pattern. For instance, if a child is found to have one of the recessive forms of mental subnormality, such as phenylketonuria or Tay-Sach's disease, the risk of another child being affected is 1 in 4, while for nonspecific forms of mental subnormality the risk is of the order of 1 in 30. Chromosomal studies are necessary before one can give genetic advice in the case of Down's syndrome. The overall risk of a child with Down's syndrome being born is 0.15%, rising to 2.5% for a mother of 45 years; but if a mother under 25 had a chromosomal translocation, there is a 2 in 3 chance that her child will have Down's syndrome or carry the translocation. In the unlikely case of a woman with Down's syndrome becoming pregnant, there is an approximately one in two chance that the child will be normal. It was our practice at the Children's Hospital, Sheffield, to perform a 48-hour 'work-up' on all mentally subnormal infants, largely in order that genetic advice could be given, and partly to institute appropriate treatment, if possible. The investigation included plasma and urine aminoacids, fasting blood glucose, blood calcium, phosphorus, sodium, potassium, bicarbonate, urea, phenylalanine, Wassermann reaction, motor nerve conduction time, karyotype, and where relevant blood lead, urine homovanillic acid, and tests for thyroid function.

The outlook for a child of a mentally subnormal parent is not as gloomy as was once thought. Skodak[119] studied 16 children whose mothers were feeble-minded, with a mean IQ of 66.4, and found that the mean IQ of the children was 116.4. In my own study of babies seen for adoption purposes, 22 children of certified mentally subnormal mothers had a mean IQ of 100.1. This is less than the average IQ for adopted children (Ch. 3).

Hereditary conditions related to development include gross anomalies of the central nervous system. The risk of a child being born with a gross anomaly of the central nervous system when the parents are normal is 0.6%. When the parents are normal the risk of their having a child with hydrocephalus alone is 1 in 1000, and of having a child with hydrocephalus and spina bifida is 1 in 3000. It has been found in Sheffield that the risk of a subsequent child being affected with hydrocephalus, spina bifida or anencephaly is about 1 in 15[82]. If two affected infants are born, the risk is even greater. In the case of epilepsy, the risk of a normal parent having an epileptic child is 0.4%; if one is affected, the risk of another being abnormal is 2.4%. The risk of an affected parent having an affected child is 2.5 to 5.0%. About 3.2% of parents, siblings or children of epileptic patients have fits.

There is a genetic factor for cerebral palsy, apart from that in kernicterus when due to blood group incompatibility. In my series of 760 children with cerebral palsy, excluding kernicterus, 4% had an affected sibling. (Kernicterus is also caused by hyperbilirubinaemia resulting from neonatal septicaemia: kernicterus due to prematurity is now rarely seen because of improved care.)

Metabolic diseases

Hereditary metabolic defects include in particular diabetes mellitus, hypothyroidism, phenylketonuria and the Lesch Nyhan syndrome. Maternal diabetes is associated with an increased risk of fetal anomalies, including sacral agenesis. It has been suggested that the level of thyroid hormone in women with thyroid disease is a factor related to the motor competence of their children.[103]

In a review of the effect of maternal phenylketonuria on the fetus,[80] involving 524 pregnancies in 155 women, it was emphasised that the child's prospects depended largely on the time when the low phenylalanine diet was instituted, and the level of phenylalanine in the pregnancy. Ninety-five per cent of mothers with a blood phenylalanine above 20 mg/l had at least one mentally subnormal child.

Chromosomal abnormalities

Many hereditary diseases are related to chromosomal defects, such as that in Turner's syndrome or Down's syndrome.[131] In a Swedish study of mental subnormality[57] 29% of cases of severe subnormality and 4% of milder subnormality were of chromosomal origin; 4% of severe subnormality and 10% of slight subnormality in boys were associated with the fragile X syndrome. Five per cent were due to inborn errors of metabolism. The role of the fragile X in mental subnormality is still uncertain.

Hereditary factors are also concerned with the child's personality, though the inherited characteristics are profoundly affected by his environment. Other genetic factors include hereditary disease, and a tendency to premature or postmature delivery.

The parents' own childhood, the amount of love which they received, the way in which they were punished, is likely to have an effect on their children. Children subjected to corporal punishment are likely to use the same method on their own children in later years. Children who are happy and loved are more likely themselves to have happy children than those who had an unhappy childhood.

Personal factors

A couple's desire for a child of a given sex may affect development. If the child is of the the desired sex, overprotection and favouritism may occur: if not, there may be rejection.

Genetic and environmental factors interact with each other.

Incest

There is much confusion amongst lay people concerning the significance of incest: the most important result of incest is genetic abnormalities.[92]

Connell[25] described incest as 'one facet of gross family pathology', with a high incidence of large families, overcrowding, unemployment, inadequate education, alcoholism, mental illness in the father, with violent temper,[10] unsatisfactory work performance, and criminal records. This home background greatly adds to the results of incest.

There have been many studies of the genetic consequences of incest.[16,114] In Seeminova's study of 161 cases in Czechoslovakia, 20% of 141 mothers were mentally retarded and 8 of the 138 fathers. There was a high mortality in the children, and around 40% of them were severely retarded. In another study 6 out 18 died or had major defects. Bundey wrote that the risks lay in recessive conditions or in polygenic disease; less than half of all the children were normal; a quarter were seriously retarded, a quarter to a third mildly so. Recognisable recessive diseases occurred in 14% and congenital malformations in 12%. By 1 year of age most but not all the recessive diseases had become apparent.

Other early factors

Several workers have indicated that there may be a seasonal factor for conception resulting in handicaps such as mental subnormality, spina bifida, cerebral palsy, Down's syndrome and congenital dislocation of the hip.[78]

Illegitimacy is often relevant to a child's development, partly because of its association with younger mothers, poor antenatal care, increased incidence of preterm delivery, and later factors concerning foster home, institutional care or one-parent family.

The possible role of the time of ovulation and fertilisation, with over-ripeness of the gamete, may be relevant to congenital defects, as it is in experimental animals.[51,55,60,79,122]

Multiple pregnancy

There is evidence that multiple pregnancy is associated with a higher incidence of mental retardation, of cerebral palsy and many other abnormalities[52a] than single pregnancies.[6] The reasons are probably complex and interwoven. They include prematurity, abnormal delivery, hypoglycaemia in the second twin and placental abnormalities or insufficiency. In a study of 80 twin pairs[135], it was found that the second-born twin was more susceptible to hypoxia and birth trauma. Twins are more often born to an older mother, and in multiple pregnancies there is a higher incidence of toxaemia and hydramnios, both conditions which tend to be associated with fetal abnormalities. There is a high perinatal mortality in a co-twin of a twin who has cerebral palsy, suggesting that there had been an antenatal factor acting on both twins. The smaller of twins is liable to suffer from hypoglycaemia in the newborn period, and so to suffer brain damage if it is severe and inadequately treated. Yet an American study of 75 twin sets,[50] in which white and coloured twins were investigated separately, revealed no difference in the performance of identical twins of dissimilar birthweight when assessed on the Bayley mental and motor examination at 8 months, and the Stanford-Binet scale at 4 years. The zygosity was determined on the basis of 37 major and minor blood group antigens or on histological examination of divided membranes in monochorionic placentas.

The twin transfusion syndrome,[106] sometimes associated with hydramnios, is associated with a high fetal mortality and morbidity, including mental subnormality and cerebral palsy, because one twin may suffer hypoxia in utero, and may be anaemic at birth. The other is born plethoric with a risk of thromboses, heart failure and hyperbilirubinaemia.

In a study of prematurity and multiple pregnancy in relation to mental retardation and cerebral palsy, we found that of 729 mentally retarded children without cerebral palsy, 20.9% were born prematurely and the incidence of twins was 3.8%. In 651 children with cerebral palsy, the incidence of prematurity was 35.9%, and that of twins was 8.4%. By statistical analysis it was shown that the high incidence of twins in cerebral palsy was not related to the high incidence of prematurity. Zazzo's book[138] on the personality and development of twins should be read by those interested in the subject. He pointed out that a genetic influence is not proved by the fact that there is greater concordance in monozygotic twins than in dizygotic ones. Monozygotic twins may be treated by parents as more alike than dizygotic twins, and monozygotic twins tend to be more firmly attached to each other and therefore to develop similar attitudes. Twins score on the average five points less than singletons[86] — and this is not due to differences in social class, family size or home conditions. Postnatal factors must be important, for if co-twins are stillborn or die in infancy, the mean IQ of the surviving twin is unlikely to be lower than that of a singleton.

Monozygotic twins tend to be smaller at birth, more prematurely born, to have a higher perinatal mortality and to be more delicate than dizygotic twins. They are more unsociable, introverted and timid than dizygotic twins (or singletons). The average age of mothers of dizygotic twins is higher than that of mothers of monozygotic twins. All these factors have an obvious bearing on development and indicate the complexity of the problem of the effect of nature and nurture on a child's personality and performance.

I have discussed the problems of multiple pregnancy and of twins in greater detail elsewhere.[65]

Irradiation

Accidental irradiation of the fetus in utero may cause severe brain damage. Babies born by mothers in Hiroshima and Nagasaki at the time of the explosion of the atomic bomb were severely mentally subnormal, with microcephaly and often cataracts. The defects were almost entirely confined to those exposed to the irradiation before 18 weeks' gestation. None of the follow-up studies noted cerebral palsy as a feature.[46]

Exposure of the male to irradiation may cause fetal abnormalities.

Drugs taken in pregnancy

Most drugs taken by a pregnant woman are transferred across the placenta to the fetus.[5] The number of drugs now known occasionally to affect the fetus is vast: they include antidiabetic drugs, antimitotic drugs, antidepressants, antibiotics, antiemetic and antiepileptic drugs, analgesics, amphetamines, diphenhydramine, salicylates, warfarin, lithium, magnesium sulphate and stilboestrol.

Forfar and Nelson[48] in a Scottish survey of 906 pregnant women, found that 82% were taking prescribed drugs (excluding iron): and 65% were also taking unprescribed drugs. Brackbill[11] quoted a study to the effect that the average number of drugs being taken by 168 clinic mothers was 11.0. In his review (with 178 references) he reported that obstetrical medication has a considerable effect on the newborn infant's behaviour, sucking and feeding: almost all studies show a significant effect on the fetus, all disadvantageous: the effect lasted up to a year after birth.

Drugs taken during labour are likely to depress the respiratory centre and adversely affect the baby's behaviour responses and sucking. Barbiturates cause significant depression. Diazepam may cause some degree of hypotonia. Oxytocin may increase the level of serum bilirubin in girls.[104] Too large a dose interferes with placental circulation and increases the risk of fetal distress.[11]

Smoking in pregnancy reduces the birthweight of the fetus (possibly by underperfusion), increases the risk of stillbirth, placenta praevia, abruptio placentae,[91] mental and physical retardation,[24] with an adverse effect on the Apgar and Bayley scores.[52] It may be a factor in later learning disorders and overactivity. It has been said[40] to increase the risk of cleft lip and palate.

The serious effect of alcohol taken in excess in pregnancy, in causing the fetal alcohol syndrome, and of other forms of drug addiction, is now well recognised. It is associated[121] with intrauterine and postnatal growth retardation, a characteristic facies, mental subnormality and cardiac, skeletal and other abnormalities. In a Swedish study[57,58] the fetal alcohol syndrome was thought to be the cause of the mental subnormality in 8% of urban males.

Children born to heroin addicts[134] may be irritable and overactive, with tremors and poor concentration for at least a year.

Mercury poisoning of pregnant women, due to eating contaminated fish, may be seriously toxic to the fetus; in Japan it caused microcephaly and cerebral palsy (Minamata disease). There is a danger of mercury poisoning elsewhere[76] as a result of contamination of sea water by effluents from factories. In Iraq serious fetal damage resulted from pregnant women ingesting seeds contaminated by mercury.[3]

The number of drugs taken by a pregnant woman, and known sometimes to affect the fetus, is now so vast that the history of drugs taken in pregnancy must be part of the history taken when assessing infants in whom there is some doubt about their development.

Drugs of addiction and other drugs may affect the father's sperm, as may lead and other toxic substances (such as herbicides), and so damage the fetus. Of 127 cases of the fetal alcohol syndrome, in 15 only the father had taken alcohol.[69] Smoking by the father in pregnancy may lower the birth weight.[108a]

Infections in pregnancy

The principal infections in pregnancy which may damage the fetus are rubella, herpes simplex, cytomegalovirus and toxoplasmosis. Of lesser importance are chickenpox, Coxsackie, Echovirus, hepatitis virus, influenza virus, poliomyelitis, measles, listeriosis, leptospira, mycoplasma, syphilis and malaria. A recent addition is infection by the AIDS virus.[115]

It has been suggested that hyperthermia due to any cause in pregnancy may damage the fetus.[120]

Social factors

The age of the mother has a bearing on fetal development. The older the mother, the greater is the incidence of anomalies of the central nervous system, Down's syndrome, mental subnormality, premature labour and dizygotic twins.

The age of the father is relevant. Advanced paternal age is associated with an increased incidence of achondroplasia, craniostenosis with syndactyly (Apert's syndrome), Down's syndrome associated with fusion of chromosomes 21 and 22,[102] osteogenesis imperfecta, congenital deafness and certain forms of congenital heart disease.[28,98]

Poverty and defective maternal nutrition increase infant and child morbidity, preterm delivery, maternal toxaemia, anaemia and perinatal mortality. Studies in Aberdeen showed the important influence of social factors on obstetrical complications. They indicated the need for caution in ascribing abnormalities in the infant to birth injury unless due consideration has been given to social class differences in their relation to the events of pregnancy.

Experimental work has shown that maternal malnutrition in pregnancy may damage the fetal brain.[31a] It reduces brain cell mitosis and the number of brain cells and reduces the number of axon terminals from each neurone; it causes a reduction in the DNA content of the animal brain, the number of brain cells, the brain weight, the myelin lipids — cholesterol, cerebroside and sulphatide, thought essential for brain function, and alters the enzyme system in the brain, affecting the succinate dehydrogenase, fructosediphosphate aldolase and the acetylcholinesterase. It is estimated that over 300 million children are at risk of permanent brain damage because of malnutrition in utero and the first 2 years after birth.[81] The cerebellum is particularly liable to suffer; it begins to grow later than the rest of the brain but completes its growth sooner. Malnutrition in late pregnancy may reduce the number of neurones in the cerebellum. Malnutrition reduces the brain size and the interneurone connections.

Relative infertility

When a child has cerebral palsy or mental subnormality, there is often a history of 'reproductive inefficiency' — a long period of marriage before conception occurred, or a history of repeated miscarriages, a stillbirth or a handicapped child. Chefetz,[20] in his study of 275 children with cerebral palsy, found such a history in 78.4%.

Placental and other uterine problems

Intrauterine growth retardation, causing the fetus to be 'small for dates', accounts for about a third of all low birthweight babies (those less than

2500 g at birth).[21] It is associated with placental insufficiency, hydramnios, hypertension, pre-eclampsia and toxaemia, antepartum haemorrhage, zinc deficiency, multiple pregnancy, twin transfusion syndrome, infections, congenital heart disease, uterine anomalies, diabetes, phenylketonuria, collagen vascular disease, malnutrition, smoking, alcohol, hard drugs and other drug-taking (e.g. phenytoin, antimetabolites, warfarin, propranolol). It has also occurred after exposure to toxic substances such as mercury. Chiswick[21] found that 5–15% of children with intrauterine growth retardation had congenital malformations, some with chromosome defects. There is a higher incidence of perinatal hypoxia, meconium aspiration, hyponatraemia, hypocalcaemia, hypoglycaemia, hyperglycaemia, polycythaemia, massive pulmonary haemorrhage, and later a higher incidence of mental subnormality, cerebral palsy, learning disorders and the attention deficit disorder.

An abnormal position of the placenta (e.g. placenta praevia) and antepartum haemorrhage are associated with preterm delivery. Hydramnios is associated with obstruction of the alimentary tract, achondroplasia, meningocele and other anomalies.

The position of the fetus in utero is important with regard to talipes, dislocation of the hip, congenital torticollis, facial palsy and craniotabes.

Maternal stress

Many efforts have been made to relate psychological stress in pregnancy to psychological abnormalities in the infant and child. Those interested should read Joffe's[68] critical review of the experimental work on animals and of published work on human beings. Joffe discussed in detail the difficulties in setting up suitable experiments and in interpreting work already done.

Stress in the pregnant animal has an adverse effect on the fetus. Thomson engendered strong anxiety in rats by exposing them to the fear of electric shocks at the sound of a buzzer; they were able to escape through a door. The rats were then mated and became pregnant, and were then exposed to the same fear, but the door was blocked so that they could not escape. Their offspring showed striking differences from controls when examined at 30 to 40 days and 130 to 140 days. Their responses were more slow, and in various ways they showed more 'emotionality' all through their adult life.

Keeley[71] subjected pregnant albino mice to stress by overcrowding. When their litters encountered unfamiliar stimuli they were less active than controls, they were slower to respond and their reaction times were longer. The differences persisted at 30 and 100 days of age. These experiments appeared to indicate that prenatal stress had an effect on the performance in later life.

Stott[124] reviewed the literature concerning the possible effect of stressful experiences in pregnancy on the human fetus. He considered that there is good evidence that psychological stress during pregnancy, such as that in wartime, is associated with an increased incidence of anomalies in the fetus. He quoted Klebanov as finding that when women gave birth to children within a year or so of release from concentration camps, the incidence of Down's syndrome and of malformations in the children was four or five times greater than normal. Drillien[33] and Wilkinson[34] provided confirmation of Stott's work. They studied the events during the pregnancies which had resulted in the birth of 227 mentally subnormal children, of whom a third were Down's syndrome babies. There was a significantly higher incidence of severe emotional stress in the pregnancy of mothers giving birth to Down's syndrome babies than there was in the mothers of other mentally subnormal children. This difference applied particularly when the mother was over 40.

Gunther[56] studied stress in pregnancy as a possible cause of premature labour, investigating 20 married mothers with no apparent physical cause for prematurity and 20 controls. Mothers with many psychosomatic symptoms and domestic crises were more likely to have infants of low birthweight.

Taft and Goldfarb[125] carried out a retrospective study of 29 schizophrenic children of school age, 39 siblings of schizophrenic children, and 34 public school children. There was a greater incidence of prenatal and perinatal complications in the case of the schizophrenic children, especially in boys. The complications included advanced maternal age, hyperemesis, antepartum haemorrhage, eclampsia and hypertension. Dodge[32] showed that there is an association between stress in pregnancy and the development of congenital pyloric stenosis.

Abnormal presentation

It is commonly assumed that if a mentally subnormal child, or a child with cerebral palsy, was born by breech, then the breech delivery is the cause of the child's handicap. This is irrational. There are many causes of breech presentation — a subject comprehensively reviewed by Braun, Jones and Smith.[13] They include multiple pregnancy, smallness-for-dates and prematurity, hydramnios, oligohydramnios, placenta praevia, bicornuate uterus, the Prader-Willi syndrome, Smith Lemli Opitz syndrome, Potter's syndrome, Zellweger's syndrome, Werdnig Hoffmann disease, myotonic dystrophy, De Lange's syndrome, fetal alcoholism and trisomy 13, 18 or 21. Other associations are congenital (fetal) torticollis (which may be the cause of the breech presentation), familial dysautonomia,[4] congenital dislocation of the hip, hydrocephalus, anencephaly and meningomyelocele. (In Sheffield it was found that breech delivery was five times more common in spina bifida than in others.) In a study of 281 babies delivered by breech,[43] it was found that the danger was not in the delivery, but in the causes of the breech presentation.

Abnormal presentations carry the risk of prolapse of the cord; but with proper management the risk to the fetus is small.[20,27]

Low birthweight babies

The term 'low birthweight baby' refers to a birth weight of 2500 g or less: the term 'preterm baby' refers to a gestation of 37 weeks or less: the 'small for dates' baby is usually regarded as one with a birthweight of two standard deviations (approximately the 5th centile) below the average weight for the gestational age, and this is usually due to intrauterine growth retardation (above). In many ways preterm delivery has similar aetiological factors to those of the small for dates baby. There may be a familial tendency to preterm birth: it is more common in the very young or older mother. It is related to socioeconomic problems, including malnutrition and low level of intelligence, multiple pregnancy, smoking, infections in pregnancy, placenta praevia, pre-eclampsia, and damage to the cervix by previous termination.

In the last edition of this book, after reviewing the literature I suggested that the incidence of handicaps in children born weighing less than 800 g was 10 to 40%, and 10 to 18% for those weighing 1000–1500 g. The handicaps associated with preterm delivery include cerebral palsy, especially spastic diplegia, sensorineural deafness, visual defects, mental subnormality, clumsiness, learning disorders and the attention deficit disorder.[8,17,35a,118,129] The incidence of congenital anomalies is eight times more than that in full-term babies. The lower the birthweight, especially if small for dates, the smaller the child is likely to be in later years.[65]

There is no exact definition of 'very low birthweight', and this makes it difficult to compare results obtained in different centres. In an American collaborative study[74] of 259 long-term survivors who had weighed 500–1500 g, seen at 2 years of age, 18.6% had a major handicap of cerebral palsy, mental subnormality or epilepsy. In Finland[87] of 57 survivors whose birthweight was 1500 g or less, four had severe mental or physical defects, and three were blind with retrolental fibroplasia. The others were less good than controls in motor and speech development and behaviour in school. In a Canadian study[111] of 110 children whose birthweight had been 500–1000 g, followed for a minimum of 2 years, 24% had sensory handicaps, 26% neurological handicaps, and the remainder were normal. Yu and colleagues[136,137] in Australia followed 261 infants weighing 500–999 g at birth. The 7-year survival rate was 46%. Of 108 survivors followed for at least 2 years, 28% had a disability. Hirata[62] followed 24 survivors with a birthweight of 501–750 g; they were small in weight and head size; four had low intelligence, two had neurological sequelae and the rest were normal. Kumar[77] followed 50 survivors, who had weighed 1250 g or less; at 1 year 46% of those who had been small for dates and 8% of those of weight appropriate for dates were lower than the third centile in weight. Cohen[23] followed 87 survivors whose birthweight had been 751–1000 g: eight died later; four could not be traced. Of the 72 remaining at 3 years, four had severe and 14 moderate handicaps. Klein[75] in a 5-year follow-up study of 80 with a mean birthweight of 1.2 g, noted the frequency of visual and perceptual difficulties even when the IQ was normal. Morgan[88] discussed their raised mortality, morbidity and cost and care.

The outlook for the small for dates baby is less good than that of the baby of the same weight which was appropriate for the duration of gestation.[94] Allen,[1] in a review (with 248 references) found a higher mortality, more perinatal complications, more neurological handicaps, congenital anomalies and chromosome anomalies than in the appropriate for dates group. Frances-Williams[49] conducted Wechsler, Gestalt and reading tests on 105 children who had weighed less than 1500 g at birth; the mean IQ for the small for dates children was 92, as compared with 99.2 for those appropriate for dates. Others made similar observations.[101] The physical growth of those small for dates babies tends to be less good than those who had been appropriate for dates. The head circumference at 3 years, usually small in those children, was found to predict later IQ scores.[64] At the age of 8, in general the very low birthweight babies fared less well than controls in perceptual, visuomotor and language development.

There are many difficulties in interpreting the follow-up studies of low birthweight babies. The causes of the low birthweight may vary from place to place, especially with regard to socioeconomic factors and nutrition, and I think that no study relates the prognosis to the cause of the low birthweight. Many studies have not distinguished small for dates babies from those appropriate for dates. Few follow-up studies made an allowance for prematurity in their early developmental assessments. There has been no uniformity in the birthweight groups studied. As far as I know, no studies have related the outcome to the individual items of neonatal care (e.g. with regard to management of apnoea, acidosis, hypothermia, hypoglycaemia, hypoxia, convulsions or respiratory distress syndrome).

Derham[29] regarded early seizures as indicating the quality of perinatal care. Several have related the later unsatisfactory prognosis to overall management in the intensive care unit[7,15,73] and to intermittent positive pressure ventilation.[44,47,85] Some[8,70] found that those who had had the respiratory distress syndrome later had more neurological handicaps than controls.

Various workers have discussed the value of ultrasound in the newborn with regard to the prognosis of cerebral haemorrhage.[9,26,31,67] Around 40–50% of very low birthweight babies have some periventricular or intraventricular haemorrhage. Severe cystic leucomalacia is a strong predictor of severe cerebral palsy, mental subnormality or cortical blindness. Haemorrhage alone has a better prognosis.

The neurological assessment of the preterm newborn infant by scan and ultrasound correlated well with the outcome at 1 year.[35] Ninety-one per cent of the 62 found at 40 weeks gestation to be normal were normal at 1 year; but only 35% of those abnormal at 40 weeks were normal on follow-up. We badly need long-term follow-up studies to point to the best methods of management and treatment. The Cardiff Workers[18,19] reported that comparison of the results obtained by two obstetrical teams, with 40 000 deliveries, failed to demonstrate significant advantages in fetal monitoring, ultrasound cephalometry, induction of labour or urinary oestrogen assays. These findings were not confined to low birthweight babies: but an Australian study[136,137] found no improvement in the incidence of handicap in very low birthweight babies in the last 20–30 years. Others have expressed similar doubts.[18,19]

Postmaturity

It is said that postmaturity is a danger to the fetus, partly because of placental insufficiency. Lovell[83] studied 106 postmature babies of 42 weeks gestation or more. He pointed out that when there is postmaturity there is a high incidence of fetal distress, of hypoxia at birth and of abnormal neurological signs in the newborn period. There was a significantly higher morbidity in the first year than in controls. He thought that the children were less socially mature than controls when they reached their first birthday. It had long been recognised that fetal hypoxia increases pari passu with each postnatal week: and that postmaturity ranks only second to prematurity as a cause of fetal morbidity and mortality, especially in the case of primiparae. Alberman found that 10% of 159 cases of spastic diplegia had been the product of pregnancies lasting over 42 weeks. Wagner[130] found that 28% of 100 children with cerebral palsy had experienced a gestation period of 41 weeks or more. When 40 postmature babies were compared with 40 controls,[45] it was found that they had had more illness, more feeding and sleep disturbance, and scored less well on the Denver and Bayley scales.

Neonatal hypoxia

Windle, Courville and others have demonstrated the pathological changes in the brain resulting from hypoxia: they include oedema, diffuse or focal atrophy, scarring, petechial haemorrhages, vascular occlusion with cerebral softening, demyelination and cyst formation. Hypoxia in later childhood, due, for instance to anaesthetic mishaps, strangling, drowning or carbon monoxide poisoning, may cause extrapyramidal rigidity, athetosis and gross mental impairment. In view of all this, it is surprising that follow-up studies of babies severely asphyxiated at birth, have shown how good a prognosis can usually be expected.[96] In a study of 31 children who had an Apgar score of 0 at 1 minute, and less than 4 at 5 minutes, compared with controls at 5 to 10 years,[126] 93% had no neurological or mental handicap. Of 48 very severely asphyxiated babies, three out of four survivors at 3 to 7 years were normal.[112] In an extensive study of 355 children at the age of 3, 116 of whom had had severe hypoxia and 159 had been normal at birth,[41] the only significant psychological difference was some impairment of conceptional skill as compared with vocabulary skill. There were no more abnormal neurological findings in the hypoxic group.

In the American collaberative perinatal project,[100] covering 40 000 deliveries, it was found that when the Apgar score was 3 or less, 96.1% proved on follow-up to be normal. When 39 full-term infants, who had episodes of hypoxia in utero,[84] were compared with 59 controls at the age of 1 to 6 years, no difference was found. In a study of nine children who achieved regular breathing only after 20 minutes, two were normal later.[39] A 3–5-year follow-up study of 167 term infants[108] who had experienced hypoxic–ischaemic encephalopathy at birth, showed that all 66 whose encephalopathy had been mild were normal; of 94 who had had moderate signs, 21.3% were moderately handicapped, while all seven who had severe signs at birth were severely handicapped. The mean IQ was significantly related to the severity of the encephalopathy.

In another study[134] only 1% of infants having an Apgar score of 0 to 3 at 5 minutes were later found to have cerebral palsy, and 9% of those having an Apgar score of 0 to 3 at 15 minutes. In another study,[96] 80% of those with an Apgar score of 0 to 3 at 10 minutes were free from handicap at school age. On the other hand 55% of children with cerebral palsy had an Apgar score of 7 to 10 at 1 minute, and 73% had an Apgar score to 10 at 5 minutes. It has been said that less than 1% of survivors are at risk of permanent damage. A good guide to the prognosis is the time of onset of regular respirations: the prognosis is good if that occurs under about 20 minutes after delivery.[42]

There are many difficulties in the assessment of the numerous follow-up studies of perinatal hypoxia. They depend on difficulties in the definition and assessment of the severity of the hypoxia, the duration of follow-up, and the accuracy and comprehensiveness of the follow-up examination. Another vital factor must be the cause of the hypoxia. Factors causing prolonged partial hypoxia in utero are more harmful than acute periods of anoxia at birth.[113] Experimental prolonged repeated partial hypoxia leads to pathological changes identical with those of cerebral palsy in infants, but complete hypoxia does not.[12,89,90]

There is often confusion about the role of the umbilical cord round the neck. Around 30 to 40% of infants are born with the cord round the neck. Horwitz[63] studied 276 infants born with the cord round the neck and found that they had no more fetal distress or perinatal mortality (unless someone cut the cord before delivery) than other babies, and there was no difference in the Apgar score. Ten infants with a true knot in the cord survived without complications.

The cause of the hypoxia, such as a prolapsed cord, may be obvious, but commonly it is not so. Sometimes the cord may be compressed by the head before·delivery. When there is no obvious cause, there is a much greater likelihood of an underlying brain defect or other reason for the fetal deprivation in utero. In a study of 100 infants in St Louis, with 'hypoxic–ischaemic' brain damage[61] there was evidence of prenatal anoxia in 90%.

It is irrational to say that if a child is subnormal, and there was hypoxia at birth, then the defect is due to the perinatal hypoxia: one has to look further back for the cause of the hypoxia. A further difficulty, similar to that in the case of the low birthweight babies, lies in socioeconomic variables. When the environmental conditions are good, adverse effects of hypoxia are likely to disappear more rapidly than they do when there are severe socioeconomic difficulties. There is no specific defect which results from hypoxia at birth:[53] but any follow-up study must be long enough to detect visuospatial defects, overactivity, defective concentration or learning disorders.

Neonatal convulsions

The prognosis of neonatal convulsions depends on the cause. The most important causes are hypoglycaemia, hypocalcaemia and cerebral oedema or haemorrhage. Other causes include hyponatraemia, hypernatraemia, hypomagnesaemia, tetanus, meningitis and other infections, galactosaemia, fructosaemia, leucine sensitivity and other metabolic causes. Many of these causes are themselves of prenatal origin. For instance, it has been suggested that neonatal hypoglycaemia may result from a prenatal brain defect. Hence a satisfactory statement of the relationship between neonatal convulsions and subsequent development could only follow the fullest laboratory investigation with follow-up examination over a period of several years.

Birth injury, brain damage and cerebral palsy

The term 'minimal brain dysfunction' should be abandoned as being useless and irrational.[30,109] Up to 100 symptoms have been ascrined to it.[112] In a symposium of 396 pages, with 772 references, various experts combined to criticise the concept of 'minimal brain dysfunction'; and similar views were expressed in a textbook on the subject.[107] There is now increasing evidence that those symptoms have a metabolic basis, probably inherited, and depend on the metabolism of cerebral monoamines.[116]

The recent serious increase in litigation for so-called 'brain damage', especially after obstetric procedures or immunisation, makes the understanding of the problem a matter of urgency. Niswander[99] wrote 'currently, in many parts of the country, the delivery of a child who is found to suffer from cerebral palsy or other major neurological deficit can be expected to lead to malpractice action against the obstetricians. This is almost a reflex action'. Unfortunately, there is still a prevalent simplistic practice of ascribing all mental or physical handicap to the indisputable fact that the child was born, and that birth can be dangerous.

I have always disliked the terms 'brain damage' and 'birth injury' — unless the latter refers to Erb's palsy or a fractured humerus or other externally obvious result of delivery. Psychologists who use the term 'brain damage' may include the effect of noxious factors during pregnancy, such as maternal rubella, but parents inevitably interpret the words as indicating damage during birth.

Some psychologists refer to a child as being 'brain injured' or having suffered 'brain damage' or 'birth injury' if he is overactive, clumsy, impulsive, concentrates badly, is excessively talkative, and shows a discrepancy between verbal and performance tests — features now termed 'attention deficit disorder' (Ch. 13).

I object to the words birth injury, brain damage, for the following reasons.

1. They distress the parents. If a tragedy should befall any of us, it would be better if we were to feel that it was entirely unavoidable, than that we should feel that if more care had been taken by us, or someone else, it could have been avoided. It must be particularly distressing for a mother who has nurtured her fetus in utero for 9 months to be told that her baby's brain has been damaged during delivery.

2. The words brain damage and birth injury inevitably imply that the obstetrician, family doctor or midwife was to blame for the tragedy. This is unfortunate, because parents are likely to try to find something which they or others have done to cause the child's handicap.

3. It attaches a 'label' to a child; when he starts school he is liable to be regarded as abnormal because of 'brain damage' — and such a label may affect the teachers' attitudes and harm the child.

4. The diagnosis is usually wrong. It would be extremely difficult to prove to a scientific audience that the diagnosis of brain damage at birth is correct if the child survives. How could one prove that a child's mental subnormality, cerebral palsy, overactivity or failure to concentrate was due to birth injury, a term which implies that we understand the cause? It is irrational to ascribe a child's mental or neurological handicap to birth injury without considering possible prenatal factors which might have caused or contributed to his brain damage.[13] For instance, in the case of cerebral palsy there are many prenatal factors which occur much more frequently than in normal children. A third of all children are preterm or 'small-for-dates': relative infertility is frequent — occurring in 78.4% of the 275 cases of cerebral palsy analysed by Chefetz:[20] multiple pregnancy is found in 7–10% of all cases: bleeding during pregnancy occurs six to seven times more often than in pregnancies producing normal children[20,59,61]: there was a family history of cerebral palsy in 5% of 762 cases of cerebral palsy seen by me in Sheffield; there is a higher incidence of congenital deformities than in normal children (in 7.5% of 762 cases of cerebral palsy seen by me in Sheffield — but

in 29.3% of 1068 children with mental subnormality without cerebral palsy, Down's syndrome, Hypothyroidism, or hydrocephalus): and there is a higher incidence of abnormal presentation in labour.

An American Committee[93] concluded that the causes of severe mental retardation are primarily genetic, biochemical, viral and developmental, and are not related to birth. Severe mental retardation is possibly linked to hypoxia only when associated with cerebral palsy. Mild mental retardation was said to be unrelated to pregnancy or birth, but rather to socioeconomic circumstances. Epilepsy was not related to perinatal events except possibly when there is cerebral palsy. The Committee felt that in 75% of cases of cerebral palsy there were no known prenatal or perinatal factors. 'Few infants who experience difficult labour and birth later develop neurological handicap; most infants who experienced such difficulties had no evidence of problems during the perinatal period.'

I reviewed the aetiology of 'brain damage' or 'birth injury' in the British Journal of Obstetrics and Gynaecology,[66] in an article entitled 'A paediatrician asks — Why is it called birth injury?', emphasising that

1. 'brain damage' (such as cerebral palsy) frequently occurs with no history of hypoxia or other obstetrical problem, and Caesarean section does not prevent it.
2. When there has been serious difficulty in delivery, or there has been severe perinatal hypoxia, the great majority of children prove to be normal. In the case of cerebral palsy, a third were low birthweight or preterm; relative infertility was frequent, being found in 78.4% of 275 cases analysed by Chefetz[20]: multiple pregnancy is a factor in 7–10%; there is commonly a family history of cerebral palsy, with a high incidence of congenital anomalies. Dental enamel defects indicate of a prenatal insult.[22] Further evidence of prenatal damage was provided by other pathological studies[37,38,54,127,128] and by dermatoglyphics.[105]

Towbin[127,128] studied the central nervous system in 600 infant deaths. He found that a major part of CNS lesions present at birth are due to prenatal conditions. Emminger[38] in Augsburg conducted 191 autopsies on fetuses with rupture of the tentorium or falx cerebri, and found that in 150 cerebral haemorrhage had been diagnosed as a result of severe hypoxia or neonatal difficulties, but no cerebral haemorrhage was found at autopsy. He found no connection between complications of birth or mode of delivery and rupture of the tentorium. He thought that hypoxia during fetal development may have rendered the fetus more liable to injury at birth. He wrote 'Prenatal lesions are the cause of neonatal anoxia, falsely ascribed to birth trauma. The primary cause is fetal maldevelopment, with birth only a secondary factor'. Gross and colleagues[54] found that at autopsy there was morphological brain damage which could reasonably be ascribed to birth injury in less than half of those who had an abnormal delivery. Perinatal accidents were reported in one-third of all morphologically confirmed cerebral malformations. They wrote that perinatal distress may be regarded not as the cause but as the result of organic brain damage in a considerable proportion of cases. Myers[89,90] reported extensive softening of the hemispherical white matter in low birthweight infants whose mothers had severe anaemia in pregnancy. Stanley and Alberman,[123] in an extensive review of the causes of cerebral palsy, suggested that genetic factors may decide the response of the brain to perinatal noxious factors.

Durkin,[36] in a study of 281 children with mental subnormality or cerebral palsy, found that in a third there were significant perinatal factors, in a third only trivial difficulties in labour, and in a third no problems at all. Nelson,[97] in 189 cases of cerebral palsy, found no relation to the duration of labour, whether it was precipitate or prolonged. In a collaborative study of 51 285 pregnancies[95,97] the cerebral palsy was only rarely related to perinatal factors. Amiel-Tison[2] followed 41 children who had experienced a particularly traumatic delivery: none had cerebral palsy. I have long been impressed in my own experience that very serious obstetrical problems are so rarely followed by handicaps on follow-up examination of the children.

Kerr and Forfar[72] commented that 'the idea that physical violence, possibly aggravated by the use of instruments, is a common cause of cerebral birth injury, has now been discarded. Indeed, the evidence is that the competent use of instruments, where necessary, in the delivery of the infant, prevents injury.'

Numerous prenatal and perinatal factors affect development. They include in particular chronic hypoxia in utero, placental insufficiency and preterm delivery.

The too-frequent practice of almost automatically ascribing mental subnormality, epilepsy and cerebral palsy to birth injury is condemned: it is important to look further than the perinatal hypoxia, breech or forceps delivery, or neonatal complications, to their possible or likely prenatal causes.

REFERENCES

1. Allen, M. C. Developmental outcome and follow up of the small for gestational age infant. Sem. Perinatol. 1984.8.123.
2. Amiel-Tison, C. Cerebral damage in full term newborn. Aetiological factors, neonatal status and long term follow-up. Biolog. Neonat. 1969.14.234.
3. Amin-Zaki, L., Majeed, M., Elhassani, S. et al. Prenatal methyl mercury poisoning. Am. J. Dis. Child. 1979.133.172.
4. Axelrod, F. B., Leistner, H. L., Porges, R. F. Breech presentation among infants with familial dysautonomia. J. Pediatr. 1974.84.107.
5. Barber, H. R. K. et al. Symposium on drugs in pregnancy. Obstet. Gynecol. 1981.58. Suppl 5, pp. 1–105s.
6. Benirschke, K., Kim, C. Multiple pregnancy. N. Engl. J. Med. 1973.288.1276.1329.
7. Bennett, F. C., Robinson, N. M., Sells, C. J. Hyaline membrane disease, birth weight and gestational age. Effect of development in the first two years. Am. J. Dis. Child. 1982.136.888.

8. Bennett, F. C., Chandler, L. S., Robinson, N. M., Sells, C. J. Spastic diplegia in premature infants. Am J Dis. Child. 1981.135.732.
9. Beverley, D. W., Chance, G. W., Coates, C. F. Intraventricular haemorrhage — timing of occurrence and relationship to perinatal events. Br. J. Obstet. Gynaecol. 1984.91.1007.
10. Blugass, R. Incest. Br. J. Hosp. Med. 1979.22.152.
11. Brackbill, Y. Obstetric medication and infant behavior. In Osofsky, J. D. (Ed.) Handbook of infant development. New York. Wiley — Interscience publications 1979. p. 76.
12. Brann, A. W., Myers, R. E. Central nervous system findings in the newborn monkey following severe in-utero partial asphyxia. Neurology. 1975.25.327.
13. Braun, F. H. T., Jones, K. L., Smith, D. W. Breech presentation as an indicator of fetal abnormality. J. Pediatr. 1975.86.419.
14. British Medical Journal. Genes for superior intelligence. Leading article 1976.1.415.
15. Britton, S. B., Fitzhardinge, R. M., Ashby, S. Is intensive care justified for infants weighing less than 801 g at birth? J. Pediatr. 1981.99.937.
16. Bundey, S. The child of an incestuous union. In Wolkind, S. (Ed.) Medical aspects of adoption and foster care. Spastics International Medical Publications. 1979.
17. Burns, R., Bullock, M. I. Comparison of abilities of preterm and maturely born children at 5 years of age. Austr. Paediatr. J. 1985.21.31.
18. Chalmers, I. British debate on obstetric practice. Pediatrics. 1976.58.308.
19. Chalmers, I., Mutch, L. Are current trends in perinatal practice associated with an increase or decrease in handicapping conditions? Lancet. 1981.1.1415.
20. Chefetz, M. D. Etiology of cerebral palsy. Role of reproductive insufficiency and the multiplicity of factors. Obstet. Gynecol. 1965.25.635.
21. Chiswick, M. L. Intrauterine growth retardation. Br. Med. J. 1985.2.845.
22. Cohen, H. J., Diner, H. The significance of developmental dental enamel defects in neurological disease. Pediatrics 1970.46.737.
23. Cohen, R. S., Stevenson, D. K., Ariagno, R. L., Sunshine, P. Survival and morbidity of our smallest babies. Is there a limit to neonatal care? Pediatrics. 1984.73.415.
24. Committee on smoking and health. Mothers who smoke and their children. Practitioner. 1980.224.735.
25. Connell, H. M. Incest — a family problem. Med. J. Austr. 1978.2.362.
26. Cooke, R. W. neonatal cranial ultrasound and neurological development at follow up. Lancet. 1985.2.494.
27. Cushner, I. M. Prolapse of the umbilical cord, including a late follow-up of fetal survivors. Am. J. Obstet. Gynecol. 1961.81.666.
28. Day, R. L. Factors influencing offspring. Am. J. Dis. Child. 1967.113.179.
29. Derham, R. J., Matthews, T. G., Clarke, T. A. Early seizures indicate quality of perinatal care. Arch. Dis. Child. 1985.60.809.
30. De la Cruz, F. F., Fox, B. H., Roberts, R. H. Minimal brain dysfunction. Ann. N.Y. Acad. Sci. 1973.205.1.390.
31. Devries, L. S., Dubowitz, L. M. S., Dubowitz, V. et al. Predictive value of cranial ultrasound in the newborn. Lancet. 1985.2.137.
31a. Dobbing, J. Undernutrition and the developing brain. Am. J. Dis. Child 1970.120.411.
32. Dodge, J. A. Pyloric stenosis. Irish J. Med. Sci. 1973.142.6.
33. Drillien, C. M. Aetiology and outcome in low birth weight infants. Dev. Med. Child Neurol. 1972.14.563.
34. Drillien, C. M., Wilkinson, E. M. Emotional stress and mongoloid births. Dev. Med. Child Neurol. 1964.6.140.
35. Dubovitz, L. M. S., Dubovitz, V, Palmer, P. G. et al. Correlation of neurologic assessment in the preterm newborn infant with outcome at one year. J. Pediatr. 1984.105.452.
35a. Dunn, H. Q. Sequelae of low birthweight. The Vancouver Study. Clin. Dev. Med. 95–96, p. 1–306. Oxford. Blackwell.
36. Durkin, M. V., Kaveggia, E. G., Pendleton, E., Neuhauser, G., Opitz, J. M. Analysis of etiologic factors in cerebral palsy with severe mental retardation. Eur. J. Pediatr. 1976.123.67
37. Emery, J, Kalpaktsoglou, P. K. The costochondral junction during later stages of

intrauterine life, and abnormal growth patterns found in association with perinatal
death. Arch. Dis. Child. 1967.42.1.

38. Emminger, E. Prenatal lesions and birth trauma. German Medical Monthly. 1956.1.58.
39. Ergander, U, Eriksson, M, Zetterstrom, R. Severe neonatal asphyxia. Acta Paediatr.
Scand. 1983.72.321.
40. Ericson, A., Kallen, B., Westerholm, P Cigarette smoking as an etiologic factor in cleft
lip and palate. Am. J. Obstet Gynecol. 1979.135.348.
41. Erhart, C. B., Graham, F. K., Thurston, D., Ernhart, T. The relationship of neonatal
apnea to development at 3 years. Arch. Neurol. (Chic) 1960.2.504.
42. Eyre, J. A., Wilkinson, A. R., Tizard, P. Birth asphyxia. Br. Med. J. 1982.2.649.
43. Faber-Nijholt, R, Huisjes, H. J., Touwen, B. C. L., Fidler, V. J. Neurological follow
up of 281 children born in breech presentation. Br. Med. J. 1983.1.9.
44. Fitzhardinge, P. M., Pape, K, Arstikaitis, M. et al. Mechanical ventilation of infants
less than 1501 g. at birth. Health, growth and neurological sequelae. J. Pediatr.
1976.88.531.
45. Field, T. M., Dabiri, C., Hallock, N., Shuman, H. H. Developmental effects of
prolonged pregnancy and the postmaturity syndrome. J. Pediatr. 1977.90.836.
46. Finch, S. C. The study of atomic bomb survivors in Japan. Am. J. Med. 1979.66.899.
47. Fitzhardinge, P. M., Pape, K., Arstikaitis, M., Boyle, M., Ashby, S., Rowley, A.,
Netley, C., Swyer, P. R. Subsequent development of mechanically ventilated LBW
neonates. J. Pediatr. 1976.88.531.
48. Forfar, J. O., Nelson, M. M. Epidemiology of drugs taken by pregnant women. Clin.
Pharmacol. Therap. 1973.14.632.
49. Francis-Williams, J. & Davies, P. A. Very low birth weight and later intelligence. Dev.
Med. Child Neurol. 1974.16.709.
50. Fujikura, T., Froehlich, L. A. Mental and motor development in monozygotic co-twins
with dissimilar birth-weight. Pediatrics. 1974.53.884.
51. Furuhjelm, M., Jonson, B., Landgren, C., Lindgren, L. The quality of the human
semen in relation to perinatal mortality. Acta Obstet. Gynecol. Scand. 1960.39.499.
52. Garn, S. M., Petzold, A. S., Ridella, S. A., Johnston, M. Effect of smoking in
pregnancy on Apgar and Bayley scores. Lancet. 1980.1.912.
52a. Gericke, G. S. Genetic and teratological considerations in the analysis of concordant
and discordant abnormalities in twins. S. Afr. Med. J. 1986.69.111.
53. Gottfried, A. W. Intellectual consequences of perinatal anoxia. Psychol. Bull.
1973.80.231.
54. Gross, H., Jellinger, K., Kaltenbach, E., Rett, A. Infantile cerebral disorders. Clinical
— neuropathological corelations to elucidate the aetiological factors. J. Neurol. Sci.
1968.7.551.
55. Guerrero, R., Rojas, O.I. Spontaneous abortion and aging of human ova and sperm.
N. Engl. J. Med. 1975.293.573.
56. Gunther, L. M. Psychopathology and stress in the life experience of mothers of
premature infants. Am. J. Obstet Gynecol. 1963.86.333.
57. Hagberg, B., Kyllerman, M. Epidemiology of mental retardation. A Swedish survey.
Brain Dev. 1983.5.441.
58. Hagberg, B. Epidemiological and preventive aspects of cerebral palsy and severe mental
retardation in Sweden. Eur. J. Pediatr. 1979.130.71.
59. Hagberg, B., Hagberg, G., Olow, I. The changing panorama of cerebral palsy in
Sweden 1954–70. Acta Paediatr. Scand. 1975.64.187.192.
60. Hecht, F., Pernoll, M. L., McCaw, B. K. Concept of overripeness of gamete causing
congenital malformation and mental retardation. N. Engl. J. Med. 1975.293.604.
61. Hill, A., Volpe, J. J. Hypoxic-ischemic brain injury in the newborn. Seminars in
Perinatology. 1982.6.25.
62. Hirata, T., Epcar, J. T., Walsh, A. et al. Survival and outcome of infants 501–750 g.
A six year experience. J. Pediatr. 1983.102.741.
63. Horwitz, S. T., Finn, W. F., Mastrota, V. A study of umbilical cord encirclement.
Am. J. Obstet. Gynecol. 1964.89.970.
64. Hunt, J. V., Tooley, W. H., Cooper, B. A. Performance of children to 8 years who
received neonatal intensive care. Pediatr. Res. 1985.9.115A.
65. Illingworth, R. S. The normal child. Edinburgh. Churchill Livingstone. 9th Edn. 1987.

66. Illingworth, R. S. A paediatrician asks — why is it called birth injury? Br. J. Obstet. Gynaecol. 1985.92.122.
67. Imura, S., Ohno, T., Takada, M. Periventricular–intraventricular hemorrage in small premature infants. Acta Paediatr. Japon, 1985.27.106.
68. Joffe, J. M. Prenatal determinants of behaviour. Oxford. Pergamon. 1969.
69. Joffe, J. M., Soyka, L. F. Paternal drug exposure: effects on reproduction and progeny. Seminars in Perinatology. 1982.6.116.
70. Kamper, J. Long term prognosis of infants with severe idiopathic respiratory distress syndrome. Acta Paediatr. Scand. 1978.67.53, 61, 71.
71. Keeley, K. Prenatal influence on behaviour of offspring of crowded mice. Science. 1962.135.44.
72. Kerr, M. M., Forfar, J. O. Cerebral birth injury. In Forfar, J. O., Arneil, G. C. (Eds), Textbook of paediatrics. Edinburgh. Churchill Livingstone. 1984, p. 151.
73. Kiely, J. L., Paneth, N., Stein, Z., Susser, M. Cerebral palsy and newborn care. Dev. Med. Child. Neurol. 1981.23.533.
74. Kitchen, W. H., Yu, V. H., Orgill, A. A. et al. Colloborative study of very low birth weight infants. Am. J. Dis. Child. 1983.137.555.
75. Klein, N., Hack, M., Gallacher, J., Fanaroff, A. A. Preschool performance of children with normal intelligence who were very low birth weight infants. Pediatrics 1985.75.531.
76. Koos, B. J., Longo, L. D. Mercury toxicity in the pregnant woman, fetus and newborn infant. Am. J. Obstet. Gynecol. 1976.126.390.
77. Kumar, S. P., Anday, E. K., Sacks, L. M. et al. Follow up studies of very low birth weight infants (1250 g. or less) born and treated within a perinatal center. Pediatrics 1980.66.438.
78. Lander, E., Forssman, H., Akesson, H. O. Season of birth and mental deficiency. Acta Genet. (Basel) 1964.14.265.
79. Lanman, J. T. Delays during reproduction and their effects on the embryo and foetus. N. Engl. J. Med. 1968.278.993.
80. Lenke, R. R., Levy, H. L. Maternal phenylketonuria and hyperphenylalaninaemia. N. Engl. J. Med. 1980.303.1202.
81. Lewin, R. The poverty of undernourished brains. New Scientist. 1974.64.237.
82. Lorber, J. The family history of spina bifida cystica. Pediatrics 1965.35.589.
83. Lovell, K. E. The effect of postmaturity on the developing child. Med. J. Austr. 1973.1.13.
84. Low, J. A., Galbraith, R. S., Muir, D. W., Killen, H. L., Pater, E. A., Karchmar, E. J. Intrapartum fetal hypoxia; a study of long term morbidity. Am. J. Obstet. Gynecol. 1983.145.129.
85. Marriage, K. J., Davies, P. A. Neurological sequelae in children surviving mechanical ventilation in the new born period. Arch. Dis. Child. 1977.52.176.
86. McKeown, T., Record, R. G. Early environmental influences on the development of intelligence. Br. Med. Bull. 1971.27.48.
87. Michelsson, K., Lindahl, E., Parre, M., Helenius, M. Nine year follow up of infants weighing 1500 g. or less at birth. Acta Paediatr. Scand. 1984.73.835.
88. Morgan, M. E. I. Late morbidity in very low birth weight infants. Br. Med. J. 1985.2.171.
89. Myers, R. E. Fetal asphyxia and perinatal brain damage. In Perinatal factors affecting human development. WHO. Scientific publication No. 185. 1969. p. 405.
90. Myers, R. E. Two patterns of perinatal brain damage and their conditions of occurrence. Am. J. Obstet Gynecol. 1972.112.246.
91. Naeye, R. L. The duration of maternal cigarette smoking, fetal and placental disorders. Early Human Development. 1979.3.229.
92. Nakashima, I. I., Zakus, G. E. Incest. A review and clinical experience. Pediatrics. 1977.60.696.
93. National Institute of Health Report on causes of mental retardation and cerebral palsy. Task force on joint assessment of prenatal and perinatal factors associated with brain disorders. Pediatrics 1985.76.457.
94. Neligan, G. A., Scott, D. McL., Kolvin, I., Garside, R. Born too soon or born too small. Clinics in Dev. Med. No. 61. 1976. London. Heinemann.

95. Nelson, J. B., Ellenberg, J. H. Obstetric complications as risk factors to cerebral palsy or seizure disorders. J. Am. Med. Assoc. 1984.251.1843 (Leading article 1868).

96. Nelson, K. B., Ellenberg, J. H. Apgar scores as predictors of chronic neurologic disability. Pediatrics. 1981.68.36.

97. Nelson, K. B., Ellenberg, J. H. Antecedents of cerebral palsy. Am. J. Dis. Child. 1985.139.1031.

98. Newcombe, H. B., Tavendale, O. C. Effect of father's age on the risk of child handicap or death. Am. J. Human Genetics. 1965.17.163.

99. Niswander, K. R. The obstetrician, fetal asphyxia and cerebral palsy. Am. J. Obstet. Gynecol. 1979.133.358.

100. Paneth, N., Fox, H. E. The relationship of Apgar score to neurologic handicap: a survey of clinicians. Obstet. Gynecol. 1983.61.547.

101. Parkinson, C. E., Wallis, S., Harvey, D. School achievement and behaviour of children who were small for dates at birth. Dev. Med. Child Neurol. 1981.23.41.

102. Penrose, L. S. Paternal age in mongolism. Lancet. 1962.1.1101.

103. Pharoah, P, Connolly, K., Hetzel, R., Ekins, R. Maternal thyroid function and motor competence in the child. Dev. Med. Child Neurol. 1981.23.76.

104. Pocock, S. J., Turner, T. L. Neonatal hyperbilirubinaemia, oxytocin and sex of infant. Lancet. 1982.2.43.

105. Preus, M., Fraser, F. T. Dermatoglyphics and syndromes. Am. J. Dis. Child. 1972.124.933.

106. Raussen, A. R., Seki, M., Strauss, L. Twin transfusion syndrome. J. Pediatr. 1965.66.613.

107. Rie, H. E., Rie, E. D. Handbook of minimal brain dysfunctions. New York. Wiley. 1980.

108. Robertson, C., Finer, N. Term infants with hypoxic-ischemic encephalopathy: outcome at 3.5 years. Dev. Med. Child Neurol. 1985.27.473.

108a. Rubin, D. et al. Father's drinking (and smoking) and infant's birth weight. New Engl. J. Med. 1986.315.1551.

109. Rutter, M. Developmental neuropsychiatry. London. Churchill. 1984.

110. Rutter, M. Family and school influences on cognitive development. J. Child Psychol. Psychiatry 1985.26.683.

111. Saigal S., Rosenbaum P., Stoskopf B., Sinclair J. C. Outcome in infants 501–1000 g. birth weight delivered by residents of the McMaster Health Region. J. Pediatr. 1984.105.969.

112. Schmitt, B. D. The minimal brain dysfunction myth. Am. J. Dis. Child. 1975.129.1313.

113. Scott, H. Outcome of very severe birth asphyxia. Arch. Dis. Child. 1976.51.712.

114. Seeminova, E. A study of children of incestuous matings. Human heredity. 1971.21.108.

115. Shannon, K. M., Amman, A. J. Acquired immune deficiency syndrome in children. J. Pediatr. 1985.106.332.

116. Shaywitz, S., Shaywitz, B., Grossman, H. J. Learning disorders. Pediatr. Clin. N. Am. 1984.31.277 (Symposium).

117. Shinnar, S., Molteni, R. A., Gammon, K. et al. Intraventricular hemorrhage in the premature infant. N. Engl. J. Med. 1982.306.1464.

118. Siegel, L. Infant perceptual, cognitive and motor behavior as predictors of subsequent cognitive and language development. Canad. J. Psychol. 1979.33.382.

119. Skodak, M. The mental development of adopted children whose true mothers are feeble minded. Child Development. 1938.9.303.

120. Smith, D. W., Clarren, S. K., Harvey, M. A. Hyperthermia as a possible teratogenic agent. J. Pediatr. 1978.92.878.

121. Smithells, R. Alcohol and the fetus. Arch. Dis. Child. 1984.59.1113

122. Spector, R. Abnormal spermatozoa and perinatal disease. Dev. Med. Child. Neurol. 1964.6.523.

123. Stanley, F., Alberman, E. The epidemiology of the cerebral palsies. Clin. Dev. Med. No. 87. Oxford. Blackwell. 1984.

124. Stott, D. H. Abnormal mothering as a cause of mental subnormality. J. Child Psychol. 1962.3.79.

125. Taft, L. T. & Goldfarb, W. Prenatal and perinatal factors in childhood schizophrenia. Dev. Med. Child Neurol. 1964.6.32.
126. Thomson, A. J., Searle, M., Russell, G. Quality of survival after severe birth asphyzia. Arch. Dis. Child. 1977.52.620.
127. Towbin, A. Central nervous system damage in the human fetus and newborn infant. Am. J. Dis. Child. 1970.119.529.
128. Towbin, A. Organic causes of minimal brain dysfunction. J. Am. Med. Assoc. 1971.217.1207.
129. Ungerer, G., Sigman, M. Developmental lags in preterm infants from one to three years of age. Child Dev. 1983.54.1217.
130. Wagner, M. G., Arndt, R. Postmaturity as an aetiological factor in 124 cases of neurologically handicapped children. Clin. Dev. Med. No. 27. p. 89. 1968.
131. Walzer, S. X chromosome abnormalities and cognitive development: implications for understanding normal human development. J. Child Psychol. Psychiatry 1985.26.177.
132. Wenzel, U., Schneider, M., Zachman, M., Knorr-Mürset, G., Weber, A., Prader, A. Intelligence of patients with congenital adrenal hyperplasia due to 21-hydroxylase deficiency, their parents and unaffected siblings. Helvetica Paediatrica Acta. 1978.33.11.
133. Whitelaw, A. When to give up in severe intrapartum asphyxia? Br. J. Obstet. Gynaecol. 1982.89.1.
134. Wilson, G. S., Desmond, M. M., Verniaud, N. M. Early development of infants of heroin addicted mothers. Am. J. Dis. Child. 1973.126.457.
135. Young, B. H., Suidan, J., Antoine, C. et al. Differences in twins: the importance of birth order. Am. J. Obstet. Gynecol. 1985.151.915.
136. Yu, V. Y. H. Effectiveness of neonatal intensive care. Austr. Paediatr. J. 1984.20.85.
137. Yu, V. Y. H., Wong., P. Y., Bajuk, B. et al. Outcome of extremely low birth weight infants. Br. J. Obstet. Gynaecol. 1986.93.162.
138. Zazzo, R. Les Jumeaux, le Couple et la Personne. Paris. Presse Universitaires de France. 1960.

3

Environmental factors and development

In Chapter 2 I provided abundant evidence that for the purpose of developmental assessment, especially in infancy, it is essential to know about and to try to understand prenatal factors which may have a considerable effect on a child's development. In this chapter I shall discuss another subject of vital importance to a child's development — environmental factors. In my opinion these must be taken into consideration in assessing a child. Purely objective tests which ignore these factors must inevitably miss important information which is necessary for a proper assessment.

Experimental work

Ethology, the study of the behaviour of animals, has much of relevance to the behaviour of the child.[33,37] When rats, cats, goats, sheep and many other animals are separated from the mother at birth, so that she cannot lick and inspect them, they are likely to be rejected, even though they are returned to her a few hours after birth. As little as 5 or 10 minutes' licking and contact prevents this rejection. The effect on the young may persist throughout life, modifying behaviour. Rats handled daily between birth and weaning are more active than those which have not been handled. Newborn lambs may die if left without stimulation for as little as an hour.

There are increasingly sophisticated methods of studying the effect of environment on animals. Rats kept in a lively and active environment for 30 days[61] showed distinct changes in brain anatomy and chemistry as compared with animals kept in a dull non-stimulating environment. The cerebral cortex was thicker and weighed more; there were more glial cells, there was more synaptic contact, and more neuronal volume: there was greater acetylcholine and cholinesterase activity and an increased ratio of RNA and DNA. Puppies kept in a kennel for the first seven weeks are not as affectionate as those kept in a more happy environment. Denenberg went further, and showed that one can determine the animal's personality by appropriate manipulation of the environment: one can make a rat emotional, aggressive, poor when exposed to stress, inefficient in sex, bad at learning, and almost psychotic in behaviour.[23]

Psychologists adopt many ways of regulating an animal's environment in order to determine the effect of environmental factors on behaviour. Denenberg wrote as follows:

> 'We can take an animal and, within broad limits, we can specify the "personality" of that animal as well as some of its behavioral capabilities by the appropriate manipulation of experiences in early life. For example, one can take a newborn rat and raise it under certain conditions so that in adulthood it will be highly emotional, relatively inefficient in learning, and less capable of withstanding environmental stresses and thus more likely to die from such stresses. On the other hand, we can also produce rats, through appropriate experiences in early life, which are non-emotional, highly curious and investigatory, efficient in learning, and which are less prone to psychological upset when exposed to mildly stressful situations. Other research has shown that we can create animals which are more intelligent in the sense of being better able to solve problems to get to a goal. Turning to a different realm of behaviour, one can restrict the early experience of rhesus monkeys so that, when adults, they act in a bizarre psychotic-like manner, show almost a complete absence of appropriate sexual behaviour (this is true both for the male and for the female) and, in the few instances where the females have become pregnant, they exhibit a profound lack of appropriate maternal behaviour.'

Concept of the sensitive period

There is abundant evidence that in many animals there is a particular stage of their development at which learning in response to the appropriate stimuli is easier than at other times. This is termed the sensitive period. Sometimes a stage of development comes beyond which learning is impossible: this is the so-called critical period. Psychologists disagree about the concept of the sensitive period in the case of human beings; some[17,62] have thought that there is no satisfactory evidence for a sensitive period either for behaviour or early learning (or the lack of learning opportunities) in the first 3 years. With a colleague, I reviewed the literature concerning the sensitive period and adduced evidence that there is a sensitive period for learning in human beings.[38] For instance, if a baby is not given solid foods when he can chew (usually at 6 to 7 months) it becomes increasingly difficult to get him to take solids later.[54] Red squirrels, if not given nuts to crack by a certain age, never acquire the skill of cracking them. If chimpanzees are not given bananas to peel within a certain age, they can never learn to remove the skin.

If a child's congenital cataract is not removed by a certain age, the child will not be able to see. If a squint is not corrected in time, the child will become blind in the affected eye. If a cleft palate is not operated on by the age of 2 or 3, it becomes increasingly difficult to obtain normal speech. The longer congenital deafness remains undiagnosed, the more difficult it becomes to teach the child to speak. Whereas young children may learn to speak a foreign language fluently with a good accent, adults settling in a country may never learn to speak the language of that country fluently, however intelligent they are. It is possible that there is a sensitive period for each subject of the school curriculum for each child. If a child is taught arithmetic too soon, he will find it difficult and may develop such a dislike for it that he never learns it well: but if he is taught it too late, he may have lost interest in it, and find it difficult to learn.

There is much interest amongst educationalists in the application of the concept of the sensitive or critical period to the development of the preschool child. Maria Montessori was one of the first to recognise the importance of these periods in the teaching of children. She found that children are more receptive for learning involving the sensory system, such as the learning of colour, shape, sound and texture, at the age of 2½ to 6 years than in later years. It may be that the nursery school improves the performance of children from poor homes where the necessary stimulation at home is lacking.

It is said[21] that absolute pitch in music depends on the age at which training begins. In a study of 1000 professional musicians, 95% of those who began their training before age 4 had absolute pitch, as compared with only 5% of those who began at the age of 12 to 14 years.

Difficulties in spatial appreciation are common among black Africans. Diagrams confuse Bantus, and they often find it difficult to understand pictures in which near objects (e.g. a mouse) appear to be larger than more distant objects (e.g. an elephant). Biescheuvel,[4-6] who has carried out extensive studies on the learning difficulties of black Africans, ascribed these and similar problems to lack of early stimuli at the time of the sensitive period. He wrote 'The evidence suggests that for various functions there are critical maturational periods, during which physical well-being, mental stimulation, environmental interactions, have their optimum effect, and during which development of potentialities can be permanently affected, either positively or negatively.' He thought that failure to show Bantu children pictures (e.g. in books) in early childhood was responsible for the visuospatial difficulties later.

Bayley[2] and others have shown that there is no difference in the test scores of negro and white infants in the first 15 to 18 months of their life, but that after this age there is an increasing gap between the performance of the whites and negroes, so that in early school life the mean IQ score of negro children is significantly less than that of white children. Schaefer, in Denenberg's book, wrote that the need for early education is suggested by studies that find that schools do not increase the low levels of intellectual functioning that disadvantaged children acquire prior to school entrance.

Baughman and Dahlstrom,[1] in a study of negro and white children in the Southern States of North America, wrote that 'the need to establish comprehensive preschool programmes for children from culturally disadvantaged families has been demonstrated in many studies and in many settings. As matters stand now, great numbers of these children are psychologically handicapped when they enter the first grade: they are prepared neither for normal first grade work nor for competition with their peers who have come out of more favourable home circumstances.'

Bloom[8] suggested that the whole pattern of learning is established before the child starts school. 'We are inclined to believe', he wrote, 'that this is the most important growing period for academic achievement.' He remarked that it is much easier to learn something new than it is to stamp out one set of learned behaviour and replace it by a new set. He wrote that the environment in the first years of life was vital for the child's subsequent learning, and laid down the pattern for the future. He suggested that failure to develop a good learning pattern in these years is likely to lead to continued failure later. He pointed out that the easiest time for a child to learn is when he is developmentally ready to learn, when he has no undesirable patterns to eliminate before he can learn new ones. Others disagree with this, and consider that the great importance of early learning has been exaggerated.

Early learning

In our book *Lessons from Childhood*[39] we described many examples of children destined for fame who were given intensive teaching in the pre-school years and who later displayed remarkable precocity. Well documented examples were those of John Stuart Mill, Karl Witte, Lord Kelvin and Blaise Pascal. Kellmer Pringle[60] showed that children starting at school early (4 years 6 months to 4 years 11 months) were considerably better at reading and arithmetic than late starters (5.0 years to 5 years 6 months). Elsewhere[59] she wrote that during the first 5 years of life, 'children learn more than during any other comparable period of time thereafter. What is more important, they learn how to learn, and whether learning is a pleasurable challenge or a disagreeable effort to be resisted as far as possible. Evidence is accumulating to show that early failure to stimulate a child's desire to learn may result in a permanent impairment of learning ability to intelligence. Learning to learn does not mean beginning to teach reading or arithmetic at the earliest possible time. It is far more basic and subtle and includes motivating the child to find pleasure in learning to develop his ability to pay attention to others, to engage in purposeful activity.'

Wolff and Feinbloom[80] uttered a word of warning about efforts to teach a child in his first 2 years, rightly deprecating an atmosphere of urgency. They wrote that, 'there is no evidence at present to support the assertion that biologically fixed critical periods control the sequence of cognitive development, no evidence that scientifically designed toys are in any way superior to the usual household items available to most infants, no evidence that systematic application of such toys accelerates intellectual development, and no persuasive evidence that acceleration of specific skills during the motor phase of development, even if possible, has any lasting effects on intellectual competence'.

It is true that we do not know for certain how to help children to achieve their best. We do not know at what age positive steps should be taken to this end. We do not know what these steps should be — what toys to supply, neither do we know how successful those steps will be.

The problem is not just one of when teaching should begin and what should be taught. The problem is that of identifying factors which affect the child's development. Douglas[26] pointed to one of the factors in his follow-up study of 5000 children born in the first week of March 1946. He showed how children in lower social classes are likely to be sent to schools where the standard of work is lower than that of schools to which children of the middle or upper classes are sent. Those in lower social classes tend to be placed in a lower stream than those of the middle classes and less is expected of them, so that they achieve less than others of the same level of intelligence. In addition, less is expected of children in poor homes, and they receive less stimulation at home — and so achieve less.

Nutrition and development

Malnutrition is the commonest disease in the world. Part of the tragedy of malnutrition lies in the damage which it can inflict on the developing brain. There is evidence from Mexico, South Africa, the United States and Britain[19,20,74] that malnutrition in infancy has a harmful effect on subsequent mental development if the malnutrition is not corrected in the early weeks of infancy.

Winick[79] in America and Dobbing[25] in England have shown that malnutrition reduces the number and size of cells in the brain together with the lipid, nucleic acid, enzyme and protein content. Winick studied the DNA content of the brain because it determines the total number of cells present; the amount of DNA in each cell is fixed, and an increase in DNA reflects that aspect of tissue growth which is due mainly to cell division; a reduced head circumference accurately reflects these changes. Undernutrition of the rat and pig in the early days caused permanent reduction in the weight of the brain. Even a brief period of postnatal fasting in newborn rabbits reduced the RNA, DNA, protein and cholesterol content of the brain.[66] Winick compared 10 normal brains from well nourished Chilean children who died accidentally with the brains of nine infants who died of severe malnutrition during the first year of life. The latter were smaller in weight, protein content, RNA, DNA content and the number of cells.

In a 20-year follow-up study,[74] 20 grossly malnourished Cape coloured infants after correction of their malnutrition fared significantly less well than controls in head circumference, weight, height, IQ score, verbal and non-verbal quotients and visuomotor perceptual function.

In an earlier study,[30] one newborn baby was selected from each of 14 families in which kwashiorkor had occurred, and malnutrition was prevented by supplementary diet. At the mean age of 8.9 years the children were tested and compared with the preceding and subsequent child in the family. The children given dietary supplements in the first 2 years had a significantly higher IQ score, especially in the verbal tests.

When 101 children in Barbados,[34] having suffered malnutrition in the first year, were examined at the age of 4–11 years, and compared with 101 controls, it was found that the former, especially the boys, tended to be clumsy, faring badly on timed motor tests (repetitive movements of one or more fingers, hand patting, pronation, supination, flexion and extension of the hands, toe tapping and heel–toe tapping). They also had features of the attention deficit disorder — poor concentration and other learning difficulties.

Severe intellectual impairment was not reversed by subsequent improvement in the environment. Cravioto[19,20] found that recovery from malnutrition is accompanied by mental improvement except when there was severe malnutrition before the age of 6 months. He remarked that the human brain is growing at its most rapid rate in the early weeks (gaining 1–2 mg per minute in the perinatal period), and that damage at the period of maximum growth may be irremediable. Birch and colleagues[7] estimated the WISC score of 37 children who had been treated for kwashiorkor at the age of 6 to 30 months, and compared it with that of unaffected siblings. The mean score of the index cases was 68.5, compared with 81.5 in siblings. Compared with the controls, twice as many of the index cases had an IQ of below 70; four of the index cases and 10 of the controls had an IQ of 90 or more. One effect of malnutrition is apathy, which in turn affects the mother child interaction, so that the mother responds less to her baby and the baby receives less stimulation from the mother. Studies all over the world have shown that severe growth retardation in the first year retards later mental development, and the longer the duration of the growth retardation, the greater is the effect on mental development.

Even severe malnutrition arising from untreated congenital pyloric stenosis may be reflected by reduced visuomotor coordination and auditory memory in later years.[43] These findings on the effect of postnatal malnutrition should be considered in conjunction with the effect of intrauterine malnutrition described in the previous chapter. Chase and Martin[15] compared 19 children at a mean age of 3½ years of age who had suffered from malnutrition in the first year of life with controls of similar sex, race, social background and birthweight. The mean DQ of the controls was 99.4 and that of the test children was 82.1; but all those rehabilitated before the age of 4 months had a DQ above 80, but only in 10 admitted after 4 months was there a DQ over 80.

Practice and development

An essential factor in development is the maturation of the nervous system.

Swaddling is still practised in many parts of the world, including Russia and Iraq. Studies have shown that on release from swaddling at the end of the first year, babies in a matter of hours develop motor skills comparable with those of children who have been free to move their limbs. Though practice had been denied them, maturation of the nervous system had progressed, so that no subsequent retardation occurred. Futile efforts have been made to cause children to walk early by giving them special motor practice. The efforts failed because children cannot walk until there is the appropriate degree of maturation of the nervous system, particularly myelination. Similar futile efforts have been made to teach children early sphincter control.

Intelligence and family size

There is an inverse relationship between the size of the family and the intelligence of the child.[53] In a study of 184 American students from multiple-child families,[22] the larger and more closely spaced the family, the lower was the IQ score of the children. Complex socioeconomic factors must be involved. Surveys have shown that the eldest, the youngest and only children tend to be more intelligent than intermediate ones. This cannot be of genetic origin: environmental factors, such as the amount of time which the mother can devote to her first or only child, must be relevant. In a study of 2523 children the first and only children were superior in reading ability.[35] In two-child families the mean IQ of the children is higher when there is a longer interval between births.

Emotional deprivation

For an interesting insight into the grossest possible emotional deprivation, and lack of stimulation and opportunity to learn, the book by Jean Itard[42] is of great interest. It discusses the authenticity of stories of 53 children brought up by animals, and describes in detail three examples for which the evidence seemed convincing — Kaspar of Nuremberg, Kamala of Midnapore and Victor of Aveyron. All children, when found, walked on all fours, all were mute and all had gross defects of spatial appreciation. A vivid description of Victor included the following summary: 'His eyes looked but did not see: his ears heard but did not listen, and the organs of touch, limited to the mechanical operation of seizing and holding, had never been used to verify the shape or the existence of any object.' The rehabilitation of Victor, enabling him for instance, to take a meal in a restaurant, is a fascinating and gripping psychological study.

Emotional deprivation retards children physically and mentally. Children need love throughout their childhood and subsequently, but deprivation of love in their first 3 years may have a profound effect. It retards them in their development and in their physical growth and may cause dwarfism with decreased human growth hormone secretion from the pituitary.[71] Children brought up in an institution are likely to be retarded in sitting, walking, sphincter control and in speech. In later childhood they may display aggressiveness, selfishness, excessive thumbsucking or other body manipulations and defective verbal reasoning. Motor behaviour is relatively less retarded than verbal, adaptive and other aspects of development.

I can never forget a visit to a home for illegitimate children in a foreign city. In an upstairs room there were 20 to 30 children, aged 12 months to 3 years, sitting on the floor with no toys and no furniture apart from their cots, which had solid wooden sides. The children were not talking or crying or playing: they were sitting immobile. The most startling feature was an open window reaching down to the level of the floor, with no bar or other obstacle to prevent children falling out. When we exclaimed in astonishment, we were told that no children had ever fallen out. Seeing their immobility, we felt that they probably never would.

Recent work has indicated that progressive retardation may be arrested or reversed if there is no further emotional deprivation after the first 2 or 3 years:[17] though continuing emotional deprivation may cause permanent personality changes, including the inability to give or receive affection. It is a commonplace to find that parents guilty of child abuse or baby-battering were deprived of love and affection in their own childhood, and were battered themselves.

The book by Pavenstedt, entitled *The Drifters*,[55] a study of slum children, gave a valuable insight into the effect of a bad home. It describes the superior motor coordination of these children, combined with a lack of caution and self protective measures, resulting in frequent accidents, from which, however, they failed to learn. Pain was rarely expressed. The children tended to avoid difficult tasks instead of trying. In their relationship to others they were need-oriented, distrustful and shallow, constantly fearing aggression, retaliation and blame. They had no interest in books or stories, they were unable to take part in back and forth conversation, and their language development was poor, with a limited vocabulary.

The poor school performance of slum children is contributed to by the impairment of health and general knowledge, inadequate sleep and over-crowding, employment out of school hours, domestic duties, lack of room to play, and non-attendance at school. In middle-class families there are more verbal interactions, more stimuli to learning and greater expectations.[78]

An educational study[81] found that 'it is becoming clear that the educational handicaps of the deprived child derive not so much from the physical factors of poverty, dirt and squalor, as from the intellectual impoverishment of the home, and from the parents' attitudes towards education, towards school and towards teachers'. Parents of disadvantaged children do not expect their children to succeed; they instil an attitude of hopelessness and expectancy of failure. Many studies have indicated the lack of intelligent conversation between child and parent in these homes. Children are not questioned, and their questions are not answered — so that the children stop asking them. Parents in these homes tend to the punitive, critical and constantly derogatory towards their children.

Children react differently to emotional deprivation and separation from a parent. There may be genetic or constitutional factors which govern a child's response to his environment. Other factors are the quality of the parent-child relationship before the deprivation occurred, the age at which it occurred, the length of separation, the experiences during the period of separation, the completeness of the separation, and the attitude of the parents when the child is returned to them.

It is a mistake to suppose that emotional deprivation is confined to institutions. Some parents are afraid of loving their children, and so are afraid of picking the baby up when he cries. There are mothers who turn a deaf ear to the 12-month-old baby who is left crying all day in a pram outside with nothing but a brick wall to see. Koupernik of Paris coined the phrase 'intrafamilial hospitalism' for this condition. Children subjected to child abuse[47] almost invariably exhibit delay in speech development. Rutter[62] argued that single stresses, such as admission to hospital, rarely have a long-term effect, but that repeated stresses may. He suggested that experiences may influence later vulnerability by affecting sensitivity to later stresses.

In recent years determined efforts have been made to reduce the risk of psychological trauma in young children, especially in those who have to be separated from their mothers in the first 3 years. Local authorities now avoid placing illegitimate infants in institutions, but place them in foster homes within 2 or 3 weeks of birth. In view of early placement in foster homes it seems likely that psychological trauma from emotional deprivation, such as that described by Bowlby, is now much more rare than it used to be.

Many children have to be admitted to hospital in the first 3 years, but with the greater consciousness of the possibility of psychological trauma to such children, paediatricians and others have done much to reduce or prevent emotional disturbance by such steps as the encouragement of daily visiting by the parents, admitting mothers with their children, and the adoption of a more humane approach to the sick child.

The mode of action of emotional deprivation is uncertain. Some of the retardation of deprived children can be explained by lack of opportunity: the baby who is ready to sit or walk may miss the help which he needs. No one has time to talk to him much, to play with him and towards the end of the first year to read to him — so that the development of speech is delayed. When normally he would acquire control of the bladder, no one gives him the opportunity to use a suitable receptable, so that sphincter control is delayed. Emotional deprivation, in addition to damaging mental development, may also cause growth retardation: the mechanism of this is not fully understood.

Enrichment programmes

Many efforts have been made to prevent or undo the damaging effects of the disadvantaged home on children's intellectual development.[11,13,24,32,73] They aimed to provide stimulation which the children would otherwise have missed, to instruct parents in ways to provide emotional, sensory and play stimulation, to encourage the mothers to show love, to handle and talk to their children more, to help the children to acquire independence, to improve language and communication.

Similar methods have been used to help mentally subnormal children,[9] who are particularly liable to be 'underachievers'. But it has been argued that preschool education by itself cannot affect the cycle of disadvantage.[17] Some feel that the schemes began too late in the child's life, do not radically affect the quality of the home, and do not last long enough, so that initial improvement is followed by a decline when the extra stimulation ceases.

Environment and adopted children

Though it is said[64] that the correlation for IQ between biological children and their parents is twice as high as that between adopted children and adopting parents, there is evidence that the mean IQ of adopted children is higher than the mean for the population — perhaps because adopted children are usually much wanted, or perhaps because of socioeconomic reasons. In my own follow-up study of 240 adopted children, the mean IQ at the age of 7 or 8 was 106. In another study[72] it was stated that the IQ of adopted children was definitely superior to that of the parents. In a study of black children adopted by white parents[65] the adopted black children had a mean IQ of 106, while that of adopted white children was 111. Black children whose biological parents had an average IQ, scored above the average when adopted by white parents.

Desirable qualities in the home

I have tried to summarise those qualities of the home which enable a preschool child to achieve his best.
Qualities suggested were:
Love and security; the constant avoidance of nagging, criticism, belittling, derogation, favouritism. Avoidance of prolonged separation from the parents.

Acceptance of the child, however meagre his performance; praise for effort rather than achievement.

Firm loving discipline, with a minimum of punishment. The teaching of behaviour acceptable to others. Inculcation of thoughtfulness for others, unselfishness, good moral values: avoidance of cheating; giving him a chance to practise his new skills, to develop any special interest which he shows.

Encouragement to try to find out, to explore, to be curious; but it is unwise to allow him to fail. Success breeds success, and failure may lead to failure and refusal to try.

Encouragement, praise and reward rather than discouragement.

Encouragement of independence, and avoidance of over-protection. Calculated risks as distinct from thoughtlessness and carelessness.

Tolerance and understanding of the developing mind of the child, of his normal negativeness and aggressiveness.

Setting a good example — not only in behaviour, but in reading, television programmes, efforts to find out the causes of things.

Ambition for the child, but not over-ambition (expecting more of him than his endowment will permit). Expectation of success, of good behaviour.

Instillation of a sensible attitude to illness, without exaggeration of symptoms.

Instillation of a sensible attitude to sex.

Instillation of a tolerant attitude to others. Avoidance of criticism of others in his presence; instead teaching him to look for the good in people. Tolerance of nonconformity.

Provision of suitable play material — which will help him to use his hands, to think, to use his imagination, to construct, to determine how things work (e.g. interlocking bricks, pencils, crayons and paper, bead threading, picture dominoes, jigsaws, constructional toys such as bildit — but not mechanical toys).

Provision of suitable material which will help him to obtain the answer to questions which he has raised. Letting him develop his own play rather than telling him what to do. Encouragement of self-initiated learning without providing all the ideas.

Encouragement of accuracy, thoroughness, self confidence, initiative, leadership.

Allowing him to make mistakes and learn from them.

Teaching him to argue, to ask for the reason why, to ask questions, to think round a subject, to question what the parent says, what the radio says, to seek evidence. To evaluate, determine what causes what, to seek similarities and dissimilarities.

Teaching persistence, creativity. It is thought that creativity is implanted in the home.

Giving opportunity to enlarge his vocabulary. Accuracy and clarity of speech.

Reading to the child (e.g. from 12 months onwards or sooner).

Providing experiences outside the home — visiting the countryside, seeing natural phenomena, visiting museums, factories.

Linguistic stimulation. Teaching clarity of concepts, intelligent conversation with the child.

Demanding but democratic family environment, emphasising self-control and responsibility.

Tolerance of nonconformity

Regular and prolonged schooling, emphasising discovery rather than rote learning.

Much interest has been shown in recent years in the emotional problems of the mentally handicapped child. It is generally agreed that the mentally subnormal child is further retarded by being placed early in an institution. Mentally retarded children can improve considerably with suitable education in the preschool period or later, but can deteriorate as a result of emotional deprivation.[76]

Any chronic illness must be expected to have a considerable psychological effect on the child. Such illnesses include juvenile chronic arthritis, haemophilia, severe asthma, cystic fibrosis, severe congenital heart disease, meningomyelocele or diabetes mellitus. Diabetes has been related to learning problems at school, cognitive difficulties, the attention deficit disorder and underachievement.[67]

The environment is of such importance for the handicapped child that it must always be borne in mind in assessing his intellectual potential. It is easy to underestimate a child's ability, because due attention has not been paid to the retarding effect of his environment. One might add that it is possible to make too much allowance for his environmental difficulties.

The aim should always be to assess the mentally or physically handicapped child's maximum potential and to help him to achieve it. When one first sees a handicapped child one must remember that owing to adverse environmental factors he may be functioning at an unnecessarily low level.

Estimation of the part played by environment

It has not proved to be a profitable exercise to try to determine how much of what we term intelligence is the product of nature and how much is the product of nurture or environment. The environment can greatly lower or raise the IQ score, and some feel that a really bad home can cause mental subnormality.[75] The Clarkes,[17] discussing environmental factors in mental subnormality, concluded on the basis of measured recovery being equivalent to the degree of organic psychological damage, that cruelty and neglect may retard intellectual development by at least 17 points. In twin studies they calculated that the environment might have an even bigger effect on the IQ.

The follow up studies of Knobloch and Pasamanick[44] cast light on the problem. They studied the development of white and negro children and found that whereas motor development remained comparable in the two groups, those aspects of development most subject to social influences showed considerable differences with increasing age. The adaptive behaviour quotient rose from 105.4 to 110.9 for the white children and fell from 104.5 to 97.4 for the negroes. Language ability likewise improved in the white children and decreased in the negroes. There were corresponding changes in the overall IQ scores. Drillien[27] made similar observations in the premature babies which she followed up at Edinburgh. The difference in performance between the babies in different social classes increased with increasing age.

Barbara Tizard,[76] interested in Jensen's theory that in the United States genetic factors explain much of the IQ differences between coloured and white races, studied the progress of children of different races in the identical environment of nurseries for illegitimate children. In one study of 39 children aged 24 to 59 months — two white, 22 West African or African and 24 mixed, in the nursery for at least 6 months, 70% of them admitted before the first birthday and 86 per cent before the second — the mean test score for non-verbal intelligence, language and comprehension were similar, slightly favouring the coloured children. In another study of 64 children aged 53 months admitted by 4 months and staying in the nursery for at least 2 years, 36 were white, nine black and 19 mixed: 24 were still in the institution, 24 were adopted into white families at the mean age of 37 months, and 15 were restored to their mothers. The occupations of the fathers were equated. The mean IQ scores of the racial group were similar, but those of the adopted children were the highest.

If parents are to bring the best out of their children, they should begin in their child's first days to give him all the love which he wants: to talk to him, play with him and let him see the activities of the home. One cannot expect a child who is kept lying in a pram all day with nothing but a brick wall to see in his first year or so to be as advanced as a baby whose mother plays with him, gives him play material, talks to him, and reads to him.

Environment and the handicapped child

The environment is important not only to the normal child, but to the handicapped child.

There is abundant scope for research into the effect of environment on handicapped children. In one way or another the environment of the child with any but the mildest handicap is almost bound to be different from that of normal children. He is likely to be over-protected at home, so that his physical or sensory handicap is augmented by lack of practice and opportunity to learn. He may be the subject of favouritism or rejection. He may be the target of unkind criticism or comments made by neighbours in his presence. He may be deprived of normal tactile and manipulative experience with toys and other materials. He may be isolated from his fellows and lack their companionship. His activities outside school hours are restricted. He has to be treated differently from normal children owing to his dependence on others. He may have to be separated from his parents at an early age in order that he can be trained in a residential school suitable for his handicap, and the problem of emotional deprivation is added to the physical defect. Blind children, in particular, may suffer 'pseudo-retardation' as a result of deprivation of the normal opportunities to learn. Delay in giving solid foods may cause difficulty in chewing and eating: toilet training is delayed: they may be deprived of the opportunity to learn to dress themselves when developmentally ready to learn: they may lack the normal sensory stimuli because they are not given suitable toys: they may be stopped from placing objects in the mouth: the parents are liable to read to them less, so that their speech is retarded.

McKeown and Record[49] found that the mean IQ of twins reared together is five points less than that of twins separated at birth — and concluded that this was due to the retarding influence of one twin on the other. But I think that there is another and better explanation: parents of twins reared together have less time to talk to their twins, to play with them and read to them, than have parents of a singleton or one twin when he is separated from his co-twin.

In conclusion, the extent to which environment can advance or retard intellectual development is uncertain. The general opinion, based mostly on studies of identical twins reared apart, seems to be that not more than 20–40% of an intelligence test score is likely to be the product of environment, the rest being the product of heredity. A more exact estimate cannot be given. There are difficulties in the two main methods of study — those of twins brought up in different environments, and of children brought up in foster homes. When identical twins are reared apart, one feels that some degree of selection of the environment is almost bound to occur, and that the environment selected is likely to be similar for each sibling. In the case of foster home studies, the main difficulty is the selection of the foster home and the attempt to match the infant's supposed mental qualities with those of foster parents. There are difficulties in the equating of the environment of monozygotic twins: the twins are apt to be managed differently by their parents: they may have different appetites and different illnesses: they may differ in personality and in physical growth — all factors which may affect their mental development.

The effect of drugs

Numerous drugs may affect mental development and behaviour.[40,48] Drugs may affect powers of concentration and memory, cause aggressiveness, irritability, overactivity, speed of cerebration, excitement, insomnia, confusion, depression, drowsiness, tremors, ataxia, clumsiness, dysphagia, dysarthria, auditory and visual defects, convulsions and general mental deterioration.[40] Drugs of addiction are of particular importance. It follows that when assessing a child, a full history of all drugs taken is essential.

Numerous toxic substances, such as lead and atmospheric pollutants, may lower the child's intelligence.

Cerebral irradiation in malignant disease

In a study of 28 children in remission for at least 2 years after completing chemotherapy for acute lymphoblastic anaemia,[28,29] nine children receiving prophylactic irradiation at least 6 months after the diagnosis of leukaemia had an average or above average IQ score, but 10 who received prophylactic irradiation within 2 months of the diagnosis had a lowered score, three markedly so. This was more serious in the younger child. Verbal achievements were unaffected. In another study[29] the relevant factors were discussed — the period of maximum brain growth (2 years), so that the younger the child the greater is the risk, the nature of the treatment (irradiation alone, or irradiation with methotrexate, which may potentiate the effect of the irradiation), and later environmental factors such as stress and anxiety and loss of time from school. It was thought that the reduction of IQ score was only trivial: it is possible that the treatment may interfere with the acquisition of new learning rather than cause loss of established learning.

Children exposed to prophylactic central nervous system irradiation[16] were found on follow-up examination to have defects in cognitive function, attention span, memory, auditory learning and speed of processing information. They were more liable to psychological problems — aggressiveness, depression, suicide attempts and alcoholism[52] — apart from the frequent growth retardation due to action on the hypothalamic–pituitary function, the thyroid, ovary and testes.[70] One investigation[77] found that after treatment for leukaemia there was no immediate deterioration, but it became progressive later — especially if the irradiation occurred under the age of three.

Severe head injury

Every year in Britain thousands of children suffer head injuries as a result of accidents or child abuse; some suffer brain damage by hypoxia or cerebral vascular problems. But the great majority recover promptly without sequelae, such as headaches or more serious neurological symptoms. Behaviour before the injury, including the various components of accident proneness, may be relevant to apparent behaviour changes after the accident. Other factors relevant to the prognosis are age, sex, social class, family reaction, and the child's temperament.[63]

In a study of 344 children[10] under the age of 18, in coma for over 24 hours, followed for a year or more, there was a favourable prognosis for motor function if coma lasted less than 3 months. Seventy-three per cent regained independence in ambulation and self care, 10% were partly dependent, 9% were totally dependent and 8% remained in coma. In a Finnish study of 34 children who were unconscious for over 24 hours,[36] and were examined 4 to 10 years after the accident. Eight were unable to attend normal schools, nine performed below the pre-accident level, and 17 were within normal limits at school. Those unconscious for 2 weeks or more rarely managed well at school: 10 suffered a marked decline in intellectual level and five had fits.

In a study of the psychiatric aspect of brain injury,[69] behaviour problems (some present before the injury) included defective control of anger, poor concentration and overactivity — especially in boys. Headache was uncommon. In another study[14] the effects were worse in younger children. Cognitive difficulties are an important result.

Meningitis and encephalitis

Pyogenic meningitis in the infant is much more likely to result in serious sequelae than in the older child: the most serious type is that due to Haemophilus influenzae. The incidence of sequelae after this infection is difficult to determine, as it varies considerably in different reports — all describing results which presumably were thought to be reasonably good and worthy of publication. Feigin et al[31] found that four of 50 infant survivors suffered severe neurological and intellectual defects, and a further 14 had an IQ score of 70 to 80. Lindberg et al[50] found that 26.8% of 82 survivors had neurological or psychological sequelae: the commonest was deafness. Sell et al[68] found that 29% of 86 had severe handicaps, only 43% escaping damage. Bell and McGuiness[3] in a review suggested that between 31 and 56% had sequelae. In some there would be later convulsions.

Many years ago Miller[50] analysed the incidence of sequelae following postinfectious encephalomyelitis. Severe sequelae followed in 2 to 5% of those with encephalitis following rubella, 20% of those following chickenpox, 30% after mumps, 35% after pertussis, 35% after measles and 45% after scarlet fever. The incidence of encephalitis in measles is around 1 in 500 and of encephalitis following rubella is 1 in 6000. (The incidence of encephalitis following measles immunisation is 1 in a million, and that following rubella immunisation is 1 in 500 000.)

Vaccine damage

The controversy about the incidence of neurological sequelae following whooping cough immunisation has led to many conflicting reports, summarised by me elsewhere.[41] A thorough search of the literature has failed to provide evidence that whooping cough vaccine causes permanent brain damage. The rise of temperature which occurs in 10% of infants a few hours after the injection may, in a susceptible child, cause a benign febrile convulsion, or, in a child liable to epilepsy, an epileptic fit: but in neither case does it cause permanent brain damage.

There are no symptoms, signs, special investigations or autopsy findings which characterise brain damage following the vaccine, or which are in any way different from those in unimmunised children. It is irrational to attribute brain damage to the vaccine merely because there is no other attributable cause, for in the majority of cases of brain damage, such as that due to encephalitis, developing in children who have not been recently immunised, there is equally no attributable cause, though in some there is evidence of a neurotropic virus. It is equally irrational to ascribe 'brain damage' to the vaccine merely because symptoms developed some time after the injection. The vaccine is normally given at the time that benign febrile convulsions, infantile spasms and infections such as otitis media, a common cause of febrile fits, are liable to occur.

Near-drowning

Reports about brain damage from near-drowning are conflicting. Some[45,56,57] claim that neurological sequelae after prompt and correct management are rare: others[12,18,51,58] found that up to 20% or 30% have severe sequelae, including mental subnormality, quadriplegia and extrapyramidal signs. Near drowning in warm water is more dangerous than that in cold water. Bad prognostic signs on admission include fixed dilated pupils, coma, initial pH less than 7.0, absence of respiration, and flaccidity.

There have been considerable recent advances in the management of hypothermia and other complications of near drowning, and with good management the prognosis for survivors has improved.

Summary

The environment — the home, the neighbourhood, the school — has a profound effect on the child's development.

The concept of the sensitive or critical period described by ethologists may be applied to the developing child. Evidence is adduced to the effect that the child should be enabled to learn when he is first ready to learn.

The rôle of nutrition in the early years, of love and security, of the opportunity to practice and to develop independence, are all emphasised.

The qualities of a bad home and of a good home are discussed. I have listed some of the ways of helping a child to achieve his best.

Postnatal 'brain damage' is discussed, with particular regard to the greatly exaggerated risks of brain damage from vaccines. A considerable variety of drugs, however, can significantly lower a child's performance at school.

The effect of environment on the handicapped child is discussed.

In conclusion, a child's IQ can be considerably raised or lowered by his environment. Genetic factors contribute a major part to the child's intelligence and ability; but the effects of nature and nurture are so intimately and intricately intermingled, that efforts to separate the effects of one from the effects of the other are doomed to failure, and are an unprofitable occupation.

REFERENCES

1. Baughman, E. E., Dahlstrom, W. G. Negro and white children. A psychological study in the rural South. New York, Academic Press. 1968.
2. Bayley, N. Comparisons of mental and motor test scores for ages 1–15 months by sex, birth order, race, geographical location, and education of parents. Child Dev. 1965.36.379.
3. Bell, J. E., McGuiness, G. A. Suppurative central nervous system infections in the neonate. Seminars in Perinatology. 1982.6.1.
4. Biesheuvel, S. Symposium on current problems in the behavioural sciences in South Africa. S. Afr. J. Sci. 1963. p. 375.
5. Biescheuvel, S. An examination of Jensen's theory concerning educability, heritability and population differences. Psychol. Africana. 1972.14.87.
6. Biescheuvel, S. The study of African ability. African Studies. 1952.11.45.105.
7. Birch, H. G., Pineiro, C., Alcade, E., Toca, T., Cravioto, J. Relational of kwashiorkor in early childhood and intelligence at school age. Pediatr. Res. 1971.5.579.
8. Bloom, B. S. Stability and change in human characteristics. New York. Wiley. 1964.
9. Bricker, D., Carlson, L., Schwarz, R. A discussion on early intervention for infants with Down's syndrome. Pediatrics. 1981.67.45.
10. Brink, J. D., Imbus, C., Woo-Sam, J. Physical recovery after severe child health trauma in children and adolescence. J. Pediatr. 1980.97.721.
11. British Medical Journal. Helping the child at risk. Leading article. 1981.1.1647.
12. Brooks, J. G. The child who nearly drowns. Am. J. Dis. Child. 1981.135.998,1006.
13. Browder, J. A. The pediatrician's orientation to infant stimulation programs. Pediatrics. 1981.67.42.
14. Chadwick, O., Rutter, M., Thompson J., Shaffer, D. Intellectual performance and reading skills after localised head injury in childhood. J. Child Psychol. Psychiatry. 1981.22.117.
15. Chase, H. P., Martin, H. P. Undernutrition and child development. N. Engl. J. Med. 1970.282.933.
16. Chessells, J. M. Cranial irradiation in childhood lymphoblastic leukaemia: time for reappraisal? Br. Med. J. 1985.2.686.
17. Clarke, A. M., Clarke, A. D. B. Early experience: myth and evidence. London. Open Books. 1976.
18. Conn, A. W., Edmonds, J. F., Barker, G. A. Cerebral resuscitation in near drowning. Pediatr. Clin. North. Am. 1979.26.691.
19. Cravioto, J., Delicardie, E. R. Mental performance in school age children. Am. J. Dis. Child. 1970.120.404.
20. Cravioto, J., Robles, B. Evolution of adaptive and motor behaviour during rehabilitation from kwashiorkor. Am. J. Orthopsychiat. 1965.35.449.
21. Critchley, M., Henson, R. A. Music and the brain. London. Heinemann. 1977.
22. Dandes, H. M. Dow, E. Relation of intelligence to family size and density. Child Dev. 1969.40.641.
23. Denenberg, V. H. Education of the infant and young child. New York. Academic Press. 1970.
24. Denhoff, E. Current status of infant stimulation or enrichment program for children with developmental disabilities. Pediatrics. 1981.67.32.
25. Dobbing, J. Undernutrition and the developing brain. Am. J. Dis. Child. 1970.120.411.
26. Douglas, J. W. B. The home and the school. London. Macgibbon & Kee. 1964.

27. Drillien, C. M. Longitudinal study of growth and development of prematurely and maturely born children. Mental development 2–5 years. Arch. Dis. Child. 1961.36.233.
28. Eiser, C. Intellectual abilities among survivors of childhood leukaemia as a function of CNS irradiation. Arch. Dis. Child. 1978.53.391.
29. Eiser, C. Intellectual development following treatment for childhood leukaemia. In: Whitehouse, J. M. A., Kay, H. (Eds.) Central nervous system complications of malignant disease. London. Macmillan. 1979. p. 236.
30. Evans, D., Bowie, M. D., Hansen, J. D. L. et al. Intellectual development and nutrition. J. Pediatr. 1980.97.358.
31. Feigin, R. D., Stechenberg, B. W., Chang, M. J. et al. Prospective evaluation of treatment of Hemophilus influenzae meningitis. J. Pediatr. 1976.88.542.
32. Ferry, P. C. On growing new neurons; are early intervention programs effective? Pediatrics 1981.67.38.
33. Foss, B. M. Determinants of infant behaviour. Vol. 1 (1961), Vol. 2 (1963), Vol. 3 (1965), Vol. 4 (1969). London. Methuen.
34. Galler, J. R., Ramsey, F., Solimano, G., Ku Charski, L. T., Harrison, R. The influence of early malnutrition on subsequent behavioral development. Pediatr. Res. 1984.18.826.
35. Glass, D. C., Neulinger, J., Brim, O. G. Birth order, verbal intelligence and educational aspiration. Child Dev. 1974.45.807.
36. Heiskanen, O., Kaste, M. Late prognosis of severe brain injury in children. Dev. Med. Child Neurol. 1974.16.11.
37. Hinde, R. A. Animal behaviour. New York. McGraw Hill. 1966.
38. Illingworth, R. S., Lister, J. The critical or sensitive period, with special reference to certain feeding problems in infants and children. J. Pediatr. 1964.65.839.
39. Illingworth, R. S., Illingworth, C. M. Lessons from childhood. Edinburgh. Livingstone. 1966.
40. Illingworth, R. S. Developmental variations in relation to minimai brain dysfunction. In: Rie, H. L., Rie, E. D. (Eds.) Handbook of brain dysfunctions. New York. Wiley. 1980.
41. Illingworth, R. S. The normal child. London. Churchill Livingstone. 9th Edn. 1987.
42. Itard, J. The wild boy of Aveyron. London. NLB. 1972.
43. Klein, P. S., Forbes, G. B., Nader, P. R. Effects of starvation in infancy on subsequent learning abilities. Pediatr. Res. 1974.8.344.
44. Knobloch, H., Pasamanick, B. Mental subnormality. N. Engl. J. Med. 1962.266.1092.
45. Kruus, S., Bergström, L., Suutarinen, T., Hyvönen, R. The prognosis of near drowned children. Acta Paediatr. Scand. 1979.68.315.
46. Lindberg, J., Rosenthall, V., Nylen, O., Ringner, A. Long term outcome of Hemophilus influenzae meningitis related to antibiotic treatment. Pediatrics. 1977.60.1.
47. Lynch, M. A. The prognosis of child abuse. J. Child Psychol. Psychiatry. 1978.18.175, 180.
48. McClelland, H. A. Psychiatric complications of drug therapy. Adverse Drug Reaction Bulletin 1973. No 41.132.
49. McKeown, T., Record, R. G. Early environmental influences on the development of intelligence. Br. Med. Bull. 1971.27.48.
50. Miller, H. G., Stanton, J. B., Gibbons, J. L. Para-infectious encephalomyelitis and related syndromes. Q.J. Med. 1956.25.427.
51. Modell, J. H. et al. Near-drowning: correlation of level of consciousness and survival. Canadian Anaesthetic Soc. J. 1980.27.211.
52. Morris Jones, P. H. The long term effects of therapy for malignant disease in childhood. J. Roy. Coll. Phys. 1980.14.178.
53. Nisbet, J. D., Entwistle, N. J. Intelligence and family size. Br. J. Educ. Psychol. 1964.37.188.
54. Palmer, S., Thompson, R. J., Linscheid, T. R. Applied behaviour analysis in the treatment of childhood feeding problems. Dev. Med. Child Neurol. 1975.17.333.
55. Pavenstedt, E. The Drifters. Children of disorganised lower class families. London. Churchill. 1967.

56. Pearn, J., Nixon, J. Prevention of childhood drowning accidents. Med. J. Austr. 1977.1.616.
57. Pearn, J. H., Bart, R. D., Yamaoka, R. Neurologic sequelae after childhood near-drowning: a total population study from Hawaii. Pediatrics 1979.64.187.
58. Peterson, B. Morbidity of childhood near-drowning. Pediatrics 1977.59.364.
59. Pringle, Kellmer, M. L. Speech, learning and child health. Proc. Roy. Soc. Med. 1967.60.885.
60. Pringle, Kellmer, M. L., Butler, N. R., Davies, R. 11,000 Seven year olds. London. Langham. 1966.
61. Rosenzweigh, M. R., Bennett, E. L., Diamond, M. C. Sci. Amer. 1972.226.22.
62. Rutter, M. The long term effects of early experience. Dev. Med. Child Neurol. 1980.22.800.
63. Rutter, M., Chadwick, O., Shaffer, D. Head injury. In Rutter, M. (Ed). Developmental neuropsychiatry. London. Churchill Livingstone. 1984, p. 83.
64. Rutter, M. Family and school influences on cognitive development. J. Child Psychol. Psychiatry. 1985.26.683.
65. Scarr S., Weinberg R. A. IQ test performance of black children adopted by white parents. Amer. Psychol. 1976.31.726.
66. Schain, R. J., Watanabe, K., Harel, S. Effects of brief postnatal fasting on brain development of rabbits. Pediatrics. 1973.51.240.
67. Schlieper, A. Chronic illness and school achievement. Dev. Med. Child Neurol. 1985.27.75.
68. Sell, S. H. W., Merrill, R. E., Doyne, E. O., Zimsky, E. P. Long-term sequelae of Hemophilus influenzae meningitis. Pediatrics. 1972.49.206.
69. Shaffer, D. Psychiatric aspects of brain injury in childhood. Dev. Med. Child Neurol. 1973.15.211.
70. Shalet, S. M., Beardwell, C. G. Endocrine consequences of treatment of malignant disease in childhood: a review. J. Roy. Soc. Med. 1979.72.39.
71. Silver, H. K., Finkelstein, M. Deprivation dwarfism. J. Pediatr. 1967.70.317.
72. Skodak, M., Skeels, H. M. A follow up study of one hundred adopted children. In Bronfenbrenner, U., Mahoney, M. A. (Eds) Influences on human development. Illinois. Dryden Press. 1975, p. 60.
73. Soboloff, H. R. Development enrichment programmes. Dev. Med. Child Neurol. 1979.21.423.
74. Stoch, M. B., Smythe, P. M., Moodie, A. D., Bradshaw, D. Psychosocial outcome and CT findings after gross undernourishment during infancy: a 20 year developmental study. Dev. Med. Child Neurol. 1982.24.419.
75. Stott, D. H. Abnormal mothering as a cause of mental subnormality. J. Child Psychol. Psychiatry. 1962.3.79.
76. Tizard, B. I.Q. and race. Nature. 1974.247.316.
77. Traddle, V., Britton, P. G., Craft, A. C., Noble, T. C., Kernahan, J. Intellectual function after treatment for leukaemia or solid tumors. Arch. Dis. Child. 1983.58.949.
78. Tulkin, S. R., Kagan, J. In Bronfenbrenner, U., Mohoney, M. A. (Eds) Influences on human development. Illinois. Dryden Press. 1975.
79. Winick, M. Nutrition and development. New York. Wiley. 1972.
80. Wolff, P. H., Feinbloom, R. I. Critical periods and cognitive development in the first two years. Pediatrics 1969.44.999.
81. Working Party for Schools Council No. 27 Cross'd with adversity. The education of socially disadvantaged children in secondary schools. London. Evans and Methuen International. 1970.

4

Abilities and reflexes of the newborn

Knowledge of the abilities of the newborn, and of his primitive reflexes, is important not only for the understanding of human development as a whole, but also for research into its application for the overall assessment of a baby, for the recognition of possible neurological damage in the prenatal and perinatal period, and for establishment of the prognosis for his future. At present we know little firm evidence concerning the practical application of such knowledge: but knowing that all mentally subnormal infants are retarded in all aspects of development (except later sometimes in gross motor development), it would be reasonable to assume that a study of the quality of the responses of the newborn, the ease or difficulty with which they are elicited, and a study of his primitive reflexes, would be likely to throw light on his maturation in utero and its possible significance for the future. For example, the strength of the grasp reflex in a full term baby may be an index of his maturation: a notably 'advanced' newborn may show virtually no grasp reflex, while a persistent grasp reflex long after the newborn period is a pointer to neurological damage. I believe that the recently developed sophisticated methods of studying the abilities of the newborn may provide important material for predicting a child's future potential. It offers a wide field for research.

Abilities of the newborn

It has long been known that the fetus can hear in utero. New tests by ultrasound and other methods indicate that from 26 weeks' gestation hearing can be demonstrated by the startle response.[3] Drife[10] wrote that early in pregnancy the fetus responds to amniocentesis and touching the mother's abdomen, and responds to noise by 24 to 25 weeks' gestation. Habituation to the stimulus is learnt in utero. The response to sound had been used in the perinatal period to detect fetal distress.[23] Lack of fetal heart rate acceleration to sound stimulation indicated fetal hypoxia.

While a vast amount has been written about the development of the infant and young child, the neurological examination of the newborn baby has until recently been relatively neglected. The subject was barely mentioned by Arnold Gesell, whose developmental studies began with the child at 4 to 6 weeks of age. We owe our knowledge of the neurological and developmental examination of the newborn baby to a small body of workers, which includes especially Albrecht Peiper, André Thomas, Madame Saint-Anne Dargassies and Heinz Prechtl. Their writings have been used extensively in the preparation of this section. Minkowski and Dargassies[18] have given me permission to quote their work at length.

In recent years psychologists have somewhat belatedly found that the human infant is a fascinating creature to study, and by various sophisticated devices have demonstrated his previously inadequately recognised visual, auditory and perceptual abilities, even in the newborn period.[6,9,13,17,24] Within minutes of birth the infant follows a face-like pattern more than other patterns of similar brightness.[7,15] He turns to and prefers milk smells to those of other substances[4,5,] he can taste and can show by altered sucking patterns that he can tell the difference between human milk and cow's milk formula designed to reproduce the content of human milk. In a study of 40 newborn babies, at a median age of 9 minutes, moving stimuli caused turning of head and eyes.[4,5] There was a greater response to a proper picture of a face than to a scrambled one, indicating that organised visual perception is an unlearned capacity. He shows more interest in a black and white pattern than in a blank grey card:[1] he will look at a black on white drawing of a face longer than three black dots on white: At birth he can detect the difference between a pattern of stripes and a mere green patch, or between vertical and oblique gratings, and between straight and curved lines.[12] When the infant becomes bored with a picture, he shows increased attention to a different one. If shown two identical red spheres until he looks away in boredom, and is then shown one red sphere next to a red cube, he shows more interest in a red cube. Horizontal tracking is present at birth, and vertical tracking at 4 to 6 weeks.[8] He can focus, and can follow his mother over an angle of 180 °. As early as 2 weeks of age he will watch his mother's face longer than that of a stranger.[7] He can adjust to distance: if an object is moved towards his face he pulls his head back in defence. At 3 to 4 weeks he fixates more on the edge of a face than on any facial feature, but at 7 weeks looks much more at the eyes, especially when his mother is speaking to him. He can discriminate colour. At 4 weeks he shows a rudimentary judgment of the size of two objects when they are presented at different distances from his eyes.[26] Long before he begins to smile, he begins to watch his mother intently as she speaks to him — and this helps to strengthen the bond between mother and baby, causing each to respond to the other. When the baby cries and is picked up, his visual alertness is increased.[13] He will turn his head to a human voice, and his face alerts as he searches for its source.[5] He prefers human sounds to pure tones of the same pitch. It has been shown that even in the first month he will imitate protrusion of the tongue: this ability is likely to disappear, like the walking reflex, before the more voluntary act begins.[15]

The newborn infant turns his eyes to sound. In one study when a mother spoke through a glass screen, the baby could see her but only hear her by means of two stereo speakers: the balance on the stereo system could be adjusted so that the sound could appear to come from straight ahead or from other positions. The baby was seen to be contented if the sound appeared to come from straight ahead, but if the mother's voice and mouth, as seen by the baby, did not coincide, the baby was disturbed. The infant thus shows auditory localisation, auditory-visual coordination, and expectation that the sound comes from the mouth. The newborn infant responds more to the female voice than to the voice of a male. In his review, containing 390 references, Appleton[1] wrote that the newborn has well-developed auditory skills, showing wide discrimination of auditory signals involving that of intensity, duration and location of sound. Certain types of auditory stimulation, especially rhythmical or low frequency sounds, are soothing, while others distress him. A sudden sound causes a startle reflex, blinking of the eyes or a change in the respiratory rhythm.

Within 6 to 10 days the baby responds to smell by turning to his mother's breast:[15] and he can differentiate his mother's smell from that of strangers.[17] It is fascinating to see the young baby begin to root for milk when brought near to his mother's breast when it is completely covered by her clothes. He can be shown to localise smell by turning his head away from an unpleasant one. Within a week he shows a preference for his mother's smell, voice and appearance.

A sugar-coated finger in the mouth elicits sucking and licking: the finger is followed when it is withdrawn. A salt-coated finger causes a grimace, with little or no sucking movement. The finger is forced back with the tongue towards the lip, along with irregular head movements. The finger is not followed.

The new infant communicates with his mother by watching her (and later by smiling and a week or two later by vocalising), by crying, clinging and holding his arms out for her. Babies kept at the mother's bedside (i.e. rooming in) establish the day-night rhythm sooner, organising their sleep rhythm better than if they are cared for by a variety of personnel in a nursery. The baby communicates by different types of cry — the cry of hunger or pain, loneliness, thwarting, fear or change of posture. It is notable that his various perceptual functions, involving vision, hearing and smell, are far in advance of the development of his motor skills.

Conditioning can be developed during the first week. A 3-day-old infant can learn to turn his head to one side to obtain a reward when a bell sounds and to the opposite side when a buzzer sounds.

Habituation occurs, for when he sees a pattern repeatedly, he turns away to look at a new one. Though he responds to a sound stimulus, he will not respond repeatedly unless the tone or frequency changes (dishabituation).[15] For this he has to remember. The speed at which habituation occurs increases with the maturity of the baby: it is slower in children of the lowest social class, or in those who had a low Apgar score.

The rate of habituation at 3 months is said to correlate with Binet tests at $3\frac{1}{2}$ years. I feel that psychologists should attempt, by follow-up studies, to correlate the rapidity and maturity of these visual, auditory and perceptual responses to the maturity of the baby and to subsequent developmental quotients. A mentally subnormal child is late in responding to his mother by smiling and vocalising and slow in developing conditioned responses.[11]

Reflexes and reactions in the newborn period

The primitive reflexes are of great interest: but for practical developmental assessment in a busy clinic one has to distinguish that which is interesting from that which is important. These primitive reflexes may, however, repay further study, and because their status for the purposes of diagnosis and prognosis has yet to be established, I felt that some of them should be described in detail here.

Oral reflexes

Sucking and swallowing reflexes are present in full-term babies and all but the smallest preterm baby. Their absence in a full-term baby would suggest a developmental defect. The sucking reflex is tested by introducing a finger or teat into the mouth, when vigorous sucking will occur.

The 'rooting' or 'search' reflex is present in normal full-term babies. When the baby's cheek contacts the mother's breast or other part, he 'roots' for milk. It enables him to find the nipple without his being directed to it. When the corner of the mouth is lightly touched, the bottom lip is lowered on the same side, and the tongue moved towards the point of stimulation. When the examiner's finger slides away from that point, the head turns to follow it. When the centre of the upper lip is stimulated, the lip elevates, baring the gums, and the tongue moves towards the place stimulated. If the finger slides along the oronasal groove, the head extends. When the centre of the bottom lip is stroked, the lip is lowered and the tongue is directed to the site of stimulation. If the finger moves towards the chin, the mandible is lowered and the head flexes. The above reflexes are termed 'the cardinal points reflexes' of the French writers.

We have found that these reflexes are difficult to elicit except when the child is near his feed time. They presumably correspond to the mouthing reflex described by Gesell.

Eye reflexes

Blink reflexes. Various stimuli will provoke blinking, even if the child is asleep, or tensing of the eyelids if the eyes are closed. For example, a sharp

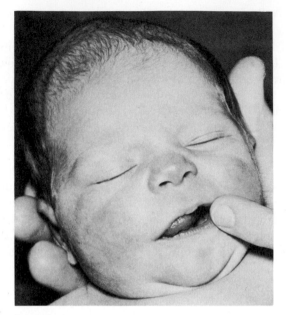

Fig. 1 Cardinal points reflex.

noise elicits the cochleo-palpebral reflex; a bright light elicits the visuo-palpebral or 'dazzle' reflex, in which there is blinking or closure of the eyes, and a painful touch elicits the cutaneo-palpebral reflex. The naso-palpebral reflex consists of blinking is response to tapping the bridge of the nose. Peiper's optic reflex consists of opisthotonos when a bright light shines on the eyes. The ciliary reflex is blinking on stroking the eyelashes. McCarthy's reflex is homolateral blinking on tapping the supraorbital area. In abnormal babies the reflex is produced by stimulation at a distance from the supraorbital region — e.g. over the vertex of the skull. If it is difficult to elicit the reflex because if the eyes are closed, stimulation of the circumoral region may cause the baby to open the eyes, so that the test can be more easily performed. The corneal reflex consists of blinking when the cornea is touched. The satisfactory demonstration of these reflexes shows that the stimulus, whether sound, light or touch, has been received, that cerebral depression is unlikely, and that the appropriate muscles can contract in response.

The doll's eye response. This is so named because there is a delay in the movement of the eyes after the head has been turned. If the head is turned slowly to the right or left, the eyes do not normally move with the head. The reflex is always present in the first 10 days, disappearing thereafter as fixation develops. It would be asymmetrical in abducens paralysis. The reflex may persist beyond the first few days in abnormal babies (see p 259).

Response to rotation. The subject of rotational nystagmus in neonates was discussed by Peiper.[21] The examiner holds the baby facing him and tilted forwards at about 30 °. He then spins round two or three times. During rotation the eyes deviate in the direction of the movement; on stopping they deviate in the reverse direction and coarse nystagmus occurs. This test depends on vestibular function, but it is useful for demonstrating ocular palsies.

Pupil reflexes. The pupil reacts to light, but in the preterm baby and some full term babies the duration of exposure to the light may have to be prolonged to elicit the reflex. The light used should not be bright, for a bright light will cause closure of the eyes. Thomas described the remarkable integration of reflexes which enables a newborn baby to turn his head towards the source of light.

The photic sneeze reflex consists of a sneeze when a bright light is shone into the eyes.

Resistance to passive opening of the eyes. This is present from birth.

André Thomas wrote that the baby only begins to respond to the rapid approach of objects to the eyes after 7 or 8 weeks or later.

Moro reflex

The Moro reflex can be elicited in two ways. The preferred method (Fig. 2) is to hold the baby at an angle of about 45 ° from the couch, and then

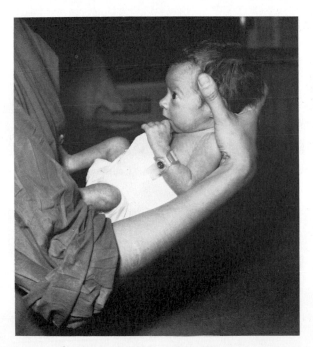

Fig. 2 Preferred position for eliciting the Moro reflex: child supported at angle of 45° from the couch. (Courtesy Professor Dubowitz.)

suddenly let the head fall back a short way. Figure 3 shows the full response. Figure 4 shows an alternative method. The baby is placed supine and the back of the head is supported on the palm of the hand an inch or so above the table. Rapid release of the hands causes the sudden movement of the cervical region which initiates the reflex.

The reflex consists of abduction and extension of the arms. The hands open, but the fingers often remain curved. This is shown well in Figure 3. This phase is followed by adduction of the arms as if an embrace. The reflex is also accompanied by crying, extension of the trunk and head with movement of the legs (the nature of which depends upon their original position). The Moro reflex is present in preterm babies, except the very small ones, but the arms tend to fall backwards on to the table during the adduction phase because the anti-gravity muscles are weaker than in the full-term baby. After a month or two the hand of the full-term baby does not open as fully as that of the newborn child.

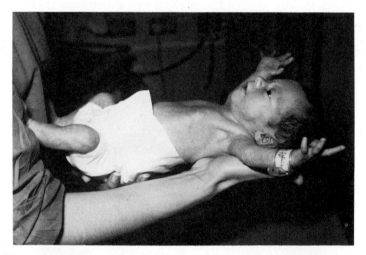

Fig. 3 Moro reflex, abduction phase, hands open. (Courtesy Professor Dubowitz.)

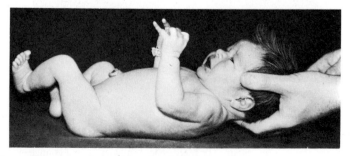

Fig. 4 Moro reflex, alternative position for eliciting the reflex.

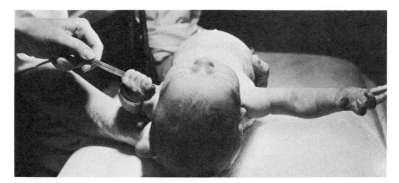

Fig. 5 Inhibition of Moro response in left hand because it is holding on object.

The reflex is less extensive in hypertonia; the full movement of the arm is prevented by the increased muscle tone. In severe hypertonia the reflex cannot be elicited at all: in less severe hypertonia there is little movement of the arms and the hands may fail to open. In severe hypotonia it is difficult to obtain the reflex: and it is reduced if the mother has been heavily sedated or if there is cerebral damage. It is asymmetrical if there is an Erb's palsy, a fractured clavicle or humerus, or a hemiplegia. It is inhibited on one side if the hand is holding an object. When eliciting the response the head should be in the midline and the hands should be open.

The reflex may be difficult to obtain in preterm babies, but it is always present when they are awake and otherwise normal.

The Moro response is a vestibular reflex. It disappears by about 3 or 4 months of age.

The startle reflex

This is often confused with the Moro reflex. In the startle reflex, obtained by a sudden loud noise or by tapping the sternum, the elbow is flexed (not extended, as in the Moro reflex), and the hand remains closed.[20] Based on observations of 12 normal newborn infants, it was said that in the Moro reflex there are more outward and inward arm movements than in the startle reflex, and they are more simultaneous and more symmetrical in distance of movement.[2]

The grasp reflex

This reflex consists of two parts, the grasp reflex, and the response to traction. The grasp reflex is elicited by introducing a finger or other suitable object into the palm from the ulnar side. When the palm is stimulated the fingers flex and grip the object. The head should be in the midline during this test. If it is not, it will be found that the grasp reflex is more easily elicited on the side to which the occiput is directed. The dorsum of the

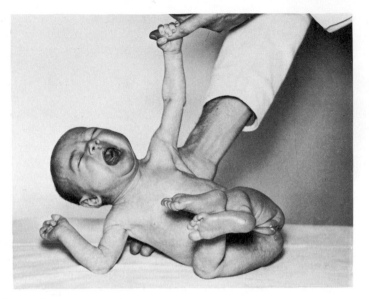

Fig. 6 Grasp reflex.

hand should not be touched during the test because this excites the opposite reflex and the hand opens. This is one of the best examples of the conflict between reflexes, a phenomenon which is discussed in the writings of André Thomas and his colleagues.[25]

Once the grasp reflex is obtained the finger can be drawn gently upwards. As this is done in the full term baby the grip is reinforced and there is a progressive tensing of the muscles from the wrist to the shoulder, until the baby hangs from the finger momentarily. It is facilitated by the initiation

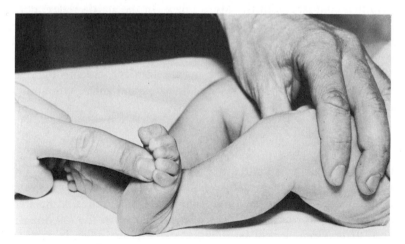

Fig. 7 Plantar grasp reflex.

of sucking movements. In the preterm baby the arm can be drawn upwards, but when traction is applied the grip opens and there is much less tensing of the arm muscles. A similar response can be demonstrated by gently stroking the sole of the foot behind the toes.

The grasp reflex is assessed partly with regard to intensity, partly with regard to symmetry, and partly with regard to persistence after it should have disappeared. An exceptionally strong grasp reflex may be found in the spastic form of cerebral palsy and in kernicterus. It may be asymmetrical in hemiplegia and in cases of cerebral damage. It should have disappeared in 2 or 3 months and persistence may indicate the spastic form of cerebral palsy.

Foot reflexes

The grasp reflex of the foot is mentioned above. The withdrawal reflex consists of a brisk flexion of the limb and occurs in response to a noxious stimulus such as a pin prick applied to the sole of the foot. It is commonly unobtainable in children with a meningomyelocele. It may be absent or weak in a baby born as a breech with extended legs.

The crossed extension reflex is obtained by holding one leg extended at the knee and applying firm pressure to the sole or stroking it on the same side. The free leg flexes, adducts and then extends, giving the impression of attempting to push away the stimulating agent. It is not normally obtained after the first month. It may be obtained in the preterm baby, but the adduction component of the reflex does not appear until the 37th week of gestation.

It is remarkable that many doctors think that the plantar response in term infants in the early months is extensor. It is not — as can be readily demonstrated in a baby clinic. The reflex is tested by the finger — and never by a key or other instrument. The stimulating finger should not be taken across the sole of the foot, for that would elicit the plantar grasp reflex: the stimulus should be applied to the distal half of the outer side of the foot.

A false extensor response can sometimes be obtained merely by flexing the hips: a false flexor response is obtained by conveying the stimulus across the sole of the foot, thus introducing the plantar grasp reflex; the stimulus should be confined to the distal half of the outer side of the foot. I have examined the plantar response in many hundreds of babies at 6 weeks of age in well-baby clinics, and find that it is almost invariably flexor unless the child has cerebral palsy of the spastic type.

In disease of the pyramidal tracts (Ch. 16) in older infants and children the extensor plantar response may be obtained over a wide area — by stroking the tibia (Oppenheim's sign), squeezing the gastrocnemius (Gordon's sign), flexing the hip against resistance, and often by stimulating the skin of the abdomen, thorax or even the neck.

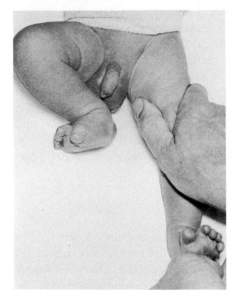

Fig. 8 Crossed extension reflex. First phase: flexion of contralateral leg.

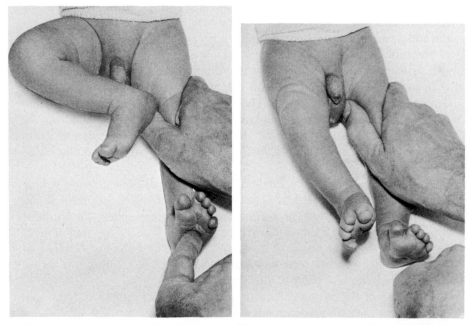

Fig. 9. Crossed extension reflex. Second stage: adduction.

Fig. 10 Crossed extension reflex. Third stage: extension.

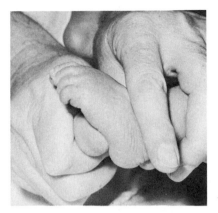

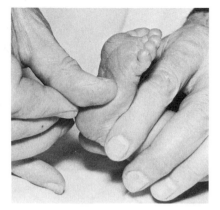

Fig. 11 Plantar response — incorrect method. Stimulation across sole of foot has elicited the grasp reflex.

Fig. 12 Plantar response — correct method of eliciting it, stimulation of distal half of outside of foot.

Hip reflexes

When one leg is flexed at the hip the other leg flexes. If strong pressure is applied to the femoral nerve in the inguinal canal the contralateral and less often the homolateral leg extends. A flexion reflex in response to strong inguinal pressure has been described as a sign of meningitis.

Placing and walking reflexes

The placing or limb placement reaction is elicited by bringing the anterior aspect of the tibia or ulna against the edge of a table. The child lifts the leg up to step onto the table, or elevates the arm to place the hand on the table. The reflex is constantly present at birth in full-term babies weighing over 1800 g, and after the first 24 hours in preterm babies weighing over 1700 g.

The walking or stepping reflex is obtained by holding the baby upright over a table, so that the sole of the foot presses against the table. This initiates reciprocal flexion and extension of the legs, simulating walking. Owing to the action of the adductor muscles, one leg often gets caught behind the other. This must not be confused with adductor spasm. A walking reflex can be demonstrated in preterm babies, but they differ from full-term babies in walking on their toes. The walking reflex disappears in normal children by the age of 5 or 6 weeks, but can be demonstrated for several more weeks if the baby's head is extended when his foot is flat on the couch.[16]

Heel reflex

Percussion of the heel or pressure on the sole of the foot causes extension of the limb.

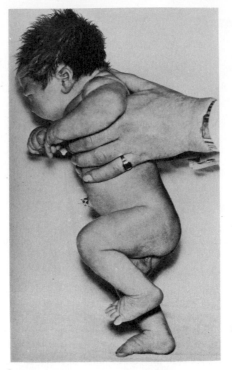

Fig. 13 The walking reflex.

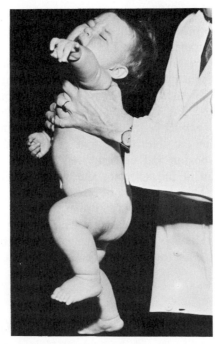

Fig. 14 Walking reflex in 5-month-old baby, seen when the neck was extended.

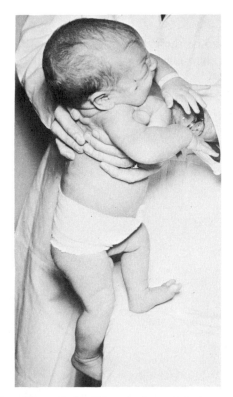

Fig. 15 Placing reaction of lower limbs. When the front of the leg touches the edge of the table, the baby steps over the edge.

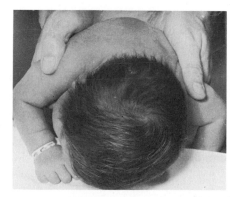

Fig. 16 Placing reaction of upper limbs.

Leg straightening reflex (a righting reflex)

When the sole of the foot is pressed on to the couch, the legs and body straighten.

The magnet reflex

When the child is supine the examiner's finger is pushed against the sole of the foot, and the knee and hip flex, and as the finger is withdrawn, the foot follows the finger.

Trunk incurvation (Galant's reflex)

When the child is held in ventral suspension or is placed in the prone position, stimulation of the back lateral to the spine, or of the lumbar region, causes flexion of the trunk towards the side of the stimulus (Fig. 17).

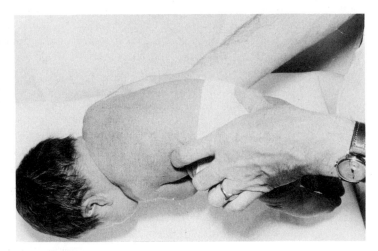

Fig. 17 Galant's reflex (trunk incurvation).

The Perez reflex

All newborn babies show this. When the child is in the prone or ventral suspension, pressure is applied upwards along the spine from the sacrum towards the head. The infant flexes the arms and legs, extends the neck and cries.

When the glutei are pricked on the outer side of the buttocks, the trunk flexes to the side stimulated.

Redressement du tronc

This is another reflex derived from the French workers. The baby is held with his back to the examiner. Firm stimulation of the soles of the feet causes extention at the hips and elevation of the trunk. The reflex appears at about 35 weeks' gestation, but extension of the spine does not begin until about 37 weeks.

The tonic neck reflexes

These are asymmetrical and symmetrical. The asymmetrical one is the better known, and is seen at intervals in young babies in the first 2 months. When the child is in the supine position and not crying, he may be seen to lie with the head turned to one side with the arm extended to the same side. The contralateral knee is often flexed. In normal babies passive rotation of the head causes some increase of tone of the upper limb on the side to which the rotation occurs, but one rarely sees full extension of the limb. The reflex normally disappears by the age of 2 or 3 months. In severe cerebral palsy the reflex persists and may increase. One may see obvious extension of the arm when the head is passively rotated.

The reflex is more marked in spastic babies, and persists longer than in normal babies. The reflex is partly responsible for preventing the child rolling from prone to supine or vice versa is the early weeks. The symmetrical tonic neck reflex is evoked by flexion or extension of the neck.

On raising the head of a kneeling child, extensor tone increases in the arms, and flexor tone increases in the legs. If the reflex is strong, the child extends the arms and flexes the legs. Flexing the neck has the opposite effect. The influence of this reflex is seen in normal children when they raise the head and shoulders in the prone: it helps them to support themselves on the arms and to get on to hands and knees. The reflex disappears when they learn to crawl, a movement which demands independence of movement of the limbs from the position of the head. In cerebral palsy the reflex is usually overactive. The child can only extend his arms in kneeling when the head is raised: the legs are then fixed in flexion. As long as the head is raised the child is unable to extend his legs. If the head is lowered, the arms flex, the legs extend and the child falls on his face, so that he is unable to crawl.

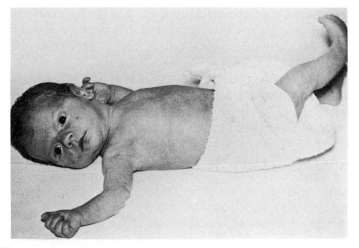

Fig. 18 The asymmetrical tonic neck reflex.

Tonic labyrinthine reflexes

These reflexes affect all four limbs and interact closely with the tonic neck reflexes. Their action in normal children in uncertain, but in children with cerebral palsy they cause marked changes in muscle tone. Their effect is most clearly seen on the head, shoulders, arms and trunk. While lying supine, the head of the child with cerebral palsy is pulled backwards and passive flexion may be strongly resisted. In the prone position, flexion of the head, neck and spine occurs and passive raising of the head is resisted.

When the normal child of 4 months or more is in the prone position and the chin is passively raised, there is a protective extension of the arms, with the use of the hands for support. In the child with cerebral palsy, the response depends on the relative predominance of the tonic labyrinth and the symmetrical tonic neck reflexes. If the former predominate, the child draws the arms up in flexion and remains in mid-air suspended by his head. He cannot support his body weight on his arms. He falls on his face when placed into the kneeling posture. He cannot get on to his hands and knees and cannot raise his head and extend the spine.

If the symmetrical tonic neck reflex predominates, there is tonic extension of the arms with flexion of the legs. If the head is flexed passively, the arms flex, the hips extend and the child falls on his face. He cannot crawl, because the legs show strong flexor spasticity as long as the head is raised.

Righting reflexes

These make their appearance in a definite chronological order and are responsible for certain basic motor activities. They enable the child to roll from prone to supine and supine to prone. They help him to get on to his hands and knees and to sit up. They are responsible for the ability to restore the normal position of the head in space and to maintain the normal postural relationship of the head, trunk and limbs during all activities. The reflexes include: (a) Neck righting reflex. This is present at birth and is strongest at the age of 3 months. Turning of the head to one side is followed by movement of the body as a whole. (b) Labyrinth righting reflex acting on the head. This is present at 2 months of age, and strongest at 10 months. It enables the child to lift the head up in the prone position (when 1 to 2 months old) and later when in the supine position. (c) The body righting reflex, acting on the body. This appears at 7 to 12 months. It modifies the neck righting reflex and plays an important role in the child's early attempts to sit and stand.

In severe cases of cerebral palsy the righting reflexes are absent. The child cannot turn to one side as the neck righting reflex is inhibited by the labyrinth reflex. He cannot raise the head in the supine or prone position. He has great difficulty in turning over and sitting up. In severe cases of cerebral palsy it will be found that when the examiner attempts to flex the child's head, holding the back of the head, there is strong resistance to flexion: the head will extend and the whole back may arch.

The Landau reflex

When the child is held in ventral suspension, the head, spine and legs extend: when the head is depressed, the hip, knees and elbows flex. The reaction is normally present from the age of 3 months,[19] is present in most infants in the second 6 months, and becomes increasingly difficult to evoke after the age of 1 year. Absence of the reflex over the age of 3 months is seen in cases of motor weakness, cerebral palsy and mental subnormality.

The parachute reaction

This appears at 6 to 9 months and persists throughout life. The reflex is elicited by holding the child in ventral suspension and suddenly lowering him towards the couch. The arms extend as if to protect him from falling. In children with cerebral palsy the reflex is absent or incomplete owing to the strong flexor tone in this position. In a child with hemiplegia the reflex would be normal on the unaffected side.

The propping reactions are similar: from about 5 to 7 months, when the child in the sitting position is tilted to one side or backwards, the arms extend to the appropriate position as if to protect him from falling.

Tendon reflexes

André Thomas paid surprisingly little attention to the knee jerks and other tendon jerks, and did not regard them as being important. I disagree with this attitude, because I consider that they provide information of considerable value in developmental assessment.

When the knee jerk is elicited in a newborn infant, there is commonly an associated adduction of the opposite leg. When the knee jerk is not obtained, the adduction of the opposite leg may occur alone. The jerks may be absent in a severely shocked child or in a child who has a brain defect. They are exaggerated in the spastic form of cerebral palsy.

The most useful tendon jerks and the easiest to test are the biceps, supinator jerks and knee jerks. They are likely to be exaggerated in the spastic form of cerebral palsy. In diseases of the pyramidal tracts the area over which the tendon jerks are obtained is greatly increased — just as in older children the area over which the plantar response is obtained is increased. Consequently one begins to test for the biceps jerk over the shoulder, and tap at intervals until the biceps tendon is reached. One begins to test for the knee jerk by tapping over the dorsum of the foot. One taps at intervals up the leg until the patellar tendon is reached. A brisk response over the shoulder may be the only indication that there is involvement of

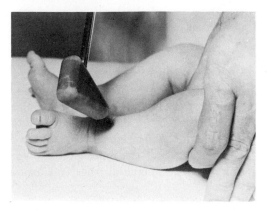

Fig. 19 Method of testing knee jerk. One begins by tapping over the dorsum of the ankle and works up to the patellar tendon. The heel must be resting on the couch, with the leg relaxed.

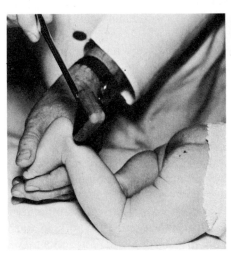

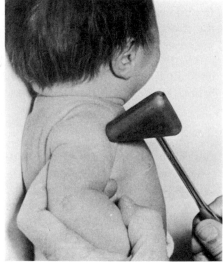

Fig. 20 Method of testing ankle jerk.

Fig. 21 Method of testing for biceps jerk — beginning over the tendon and working up to the shoulder.

the upper limbs in a child previously thought to have a spastic paraplegia: a brisk response over the dorsum of the foot may be within normal limits. As always, one can never draw the line between normal and abnormal, and only personal experience can guide one as to whether to accept the reflex as normal, or to suspect cerebral palsy of the spastic type. Asymmetry of the knee jerk would certainly suggest spastic hemiplegia. Nevertheless, asymmetry of tone or of tendon jerks may not necessarily be permanent, but it does indicate the need for follow-up examinations.

Ankle clonus

Ankle clonus is elicited by flexion and abduction of the hip, flexion of the knee, and then rapid but gentle dorsiflexion of the ankle to elicit the stretch reflex. The test should be carried out only when one feels that the limb is relaxed and the child is not resisting. Ankle clonus is an indication that the muscle tone is more marked than usual, but it by no means necessarily signifies disease, even if the clonus is fairly well sustained. The finding of unusually brisk tendon jerks and ankle clonus is merely an indication that the child should be re-examined in a month or two. It is true that the older the child with ankle clonus in the early weeks, the more likely it is to be significant. The diagnosis of cerebral palsy or other abnormality must never be made on the finding of single signs (such as unusually brisk tendon jerks with or without ankle clonus), but only on a combination of signs (see Ch. 16).

Superficial reflexes

The abdominal reflexes can always be obtained in the newborn baby when he is quiet. The reflex is reduced if the abdomen is distended, or if the skin is dry.

In addition to the usual contraction of the abdominal muscles, as seen in adults, there is commonly a curving of the trunk to the affected side, with a tendency to contraction of the muscles on the opposite side. The response is more extensive than in adults, and the zone over which the reflex is obtained is wider. During or immediately after the response there is commonly flexion of the homolateral leg or of both legs. The reflex is not obtained in babies with serious cerebral lesions.

The palmomental and similar reflexes

Babkin described a reflex consisting of opening of the mouth when the infant's palm is pressed. When the thenar or hypothenar eminences are stroked, there may be contraction of the chin muscles and uplifting of the leg. When the child is asleep in the supine position, and the neck is touched, the hand strokes it while the head rotates. If the right ear is touched, the left hand strokes the neck. If the nose is tickled, both hands reach for the face. The reflex is usually present in the first 3 years, but may persist longer is mentally retarded children.[14]

Head thrust responses

The baby is held in the sitting position, with the body leaning slightly backwards. A hand placed against the back of the head thrusts the head forwards. The head opposes the movement.

When the baby is held in the sitting position, slightly leaning to one side,

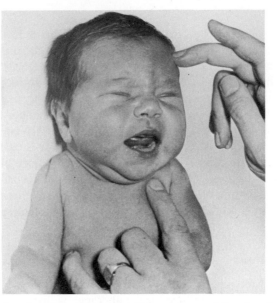

Fig. 22 Method of testing McCarthy's reflex. (Baby crying, and therefore the response is not shown.)

the head is flexed to that side. When the head is pushed to the other side, there is strong resistance by the lateral flexor muscles.

Thomas remarked that this response is marked even in preterm babies, though there is a notable head wobble when the body is passively moved. There is a less marked response when the head is thrust backwards when the child is held sitting with the body flexed. The reaction to thrust increases as the child matures and the head wobble decreases.

The jaw jerk

Tapping the chin causes elevation of the mandible.

Other reflexes

When the baby is held under the armpits and shaken, the head wobbles in all directions, but the limbs do not move. The opposite occurs in the older child.

Stimulation in the temporal region causes rotation of the head to the opposite side.

Vollmer's reflex consists of a vigorous cry, flexion of extremities, lordosis of the spine and elevation of the head, when the infant, held in ventral suspension, is firmly stroked down the spine. It is said to be present in the first months and it disappears by the age of 3 months. This corresponds to the Perez reflex.

André Thomas described a reflex in the hand. Stimulation of the ulnar border of the closed hand causes extension of the digits, beginning with the little finger.

Rubbing the ear causes rotation of the head to the opposite side.

Kratschmer's reflex consists of respiratory arrest when the baby experiences a bad smell.

Infants exhibit a protective skin reflex after about 10 days. They scratch the skin if there is an itch. Peiper remarked that a child is seriously ill if he cannot keep flies off the face.

Conclusion

There are some 73 primitive reflexes of which I am aware, but as far as I have been able to determine only about six have as yet been shown to be of value in developmental assessment. Scherzer[22] thought that Galant's reflex was of doubtful value, but that the following were useful — the asymmetrical tonic neck reflex, the grasp, Moro, rooting and sucking reflexes, parachute and Landau reflexes. He suggested that one should distinguish reflexes present at birth, the true primitive reflexes, which should disappear, from the postural reflexes, (neck and body righting, parachute and Landau reflexes), which appear later. He thought that the age of the loss of the former and of the appearance of the latter may be relevant to assessment. My own view is that the reflexes which are most relevant in the present state of our knowledge are the Moro, grasp, asymmetrical tonic neck reflex, oral reflexes, the biceps, knee jerks, plantar response and ankle clonus.

In the management of cerebral palsy other reflexes are important. They include the tonic neck and labyrinthine reflexes.

REFERENCES

1. Appleton, C., Clifton, R., Goldberg, S. The development of behavioral competence in infancy. In Horowitz, F. D. Review of child development research. Vol. 4. Chicago. Chicago University Press. 1975.
2. Bench, J., Collyer, T., Langford, C., Toms, R. A. comparison between the neonatal sound-evoked startle response and the head-drop (Moro) reflex. Dev. Med. Child. Neurol. 1972.14.308.
3. Birmholz, J., Benacerraf, B. Fetal hearing. Science. 1983.222.516.
4. Brazelton, T. B. Behavioral competence of the newborn infant. Seminars in Perinatology. 1979.3.3.
5. Brazelton, T. B. Behavioral competence of the newborn infant. In: Taylor, P. M. (Ed.) Parent–infant relationships. New York. Grune and Stratton. 1980.
6. Bryant, P. Infants' inferences. New Scientist 1974.62.68.
7. Carpenter, G. Mother's face and the newborn. New Scientist. 1974.61.742.
8. Cole, G. F., Hungerford, J., Jones, R. B. Delayed visual maturation. Arch. Dis. Child. 1984.59.107.
9. Costello, A. Are mothers stimulating? New Scientist 1974.62.742.
10. Drife, J. O. Can the fetus listen and learn? Br. J. Obstet. Gynaecol. 1985.92.777.

11. Gollin, E. S. Research trends in infant learning. In: Hellmuth, J. Exceptional infant. Seattle: Special Child Publications. 1967.
12. Kagan J. The nature of the child. New York. Basic Books. 1984.
13. Korner, A. F., Grobstein, R. Visual alertness as related to soothing in neonates: implications for maternal stimulation and early deprivation. In: Bronfenbrenner, U., Mohoney, M. A. Influences on human development. Illinois. Dryden Press. 1975.
14. Little, T. M., Masotti, R. E. The palmo-mental reflex in normal and mentally retarded subjects. Dev. Med. Child Neurol. 1974.16.59. .
15. Lozoff, B., Brittenham, G. M., Trause, M. A., Kennell, J. H., Klaus, M. H. The mother newborn relationship: limits of adaptability. J. Pediatr. 1977.91.1.
16. MacKeith, R. C. The placing response and primary walking. Guy's Hosp. Gaz. 1965.79.394.
17. Mills, M., Melhuish, E. Recognition of mother's voice in early infancy. Nature 1974.252.123.
18. Minkowski, A., Saint-Anne Dargassies, S. Le retentissement de l'anoxie foetale sur le systeme nerveux central. Rev. Franc. Etud. Clin. Biol. 1956.1.531.
19. Mitchell, R. G. The Landau reaction. Dev. Med. Child Neurol. 1962.4.65.
20. Parmelee, A. H. Critical evaluation of the Moro reflex. Pediatrics 1964.33.773.
21. Peiper, A. Cerebral function in infancy and childhood. London. Pitman. 1963.
22. Scherzer A. L. Primitive reflex profile. Dev. Med. Child Neurol. 1985.27.126.
23. Serafini, P., Lindsay, M. B., Nagey, D. A., Pupkin, M. J., Tseng, P., Crenshaw, C. Antepartum fetal heart rate response to sound stimulation: the acoustic stimulation test. Am. J. Obstet. Gynecol. 1984.148.41.
24. Stone, L. J., Smith, H. T., Murphy, L. B. The competent infant. London. Tavistock Publications 1974.
25. Thomas, A., Chesni, Y., Saint-Anne Dargassies. The neurological examination of the infant. Little Club Clin. Dev. Med. 1960.1.
26. Wolff, P. H. Mother–child interactions in the first year. N. Engl. J. Med. 1976.295.999.

5

Normal development

THE PRINCIPLES OF DEVELOPMENT

These may be summarised as follows:

1. Development is a continuous process from conception to maturity. This means that development occurs in utero, and birth is merely an event in the course of development, though it signals the beginning of extraneous environmental factors.

2. The sequence of development is the same in all children, but the rate of development varies from child to child. For example, a child has to learn to sit before he can learn to walk, but the age at which children learn to sit and to walk varies considerably.

There is a sequence of development within each developmental field, but the development in one field does not necessarily run parallel with that in another. For instance, though the stages in the development in grasping and in locomotion (sitting and walking) are clearly delineated, development in one field may be more rapid than in another. A child with cerebral palsy involving mainly the lower limbs will be late in learning to walk, but if his intelligence is normal the development of manipulation will be average. I have termed this lack of parallelism between different fields of development 'Dissociation'.

3. Development is intimately related to the maturation of the nervous system. For instance, no amount of practice can cause a child to walk until his nervous system is ready for it, but lack of opportunity to practise will retard it.

4. Generalised mass acitivity is replaced by specific individual responses. For instance, whereas the young infant wildly moves his trunk, arms and legs, and pants with excitement when he sees something interesting which he wants, the older infant merely smiles and reaches for it.

5. Development is in the cephalocaudal direction. The first step towards walking is the development of head control — of strength in the neck muscles. The infant can do much with his hands before he can walk. He

83

can crawl, pulling himself forward with his hands, before he can creep, using hands and knees.

6. Certain primitive reflexes, such as the grasp reflex and walking reflex, have to be lost before the corresponding voluntary movement is acquired.

THE SEQUENCE OF DEVELOPMENT

In the section to follow I shall outline the sequence of development in locomotion, manipulation and other fields, basing it almost entirely on the work of Arnold Gesell. In all cases the figures given are average ones. Most children acquire the skills a little earlier or later than the dates given. They refer to full-term babies: for preterm babies an appropriate addition must be made to the ages mentioned.

In order to avoid overlapping and confusion I have combined a description of the normal course of development with the results of developmental tests. The equipment needed for these tests and the method of testing will be discussed in Chapter 12.

The development of locomotion

Every child goes through an orderly sequence of development, from the development of head control, to the stage of mature walking, running and skipping. The development of locomotion can be observed when the infant is held in ventral suspension, when he is placed in the prone position and when he is pulled to the sitting position. Subsequently it is seen in the sitting and upright posture.

Ventral suspension

When the newborn baby is held off the couch in the prone position with the hand under the abdomen, there is an almost complete lack of head control. By 6 weeks he reaches an important and easily determined milestone, when he momentarily holds the head in the same plane as the rest of the body. By 8 weeks he can maintain this position, and by 12 weeks he can maintain the head well beyond the plane of the rest of the body. After this age the position of ventral suspension is not used for assessing head control in normal babies.

The position of the limbs of the young infant is important. By 4 weeks the elbows are largely flexed and there is some extension of the hips with flexion of the knees.

Prone

The newborn baby lies with his head turned to one side, the pelvis high and the knees drawn up under the abdomen. As the matures the pelvis becomes lower and hip and knees extend. By 4 weeks he can momentarily lift the chin off the couch. By 12 weeks he holds the chin and shoulders off the couch with the legs fully extended. Soon he lifts the front part of his chest off the couch, so that the plane of the face is at 90 degrees to it, bearing his weight on the forearms. By 24 weeks he keeps the chest and upper part of the abdomen off the couch, maintaining his weight on the hands with extended elbows. He rolls from prone to supine, and a month later from supine to prone. He shows the 'frog' position, with the legs abducted, the soles of the feet coming together. By 28 weeks he can bear the weight on one hand. He can usually crawl by 9 months, though the first stage is accidental progression backwards. He pulls himself forward with the hands, the legs trailing behind. A month later he creeps on hands and knees with the abdomen off the couch. Later he intermittently places one foot flat on the couch, and finally may creep like a bear on hands and feet, the last stage before walking.

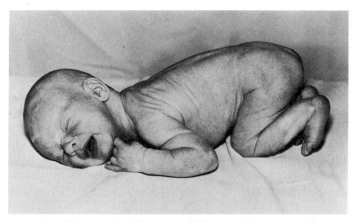

Fig. 23 About 0 to 2 weeks of age. Pelvis high, knees drawn up under abdomen.

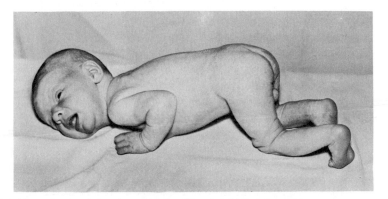

Fig. 24 About 4 to 6 weeks of age. Pelvis still rather high. Intermittent extension of hips.

Sitting

When the newborn baby is pulled to the sitting position there is complete head lag. When half pulled up he will raise his head. When in the sitting position the back is uniformly rounded: he may lift the chin up momentarily. The head lag decreases with maturation, so that by 12 weeks it is only slight and by 20 weeks there is no lag at all. A month later he lifts the head off the couch when he is about to be pulled up, and at 28 weeks he raises it spontaneously and repeatedly. Meanwhile the back is straightening, so that by 24 weeks he can sit propped up in his pram with trunk erect. A month later he sits on the floor with his arms forward for support, and at 28 weeks without support for a few seconds. He learns to sit more and more steadily so that by 40 to 44 weeks he is really steady and can perform various movements such as righting himself. By 15 months he can seat himself in a chair.

Standing and walking

The walking reflex disappears by the age of 6 to 8 weeks except when the neck is extended. At 8 weeks the baby holds his head up momentarily when held in the standing position. In the early weeks the baby sags at the hip and knee, but by 24 weeks he can bear almost all his weight if his mother has given him a chance. At 36 weeks he stands holding on to furniture and can pull himself up to the standing position, but cannot let himself down. At 44 weeks he is seen to lift one foot off the ground, at at 48 weeks he walks, holding on to the furniture. He walks without help at 13 months, with a broad base and steps of unequal direction and length, usually with the shoulder abducted and elbows flexed. At 15 months he creeps upstairs and can get into the standing position without help. At 18 months he can get up and down stairs without help, and pulls a doll or wheeled toy along the ground. At 2 years he can pick an object up without falling, can run

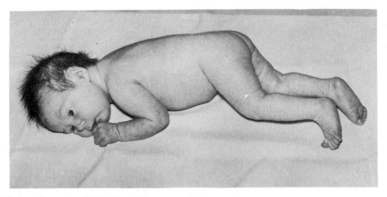

Fig. 25 6 to 8 weeks. Pelvis flat. Hips extended.

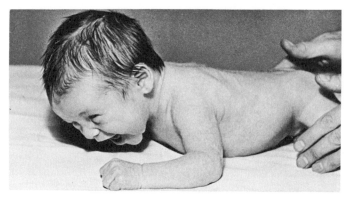

Fig. 26 6 weeks. Chin held off couch intermittently but plane of face not as much as angle of 45 ° to couch.

and walk backward. He goes up and down stairs with two feet per step. At 3 he can stand for a few seconds on one leg. He goes up stairs one foot per step, and down stairs two feet per step. He can ride a tricycle. At 4 he goes down stairs one foot per step and can skip on one foot. At 6 he can skip on both feet.

Other forms of progression

Before babies learn to walk they may learn to move from place to place by a variety of methods.

1. They may become proficient at getting about by rolling.

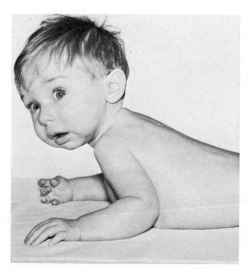

Fig. 27 10 to 12 weeks. Weight on forearms. Plane of face almost reaches angle of 90 ° to couch.

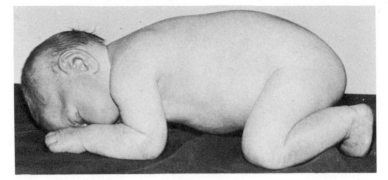

Fig. 28 Microcephalic mentally retarded child, aged 9 weeks, showing prone position similar to that of newborn baby.

2. They may lie in the supine position and elevate the buttocks and entire lower part of the body from the ground, progressing by a series of bumps on the buttocks.

3. They may hitch or shuffle — getting about on one hand and one buttock, or on both hands and both buttocks. It is said that this method of progression may be familial[19] It often continues for about 7 months. It often delays walking.[12]

4. They may crawl backwards.

Other methods are also adopted.

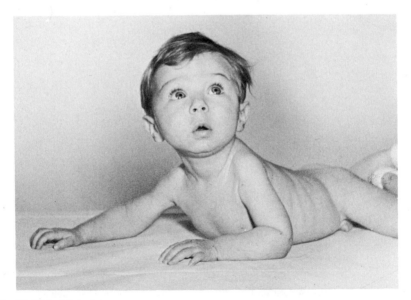

Fig. 29 12 to 14 weeks.

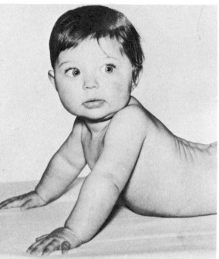

Fig. 30 16 to 20 weeks. Weight partly on extended arms. Plane of face reaches angle of 90 ° to couch.

Fig. 31 24 weeks. Weight on hands, with extended arms.

Fig. 32 44 weeks. Creep position.

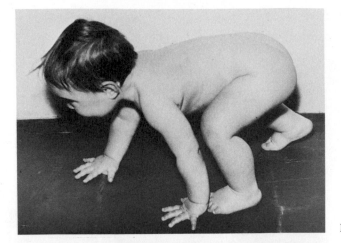

Fig. 33

Fig. 34

Fig. 35

Fig. 33 52 weeks. Walking like a bear.

Fig. 34 Full-term newborn baby, ventral suspension. Note flexion of elbows and knees, with some extension of hips.

Fig. 35 6 weeks baby, head held in same plane as rest of body.

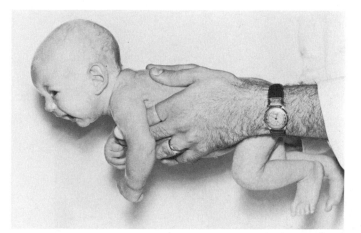

Fig. 36 Normal posture at 18 weeks. Head held up well beyond plane of rest of body.

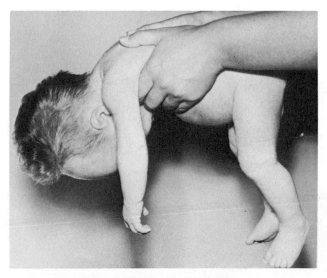

Fig. 37 Abnormal posture. Child of 6 weeks. Head hangs down too much. Arms and legs extended. No extension of hips. (Child with cerebral palsy.)

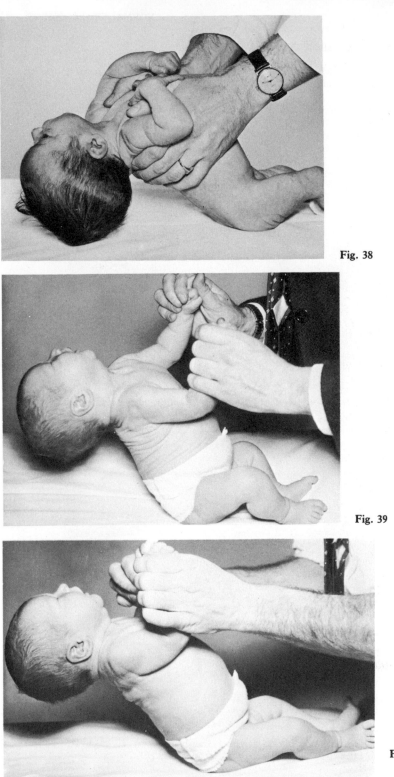

Fig. 38

Fig. 39

Fig. 40

Fig. 38 First 4 weeks or so. Complete head lag when being pulled to the sitting position.

Fig. 39 Newborn baby, half pulled to sitting position: head lag.

Fig. 40 Same as Fig. 39 seconds later, lifting head up slightly.

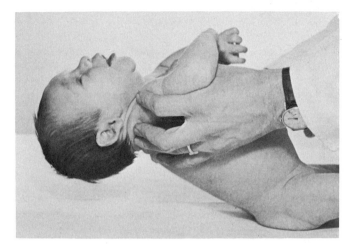

Fig. 41 About 2 months. Considerable head lag when he is pulled to the sitting position, but lag not complete.

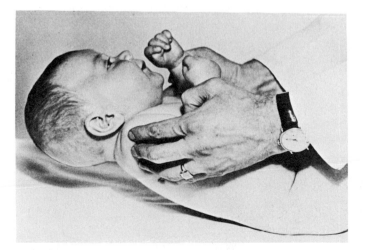

Fig. 42 4 months. No head lag when pulled to the sitting position.

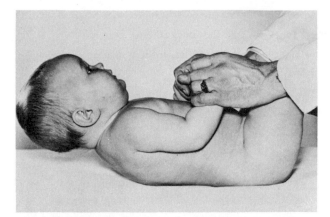

Fig. 43 5 months. Lifts head from supine when about to be pulled up.

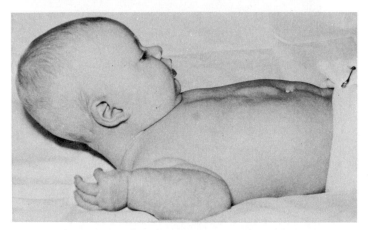

Fig. 44 6 months. Head lifted up spontaneously from supine position.

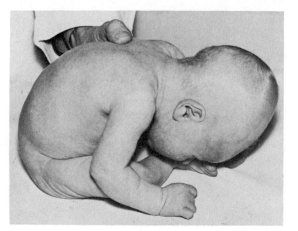

Fig. 45 First 4 weeks or so. Completely rounded back.

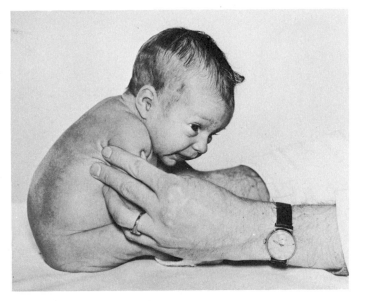

Fig. 46 4 to 6 weeks. Rounded back. Head help up intermittently.

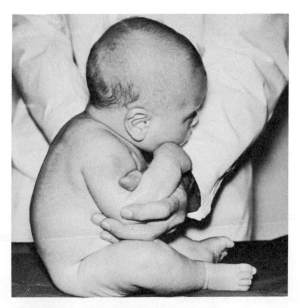

Fig. 47 8 weeks. Back still rounded. Now raising head well.

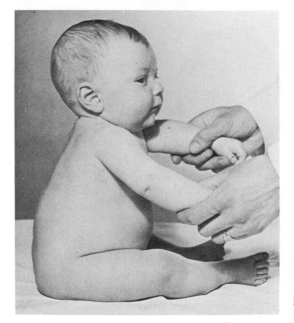

Fig. 48 16 weeks. Back much straighter.

Fig. 49 26 weeks. Sitting with the hands forward for support.

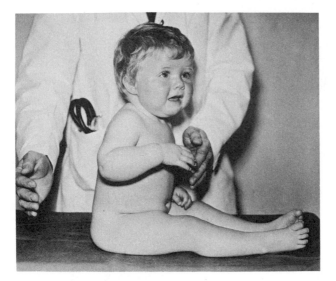

Fig. 50 7 months onwards. Sitting without support.

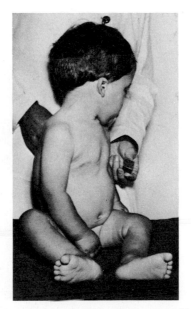

Fig. 51 11 months. Pivoting — turning round to pick up a toy without overbalancing.

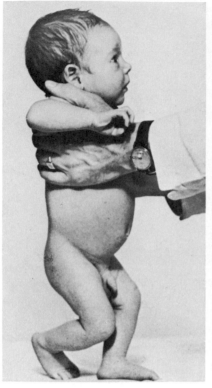

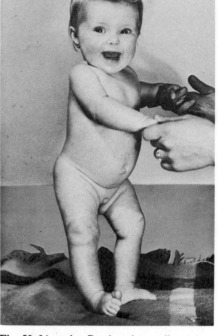

Fig. 52 About 12 weeks. Bearing much weight.

Fig. 53 24 weeks. Bearing almost all weight.

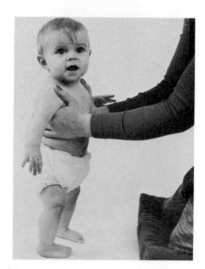

Fig. 54 28 weeks. Bears full weight.

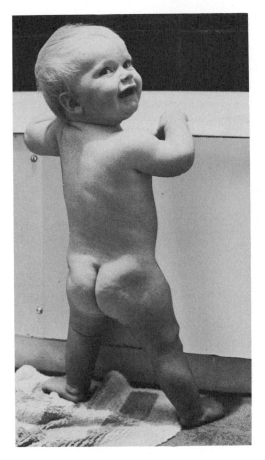

Fig. 55 48 weeks. Can stand holding on to furniture and can walk holding on to it. ('Cruises'.)

Fig. 56 52 weeks. Walks, 1 hand held.

Fig. 57 13 months. Walks, no help. Arms abducted, elbows flexed, broad base. Steps of varying length and direction.

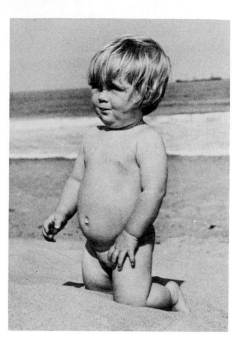

Fig. 58 15 months. Kneels without support.

Manipulation

The primitive grasp reflex of the first 2 or 3 months disappears before the voluntary grasp begins. At 4 weeks the hands are still predominantly closed, but by 12 weeks they are mostly open. One can see at this stage that the baby looks at an object as if he would like to grasp it. He will hold an object placed in the hand. At 16 weeks his hands come together as he plays, and he pulls his dress. He tries to reach for an object, but overshoots the mark. At 20 weeks he can grasp an object voluntarily. He plays with his toes. Thereafter his grasp has to go through several stages from the ulnar grasp — with the cube in the palm of the hand on the ulnar side, to the radial grasp and then to the finger-thumb grasp in the last 3 months of the first year. In the first 6 months the cube is grasped in the palm of the hand on the ulnar side: from 24 to 32 weeks it it held against the thenar eminence

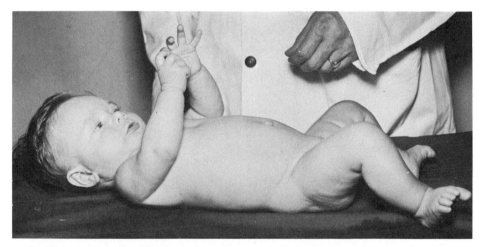

Fig. 59 11 to 20 weeks. Hand regard.

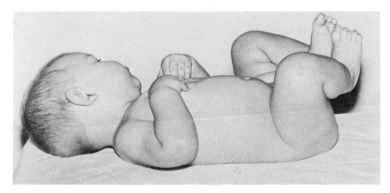

Fig. 60 12 to 16 weeks. Soles of feet come together.

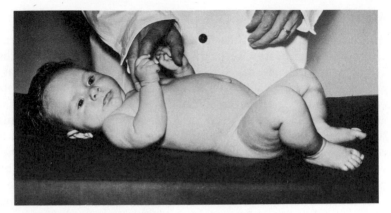

Fig. 61 16 weeks. Soles of feet on couch.

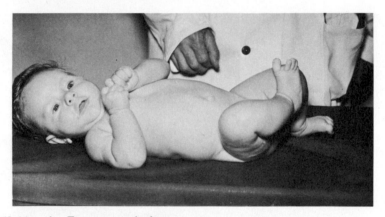

Fig. 62 16 weeks. Foot on opposite knee.

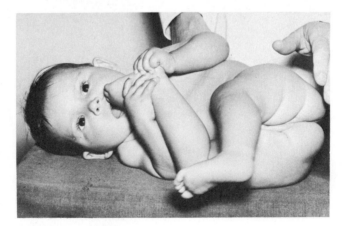

Fig. 63 20 weeks. Feet to mouth.

at the base of the thumb. From 32 to 40 weeks the index finger usually with the help of the ring and little finger presses the cube against the lower part of the thumb; and between 40 and 50 weeks the cube is grasped between the volar pads of the finger tip and the distal volar pad of the thumb. The rapidity with which he drops the cube is a good index of the maturity of the grasp. If he repeatedly drops it in a matter of seconds the grasp is unlikely to be a mature one. At first he is ataxic and overshoots the mark, but soon he is able to reach for an object with precision.

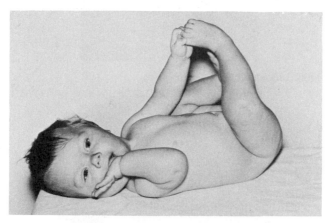

Fig. 64 20 weeks. Plays with feet.

Fig. 65 Manipulation. 6 months. Transfers objects.

Fig. 66 6 months. Immature palmar grasp of cube.

Fig. 67 8 months. Grasp, intermediate stage.

Fig. 68 1 year. Mature grasp of cube.

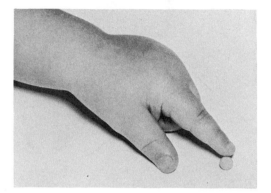

Fig. 69 40 weeks. Index finger approach to object.

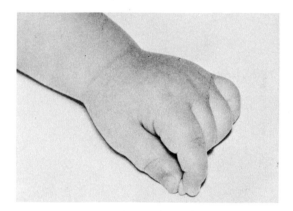

Fig. 70 40 weeks. Finger-thumb apposition, enabling child to pick up pellet.

At 6 months he transfers objects from hand to hand, and as he can now chew, he can feed himself with a biscuit. He plays with his toes in the supine position. He loves to play with paper. Everything goes to the mouth. It is not till 40 weeks that he can pick up a small object of the size of a currant, bringing finger and thumb together. He goes for objects with his index finger. He can now deliberately let go of objects, but true casting — deliberately throwing bricks on to the floor, one after the other — usually reaches its height between 12 and 13 months. Before that he learns to hand a toy to the parent, at first refusing to let it go, but later releasing it. He spends long periods at 44 weeks and onwards putting objects in and out of a basket. He stops taking things to his mouth by about a year. By 13 months he can build a tower of two 1-inch cubes, but he cannot build a tower of 10 until 3 years of age. By 15 months he can pick up a cup, drink from it and put it down without much spilling. At 18 months he turns two or three pages of a book at a time, but turns them over singly by the

Fig. 71 40 weeks. Pokes clapper of bell with index finger.

Fig. 72 10-month-old child feeding himself. Note the immature grasp.

age of 2 years. By 2 years he can put his socks on, by 2½ he can thread beads, and by 3 he can fasten buttons, dressing and undressing himself. He can draw and paint.

The use of the eyes and ears

The reflex responses of the eye of the newborn baby have been described. The baby blinks at birth in response to sound, movement or touching the cornea, but not usually on the approach of an object. He soon displays a protective response to an object moving towards him.

The pupil responds to light after about the 29th week of gestation, and the preterm baby begins to turn his head to diffuse light at about the 32nd or 36th week. The 26 to 30 week preterm baby dislikes a bright light.

At birth he shows visual perception and will follow a moving person with his eyes. He can follow a dangling ring with difficulty in a range of about

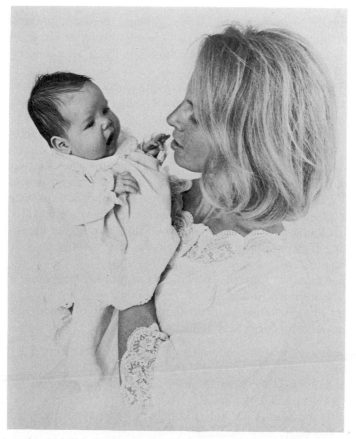

Fig. 73 4 weeks old baby, showing the baby's intent regard of his mother as she speaks to him. Note his open mouth.

45 ° when it is held 8 to 10 inches away. By 4 weeks he can follow in a range of 90 ° and by 3 months within a range of 180 °. There is little convergence before 6 weeks of age. By 3 months he can fixate well on near objects. By 3 or 4 weeks he watches his mother intently as she speaks to him, fixating on her face, and by 4 to 6 weeks he begins to smile at her as she speaks to him. He will also smile at a face-sized card with two eye dots — and still more at one with six dots. By 3 months or so he fixes his eyes well on his feeding bottle, and by 4 months he can fix his eyes on a half-inch brick ('grasping with his eyes'). The newborn baby cannot integrate head and eye movements well; the eyes lag behind if his head is passively rotated to one side (doll's eye reflex). The response disappears by 2 or 3 months.

The eyes of the newborn tend to move independently. Binocular vision begins at 6 weeks and is fairly well established by 4 months.

From 12 to 20 weeks he characteristically watches his hand (hand regard) as he lies on his back; but 'hand regard' can also occur in blind children, and so it is really a developmental pattern not requiring visual stimulation.[8]

At 5 months he excites when his feed is being prepared, and at 6 months he adjusts his position to see objects — bending back or crouching to see what he is interested in. He cannot follow rapidly moving objects until he is nearly a year old.

Mary Sheridan tested 100 5- to 7-year-old school children with the stycar method at 20 feet: she found that a visual acuity of 6/9 should be regarded as sub-optimal.

There have been several studies relating to the ability of the fetus to hear in utero. Blink startle responses to vibroacoustic stimulation was monitored by ultrasound in human fetuses of known gestational age.[5] Responses were first elicited from 24 to 25 weeks gestation, and then constantly after 28 weeks. It was suggested that this may provide a foundation for the antenatal diagnosis of deafness. The newborn full-term baby can hear: he may respond to sound by a startle reflex, by crying, by quieting if he is crying, by quieting if he is crying, by blinking, or by a momentary catch in his respirations (Ch. 4).

At 3 or 4 months of age the baby begins to turn his head more obviously towards the source of sound.

Murphy described the sequence of development of sound localisation, making a sound approximately 18 inches from the ear. These are as follows:

1. The infant turns the head to the side at which the sound is heard (3 months)
2. The infant turns the head towards the sound and the eyes look in the same direction (3 to 4 months)
3. He turns the head to one side and then downwards, if the sound is made below the ear (5 to 6 months)
4. He turns the head to one side and then upwards, when the sound is

made above the level of the ear (about 6 months); i.e. downward local-isation occurs before upward localisation.

5. He turns the head in a curving arc towards the sound source (about 6 to 8 months)
6. The head is turned diagonally and directly towards the sound (about 8 to 10 months).

He may imitate sounds by 6 months, and by 7 months he may respond to his name. By the age of 9 to 12 months he knows the meaning of several words, including the names of members of his family.

By the first year the ability to localise a sound source is almost as good as in the older child and adult. From about 9 months the baby learns to control and adjust his responses to sounds. He may delay his response or inhibit it altogether. He may listen to hear the sound again and not attempt to localise it. This represents a further step towards understanding and controlling his environment.

General understanding

The first sign of understanding can be seen in the first few days, when he begins to watch his mother when she speaks to him. He quiets, opens and closes his mouth and bobs his head up and down. By 4 to 6 weeks he begins to smile and two weeks later to vocalise. By the second or third month (or sooner) he may imitate his mother's mouth movement or tongue protrusion. Trevarthen[21] pointed out that to do so he must have a model of his mother's face in his brain, and this model must be mapped on to the motor apparatus of his own face. At 12 weeks he shows considerable interest in his surround-ings, watching the movements of people in the room. He may refuse to be left outside alone, preferring the activity of the kitchen. He excites when a toy is presented to him. He recognises his mother and turns his head to sound. He may turn his head away when his nose is being cleaned by cotton wool. Between 12 and 16 weeks he anticipates when his bottle or the breast is to be offered, by opening his mouth when he sees it approach. At 20 weeks he smiles at his mirror image and shortly after looks to see where a dropped toy has gone. At 24 weeks when lying down he stretches his arms out when he sees that his mother is going to lift him up. He smiles and vocalises at his mirror image. At 6 months he imitates acts such as tongue protrusion or a cough. He may try to establish contact by coughing. He enjoys peep-bo games. At 32 weeks he reacts to the cotton wool swab by grasping his mother's hand and pushing it away. He tries persistently to reach objects too for away. He responds to 'No'.

At 40 weeks he may pull his mother's clothes to attract her attention. He imitates 'patacake' and 'bye-bye'. He repeats a performance laughed at. At 44 weeks he helps to dress by holding his arm out for a coat, his foot out for a shoe or transferring on object from one hand to another so that a hand can go through a sleeve. At 48 weeks he begins to anticipate movements in nursery rhymes. He begins to show interest in books and understanding of words. At 11 to 12 months he may laugh when his mother puts an unusual object on her head. At 1 year he may understand a phrase such as 'where is your shoe?'

After the first birthday he shows his understanding in innumerable different ways. His increasing understanding is shown by his comprehension of what is said to him, by the execution of simple requests, by his increasing interest in toys and books, by his developing speech. His play becomes more and more complex and imaginative. He begins to appreciate form and colour and by $2\frac{1}{2}$ years he can tackle simple jig-saws. Right — left discrimination develops at about 4 years of age.

The main test objects used for observing his developing understanding are the pencil and paper, the picture book, the picture card with pictures of common objects and formboards or cut-out forms.

Pleasure and displeasure

All babies express displeasure before they learn to show pleasure, and all say 'No' before they say 'Yes'.

The first sign of pleasure shown by the baby is the quieting in the first few days when picked up. During his feeds he shows his pleasure by the splaying of his toes and by their alternate flexion and extension. The smile at 6 weeks when he is spoken to is followed in 1 or 2 weeks by vocalising. At 3 months he squeals with delight. He then shows his pleasure by a massive response — the trunk, arms and legs move, and he pants with excitement. At 16 weeks he laughs aloud. He plays with the rattle placed in his hand. He smiles when pulled up to the sitting position.

After 5 or 6 months he takes pleasure in newly-acquired skills — sitting, standing, walking and feeding himself. He enjoys games from 6 months and likes to be read to and enjoys nursery rhymes. He is ticklish by 4 or 5 months and soon responds by a laugh when he sees a finger approaching to tickle him. He enjoys games and company more and more as he gets older.

Feeding and dressing

The young baby cannot usually approximate his lips tightly round the areola of the breast or the teat of the bottle, so that milk leaks out at the corners of the mouth, he swallows air and so has 'wind'. As he matures he gets less wind because of the complete approximation of his lips to the sucking surface.

In the first 4 months or so the baby's tongue tends to push food out if food is placed on the front of the tongue. Food, therefore, should be placed well back. Babies can approximate their lips to the rim of a cup by four or five months and cup-feeding at this time is likely to be quicker than bottle-feeding.

The next milestone of importance is the beginning of chewing at 6 months, together with the ability to get hold of objects, enabling a child to feed himself with a biscuit. He likes to hold his bottle.

At any time after 6 months the baby may begin to hold his spoon, and some babies can feed themselves fully with the spoon by 9 or 10 months, though the average age for this is about 15 months. In the early days of self feeding the fingers go into the food, and much is spilt, accidentally or deliberately.

When he is first allowed to use a cup, he lets it go when he has had what he wants. If he is given a chance to learn, however, he should be able to manage the cup fully by 15 months of age. Children can manage a knife and fork by the age of $2\frac{1}{2}$ to 3 years.

The age at which children learn to dress themselves varies greatly. Much depends on how much chance the mother gives the child to dress himself. A child of average intelligence can dress himself fully by the age of 3, provided that he is advised as to back and front, and as to the appropriate shoe for the foot. He will also need help with difficult buttons. He should be able to tie his shoelaces by 4 or 5 years, and so to be fully independent.

Opening of mouth when the nose is obstructed

The young baby does not usually open his mouth spontaneously when his nose is obstructed until he is about 4 or 5 months old. This is of importance under various circumstances. For instance, the infant with choanal atresia gasps for breath and becomes cyanosed until he opens his mouth to cry or until an airway is inserted.

Speech

There have been several extensive studies on the speech of infants.[16,17]

The infant has many methods of preverbal communication.[10] He can communicate with his mother by watching her as she speaks, and later by smiling and vocalising in response. He communicates by crying, smiling, nestling, clinging, vigorous welcoming, frowning, kissing, resistive stiffening or pushing away, turning his head away, holding his mother's arm, pulling his mother, pointing or taking her hand and placing it near the object which he wants. He communicates by laughter, screaming and temper tantrums. He holds his arms out (at 5 or 6 months) to be pulled up. He communicates by spitting food out or closing his mouth when food is offered. His response is dependent on his mother's responses, on her expressions of love, tone of voice, conversation and play.

One or 2 weeks after he has begun to smile at his mother in response to her, he begins to vocalise as well as smile — beginning with vowel sounds ah, uh, eh. In 3 to 4 weeks he adds the consonants m, p, b when expressing displeasure, and j and k when pleased.

By 12 to 16 weeks he characteristically holds long 'conversations' with his mother. He begins to say gaga, ng, and ah goo. At 4 months the squeals with delight, laughs aloud, and begins to enjoy vocal play such as razzing (blowing between partly closed lips). In the second 3 months he adds syllables ma, da, ka, der, erheh, and at 7 months combines consonants to say mumum (especially when displeased) and dadada — in neither case referring to his parents. He now vocalises with many high and low pitched tones. A nasal tone may be heard and tongue-lip activity develops. At 7 or 8 months he vocalises or coughs to attract attention, and at 9 or 10 months he begins to imitate sounds — an important step towards speech. At 8 months or so he adds d, t and w. At 10 months he may say one word with meaning. He responds to 'No', and obeys orders. He responds to nursery rhymes by an appropriate action, and plays pat-a-cake and communicates by waving bye-bye. By 12 months he imitates dogs, cows and clocks, and may say two or three words with meaning. In the early stage he frequently omits the first or last part of a word, saying g for dog, and later og for dog. Between 15 and 18 months the child jargons, speaking in an unintelligible but expressive language of his own, with modulations, phrasings and dramatic inflections but with only an occasional intelligible word. If asked to repeat what he said, he makes exactly the same sounds as he did first time. He may repeat phrases such as 'Oh dear', but the average child begins to join words together spontaneously by 21 to 24 months. Substitution of letters may occur with lisping as a result of protruding the tongue between the teeth when saying 's'. By the age of 3 he is talking incessantly, but some substitution of letters and repetition of syllables is usual rather than the exception.

Sound spectographic methods have opened up a new field of research into speech characteristics, development and significance.[14,15] Karelitz and Rosenfeld[11] took 1300 recordings of normal and 'brain damaged' infants in their first two years. They described the cry of the young infant as short, staccato and repetitive. It builds up in a crescendo as the stimulus is applied. As he develops, the duration of the individual cry increases, and eventually becomes polysyllabic. The pitch becomes more varied and the inflections become more plaintive and meaningful at about 6 months of age. Later syllables (mumum) and real words and subsequently phrases can be heard as part of the cry.

The Newcastle study[18] of 1824 boys and 1747 girls, found that 3% said their first word just before 9 months of age, 10% by 10 months, 50% by 12 months, 90% by 18 months and 7% by 10 to 22 months.

In order to develop speech, the child has to learn what effect sound has on others.[13] The cry, initially reflex, becomes purposeful as memory and understanding develop. His thought is far more developed than his language: when he wants something he can show his desire long before he can say what he wants. he understands the meaning of numerous words before he can articulate them.

Sphincter control

In the newborn period, micturition is a reflex act. It can be stimulated by handling the baby and by other non-specific measures. Babies usually empty the bowel or bladder immediately after a meal. They can be conditioned at any age (e.g. at a month or so) to empty the bladder when placed on the pot, the bladder emptying when the buttocks come into contact with the rim of the pot. Voluntary control does not begin until 15 to 18 months of age when the baby first tells his mother that he has wet his pants. He then tells her just before he passes urine, but too late, and a little later he tells her in time. By about 16 to 18 months he may say 'No' if asked whether he wants to pass urine. There is great urgency at this time, so that as soon as he wants to pass urine he must be offered the pot immediately, or it will be too late. As he matures the urgency disappears — though in enuresis of the primary type diurnal urgency may continue for some years. By the age of 2 to 2½ years he can pull his pants down and climb on to the lavatory seat unaided. He is apt to forget to go to the lavatory when occupied with some new toy or play, but later can remember to look after his needs.

Most children are reasonably dry by day at 18 months. By 2 years, 50% are dry at night; by 3, 75%; and by 5 some 90% are dry. This means that about 1 in 10 at the age of 5 will still be wetting the bed at least occasionally.

Bowel control is usually acquired before control of the bladder.

Handedness

Amongst famous people who were left handed were Holbein, Durer, Landseer, Ravel, Johann Sebastian Bach, Rev. Charles Dodgson (Lewis Carroll) and Thomas Carlyle.

Gesell and Ames suggested that the first indication of handedness may be the direction of the asymmetrical tonic neck reflex. There are often shifts of handedness from side to side in the first year, with a predominance of left handedness in the earlier weeks, and a shift to the right in the second 6 months. Handedness is usually established by about 2 years, but is often not firmly established until the age of 3 or 4.

When the child is old enough, he can be tested by getting him to draw, rub with a duster, throw a ball, pick up an object from the floor, cut paper with scissors, wind a clock or place an object in a tin. The dominant foot is found by getting him to kick a ball. The dominant ear is tested by holding a watch in the midline in front of him and asking him to listen to it. The dominant eye is found by making a hollow roll of firm paper and asking him to look at an object through it.

Left handedness is not just the opposite of right handedness. Those with right handedness are usually consistent in the use of the right hand, but most left handed persons on occasion use the right hand — and are then termed mixed handers. A third of right handers prefer to use the left eye in tests and a third of left handers the right eye.[1,2,20] About 6% of children in British schools are left handed[16] (but 12% in special schools). About 4% of female adults and 6% of male adults are left handed.

There is disagreement as to how much handednes is genetically determined and how much it is related to environmental factors, such as imitation, instruction and social pressure.[9] Left handedness is three times more common in twins (uniovular or binovular) than in singletons, and it is more common in epileptics, psychotics, genius and criminals. It is more common in clumsy children.[6,7] It is said to be associated with immune disease, migraine and learning disorders.[4] There is more left handedness amongst manual workers than amongst middle and upper classes, and more amongst those of low intelligence. The number of left-handed offspring is least with two right-handed parents, greater with one left-handed parent, and greatest with two left-handed parents; but 84% of left-handed children have two right-handed parents, so that the familial tendency is only a weak one.[3] It has been suggested that there is a genetic factor for right handedness but not left handedness. In mentally subnormal children there may be maturational delay in the establishment of laterality.

There is disagreement as to the relationship between laterality and reading difficulties and related learning disorders. There is no evidence that left or mixed handers are typically retarded in verbal tests.[1,2] It is now accepted that training a left-handed child to use the right hand does not per se cause stuttering, unless there is stress in the manner of teaching. Zangwill[17] considered that handedress and speech are in some way related, but others disagree. There is no significant difference in the writing ability of right and left handers, but left handers may find mechanical difficulties in writing, and become tired as a result. Vernon thought that the relationship between laterality and reading difficulties is at least tenuous.

In conclusion, there are many problems of handedness which remain unsolved. Handedness is partly genetic and partly environmental in origin. The role of handedness in reading and writing difficulties has been exaggerated in the past, and it is probable that handedness is of little importance in these problems. Left handedness is more common in mentally subnormal children, but the reason for this is not obvious.

THE AVERAGE LEVEL OF DEVELOPMENT AT DIFFERENT AGES

In this section I have put together the main features of development at different ages. I have combined with these milestones a variety of simple developmental tests, mainly culled from Gesell.

4 Weeks

Gross motor. Ventral suspension — (held in prone position with hand under abdomen), head held up momentarily. Elbows flexed, hips partly extended, kness flexed.

Prone — pelvis high, knees drawn up largely under abdomen. Intermittent partial extension of hip and knee. Momentarily lifts chin off couch. Head predominantly to one side.

Pulled to sit — almost complete head lag.

Held in sitting position — back uniformly rounded. May hold head up momentarily.

Supine — asymmetrical tonic neck reflex seen when at rest.

Held standing — flops at knees and hips. Walking reflex when sole of foot is pressed on flat surface.

Hands. Hands predominantly closed.

Grasp reflex.

General understanding. Watches mother's face when she talks to him and he is not crying. Opens and closes mouth. Bobs head up and down.

Vision. In supine — regards dangling object (e.g. ring on string) when brought into line of vision (3 feet from the eyes), but not otherwise when in midline. Follows it less than 90 degrees.

Sound. Quiets when bell is rung.

6 Weeks

Gross motor. Ventral suspension — head held up momentarily in same plane as rest of body. Some extension of hips and flexion of kness. Flexion of elbows.

Prone — pelvis high, but knees no longer under abdomen. Much intermittent extension of hips. Chin raised intermittently off couch. Head turned to one side.

Pulled to sit — head lag considerable but not complete.

Held in sitting position — intermittently holds head up.

Held standing — head sags forward. May hold head up momentarily.

Supine — asymmetrical tonic neck reflex at rest intermittently seen.

Hands. Often open. Grasp reflex may be lost.

General understanding. Smiles at mother in response to overtures.

Vision. Eyes fixate on objects, and follow moving persons.

In supine — looks at object held in midline, following it as it moves from the side to midline. (90 degrees.)

8 Weeks

Gross motor. Ventral suspension — can maintain head in same plane as rest of body.

Prone — head mostly in midline. Intermittently lifts chin off couch so that plane of face is at angle of 45 degrees to couch.

Pulled to sit — less head lag.

Head in sitting position — less rounding of back. Head is held up but recurrently bobs forward.

Supine — head chiefly to side. Asymmetrical tonic neck reflex seen intermittently at rest.

Held in standing position — able to hold head up more than momentarily.

Hands. Frequently open. Only slight grasp reflex.

Vocalisation. Smiles and vocalises when talked to.

Vision. Fixation, convergence and focusing. Follows moving person.

In supine — follows dangling toy from side to point beyond midline.

12 Weeks

Gross motor. Ventral suspension — head held up for prolonged period beyond plane of rest of body.

Prone — pelvis flat on couch. Holds chin and shoulders off couch for prolonged period so that plane of face is at angle of 45 degrees to 90 degrees from couch, weight borne on forearms.

Pulled to sit — only slight head lag.

Held in sitting position — head mostly held up, but still bobs forward.

Supine — no more asymmetrical tonic neck reflex.

Hands. No grasp reflex.

Hands loosely open.

When rattle is placed in hand, holds it for a minute or more.

Looks as if he would like to grasp object, but cannot without it being placed in hand.

Vocalisation. Squeals of pleasure.

'Talks' a great deal when spoken to.

Vision. Supine — characteristically watches movements of his own hands. ('Hand regard').

Follows dangling toy from side to side. (180 degrees.)

Promptly looks at object in midline.

Hearing. Turns head to sound.

16 Weeks

Gross motor. Prone — head and chest off couch so that plane of face is at angle of 90 degrees to couch.

'Swimming' — limbs stretched out in full extension.

Pulled to sit — only slight head lag in beginning of movement.

Held in sitting position — head held up constantly.

Child looks actively around.

Head wobbles when examiner suddenly sways child, indicating that head control is incomplete.

Back now curved only in lumbar region.

Supine — head in midline.

Hands. Hands come together as he plays. Hand regard still present.

Pulls dress over face in play.

Tries to reach object with hands but overshoots it.

Plays with rattle placed in hand for long period and shakes it, but cannot pick it up if he drops it.

General understanding Excites when food prepared, toys seen, showing massive reaction involving all four limbs and respirations.

Shows pleasure when pulled to sitting position. Likes to be propped up.

Vocalisation. Laughs aloud.

Vision. Supine — immediate regard of dangling object.

20 Weeks

Gross motor. Prone — weight on forearms.

Pulled to sit — no head lag.

Held in sitting position — no head wobble when body swayed by examiner.

Back straight.

Supine — feet to mouth.

Held in standing position — bears most of weight.

Hands. Able to grasp objects voluntarily.

Plays with toes. Crumples paper.

Splashes in bath. Objects taken to mouth.

Cube. Grasps; bidextrous approach; takes it to mouth.

Vocalisations. Razzing; 'Ah-goo'.

General understanding. Smiles at mirror image.

Pats bottle.

No more hand regard.

24 Weeks

Gross motor. Prone — weight on hands, not forearms; chest and upper part of abdomen off couch.
   When about to be pulled to sit, lifts head off couch.
   Sits supported in high chair.
   Held in standing position — almost full weight on legs.
   Rolls prone to supine.

Hands. Holds bottle.
   Grasps his feet.

Cube. Palmar grasp of cube.
   Drops one cube when another is given.

Feeding. Drinks from cup when it is held to lips.

General understanding. When he drops a toy he looks to see where it has gone to and tries to recover it.
   May excite on hearing steps.
   Mirror — smiles and vocalises at mirror image.
   Stretches arms out to be taken.
   Shows likes and dislikes.
   Many show fear of strangers and are 'coy'.
   Displeasure at removal of toy.

Play. Laughs when head is hidden in towel.

Imitation. Imitates cough or protrusion of tongue.

28 Weeks

Gross motor. Prone — bears weight on one hand.
   Sits with hands on couch for support.
   Rolls from supine to prone.
   Supine — spontaneously lifts head off couch.
   Held standing — bounces with pleasure.

Hands. Feeds self with biscuit.
   Likes to play with paper.
   Unidextrous approach.

Cubes. Bangs cube on table.
   Transfers it from hand to hand.
   If he has one cube in hand he retains it when second is offered.

Feeding. Chews.
   Keeps lips closed when he is offered more food than he wants.

General understanding. Imitates simple acts.
  Pats image of self in mirror.
  Responds to name.
  Tries to establish contact with person by cough or other method.
  Expectation in response to repetition of stimulus.

Speech. Syllables — ba, da, ka.

32 Weeks

Gross motor. Sits momentarily on floor without support.
  Adjusts posture to reach object, e.g. leans forward to reach.
  Readily bears whole weight on legs when supported. May stand holding on.

General understanding. Reaches persistently for toys out of reach.
  Responds to 'No'.
  Looks for dropped toy.

Imitation. Imitates sounds.

Speech. Combines syllables — da-da; ba-ba.

36 Weeks

Gross motor. Prone — in trying to crawl progresses backwards.
  May progress by rolling.
  Sits steadily on floor for 10 minutes.
  Leans forward and recovers balance but cannot lean over sideways.
  Stands, holding on to furniture. Pulls self to stand.

Hands. Can pick up object of size of currant between tip of finger and thumb.

Cubes. Compares two cubes by bringing them together.

General understanding. Puts arms in front of face to prevent mother washing his face.

40 Weeks

Gross motor. Prone — crawl position, on abdomen.
  Crawls by pulling self forward with hands.
  Sitting — can go over into prone, or change from prone to sitting.
  Can pull self to sitting position.
  Sits steadily with little risk of overbalancing.
  Standing — can stand holding on to furniture. Collapses with a bump.

Hands. Goes for objects with index finger.

Cubes. Beginning to let go of objects (release).

General understanding. Looks round corner for object.
Responds to words, e.g. 'Where is daddy?'
Pulls clothes of another to attract attention. Holds object to examiner but will not release it.
Repeats performance laughed at.

Imitation. Waves bye-bye. Plays patacake.

44 Weeks

Gross motor. Prone — creeps, abdomen off couch.
Standing — Lifts foot.

Cubes. Beginning to put objects in and out of containers.

Dressing. Holds arm out for sleeve or foot out for shoe.

General understanding. Will not give object to examiner: holds it but will not release it.
Drops objects deliberately so that they will be picked up.

48 Weeks

Gross motor. Prone — when creeping, sole of foot may be flat on couch.
Sitting — pivots, twisting round to pick up object.
Walks, holding on to furniture.
Walks, two hands held.

General understanding. Rolls ball to examiner.
Will now give toy to examiner, releasing it.
Anticipates body movements when nursery rhyme being said.
Shows interest in picture book.
Shakes head for 'No'.

Play. Plays peep-bo, covering face.
Plays game — 'Up, down'.

Speech. One word with meaning.

1 Year*

Gross motor. Prone — walks on hands and feet like a bear.
Walks, one hand held.
May shuffle on buttock and hand.

---

* For details and methods of examination see Chapter 12.

Hands. Mouthing virtually stopped.
Beginning to throw objects to floor ('casting').

General understanding. May understand meaning of phrases, 'Where is your shoe?'
May kiss on request.
Apt to be shy.

Speech. Two or three words with meaning.
Knows meaning of more words.

Slobbering. Virtually stopped.

15 Months*

Gross motor. Creeps up stairs. Kneels without support.
Walks without help (from 13 months).
Can get into standing position without support.
Falls by collapse.
Cannot go round corners or stop suddenly.

Hands. Casting less.

Cubes. Builds tower of two.
Holds two cubes in one hand.

Ball. Cannot throw without falling.

Dressing. Likes to take off shoes.

Feeding. Feeds self, picking up cup, drinking, putting it down.
Manages spoon but rotates it near mouth.
Feeds self fully, no help.

Pencil. Imitates scribble or scribbles spontaneously.

General understanding. Asks for objects by pointing. Mouthing stopped.
May kiss pictures of animal.
Imitates mother in domestic duties — sweeping, cleaning.

Sphincter control. Begins to tell mother that he wants to use pot.
Indicates wet pants.

Speech. Jargoning.
Several intelligible words.

Simple formboard. Inserts round block without being shown.

---

* For details and methods of examination see Chapter 12.

18 Months*

Gross motor. Gets up and down stairs, holding rail, without help.
Walks up stairs, one hand held.
Walks, pulling toy or carrying doll.
Seats self on chair.
Beginning to jump (both feet).

Cubes. Tower of three or four.

Ball. Throws ball without falling.

Dressing. Takes off gloves, socks, unzips.

Feeding. Manages spoon well without rotation.

Pencil. Spontaneous scribble.
Makes stroke imitatively.

General understanding. 'Domestic mimicry'. Copies mother in dusting, washing, cleaning. No casting.

Parts of body. Points to two or three (nose, eye, hair, etc.).

Simple orders.† Two.

Common objects.‡ One.

Picture card.§ Points to one ('Where is the . . .?')

Book. Turns pages, two or three at a time.
Points to picture of car or dog.
Shows sustained interest.

Sphincter control. Dry by day; occasional accident.

Speech. Jargon. Many intelligible words.

Simple formboard. Piles three blocks.

2 Years*

Gross motor Goes up and down stairs alone, two feet per step. Walks backward in imitation (from 21 months).
Picks up object without falling.
Runs. Kicks balls without overbalancing.

Hands. Turns door knob, unscrews lid.
Washes and dries hands.

---

* For details and method of examination, se Chapter 12.
† Take ball to mother, put it on chair, bring it to me, put it on table.
‡ Coin, shoe, pencil, knife, ball.
§ Picture card. See Figure 128.

Cubes. Tower of six or seven (five or six at 21 months.)
Imitates train of cubes, without adding chimney.

Ball. Kicks.

Dressing. Puts on shoes, socks, pants.
Takes off shoes and socks.

Pencil. Imitates vertical and circular stroke.

General understanding. Pulls people to show them toys (from 21 months).

Parts of body. Points to four.

*Simple orders.** Obeys four (three at 21 months).

Common objects.† Names three to five.

Picture card.‡ Points to five ('Where is the . . .?')
Names three ('What is this?')

Book. Turns pages singly.

Sphincter control. Dry at night if lifted out in evening.

Speech. Asks for drink, toilet, food.
Repeats things said (from 21 months).
Uses 'I', 'me', 'you'.
Joins two three words in sentences (from 21–24 months), other than in imitation.
Talks incessantly.

Simple formboard. Places all (Places two or three at 21 months.) When formboard is rotated, places three in correctly, after four errors.

Play. Wraps up doll. Puts it to bed.
Parallel play. Watches others play and plays near them, but not with them.

2½ Years§

Gross motor. Jumps with both feet.
Walks on tiptoes when asked.

Cubes. Tower of eight.
Imitates train, adding chimney.

---

* Take ball to mother, put it on chair, bring it to me, put it on table.
† Coin, shoe, pencils, knife, ball.
‡ Picture card. See Figure 128.
§ For details and method of examination, see Chapter 12.

Pencil. Holds pencil in hand instead of fist.
  Imitates vertical and horizontal stroke.
  Two or more strokes for cross.

General understanding. Helps to put things away.
  Begins to notice sex differences.
  Knows full name.
  Knows sex.

Common objects. Names five.

Picture cards. Points to seven: ('Where is the . . .?')
  Names five ('What is this . . .?')

Digits. Repeats two in one of three trials (e.g. say 'Eight five').

Coloured forms. Places one.

Sphincter control. Attends to toilet need without help, except for wiping.
  Climbs on to lavatory seat.

Colour sense. Names one colour.

Simple formboard. Inserts all three, adapting after errors.

3 Years*

Gross motor. Jumps off bottom step.
  Goes up stairs, one foot per step, and down stairs, two feet per step.
  Stands on one foot for seconds.
  Rides tricycle.

Hands. Can help to set table, not dropping china.

Cubes. Tower of nine.
  Imitates building of bridge.

Dressing. Dresses and undresses fully if helped with buttons and advised about correct shoe.
  Unbuttons front and side buttons.

Pencils. Copies circle (from a card).
  Imitates cross.
  Draws a man on request.
General understanding. Knows some nursery rhymes.
  May count up to 10.

Picture card. Names eight ('What is this?')

---

* For details and method of examination, see Chapter 12.
† Put the ball under the chair, at the side of the chair, behind the chair, on the chair.

Digits. Repeats three (one of three trials).

Coloured forms. Places three.

Uncoloured geometric forms. Places four.

Prepositions.† Obeys two.

Colour. Names two.

Simple formboard. Adapts, no error, or immediate correction.

Gesell 'incomplete man'. Adds one or two parts.

Speech. Constantly asking questions. Uses pronoun.

Play. Dresses and undresses doll; speaks to it.
    Now joins in play.

3½ Years*

Cubes. Copies bridge.

Picture card. Names 10.

Digits. Repeats three (two of three trials).

Prepositions. Obeys three.

Uncoloured geometric forms. Places six.

Goddard formboard. 56 seconds (best of three trials).

Play. Imaginary companion.

4 Years*

Gross motor. Goes down stairs, one foot per step.
    Skips on one foot.

Hands. Can button clothes fully.

Cubes. Imitates gate.

Pencil. Copies cross.

General understanding. Questioning at its height. Says which is the larger
of two lines.
    Tells tall stories. Right — left discrimination

---

* For details and method of examination, see Chapter 12.
† Put the ball under the chair, at the side of the chair, behind the chair, on the chair.

Digits. Three (three of three trials).

Coloured forms. Places all.

Uncoloured forms. Places eight.

Prepositions. Obeys four.

Sphincter control. Attends to own toilet needs.

Goddard formboard. 46 seconds: (best of three trials).

Goodenough test. Four

Gesell 'incomplete man'. Adds three parts.

Play. Imaginative play with doll (e.g. being a nurse).

4½ Years*

Cubes. Copies gate.

Pencil. Copies square.

Digits. four (one of three trials).

Uncoloured geometric forms. Places nine.

Goddard formboard. 40 seconds: (best of three trials).

Goodenough test. six

Gesell 'incomplete man'. Adds six parts.

5 Years*

Gross motor. Skips on both feet.

Cubes. Cannot make steps.

Dressing. Can tie shoelaces.

Pencil. Copies triangle.

General understanding. Gives age.
  Distinguishes morning from afternoon.
  Compares 2 weights.

Uncoloured geometric forms. All.

Digits. Repeats four (two of three trials)

Goddard formboard. 35 seconds: (best of three trials).

---

* For details and method of examination, see Chapter 12.

Goodenought test. Eight

Gesell 'incomplete man'. Adds six or seven parts.

Colours. Names four.

Preposition (triple order). Put this on the chair, open the door, then give me that book.

6 Years*

Pencil. Copies diamond.

Digits. Repeats five.

General understanding. Knows number of fingers. Names weekdays.
   Knows right from left.
   Counts 13 pennies, not in a row. Names four coins.

Goddard formboard. 27 seconds: (best of three trials).

Goodenough test. 12.

Gesell 'incomplete man'. Adds seven parts.

Essential milestones

Many milestones of development may be important, but the following are the essential milestones which anyone responsible for assessing babies needs to know:

Birth	Prone — pelvis high, knees under abdomen.
	Ventral suspension — elbows flex, hips partly extended.
4–6 weeks	Smiles at mother. Vocalises 1 to 2 weeks later.
6 weeks	Prone — pelvis flat. Ventral suspension — head up to plane of trunk
12–16 weeks	Turns head to sound.
	Holds object placed in hand.
12–20 weeks	hand regard.
20 weeks	Goes for objects and gets them, without their being placed in the hand.
26 weeks	Transfers objects, one hand to another.
	Chews.
	Sits, hands forward for support.
	Supine — lifts head up spontaneously.
	Feeds self with biscuit.
9–10 months	Index finger approach.
	Finger thumb apposition.
	Creeps.
	Patacake, byebye.
	Helps dress — holding arm out for coat, foot out for shoe, or transferring object from hand in order to insert hand in sleeve.
13 months	Casting (ceases by about 15 months).
	Walks, no help.
	Single words.

---

* For details and method of examination, see Chapter 12.

15–18 months	Domestic mimicry.
15 months	Feeds self fully if given a chance, picking up a cup, drinking, putting it down without help.
	Casting stops. Mouthing stops.
18 months	Begins to tell mother about wetting.
21–24 months	Joins two or three words together spontaneously.
2 years	Mainly dry by day.
3 years	Mainly dry by night.
	Dresses self, except for buttons at back, if given a chance.
	Stands momentarily on one foot.

REFERENCES

1. Annette, M., Turner, A. Laterality and the growth of intellectual abilities. Br. J. Educ. Psychol. 1974.44.37.
2. Bakan, P. The cause of left handedness. New Scientist. 1975.67.200.
3. Barsley, M. The left handed book. London. Souvenir Press 1966.
4. Behan, P. O. Left handed. Br. Med. J. 1982.2.652.
5. Birnholz, J. C., Benacerraf, B.R. The development of human fetal hearing. Science. 1983.222.516.
6. Bishop, D. V. M. Handedness, clumsiness and cognitive ability. Dev. Med. Child, Neurol. 1980.22.569.
7. British Medical Journal. Left hand, right hand. Leading article. 1981.1.588.
8. Freedman, D. G. Smiling in blind infants and the issue of innate VS acquired. J. Child Psychol. 1964.5.171.
9. Grist, L. Why most people are right handed. New Scientist. 1984, 16 August, p. 22.
10. Illingworth, R. S. The development of communication in the first year and factors which affect it. In Murry I., Murry J. (Eds) Infant communication: cry and early speech. Houston. College Hill Press. 1980.
11. Karelitz, S., Karelitz, R. E., Rosenfeld, L. S. In: Bowman, P. W., Mautner, H. V. (Eds.) Mental retardation. New York, Grune and Stratton. 1960.
12. Lundberg, A. Dissociated motor development. Neuropädriatrie 1979.10.xx.1.
13. Macnamara, J. Cognitive basis of language learning in infants. Psychol. Rev. 1972.79.1.
14. Michelsson, K. Cry characteristics in sound spectographic cry analysis. In Murry T., Murry J. (Eds) Infant communication: cry and early speech. Houston. College Hill Press. 1980, p. 85.
15. Michelsson, K., Wasz-Hockert, O. In Murry T., Murry J. (Eds) Infant communication: cry and early speech. Houston. College Hill Press. 1980, p. 152.
16. Morley, M. E. The development and disorders of speech in childhood. Edinburgh. Churchill Livingstone. 1972.
17. Murry, T., Murry, I. Infant communication, cry and early speech. Houston. College Hill Press. 1980.
18. Neligan, G., Prudham, D. Normals for four development milestones by sex, social class and place in family. Dev. Med. Child. Neurol. 1969.11.413.
19. Robson, P. Shuffling, hitching, scooting or sliding — some observations in 30 otherwise normal children. Dev. Med. Child. Neurol. 1970.12.608.
20. Seth, G. Eye-hand coordination and handedness. Br. J. Educ. Psychol. 1973.43.35.
21. Traverthen, C. Conversations with a two-month old. New Scientist. 1974.62.230.
22. Zangwill, O. L. In: Dorfman, A. (Ed.) Language and language disorders. Child care in health and disease. Chicago. Year Book Publishers. 1968.

6

Variations in the general pattern of development

Variations in the general pattern of development

> 'Whoever, said the old goat sheep, divided all living things into sheep and goats, was ignorant that we neutrals and nondescripts outnumber all the rest, and that your sheep and your goat are merely freak specimens of ourselves, chiefly remarkable for their rarity'. — R. L. Stevenson: Fable of the Goat Sheep.

In the study of the development of infants and children, it is essential to remember that all children are different. If they were all the same the study of development would be easy. As they are all different, and different in a wide variety of ways, the study is one of great difficulty. We can all say what the average level of development is for a child of a given age, but none can say what the normal is, for it is impossible to draw the dividing line between normal and abnormal. We can say that the further away from the average he is, the more likely he is to be abnormal.

In this and the next chapter I have described many variations from the usual pattern of development, with examples to emphasise some of the difficulties which arise in developmental diagnosis. Many similar examples were discussed in Arnold Gesell's book *Biographies of child development*, now out of print.

There are several different patterns of development. They are as follows:

1. Average.
2. Average, becoming advanced.
3. Advanced in certain fields.
4. Advanced in all fields.
5. Average or advanced, deteriorating, or slowing down in development.
6. Retarded in all fields.
7. Retarded in all fields, becoming average or advanced.
8. Retarded in some fields.
9. Lulls in development.

A child may appear to make no progress in one field of development, such as speech, for several weeks, and then for no apparent reason he rapidly advances in that field.

The truly average child, the child who is average in everything, is a rarity. Some appear to be merely average at first, but later prove to be mentally superior; it may be that the early developmental tests failed to detect the signs of superiority, or else full maturation was delayed. Some are advanced or retarded in certain fields of development — often because of a familial trait, or, in the case of retardation, because of a physical factor (such as deafness in the case of delayed speech). The course of development of some children slows down, as in Down's syndrome, while in others tragic deterioration occurs because of severe emotional deprivation, poor education, degenerative diseases, psychosis, encephalitis or metabolic diseases. Retardation in all fields usually signifies mental subnormality, but can occasionally be merely a feature of delayed maturation.

Variations in intelligence

The lowest level of intelligence is so low that it is unscorable, and therefore there are no precise figures for the lowest levels. We have only limited information about IQ levels at the other extreme of the scale — at the very top.

Bakwin and Bakwin[1] gave the following range:

150 and over	0.1
130–149	1.0
120–129	5
110–119	14
100–109	30
90–99	30
80–89	14
70–79	5
Below 70	1

Michael Smith[12] gave the following figures for the upper end of the scale:

Over 180	1 in	1 000 000
Over 170	1 in	100 000
Over 160	1 in	10 000
Over 150	1 in	1000
Over 140	1 in	170
Over 136	1 in	100
Over 125	1 in	17

Apart from variations in the level of intelligence, there are many important variations in the pattern of development.

Intelligence test scores themselves vary — partly, no doubt, because of inherent factors in the tests, partly because different aspects of development are being tested as the child gets older, partly because of differences in maturation of the individual child, but largely because of environmental circumstances. In a study of 109 London children from a varied social background,[8] IQ scores at intervals from 6 months to 17 years showed that between the ages of 3 and 17 years 50% changed by 10 points or more, and 25% by 22 points or more.

In the sections to follow I shall describe some of the important variations in development as a whole.

Mental superiority

It would seem reasonable to suppose that as the mentally subnormal infant is retarded in all aspects of development (except sometimes in gross motor development of sitting and walking) and there is not much difficulty in making an early diagnosis of all but the mildest mental subnormality, then one should be able to diagnose the opposite — mental superiority. But I know of no statistical evidence that one can diagnose mental superiority in infancy, though we provided suggestive evidence in our Sheffield adoption study (Ch. 1). I have little doubt, based only on many years of clinical impression, that there are numerous indications of mental superiority from the first few days, but up to the present many of the indications do not lend themselves to scoring methods.

Gessel[6] discussed the early signs of superiority in some detail. He emphasised the fact that superior endowment is not always manifested by quickened tempo of development, but that the signs are there for careful observation. He wrote that superiority

> 'manifests itself in dynamic excellence, in intensification and diversification of behaviour, rather than in conspicuous acceleration. The maturity level is less affected than the vividness and vitality of reaction. The young infant with superior promise is clinically distinguished not so much by an advance in developmental age, as by augmented alertness, perceptiveness and drive. The infant with superior equipment exploits his physical surroundings in a more varied manner, and is more sensitive and responsive to his social environment.'

I think that research on the development of conditioned reflexes in infancy might provide useful clues with regard to a child's maturation and so to his mental endowment.[2a,4,11] There is some evidence that in mentally subnormal infants it is more difficult to establish conditioned reflexes than in normal infants, and that they can be established at an earlier age in normal babies. The rapidity of habituation and dishabituation at different developmental levels could well be relevant.

The establishment of certain habit patterns may be worthy of investigation. In a study of the age of onset of handsucking in 140 normal newborn infants and 79 abnormal infants with cerebral palsy or Down's syndrome,[10] it was found that the abnormal infants developed the habits significantly later than the normal ones.

A study of developmental features in subnormal infants might well throw light on the development of advanced babies. Only future research can show whether these conjectures are relevant.

I think that the predictive value of primitive reflexes and responses in the newborn and subsequently would provide a useful field for research. The primitive reflexes are related to maturation (Ch. 4). I believe, from personal observation, that the early loss of the grasp reflex is one of the early signs of advanced maturation. I recorded the virtual loss of the grasp reflex in children who were in later years to prove to have an unusually high IQ. Unfortunately, with very few exceptions[2,3] the newer sophisticated methods of examining the abilities of the newborn have not been followed by later developmental examination, so that the predictive value of these responses has not been demonstrated. Arnold Gesell paid great attention to the phenomenon of 'hand regard', a feature of the 12 to 20-week full-term baby (Chs 5 and 14); he regarded loss of hand regard later than 20–22 weeks as a pointer to mental subnormality. I have seen early appearance of hand regard by 8 weeks, long before 12 weeks of age, and subsequent early loss of this feature, in children who were going to prove to have a high IQ level. Delayed disappearance of casting, mouthing and perhaps slobbering, and of the reciprocal kick, indicate mental subnormality; I believe from observation that the early appearance of casting, and the early loss of casting, mouthing and slobbering are pointers to a future high level of intelligence.

Other indications of a possible superior mental endowment are the wide-awake, alert, interested open eyes of the new baby, a sleep requirement less than the average for the age, early response to sound, and especially early smiling and vocalisation followed by advanced intonation and variety of vocalisations. One sees early manipulative development — early ability to grasp a toy, later to transfer it from hand to hand, early index finger approach, and early ability to release a toy into the mother's hand. One notes early understanding and memory — early excitement when the breast or bottle is being prepared; early imitation — peep-bo, pat-a-cake, early attempts to attract attention by the cough or sleeve-pulling; interest in stories and rhymes read by the mother, with appropriate action, response to simple instructions; determination, concentration, and good speech.

I saw a 10-month-old child respond promptly to a request by her mother 'show me the book about the caterpillar': the girl fumbled amongst a dozen books and rapidly produced the right book: she repeated the performance when told 'show me the book about farm animals'. I immediately realised that the girl by her rapid response to those two simple questions had demonstrated that she could hear, that she had listened (understanding what was said), could see, and could understand what she saw, had memory, interest, eye–hand coordination and manipulation, and was interested and cooperated: none of those items were scorable.

In the second year the examiner can observe the response in innumerable other unscorable items, for which there are no scores. They include play behaviour — imagination, fantasy play, fantasy stories, early beginnings of domestic mimicry and 'jokes' — the child changing names in nursery rhymes to those of a sibling and laughing: and choice of playmates of corresponding mental age rather than actual age. One observes the advanced memory, ability to point out objects in pictures and describe them, the advanced speech and mature questions, the early manipulative and motor development. I saw a 22-month-old girl asked by her mother to find the letter A (in a set of 26 letters). The letter A happened to be hidden under another one and after 2 or 3 minutes she said, 'Here it is. I've looked all over the place for it.' A bright boy of 24 months constantly asked 'Why?' when told to do things.

Gesell regarded consistent language acceleration before 2 years as one of the most frequent signs of superior intelligence, while general motor ability, as revealed by drawing and coordination tests, are not necessarily in advance. Elsewhere Gesell and Amatruda[6] wrote:

> 'The acceleration comes into clearer prominence in the second and third years, with the development of speech, comprehension and judgement. However, personal social adaptation and attentional characteristics are usually excellent even in the early months. The scorable end products may not be far in advance, but the manner of performance is superior.'
> They added that 'the superior infant is emotionally sensitive to his environment, looks alertly, and displays an intelligent acceptance of novel situations. He establishes rapport. He gives anticipatory action to test situations. He shows initiative, independence and imitativeness. He gives a good performance even if sleepy. He is poised, self-contained, discriminating, mature. The total output of behaviour for a day is more abundant, more complex, more subtle than that of a mediocre child.'

They described twins with an IQ of 180 who talked in sentences at 11 months. Terman described a child who walked at 7 months, and knew the alphabet at 19 months. The IQ was 188.

Mentally superior children commonly learn to read at about 3 years of age. Francis Galton and Gauss were reading before then. Numerous famous persons were reading fluently by 3; they included John Ruskin, Walter Scott, Macaulay, Samuel Johnson, Charles Dickens, Coleridge, Voltaire, Dean Swift, Lloyd George and Edith Sitwell. Mentally superior children tend to be early in perceiving differences, similarities and alternative explanations. They tend to develop hobbies early and to collect objects of interest.

Children with an IQ of over 150 talked earlier than usual. Stedman, in a discussion on the education of gifted children, found most of them friendly and cooperative, and not conceited, egotistical or vain. Hollingworth described 31 children with an IQ of over 180:12 of them were children she had seen, and 19 were cases from the literature. They tended to read a great deal, to be tall and healthy and to have a powerful imagination. Their problems included difficulty in 'learning to suffer fools gladly'; physical difficulties — their mental development having outstripped their physical development: a tendency to idleness: a tendency to be discouraged easily: and problems of immaturity. It was difficult for them to find enough interests at school, to avoid being negativistic towards authority, and to avoid becoming lonely, because of reduced contacts with others of their own age. One feels that Michal-Smith[9,12] went a little too far with regard to the difficulties of children with a superior level of intelligence when he included a chapter on 'Mentally gifted children' in his book entitled *Management of the Handicapped Child*.

Below are two personally observed examples of uniformly advanced development, in which the early promise was fully maintained in adult life. The tests used were mainly those of Gesell.

Case 1

1st day	Listened when spoken to and looked intently.
3rd day	Smiled in response to overture.
	Virtually no grasp reflex.
9th day	Advanced head control. Very interested in surroundings.
	Extremely interested in other children.
18 days	Turned head repeatedly to sound. Holding rattle placed in hand almost indefinitely.
	Vocalising.
8 weeks	Hand regard. 'Grasping with eyes' (Gesell).
11 weeks	Smiling at self in mirror.
14 weeks	Able to go for object and get it.
19 weeks	Sitting on floor for seconds without support.
	Holds arms out to be pulled up.
	Laughs at peep-bo game.
	Rapid transfer of objects. Attention-seeking noises — e.g. cough.
23 weeks	Chewing well. Feeding self with biscuits.
	Stands, holding on to furniture.
	Advanced vocalisation.
	Notably good concentration on toys.
29 weeks	Progressing backwards in attempting to crawl.
35 weeks	Laughs at familiar rhymes. Puts hands on feet and toes when hears 'This little pig went to market'. Bricks in and out of basket.
	Pulls self to stand. Casting. Crawling.
44 weeks	Single words with meaning. Picks up doll on request.
48 weeks	Standing and walking without support.
	Points to two objects in picture when asked, 'Where is the . . .?'
	Eight words with meaning.
13 months	Knows numerous objects in books and seven parts of body.

Carries out numerous errands on request. Feeds self with imaginary fruit from pictures of fruit in books.

16 months Simple formboard — all three in without error.

All pieces into Goddard formboard.

Words together into sentences.

20 months Knows several rhymes.

Answers questions intelligently, e.g. 'Where is your toothbrush?'

Answer, 'Upstairs in the bathroom.'

Spontaneously describes pictures shown to her.

Counts two objects spontaneously.

Speaking in 10 word sentences.

Asks questions.

Makes jokes — e.g. calling sibling a rogue and laughing.

24 months 'Reads' books in jargon, describing each page. Spontaneously changes name in a rhyme for sibling's name and laughs.

26 months Geometric forms — nine correct.

Goddard formboard, 76 seconds.

Repeats four digits, two of three trials.

Prepositions — four.

33 months Goddard formboard, 44 seconds.

Goodenough 'draw a man' test = 51 months.

Dressing self fully without help.

44 months Goodenough 'draw a man' test = 78 months.

Repeats five digits, three of three trials. (six not tried.)

Goddard formboard, 30 seconds.

Able to read school books.

47 months Holds imaginative conversations with doll in two voices — i.e. replying in a different voice.

49 months Qualifies statements by, 'It depends on whether . . .'

Showed memory of 18 months' span.

Reading simple books very easily.

62 months Goodenough 'draw a man' test = nine years.

Repeats seven digits easily.

Case 2

3rd day Smiles in response to social overture. Virtually no grasp reflex.

Intent gaze when spoken to.

7th day Head well off couch in prone position.

3 weeks Followed moving object 180 degrees. Very good vocalisations.

9 weeks 'Grasping with the eyes.'

Advanced vocalisations, including 'Ah-goo'.

12 weeks Able to go for objects and get them. Ticklish.

14 weeks Smiles at mirror. Full weight on legs.
Splashes in bath.

18 weeks Coughs to attract attention. Enjoys peep-bo game.

22 weeks Chews. Sitting without support on floor.
Very good concentration.

24 weeks Stands, holding on to furniture.

30 weeks Laughs loud at 'This little piggie' game.
Turns head to name.
Pulls self to standing position.
Matches cubes. Casting repeatedly.

35 weeks Great determination and concentration. Plays games of spilling milk from cup and laughing loudly.

40 weeks Hands a toy. Release.
Patacake.
Holds out foot for 'This little piggie' game.

44 weeks Knows meaning of numerous words.
Will creep for object on request.
Feeding self fully, managing cup without help.
Obeys commands — get up, sit down.
Creeping up stairs.

12 months Walks, no help. Moos or quacks when asked what cow, duck, says.
Tries to take cardigan off on request.

13 months Tower of six cubes. Spontaneously 'picks cherries off pictures' and pretends to eat them.

16 months Carries out complicated commands, e.g. 'Go into the kitchen and put this toy into the toy cupboard.'

20 months Recognises colours. Knows what page in book has certain nursery rhymes on it.
Advanced sentences.

21 months Goddard formboard, 55 seconds.
Geometric forms — all correct, immediately.
Picture identification — all correct immediately.

24 months Asks 'Why?' when told to do things.

30 months Repeats five digits easily, three of three trials.
Asks 'What does this say?' when looking at books.
Counts up to 25.

33 months Dressing self fully without help.

36 months Reading simple books readily.

39 months Goddard formboard, 20 seconds.
Goodenough 'draw a man' test = six years. (The first man he had ever drawn.)
Cubes — made gate from model immediately, and made steps from 8 cubes.

50 months Able to do 78 piece jigsaw rapidly.

60 months   Goodenough 'draw a man' test = 7 years.

Goddard formboard, 16 seconds (one attempt only).

Repeats four digits backwards (i.e. says 8-4-3-6 backwards).

Subsequent performance confirmed the early prediction of a very high IQ.

The above are two examples of consistently advanced development. They are by no means typical of all children with a high level of intelligence, in whom development in most fields appears to be merely average in the first few months, though certain features, such as unusually good concentration, interest in surroundings and social responsiveness, may be seen by the discerning eye.

Amongst many stories of prodigies, one of the best known is that of Christian Heineken, born in Lubeck. It is said that at 14 months he knew the whole Bible: at $2\frac{1}{2}$ years he was conversant with history, geography, anatomy and 800 Latin words, learning over 150 new ones weekly. He could read German and Latin, and spoke German, Latin and French fluently. When 3 years old he could add, subtract and multiply, and in his fourth year he learned 200 songs, 89 psalms, and 1500 verses and sentences of Latin writers. He died at 4 years and 4 months. Many other stories of mental precocity in childhood have been described in our book *Lessons from Childhood*.[9]

In Chapter 2 I named certain conditions associated with high test scores: they were myopia, retinoblastoma, high blood uric acid, adrenocortical hyperplasia and possibly asthma. It is said that girls with precocious puberty tend to score highly on verbal, but not performance, tests.[5]

Delayed maturation ('Slow starters')

Some children are unaccountably late in acquiring certain individual skills, such as sitting, walking, talking and sphincter control, I have ascribed these, for want of anything better, to delayed maturation of the appropriate part of the nervous system.

One occasionally sees children who were retarded in the first few weeks, not only in motor development, but in other fields as well, and who catch up to the 'normal' and are later shown to have an average level of intelligence with no mechanical or other disability. They can be termed 'slow starters'. One can only presume that it is due to widespread delay in maturation of the nervous system. These cases are rare but important because of the ease with which mental subnormality could be wrongly diagnosed. Below are brief illustrative case histories:

Case 1. This girl had a full-term normal delivery, and was well in the newborn period. At 13 weeks there was complete head lag when held in ventral suspension or when pulled to the sitting position. She did not follow with her eyes until 17 weeks or smile till 18 weeks. She appeared to 'waken up' at about 17 weeks and then made rapid headway. At 25 weeks her head control was equivalent to that of a 16 weeks' old baby. She was able to sit like an average baby at $7\frac{1}{2}$ months, to stand holding on at 10 months, to walk with one hand held and to say 10 words with meaning at 1 year. At the age of 5 years there was no mechanical disability and her IQ test score was 122.

Case 2.   This boy (birthweight, 3400 g) had a proved cerebral haemorrhage at birth, grade 3 asphyxia (using Flagg's classification), and severe neonatal convulsions. He was born at home and the facts about the duration of apnoea are uncertain. He was seen in an apnoeic state approximately half an hour after birth and was given oxygen. Three hours after birth he made one spontaneous respiration each 30 seconds, and 3½ hours after birth he made one each 20 seconds. Oxygen was continued until respirations were properly established 5 hours after birth. Blood was withdrawn under high pressure by lumbar puncture.

In the early weeks he showed gross retardation in development. At 4 weeks of age, for instance, his motor developmental corresponded to that of an average newborn baby. At 27 weeks his motor development was that of a 4 months old baby. At 1 year he was standing and walking without support, saying several words with meaning, had no mechanical disability and was normal in all respects.

I have a cinematographic record of his progress from gross retardation to normality.

Case 3.   This girl had a normal-full-term delivery. There was no abnormality in the neonatal period. She was able to grasp objects voluntarily at 6 months, but could not sit without support till 1 year or walk without help until 3 years. She was saying words with meaning at 1 year. She could not manage buttons until the age of 6 years. The diagnosis made was that of minimal birth injury, as described by Gesell, because there were minimal but non-specific neurological signs.

Her subsequent progress was good, but it was interesting to note that although she could run fast, ride a bicycle, play hockey and take a full part in sport, she had an unusual tendency to stumble in Physical Education classes, her hand movements were slow, and she could only type 50 words per minute. She was top of her class at a technical school and passed her General Certificate of Education at 17.

Case 4.   This girl (birthweight, 3685 g) had a proved cerebral haemorrhage on full-term delivery, repeated lumbar punctures having to be performed on account of severe vomiting due to increased intracranial pressure. An intravenous drip had to be given on the fourth day with considerable reluctance on account of dehydration resulting from the vomiting. Bloody cerebrospinal fluid and later xanthochromic fluid was repeatedly withdrawn by lumbar puncture. There was gross retardation of motor development, but I was impressed by the fact that at 7 weeks she was beginning to take notice of her surroundings and she began to smile. At 9 weeks her head control corresponded to that of a newborn baby. At 16 weeks it corresponded to that of a 6 weeks old baby and at 24 weeks to that of a 13 weeks baby. At 28 weeks she began to go for objects with her hands and get them, and her head control was that of a 24 weeks old baby. She was able to sit for a few seconds without support at 8 months, to pull herself to the standing position at 10 months, and to feed herself (with a cup) at 14 months. She walked without help at 18 months and put words into sentences at 21 months. At 6 years her IQ was 100 and there was no mechanical disability. It is interesting to note that an epileptic fit occurred at the age of 8 years.

Case 5.   After seeing an 18 month old baby boy on account of uniform backwardness in development, I wrote to the family doctor as follows:

'I think that he is a normal boy, but I am not quite sure and will see him again in 6 months. The difficulty is that he has been backward in everything. He did not sit till a year. He is not walking or nearly walking. He was late in reaching out and getting things (9 months), in playing patacake (16 months), in waving bye bye (18 months), and in helping his mother to dress him (he has not started yet). Yet he is a bright little boy, alert and interested. He would not cooperate in tests, but I saw enough to know that he is certainly not less than 10 or 11 months in development of manipulation. His head is of normal size (47 cm). I think that he is merely a late starter. It is always a difficult diagnosis to make and time will tell whether we are right.'

At 2 years he began speaking in sentences; his performance on the simple formboard was like that of a 3 year old. At 4 years he was well above average in developmental tests, and was normal.

Case 6.   Below is another extract from a letter to a family doctor about a child referred to me at 22 months for uniform delay in development:

'The immediate impression on seeing this girl was that she was normal mentally and showed normal concentration and interest in her surroundings. Yet she has been backward in all aspects of development. She is not walking or talking. She has no sphincter control. She can't feed herself. She has only recently started to hold her arm out for a coat. She can't point out any objects in pictures on request. When I gave her 1 inch cubes she cast the lot on to the floor like a child of 13 to 15 months. She is therefore, uniformly retarded. Her head, however, is of normal circumference, and this together with her normal interest and the story of the sibling's lateness in walking and talking makes one extremely cautious about the prognosis. I told the mother that I cannot say whether she will catch up to the normal or not. Time alone will tell, but there are grounds for hoping that she will. I shall see her again in 6 months'.

She walked without help at 25 months, began to join words together into sentences at 33 months, and at that age her performance on the simple formboard was that of a 3-year-old. At 49 months she was normal, with advanced speech, and could count up to 130. There was no disability.

Many workers have remarked about the unexpected improvement seen in some mentally retarded children. Unless deterioration occurs in association with epilepsy (especially infantile spasms), and unless there is a familial degenerative disease, or certain rare syndromes, deterioration is rare: but unexpected improvement may occur, perhaps as the result of a change in the environment, the treatment of disease, the alleviation of emotional problems, or the removal of other harmful factors, such as malnutrition, which were retarding development. As stated elsewhere, it is difficult to predict the reversibility of damage done by unfavourable environmental factors. Except in the case of degenerative diseases of the nervous system, one is more likely to underestimate than to overestimate a child's potential. More commonly one sees children who were grossly retarded in the early weeks, but who make rapid progress and reach a much higher level than expected, remaining, however, below the average. This unexpected improvement is sometimes a feature of cerebral palsy — indicating the difficulty of stating the prognosis for intellectual development. Below are two examples.

Case 1. This girl, born at term, began to smile at 6 months. She began to grasp objects voluntarily at 9 months, to acquire sphincter control and say single words at 23 months, to feed herself, walk unsupported and to help to dress herself at 29 months. She put words together at 3 years. Her IQ at 5 years was 90. She had a mild cerebral palsy of the ataxic type.

Case 2. This boy was born at term, weighing 2385 g. Below is a summary of his development:

First 12 months	Took no notice of anything.
	Lay almost still. Did not kick. No response to overture.
1 year	Began to take notice. Tried to reach objects.
26 months	Major convulsions began.
39 months	Single words only. Cerebral palsy of spastic type diagnosed.
7 years	IQ score 81. Diagnosis spastic quadriplegia. Interested, alert, occasional convulsions.

Meningitis or encephalitis. Prognostic difficulties

It is impossible to predict the outcome of encephalitis or severe meningitis until sufficient time has elapsed to observe the rate of improvement.

The following is a remarkable case history which illustrates the error which can be made in assessment of such a child.

Case report. Unexpected recovery from a state of decerebrate rigidity in tuberculous meningitis. This girl was admitted to the Children's Hospital, Sheffield, at the age of 2 years and 5 months. The clinical and bacteriological diagnosis was tuberculous meningitis. She was drowsy and irritable on admission, and in spite of full intrathecal and intramuscular antibiotic treatment, she deteriorated progressively, until she became more and more deeply unconscious. Three months after admission she was in deep coma, and in a state of decerebrate rigidity. There was no evidence that she could see or hear. She had bizarre movements of the limbs, bruxism, and extreme spasticity, with opisthotonos and severe emaciation. An air encephalogram showed a moderate degree of hydrocephalus. After consultation with the parents, treatment was abandoned and she went home.

She unexpectedly made remarkable improvement at home, so that 5 months after discharge it was decided to resume treatment in order to ensure that she did not relapse. She made a complete recovery, both physically and mentally.

At the age of 7½ years she weighed 38.1 kg and was 129.5 cm tall. Her fundi, vision and hearing were normal, and there were no neurological signs. The x-ray of her skull showed calcification above the sella. Her school progress was excellent, and her IQ was 101. The EEG remained abnormal.

There was every reason to give an extremely bad prognosis here, and yet she made a complete recovery. This is a perfect example of the extreme caution needed in predicting development in the early days after an attack of meningitis or encephalitis, even though at the time the future seems as black as it could be.

I have described these cases at some length because of their great importance. On rare occasions one sees a child who is retarded in all fields of development in the early weeks, and who then reaches a normal level of intelligence. It is possible that this picture may occur when there is a 'birth injury' using the term in its broadest sense, the brain having been previously normal, and that full functional recovery may then occur. The picture may alternatively be due to delayed maturation of the nervous system for reasons unknown, perhaps familial. The problem was discussed by Edith Taylor in her book on the appraisal of children with cerebral defects.[13] She described an athetoid child who at 15 months was unable to sit, could hardly use the hands at all, could not chew, and had to have a semi-solid diet because of difficulty in swallowing and of regurgitation. The child had an expressionless face, but was said to be alert and observant. At the age of 12 years the IQ was 103.

It follows that in developmental prediction the possibility of delayed maturation and unexpected improvement must always be borne in mind, and in all cases *the rate of development* must be observed and assessed. This is based partly on the history of previous development and partly on the findings on repeated examination.

Unexplained temporary cessation of development

Lulls in development of certain skills, such as speech, have already been described. Very occasionally one sees a much more general showing down or cessation of development, without apparent reason. The following are examples:

Case report. This girl was born at term by normal delivery. She developed normally until 8 weeks, having begun to smile at 5 weeks with good motor development. At 8 weeks she had a cold, and then became drowsy, inactive and disinterested in her surroundings. She was admitted at 10 weeks. She took no notice of her surroundings and was suspected of being blind. She was drowsy and apathetic. There were no other abnormal physical signs. A subdural tap and tests for toxoplasmosis were negative. An air encephalogram was thought to show cortical atrophy. The electroencephalogram was normal. The following letter was written to the family doctor: 'I am afraid that the outlook for this child is extremely poor; although she appeared to develop normally till the age of 8 weeks, she is now obviously mentally retarded; her mental retardation is likely to be of severe degree'. She was discharged, to be followed up as an outpatient.

At 14 weeks she was smiling and alert. At 7 months she was a normal happy smiling baby, vocalising well. At 3 years and 9 months in developmental tests she was above the average in all respects.

There is a possibility that the unexplained lull in development was due to encephalitis, but there were no neurological signs and there was no other evidence of that condition. In retrospect there seemed to be every reason to give a bad prognosis.

Case report.   This baby was born by breech delivery at term, weighing 3175 g. Owing to a clerical error blood group incompatibility was not expected. She developed mild haemolytic disease of the newborn, responding to 3 simple transfusions. She began to smile at 6 weeks, and shortly after to vocalise. She developed normally until the age of 3 months. She then refused the breast, stopped playing with her toes, and just lay, with no interest in her surroundings for 4 months, without moving her arms or legs. She then appeared to waken up, began to go for objects with her hands at 9 months, and to sit up without support, walking without support at 16 months, saying 2 words with meaning. At 2 years she was well up to the average in all developmental tests and was speaking in sentences. At just under 7 years she was doing well in an ordinary school.

Summary of four cases thought to be retarded when first seen in infancy, but proving later to have a normal IQ score

Case 1.   The girl was born normally 6 weeks before term, weighing 1960 g. She began to smile at 4 months, to grasp objects voluntarily at 6 months, to imitate noises at 8 months and to cast objects at 11 months. At this age she could say 1 word with meaning. At 1 year she could say 3 words with meaning, but her head control was equivalent to that of an average 4½ months' old child. At 17 months she was examined by an expert in another city with a view to admission to a centre for cerebral palsy, but the diagnosis of simple mental deficiency was made. At 22 months she could stand holding on to furniture. I wrote that her IQ was 'only slightly below the average.' At 23 months she could sit without support, and at 25 months she began to walk, holding on to furniture. She began to walk without help at 4 years and 2 months. Her IQ at the age of 8 was 118. She was running about well, but not really nimble on her feet.

Case 2.   This child was seen by me at the age of 11 months. He was unable to sit and had not begun to chew, but was saying single words. I wrote 'There is a striking dissociation in development. I think he shows a combination of mental retardation with a physical defect. Further observation is essential'.

At 4 years he was an obvious athetoid with an IQ score of 100.

Case 3.   This child was seen by an assistant at the age of 7 months, and spastic hemiplegia with mental retardation was diagnosed. At the age of 7 years his spastic hemiplegia had persisted but the IQ score was 100.

Case 4.   This child was seen by me at the age of 8 weeks with a 3 weeks' history of convulsions. I thought that he was mentally retarded. Apart from an air encephalogram, which was thought to show cortical atrophy, all investigations were negative. He began to vocalise at 3 months, but there was complete head lag in ventral suspension and when pulled to the sitting position. At 10 months I wrote 'IQ average'. At 9 years his IQ score was 122, and there was no physical disability.

Severe microcephaly with initial normal development

I believe that sometimes a child with microcephaly may be relatively normal for the first few weeks, but that slowing down of development then occurs. I have seen several examples of this. I have cinematographic records of two such children, giving permanent evidence of the normality of early development.

Case 1. This girl (Fig. 149) was born at term, weighing 3375 g. There was gross microcephaly, and it was impossible to obtain a proper measurement of the head circumference: it was probably between 11 and 12 inches. X-ray studies eliminated craniostenosis. I followed her up at frequent intervals and recorded her progress by cinéphotography, because of the advanced development. At 26 days her motor development was equivalent to that of an average 6 to 8 weeks old baby. She was smiling and vocalising at 4 weeks. The subsequent history was as follows:

10 weeks	Laughs frequently. Tries to grasp objects.
6 months	Sitting well without support. Chewing for a month.
8½ months	Creeping. Imitating.
10 months	Playing pat-a-cake; waving bye-bye.
11 months	Pulls self to stand. Casting. Helping to dress. Very active, interested. Head circumference 148 in. (37.5 cm).
13 months	Standing alone. Walking, holding on to furniture.
15 months	Walking.
16 months	Domestic mimicry. Head circumference 15¼ in (38.7 cm) Managing cup.
18 months	Three words with meaning.
33 months	Head circumference 39.4 cm. Five or six words. IQ now 45.

The subsequent progress was one of gradual falling off in the rate of development.

A sibling was subsequently born with microcephaly. She showed a similar pattern of development. Both children at school age had an IQ score below 50.

Mental deterioration

Slowing down in development, or worse still mental deterioration, occurs in a wide variety of conditions, of which the following are the chief examples and causes:

Malnutrition in infancy
Severe emotional deprivation: insecurity: child abuse
Hyperbilirubinaemia (neonatal).
Metabolic diseases (e.g. phenylketonuria, other abnormal aminoacidurias, metachromatic leucodystrophy, Lesch-Nyhan syndrome, lipoidoses, mucopolysaccharidoses).
Thyroid deficiency.
Hypoglycaemia, hypernatraemia.
Chromosome abnormalities.
Lead poisoning: other toxic substances; pollution; drug addiction.
Cerebral irradiation for leukaemia.

Epilepsy and the effect of drugs for its treatment.

Perceptual difficulties, learning disorders, emotional and educational problems.

Hydrocephalus.

Degenerative diseases of the nervous system. AIDS.

Meningitis, encephalitis, subacute sclerosing panencephalitis, cerebral tumour.

Cerebral vascular accidents. Acute infantile hemiplegia.

Severe head injury.

Psychoses. Severe personality disorders.

Bad teaching. Effect of failure.

It is incorrect to say that children with Down's syndrome 'deteriorate' during the latter part of the first year. Their development slows down, but they do not lose skills already learnt.

Conclusions and summary

This chapter, and the next, point to some of the major difficulties in developmental diagnosis.

The difficulties in the diagnosis of mental superiority are discussed, but I have described the main features commonly found.

The chapter includes difficulties arising from unexpected improvement or mental deterioration.

The importance of follow-up studies is emphasised.

REFERENCES

1. Bakwin, H., Bakwin, R. M. Behaviour disorders in children. Philadelphia: Saunders. 1972.
2. Bierman-van Endenberg, M. E. C. Predictive value of neonatal neurological examination: a follow up study at 18 months. Dev. Med. Child Neurol. 1981.21.296.
2a. Connolly, K., Stratton, B. An exploration of some parameters in classical Conditioning in the neonate. In Stone, L. J., Smith, H. T., Murphy, L. B. (Eds). The competent infant. London. Tavistock Publications. 1974, p. 385. (See pp. 374–402.)
3. Dubowitz, L. M. S., Dubowitz, V., Palmer, P. C. et al.Correlation of neuroligic assessment in the preterm newborn infant with outcome at one year. J. Pediatr. 1984.105.452.
4. Fitzgerald, H. E., Brackbill, Y. Classical conditioning in infancy: development and constraints. Psychol. Bull. 1976.83.353.
5. Galatzer, O., Beth-Halachmi, N., Kauli,R., Laron, Z. Intellectual function of girls with precocious puberty. Pediatrics 1984.74.246.
6. Gesell, A., Amatruda, C. S. In: Knobloch, H., Pasamanick, B. (Eds.) Developmental diagnosis, 2nd Edn. Maryland. Harper and Row. 1974.
7. Gesell, A., Amatruda, C. S., Castner, B. M., Thompson H. Biographies of Child Development. London. Hamilton, 1930.
8. Hindley, C. B., Owen, C. F. The extent of individual changes in IQ for ages between 6 months and 17 years in a British longitudinal sample. J. Child Psychol. Psychiatry. 1978.19.329.
9. Illingworth, R. S., Illingworth, C. M. Lessons from childhood. Some aspects of the early life of unusual men and women. Edinburgh. Livingstone. 1966.

10. Kravitz, H., Boohm, J. J. Rhythmic habit patterns in infancy: their sequence, age of onset and frequency. Child. Dev. 1971.42.399.
11. Lobb, H., Hardwick, C. Eyelid conditioning and intellectual level: effect or repeated acquisition and extinction. Am. J. Ment.Deficiency. 1976.80.423.
12. Michal-Smith, H. Management of the handicapped child. New York. Grune and Stratton. 1957.
13. Taylor, E. M. Psychological appraisal of childen with cerebral defects. Cambridge Mass. Harvard University Press. 1959.

7

Variations in individual fields of development

In this chapter the variations in the various fields of development and the reasons for the variations will be discussed in detail.

Variations in motor activity

Infants and children vary enormously in the degree of motor activity. One knows that active wiry babies are liable to posset more than the fat placid, less active ones.

Variations in gross motor development

There are considerable normal variations in the age of sitting, walking and other manifestations of gross motor development. In many children with delayed development there is no discoverable reason for the delay. In others there is a variety of factors, such as conditions affecting muscle tone or mental retardation. It is probable that an important factor which governs the age of sitting and walking is myelination of the appropriate part of the nervous system — commonly a familial pattern.

Advanced motor development

Some children learn to sit and walk at an unusually early age. About 3% of children walk without support by the age of 9 months. One often finds that there is a family history of similarly advanced motor development. Advanced motor development can be detected early, often as soon as the third or fourth week, and early sitting can be predicted by the sixth week with a good degree of accuracy. For the purpose of demonstrating this I took cinematograph records of infants with advanced motor development in the first 8 weeks, and showed the predictive value of the early tests by refilming the infants at later ages to show the unusually early development of sitting and walking.

Advanced motor development gives no indication of mental superiority. I saw a boy who was able to creep actively at $4\frac{1}{2}$ months (not crawl), and to pull himself readily to the standing position at $5\frac{1}{2}$ months. I wrote the opinion at that time that his IQ was not better than average. At the age of

6 months he could walk holding on to furniture and at 8 months he could walk without support. At $4\frac{1}{2}$ years he could not dress himself fully, and could not draw anything or count. His IQ score at 5 years was 88. I saw another boy who could walk without support at 8 months. His IQ score at the age of 6 years was 103.

Numerous studies have suggested that the motor development of negro infants is commonly more advanced than that of white infants.[7] The advancement does not extend to adaptive, fine motor, language or personal social development. Geber and Dean[20] claimed that newborn African children behaved like European children at 3 or 4 weeks of age: later they commonly sit unsupported at 3 or 4 months for a few seconds and for half an hour or more at 5 months. At 7 months they could stand without support and walk alone at 9 months. It is not certain whether this advancement occurs in certain tribes and countries or in negro children as a whole.

The advanced motor development of Uganda infants was discussed by Mary Ainsworth.[2] She suggested that the precocious development was in some way related to close infant–mother relationship, and that social and cultural factors were responsible. Others have made similar suggestions.[61] Yet in five longitudinal European studies, carried out in England, Belgium, France, Sweden and Switzerland, no social (or sex) differences were found in the age of walking. But Super,[56] working amongst the Kipsigis in Kenya, showed that the advanced motor development described by many workers in different parts of Africa is culturally determined. The Kipsigi babies learned to sit about a month earlier than American babies: but the mothers gave them the relevant practice which would strengthen the muscles (and perhaps have other effects); from 1 month of age the babies were given bouncing movements on the legs; at 5 or 6 months the babies were seated in a special hole in the ground with back support: and later they were given constant exercise in walking when held. The babies were advanced only in the skills which were specifically taught. When compared with babies of the same cultural and genetic background living in European houses in Nairobi, they were given less of this 'training' — but more than the average baby in the USA — and their sitting and walking development proved to be intermediate between that of the village Kipsigis and the Americans. The Kipsigi babies learned to crawl later than American ones, not being given any encouragement to do so: but amongst the Teso tribes, who give actual encouragement to crawl, the age of crawling is advanced. Confirmation of Super's study was provided by Solomons in Mexico.[55] Special 'training' in this way can only operate when nervous system maturation is ready: motor development therefore depended here on a combination of maturational and cultural factors.

Lateness in gross motor development

The following are the usual factors related to delayed motor development.

Familial factors

The age at which children learn to walk is often a familial feature. It probably depends on the familial rate of myelination of the spinal cord.

Environmental factors

Children who are brought up in an institution from early infancy are likely to be late in motor development, as in other fields. This may be in part due to lack of practice. If mothers deliberately keep their infants off their legs to prevent them developing rickets, knock-knee or bow legs, they weaken the child's legs and may retard walking.

It was thought that the apparent motor retardation seen in Chinese and Japanese children in Hong Kong was a cultural matter; the children had tended to be kept on their backs, tightly wrapped.[18]

Personality

The personality of the child has some bearing on the age of walking, in that children with little confidence and much caution, or children who lose confidence as a result of falls, may be delayed in learning to walk. A child with extreme delay in learning to walk (4 years) had no mechanical difficulty and had a normal IQ. She was able to walk with one finger held for a whole year before she eventually summoned up enough courage to walk alone. When a child like this eventually walks without support, it is at once obvious that the gait is a mature one, indicating that he could have walked long before if his confidence had permitted. Slippery shoes in a child of 12 months may be enough to cause falls and delay in walking.

Mental subnormality

Most mentally retarded children are late in learning to sit, but not all (Ch. 14). Children with Down's syndrome are later in learning to walk than other mentally subnormal children of a comparable level of intelligence. The reason for this may be hypotonia.

As a general guide, one can say that a child with an IQ of less than 20 may learn to walk as long as he has no cerebral palsy: a child with an IQ of 20 to 40, in the absence of cerebral palsy, can certainly be expected to learn to walk.

Abnormalities of muscle tone

If there is excessive muscle tone, as in cerebral palsy, walking will be delayed. Some children with cerebral palsy never walk. If would not be profitable to analyse the average age at which children with different forms of cerebral palsy learn to sit or walk, because there is an additional vital factor, the intelligence, which has a profound effect on motor development.

In the case of the spastic form of cerebral palsy, the child with hemiplegia is likely to learn to walk sooner than the child with diplegia or quadriplegia, especially if his IQ is satisfactory. An occasional hemiplegic child with a good IQ learns to sit and walk at the usual age. The child with diplegia with a normal IQ may not be late in sitting, but he will be considerably delayed in learning to walk. I do not know what factors, other than the IQ, decide the age at which a child with diplegia will be able to sit unsupported. They may include the amount of spasm in the hamstrings and trunk muscles, the amount of extension thrust, and the presence and strength of the tonic neck reflex. I have seen some children with severe diplegia who could sit at the usual age without support (7 months). The usual story of diplegia with a good IQ is average or somewhat retarded sitting, with grossly delayed walking, but normal development in all other fields. I have seen a child with a mild to moderate diplegia but with a normal IQ who was able to walk without help at 18 months. The child with spastic quadriplegia is almost invariably retarded in both sitting and walking, and his IQ is usually lower than that of the child with hemiplegia or diplegia.

The child with athetosis is usually late in learning to sit and walk, but not always, provided that the IQ is normal.

The child with rigidity is virtually always severely mentally defective and may never walk.

The child with ataxia is usually late in learning to walk.

The child with hypotonia is late in learning to sit or walk, and if the condition is severe he will never learn to do either. There are probably other related conditions. The child with benign congenital hypotonia will learn to sit and walk very late. I have seen several who were able to walk between the age of 4 and 6 years.

The usual story in cases of benign congenital hypotonia is that of defective gross motor development, with normal development in other fields — smiling, chewing and manipulation, with late sitting and walking. A child who develops hypotonia as a result of severe illness or rickets will be delayed in gross motor development, but as the underlying disease improves his motor development advances.

A child with meningomyelocele with severe involvement of the lower limbs will be unable to walk without a series of skilled orthopaedic procedures, including muscle transplants.

Obesity

It is probable that obesity, unless gross, does not delay walking,[33] but there is a difference of opinion about this. I saw a grossly obese child, weighing 25.4 kg at 15 months, who walked without help at 10 months.

Neuromuscular disease

Children with Duchenne muscular dystrophy are commonly late in beginning to walk.[11] According to Gardner-Medwin[19] half of all cases have not begun to walk by 18 months of age: he advocates creatine phosphokinase estimation for all boys who have not begun to walk by that age. In another study of 31 boys with Duchenne muscular dystrophy the mean age of beginning to walk was 17.2 months (range 11 to 34 months). A contributory factor for the late walking may be the low mean IQ of affected boys. In congenital muscular dystrophy[39] there is progressive weakness of proximal muscles, including the face and neck, with delayed walking: the creatine phosphokinase is normal or only slightly raised.

A girl was referred to me when 12 months old because of lateness in walking. In all respects her previous developmental history had been normal. She showed prompt finger-thumb apposition, and could sit steadily, but bore virtually no weight on the legs. The knee jerks could not be obtained. A clinical diagnosis of spinal muscular dystrophy was made, and this was confirmed by the electrical reactions, electromyogram and muscle biopsy.

Shuffling

The peculiar mode of progression known as shuffling or hitching on one hand and one buttock may delay the onset of walking. The child learns to progress rapidly in this way. The retardation caused is not severe.

Blindness

Blind children have to be taught to walk. In one study two out of 12 children crawled before they learned to walk. A blind child's motor development may be retarded because he is not given the same chance to learn to walk as normal children. His parents may be so afraid that he will hurt himself that they do not let him practise walking.

Cause unknown

If gross motor development is considerably delayed, there is usually a good cause for it, but this is by no means always the case. I have seen 20 or more children with no physical or mental handicap, who were unable to walk without help until the second birthday or later. There was no discoverable cause for this in any of them. All were followed up and were shown to be normal children.

Case report. A girl who was delivered normally at term could grasp objects voluntarily at 4 months, manage a cup of milk without help at 10 months, and was speaking in sentences at 12 months. She sat without support at 9 months, but could not walk without help till 4 years. Her IQ at 5 years was in the region of 125. There was no physical disability.

Others walked without help at 24 months (IQ average), 24 months (with advanced speech in long sentences), 25 months (IQ just average), and 30 months (IQ 108).

Delayed walking is rarely due to congenital dislocation of the hip.

Other variations in motor development

One of my colleagues at Sheffield[27] wrote that the current tendency in the United States to place young babies in the prone position for sleep and play apparently led to an alteration of the developmental pattern in the prone and supine positions. Babies managed in this way seemed to be more advanced in the prone position than babies who are placed on their back for sleep and play. It was suggested that the relationship of posture to observed developmental variations might repay further study.

For reasons unknown some children omit the stage of creeping.

Crawling and walking before sitting

Below is a bizarre example of unusual motor development.

Case report.   This girl, aged 19 months when first seen (birthweight 1080 g) was referred because she could not sit, although she could crawl forwards and walk well with one hand held, or walk while holding on to furniture.

She had been able to go for objects and get them from 4 months. She had begun to say words with meaning at 9 months. She could pick up a cup, drink and put it down without help from one year, and she had begun to walk, holding on to furniture, at that date.

She was a bright, interested girl, talking and jargoning well. She was seen to walk well, holding on to the edge of the desk. When placed in the sitting position, although head control was full, the back was markedly rounded, but there was no spasm of the hamstrings. She repeatedly fell backwards. The grasp with each hand was normal. The knee jerks were normal and there was no ankle clonus. There was no shortening in either leg. Spinal muscles were normal and there was no evidence of vertebral or spinal anomalies. The clinical diagnosis was either congenital shortening of the gluteus maximus or congenital shortening of the hamstrings.

Another child who was able to crawl before he was able to sit had suffered from emotional deprivation by being brought up in an institution. The explanation of the anomaly of development may have lain in the fact that he could crawl without help, but needed help to sit, and the staff had not time to give him that help.

Another child who showed this variation had congenital hypotonia.

Grasping and manipulation

Voluntary grasping may begin as early as 3 months, but that is rare. It is unusual for a normal full-term child not to be able to grasp objects by 6 months.

The subsequent development of manipulation depends not only on intelligence, but on the child's aptitudes — some showing early manipulative ability greater than others of comparable intelligence.

The development of the use of the hands is retarded in mental subnormality, blindness or severe hypotonia or hypertonia (cerebral palsy).

Smiling

The earliest age at which I have personally seen a child smile in response to social overture was 3 days. From that day onwards smiling became rapidly more frequent. He was a uniformly advanced baby, holding and playing with a rattle, for instance, for several minutes at $2\frac{1}{2}$ weeks, and following an object for 180 degrees at 3 weeks. He proved to have a high IQ in later years. Although it is difficult to date the first smile accurately, the sequence of relevant aspects of development indicated that in this case (and in two other examples seen by me) the dating was likely to be correct. As with all aspects of development, due allowance must be made for preterm delivery.

Söderling[54] analysed the age of the first smile in 400 normal full-term infants. The following were the figures:

First smile	Percentage
Before 2 weeks	0
2–3 weeks	11
3–4 weeks	49
4–5 weeks	21
5–6 weeks	19

It should be noted that mothers commonly interpret any facial movement as a smile, and have the extraordinary idea that they smile when they suffer pain from wind. Mothers tickle the circumoral area of a baby to get him to smile, and the resultant reflex responses ('cardinal points reflex') may be wrongly interpreted as a smile.

Few normal full-term babies reach 8 weeks of age without having begun to smile. There is little latitude in this direction for normal babies, and the majority of full-term babies who have not begun to smile by 8 to 10 weeks will prove to be mentally subnormal. A blind child is likely to be late in smiling because he cannot see his mother's social overtures. An autistic child is likely to be late in smiling at his mother because he is unresponsive (and probably does not look at her). Nevertheless, I have seen an occasional full-term baby who did not begin to smile until 8 to 10 weeks of age, without delay in other fields, and who subsequently turned out to be normal.

I had a child referred to me with a diagnosis of mental subnormality, because of the absence of smiling by the age of 1 year. She was an example of the Möbius syndrome of congenital facial diplegia, with an IQ score of about 75. A similar difficulty would arise with a baby suffering from myotonic dystrophy.

Delayed visual maturation

The commonest cause of delayed visual maturation is mental subnormality, for the mentally subnormal child is late in all aspects of development, except occasionally in sitting and walking. I have seen numerous babies who had been thought to be blind because of their delayed visual responses, but in whom the delay was merely part of their general retardation due to mental subnormality: the pale optic disc of the normal young baby is then interpreted as optic atrophy, and blindness is confidently but wrongly diagnosed.

Delayed visual maturation is a rare feature in some normal babies.[15,23,30] I described a boy first seen by me at the age of just under 4 months, because he did not appear to see. He did not smile at his mother, or watch her face or focus his eyes. He had begun to vocalise at 7 weeks and to turn his head to sound at 12 weeks. On examination he was developmentally up to the average in all respects. On ophthalmoscopic examination (by me and by two ophthalmologists) no abnormality was found, and there was no nystagmus. The provisional diagnosis of delayed visual maturation was made, and the parents were informed that there were good grounds for optimism, though because of the rarity of the condition it was impossible to be sure. He showed signs of seeing at 5 months, and at 6 months he was following a light and beginning to follow a dangling ring. He appeared to be normal in all respects at 10 months. At the age of 5 years he showed evidence of a better than average intelligence at an ordinary preparatory school. He had a slight strabismus, for which glasses were worn, but the vision was normal.

I also saw a girl who apparently saw nothing for the first 6 months. She had spasmus nutans. No abnormality was found by an ophthalmologist. She began to show signs of seeing at 6 months and by a year of age was normal. At school age she showed a better than average intelligence, with normal vision.

It is not possible to say whether these children were genuinely unable to see, or whether they were unable to interpret what they saw (visual agnosia). In all such cases, the absence of a roving nystagmus is important as indicating the possibility of delayed visual maturation. I was told about a Canadian child[34] who was apparently blind to the age of 6 months, and then made a rapid recovery. The IQ score was normal, but there was some residual language disability and some perceptual weakness. The EEG and visually evoked responses were normal. Another report[41] described four cases, all with normal intelligence, who showed no visual fixation until 11 to 16 weeks of age: electroretinography and cortical visually evoked responses were normal. All four were normal by 4 to 9 months of age.

A London report[10] described 16 cases seen at the Moorfields Eye Hospital, using sophisticated tests. It has been suggested[24,37] that the cause may be perinatal ischaemic damage, or delayed dentritic and synaptic formation in the occipital cortex, perhaps with delayed myelination of the optic nerve. It was said that a high proportion of affected babies were preterm or small for dates.

The blind child

If blindness develops shortly after birth the muscles round the eye — the orbicularis oculis, corrugator supercilii and frontalis muscles — are not involved in facial expression, remaining rigid and motionless. If the child becomes blind sometime after birth, the facial expression is normal.

Blind children may show a variety of mannerisms, such as eye-boring, pressing the finger into the eye — beginning in the first year and ending by the fifth or sixth year.[48a] The child may show rapid symmetrical flapping of the hands, hyperextension or flexion of the head, twirling, massive to and fro body swaying, jumping backwards and forwards or facial grimacing.

The assessment of the development of a blind child is difficult; the tests used and the problems of assessment were discussed by the Bakwins.[4] They wrote that over the age of 3 the Interim Hayes Bint Intelligence Test is favoured by many. Apparent backwardness may be due to unsatisfactory tests, restricted past experiences, inadequate opportunities for learning or overprotection. The mean IQ of blind children is less than that of the normal population (see Ch. 15).

If would be expected that blindness would retard smiling.[17] Not only does the child not receive the stimulus of seeing his mother's face, but he is 'at risk' of being mentally retarded, and therefore late in his milestones of development.

Blind children may show what Gesell termed 'hand regard'. This 'hand regard', seen in normal infants from 12 to 24 weeks of age, is presumably a developmental phenomenon and not related to vision.

Under certain circumstances children may recover vision after complete blindness. Lorber[38] has described this after prolonged blindness resulting from hydrocephalus and tuberculous or other pyogenic meningitis.

Delayed auditory maturation

The commonest cause of delayed auditory maturation is mental subnormality. I have seen numerous babies who had been thought to be deaf, on account of delayed auditory responses, but in whom delayed auditory maturation was merely due to mental subnormality.

Some children who are mentally normal appear to be deaf for some weeks or months, and subsequently respond normally to sound. Ingram[31] studied several examples of this. He suggested that it may be the result of damage to the auditory nerve or its central connections before birth, and that recovery then follows. He wrote that some infants with kernicterus do not begin to respond to sound until the age of 4 or 5 months. He considered that some children with brain damage appear to be deaf in the early weeks, but later are found to hear, though they may be later in distinguishing their parent's or sibling's voices, and late in learning to perceive or distinguish what is said. Others have difficulty in perceiving sounds and distinguishing them, and are late in acquiring speech. They are slow to react to sound, and slow to differentiate them or perceive their significance. He termed this developmental auditory imperception.

Chewing

There is little variation in the age at which normal infants learn to chew. They may begin as early as 5 months, but nearly all full- term infants can chew by the age of 7 months. The age of chewing is delayed if a sufficiently mature baby is given thickened feeds only, with nothing solid to bite on. The commonest cause of lateness in beginning to chew is mental subnormality.

Feeding and dressing

The age at which children learn to feed and dress themselves depends not only on their intelligence and manipulative ability but on the opportunity to learn. The age at which they do it also depends on their personality and desire for independence. When a mother continues to feed and dress her child long after he is old enough to do it for himself, she retards his development in these matters.

Sphincter control

There are great individual variations in the age at which sphincter control develop. It is difficult to say how soon control can be acquired, because it is not easy to distinguish the early conditioning from voluntary control. I doubt whether voluntary control begins before the age of 12 months.

Many children do not acquire control of the bladder for several years[60] Thorough investigation reveals no abnormality, though some would disagree with this. In the National Child Development study of 12 000 children, it was found that 10.7% still wet occasionally at 5 to 7 years, and 4.8% at 11 years.[14] Others found a similar incidence.[42,60] When one sees a child who has never had a dry night, and has long passed the usual age for acquiring control of the bladder, there is usually a family history of the same complaint. This is usually termed primary enuresis, and it is almost certainly due basically to delayed maturation of the nervous system. This cannot be the only factor, however, because primary enuresis is more common in the lower social classes than in the upper. The quality of home care is relevant. Many of these children retain the primitive urgency into school years. It is normal for an 18–24-month-old child to have great urgency, so that he cannot wait to pass urine, but as he matures he loses this urgency; the child with primary enuresis commonly retains this urgency for several years. Day-wetting without night-wetting is unusual[6] and is commonly associated with urgency of micturition.

The Newcastle team[42] found that a low social class, emotional deprivation, deficient physical care, social dependence, marital instability, parental crime and defective family supervision were strongly related to the incidence of enuresis. I agree with Miller's conclusion,[43] on the basis of the Newcastle work, that 'the social correlations were such that it is reasonable to think that most enuresis occurs in a child with a slow pattern of maturation when that child is in a family where he does not receive sufficient care to acquire proper conditioning. We doubt if the continuous type of enuresis is caused by major psychological difficulties at the onset, though we acknowledge that psychological difficulties can occur as an overlap.' 'Enuresis is not only a disturbance of development in an individual child, but also a reflection of family relationships and attitudes.' Further evidence of the maturation factor was provided by Weir[59] in a London study of 3-year-old bed-wetters. There was no association with social class, housing conditions, single parent families, family size, birthweight, general health, family stresses or behaviour problems in the child.

The sensitive or critical period for learning may be relevant:[36] faulty training or the occurrence of psychological stress at the time when the child is first able to control the bladder may be of great importance. Maturation, which is probably genetically determined, has occurred in nearly all children by the age of 5: but when the child is developmentally ready to control the bladder, psychological stress, including overenthusiastic 'training' during the sensitive period, will delay control. Mentally subnormal children are usually late in acquiring control, probably in the main due to delayed maturation. Laziness may be a factor when housing is poor and the only lavatory is out of doors.

When a child who has been dry at night begins to wet (secondary enuresis), the cause is almost always psychological, but may be due to the development of frequency of micturition or to polyuria, in either case particularly if he has only recently acquired control of the bladder. The cause usually lies in insecurity, separation from the parents, jealousy or other emotional trauma.

The acquisition of sphincter control can be delayed by over-enthusiastic 'training' — compelling the child to sit on the pot when he is trying to get off, and punishing him for failure to do what is expected of him, so that his normal negativism comes into play. He may come to associate the potty with unpleasantness, and become conditioned against it.

Organic causes of delayed sphincter control are of great importance. The development of frequency or polyuria, especially during the sensitive period of learning, may cause incontinence. Some blame a small bladder capacity for primary enuresis. In a study[51] of 126 enuretic children, psychiatric disorders were significantly related to a lower bladder volume. It was thought that because there is so often an overlap, it is not useful to distinguish primary from secondary enuresis.

Constant dribbling incontinence in a boy suggests urethral obstruction, and in a girl it suggests an ectopic ureter entering the vagina or urethra. In either sex the incontinence may be due to a meningomyelocele, but occult spina bifida is always irrelevant. The surgical causes of enuresis were fully reviewed by Smith in Australia.[53] They include epispadias, diverticulum of the anterior urethra, absent abdominal muscles, ectopia vesicae, lipoma involving the cauda equina, sacral agenesis and diastematomyelia. The 'neurogenic bladder' is diagnosed by the dribbling of urine, the patulous anus, perineal anaesthesia, and ability to express urine by suprapubic pressure. A tuft of hair in the midline may point to a diastematomyelia. Sacral agenesis may be impossible to diagnose without x-ray studies; if only one or two segments are missing, there is usually no external sign; if three or more segments are missing, a gap may be felt on palpation. A history of maternal diabetes should alert one to the possibility.

On the basis of the papers mentioned above, the review by Kolvin, MacKeith and Meadow[36] and my own experience, I support the view that urinary incontinence is related to numerous factors, many of them interacting: they include maturation of the nervous system, conditioning, the nature, quality and timing of training methods, the sensitive or critical period, the child's ego and personality and the personality of the mother, the mother's ignorance of normal development and variations in it, psychological stress, social factors, laziness, bladder capacity, polyuria and organic disease.

Speech

The development of speech depends on a range of factors: genetic, auditory, environmental, intellectual and constitutional, one interacting with the other. As would be expected there are wide variations in speech development in children.[44] On the one hand, normal children may begin to say words with meaning by the age of 8 months, and even make sentences spontaneously before the first birthday: on the other hand many children of superior intelligence may not begin to speak at all until the third or fourth birthday and have defective speech by the age of five. Girls learn to speak earlier than boys.

Morley,[44] in her sample of 114 children from the Newcastle on Tyne 1000 family survey, found that 73% of the children were using words with meaning by the first birthday, with a range of 8 to 30 months, and 40% had begun to join words together, other than in imitation, by the age of 18 months. The range for this was 10 to 44 months. Eighty-nine per cent had begun to join words by the age of 24 months. In 10% speech was not intelligible at the age of 4 years. Seventeen per cent had defects of articulation of serious degree at 4 years, and 14% at 5 years. All these children had an IQ within the normal range. These figures, though based on a small sample in one city, give a good idea of the variations in speech development in normal children. Speech defects such as stammering were more common in social classes 4 and 5 and in homes with poor maternal care.

Gesell et al. wrote that a normal two 2-year-old may have a vocabulary of a few words or more than 2000.

Delay in the development of speech and aphasia

General analysis of causes

When analysing speech problems it is difficult to determine how selected the cases were. Only a limited number of children with delay in speech development are referred to a speech clinic.[45] Morley[44] analysed a series of 280 children referred to her speech clinic at Newcastle on Tyne, and gave the following figures:

Hearing defects	110
Developmental expressive aphasia	72
Mental retardation	71
Cerebral palsy	22
Psychogenic retardation	3
Developmental receptive aphasia (congenital auditory imperception)	2

Although I have not made a statistical analysis, I have no doubt that by far the commonest cause of delay in the development of speech as seen in an out-patient clinic is mental subnormality. Only a few of these are referred to the speech therapy department. The next commonest cause is the familial factor: lateness of speech is a feature of family development. The first born, on the average, tends to speak earlier than later born children — perhaps because the mother had more time to devote to talking to him and reading to him. Speech tends to develop earlier in girls.

Mental subnormality. There is a strong relationship between intelligence and speech, and mental subnormality has a profound effect on speech development. Speech development is relatively more retarded in mentally backward children than other fields of development. The retarded child takes less notice of what is said to him, has poor concentration, is late in imitation, and is backward in the expression and comprehension of words. Though defective articulation occurs in these children, probably to a greater degree than in children of average intelligence, the main problem is delay in the onset of speech and in its use as a means of expression. Common defects in older children include irrelevancy of ideas, echolalia (repetition of questions put instead of answering them), and perseveration — repeating phrases which have just been said.

It would be useful if one could predict the likelihood of speech development in severely retarded children. The majority of children with Down's syndrome eventually learn to speak. Karlin and Kennedy found that of 32 children with an IQ of less than 20, twenty had complete mutism and 10 had a 'jabber with an occasional intelligent word'. Of 32 children with an IQ of 20 to 50, seven had mutism, and 24 had defective speech. Of 249 children with an IQ of 50 to 70, none had mutism.

It is common for a retarded child to begin to say single words clearly and then appear to forget them, so that they are not heard again for many months.

Defects of hearing. If there is a severe defect of hearing, the child will not learn to speak until special methods of teaching him are used. If the defect is less severe, he may learn to make sounds such as b, f, w, which he can see made, but not the g, l, and r. He substitutes for these, and is apt to say 'do' for go, 'yady' for lady, 'wed' for red.

When there is only high tone deafness, involving those tones used in human speech, i.e. between 512 and 2048 double vibrations per second, the child is late in learning to talk, or more commonly his speech is defective through the omission of certain high-pitched sounds such as the 's' and 'f' which he does not hear in the speech of others. He tends to omit the final consonants in words. He does, however, respond to the low frequency whispers, clinks and clapping of hands commonly used as hearing tests. He can hear the car passing and the door banging and the aeroplane, and will listen to the wireless, so that his parents and often the doctor do not consider the possibility of deafness.

If the defect of hearing develops after speech has been acquired, speech is not severely disturbed; but a relatively slight defect at an early stage of development will cause a serious defect of speech.

Delayed maturation. It is commonly thought that the development of speech depends on the maturation of the nervous system. It follows that no amount of practice can make a child speak before his nervous system is ready for it, and that speech therapy will not help a mentally subnormal child to begin to talk — though it may possibly help him to speak more distinctly once speech has developed.

In normal children the understanding of the spoken word long precedes the ability to articulate. A patient of mine at the age of 15 months could only say four or five words with meaning, but he could readily point out 200 common objects in picture books, when asked, 'Where is the . . .?' (drum, cup, soldier, etc.). I saw another child who at $2\frac{1}{2}$ could say four or five words only. His father and sister were late in speaking. Three weeks later he was speaking freely in five-word sentences. Einstein gave his parents reason for anxiety about his mental development because of his retarded speech when he was 4. He lacked fluency of speech at 9.

Familial factors. When a child is notably late in learning to speak, and has normal hearing with a normal level of intelligence, and has no mechanical disability such as cerebral palsy, it is common to find that there is a family history of the same problem — particularly in the mother or father. The reason may lie in a familial delay in the maturation of the appropriate part of the nervous system.

Association with dyslexia. Delay in speech development is commonly associated with later dyslexia and dysgraphia.

The environment. It is customary to find in textbooks and papers the statement that overprotection is an important cause of retardation of speech. It is supposed to retard speech by making speech unnecessary, everything being done for the child before he asks for it. I have never seen evidence to this effect. If it were true, one would expect to find that speech would tend to be delayed more in the first child of a family, in whom overprotection is more likely to occur than in subsequent children. There is no such evidence, and in fact the reverse is the case, first born children tending to speak earlier than subsequent ones.

Language development is retarded in children who are brought up in an institution. It has been said that this retardation can be detected as early as the second month of life, by the variety and frequency of phonemes emitted. These children tend to be late in acquiring speech and subsequently in sentence formation. It must be exceptional for lack of stimulation to be so extreme in a private house that delay in speech development results.

Several workers have mentioned the relation of social class to speech development. In the upper social classes there is greater parent-child contact, there are better speech models in the home, and higher parental expectation regarding verbal accomplishment. In addition there is a higher mean level of intelligence. It is generally recognised that speech development occurs earlier in the upper social classes than the lower ones. Speech development and vocabulary are retarded in slum children. Parental rejection which takes the form of continuous disapproval and criticism of speech as well as of other forms of behaviour may cause the child to stop efforts to talk. It is reasonable to suggest that severe rejection might cause at least partial mutism. Late speech development is a common feature of child abuse.

It is customary to say that delay in the acquisition of speech is due to jealousy. The new baby is blamed for a lot of things, but I have never seen any reason to blame him for this. It would indeed be difficult to prove that jealousy of a sibling has delayed speech, and I have never seen evidence to that effect.

Many workers ascribe delay in speech to 'laziness'. It is argued that the child does not speak because he cannot be bothered to do so. I have never seen an example of this. I have seen serious harm done by advice given to parents by a family doctor that the child should be made to express his needs, on the ground that his failure to speak is just 'laziness'. Really troublesome behaviour problems result from the consequent thwarting. In fact the reason why the children were not speaking was that they could not. I agree with Morley that laziness is rarely if ever the cause of delayed speech development.

Speech problems, including delay in the onset of speech and indistinctness of speech or stuttering, may themselves cause psychological problems, insecurity and withdrawal from the fellowship of others. It is easy to ascribe the speech problems to the psychological difficulties, when in fact the psychological difficulties are due to the speech problem.

For good reviews of speech delay, the reader should refer to the books by Rutter[49] and Renfrew and Murphy.[47].

Psychosis. Mutism may be a manifestation of schizophrenia. I have seen one example of mutism due to hysteria. It is common in autism. In the case of elective mutism, talking is confined to a familiar situation and a small group of intimates;[35] in a study of 24 cases there was immaturity of behaviour, a high incidence of familial psychological disturbances, and a low average level of intelligence.

Speech delay in twins and triplets. The usual reason given for this is exemplified by the statement of Jersild that 'the type of companionship which twins provide each other means that there is less reason for using language to communicate with others'. Some delay may be due to their developing a language of their own:[49] if the co-twin dies in early infancy, the retardation in the surviving twin is only marginal. It is of interest that the incidence of stuttering is five times greater in twins than in singletons, and there is more left-handedness in twins.[25] Morley[44] pointed out, however, that the speech defect is rarely the same in both twins; that speech disorders may occur in one twin and not the other; and that twins may each have a speech disorder but of dissimilar type and degree. It would seem, therefore, that other factors are involved. It is said that language retardation is greater in middle class twins than in those from the 'working' class. It is likely that the main cause is the fact that the mother of twins has not as much time to devote to the two children as she would have for a singleton: she reads to them less, and has less time to teach them the names of objects. Another cause may lie in the twin imitating the speech of his co-twin instead of that of an adult.

Lulls and spurts. Many children go through phases in which the development of speech seems to come to a complete stop. When one skill is being actively learned another skill tends to go into abeyance. The child seems to make no progress for some months, and then suddenly, for no apparent reason, he makes repid headway. These lulls cause considerable anxiety to parents.

When a child is learning to speak, deterioration in the clarity of speech may occur when he has a respiratory infection, especially if there is nasal obstruction.

Lateral dominance and crossed laterality. The relationship of lateral dominance and crossed laterality to speech problems has been discussed elsewhere (Ch. 5).

Structural defects. A cleft palate in itself causes only trivial retardation of speech development, though it causes indistinctness of speech if treatment is inadequate. I have shown elsewhere, however, that the intelligence of children with cleft palate tends to be on the average somewhat less than that of other children.[28] A cleft palate may also cause some retardation because consonant sounds p, b, t, d, k, g needed by the child to establish his early vocabulary are the ones most disturbed by the open palate, with the result that some prelanguage activity is omitted. It should be remembered that deafness commonly develops in children with cleft palate — usually, however, after speech has been acquired.

A submucous cleft or adenoids cause nasal speech. Rhinolalia may follow adenoidectomy, possibly as a result of decreased postoperative movement of the palate.

Malocclusion affects speech, especially if there is micrognathia or 'an open bite'. *Tongue-tie,* unless extreme, does not affect speech.

Speech in cerebral palsy. Speech problems are common in cerebral palsy. They include both delay in beginning to speak, receptive aphasia and dysarthria. Dunsdon found speech defects in 70% of her cases, and Floyer found a speech defect in 46% of the Liverpool school age children. The figure for the athetoid children was 88%.

There are several causes for the speech problems of children with cerebral palsy. They include a low level of intelligence, hearing difficulties, incoordination or spasticity of the muscles of speech and respiration, the effect of prematurity and of multiple pregnancy, cortical defects, psychological factors and perhaps laterality problems. Defects of hearing are common, particularly in children with the athetoid form of cerebral palsy. Twenty per cent or more have a significant defect of hearing. Incoordination of the muscles of the tongue, larynx and thorax interferes with articulation, especially in athetoid children. Thirty per cent of all children with cerebral palsy were prematurely born and about 8% were products of multiple pregnancy — both factors related to speech delay. Psychological factors are important, for children with cerebral palsy may lack normal stimulation and the contact of others. In addition there are probably other factors related to the cortical defect in cerebral palsy.

Speech is not delayed by tongue tie, it is not delayed by laziness, it is not delayed by 'Everything being done for him'. A child does not speak because he cannot speak.

Aphasia

It is almost always impossible to draw the line between normal and abnormal. There are great variations in the age at which speech develops in normal children, and it is not clear at what stage of delay in development in relation to the IQ one should use the word aphasia.

One must try to distinguish the receptive form of aphasia (e.g. congenital auditory imperception) from the expressive form. Whereas the child with receptive aphasia cannot understand written or spoken language, the child with expressive aphasia can understand, but cannot use meaningful language. The two forms are often combined.

Receptive aphasia is more common in boys. The child can hear what is said, but cannot understand the spoken word when it is spoken in his hearing but out of his sight (congenital auditory imperception). The child may cause confusion by repeating words said to him, but without understanding them.

Stuttering (stammering)

Numerous famous men are said to have stuttered. They include Moses, Aristotle, Aesop, Demosthenes, Virgil, Charles I, Robert Boyle, Aneurin Bevan, Lewis Caroll, Somerset Maugham, Charles Lamb and Charles Darwin. Hippocrates, Aristotle, Galen and Celsus discussed the causes of the problem.

According to Jenks, Dieffenbach in Berlin was one of the first to attempt the cure of stuttering by dividing the lingual muscles. He wrote that Mrs Leigh and Dr Yates of New York in 1830 opened the New York institution for correcting impediments of speech. The stammerer had to press the tip of the tongue as hard as he could against the upper teeth, had to draw a deep breath every six minutes, and was instructed to keep silent for 3 days, during which period the deep respirations and tongue pressure had to be continued without interruption. For the night small rolls of linen were placed under the tongue in order to give the tongue the right direction during sleep. Other treatment included teaching the child to speak with pebbles in the mouth or with a cork between the teeth.

The onset of stuttering is usually between 2 and 4 years. Seventy per cent begin before 14, and 95% before 11. It rarely begins after 7. About 1–2% of the school population stutter. It is three times commoner in young boys than girls, but much more common in older boys than girls — indicating that girls are more likely to recover from it than boys.

About four out of five lose their stutter spontaneously. A mild stutter in a child is more likely to cure itself than a severe one. About 3 per 1000 of the adult population has a persistent stammer.[44] The average IQ of stutterers is slightly lower than that of non-stutterers.[3]

Normal children when learning to speak commonly stutter or stumble over words, particularly difficult ones, when excited or upset. They nearly all lose this normal 'stutter' unless they are ridiculed for it, or unless a parent becomes worried about it — perhaps having had his attention drawn to it by a relative: the parent may then tell the child to repeat himself, to speak clearly and distinctly, to 'take a big breath before he speaks', thus making him self-conscious and drawing his attention to his speech. True stuttering then begins. Parents should do absolutely nothing at any time, by word or deed or posture, or facial expression, that would serve to call his attention to his interruptions in speech. One is reminded of the centipede:

'The centipede was contented, quite,
Until the toad one day in spite
Said say, which foot comes after which?
This so wrought upon her mind
She lay distracted in a ditch,
Considering which came after which'.

It is probable that several other factors are involved.[12] These are:

1. The familial factor. The significance of this is not understood. There is a possibility that imitation plays a part, or that a parent who stutters or has stuttered himself shows undue anxiety about his own child's speech and so causes him to stutter.
2. Lateral dominance and crossed laterality. Though many have shown that there is a higher incidence of crossed laterality and ambidexterity in stutterers than there is in the normal population, its significance is not understood.
3. Insecurity. Though insecurity may be a factor in causing stuttering, some psychological problems may be the result rather than the cause of the stuttering. Nevertheless, there is good evidence that insecurity is a factor, provided that it operates before speech is fully established.
4. Constitutional factors. Berry compared the antecedents of 500 stutterers with those of 500 controls. He found that the stutterers were somewhat later in learning to walk than the controls. In the stuttering group there was more often retardation in the initiation of speech and the development of intelligible speech.
5. The personality of the child. It may be that if the other factors operate as well, the more sensitive child by nature is more likely to stutter than the more placid child of even temperament.

Treatment can be highly successful, but all methods have their failures.[8] The first essential is to persuade the parents to stop criticising the child for his speech, and to stop drawing his attention to his difficulty. They should ignore his problem as far as they possibly can; they should not try to help him by saying difficult words for him. They should try to remove sources of insecurity.

A favourite method of treatment is timed syllabic speech — the child being taught to pronounce all syllables equidistantly — eq-ui-dist-ant-ly. Shadowing consists of teaching the child to repeat syllables and words after the therapist. Stutterers speak fluently when they cannot hear their own voice: and in 'delayed auditory feedback', a tape recording device returns the child's voice to him in earphones after a brief delay in transmission of the order of 0.2 second. In an effort to overcome this distorted feedback the child slows his speech and prolongs sounds.[12,16]

Indistinctness of speech

In this section I have included dysarthria, indistinct and nasal speech. Many children during the process of developing go through a stage of substituting consonants or other sounds, or of repeating certain sounds. They may omit consonants and make speech difficult to understand. The commonest defect is the lisp, due usually to the protrusion of the tongue between the teeth on pronouncing an 's'. At the age of 7, 13.5% of children in a national sample were not fully intelligible:[44] this was twice as common in boys. Ten per cent were said by teachers to be difficult to understand: 10–13% at the age of 7 had some speech impairment. It seems to be due to immaturity in speech formation, but the explanation of that immaturity is not clear.

Apart from the lisp, the indistinctness usually disappears without treatment as the child matures, and it is probable that speech therapy is irrelevant except for the lisp. Children usually learn to say g, d, k and t before r, l, w, y, th and fs.

In all cases of delayed or indistinct speech, the hearing should be tested. Ingram[32] regarded many of the common speech difficulties as being grades of severity of one problem, rather than as separate and distinct problems. His four grades are as follows:

1. *Mild* — dyslalia (now termed 'phonological disorder').
2. *Moderate* — retarded acquisition of language with phonological disorder, but normal comprehension of speech.
3. *Severe* — both comprehension and expression of speech defective. Congenital word blindness.
4. *Very severe* — true auditory imperception. Defect of comprehension together with a failure to perceive the significance of sound.

In a study of 43 survivors of Reye's syndrome,[46] 60% had aphonia in convalescence, hoarseness or other speech problems.

Perceptual and allied problems in cerebral and palsy and other children

Only a brief note can be included here concerning certain sensory defects, involving particularly spatial appreciation and body image. They occur notably in children with cerebral palsy,[1] particularly those with a lesion in the right hemisphere, and especially in young children who have been deprived of experience in the handling of toys and other objects because of their physical handicap.

Children at risk of these problems include those who were small-for-dates, or had neonatal hyperbilirubinaemia,[13] or who lacked relevant sensory experiences in the early months. Vernon[57] discussed the difficulties which Bantus often experience in understanding pictures (see also Ch. 3). They may be unable, for instance, to connect a drawing of a mechanical

object with the object itself, or to see depth in a picture. Perceptual difficulties occur in otherwise normal children: sometimes there is a genetic
basis for this.

The handicaps include particularly:

1. *Difficulty in appreciating space and form*, so that an unduly poor score
is achieved on formboards, and on pattern making and pattern copying, e.g.
with bricks or with strips of cardboard. Difficulty may be expected in the
'posting box' test.

2. *Defect of body image*. The child finds it difficult to reproduce movements of the lips, tongue or other parts of the body. His drawings of the
human figure (as in the Goodenough 'draw-a-man' test) are poor. If given
the outline of a face and asked to insert cardboard models of the eyes, lips,
nose, etc., he has difficulty in placing them in the appropriate position.

3. *Difficulty in estimating size, depth, distance, time*. The child may find
it difficult to estimate depth in walking down stairs, to estimate size in
sorting out objects of different sizes, to estimate distance in jumping from
one line to another on the floor, to estimate time in beating a rhythm. When
older he may find it difficult to find his way round a page of print.

4. *Perseveration*. He finds it difficult to change from one task to another.
When writing he may repeat the last letter. When counting cubes he fails
to stop counting at the last brick in a row.

5. *Concentration*. Concentration tends to be unduly poor in relation to the
IQ. There is undue distractibility. There is a tendency for the child to be
distracted by unimportant minutiae, such as the page number in a book,
flaws in the paper, the teacher's dress. He is unduly distracted by sound
or movement in the environment.

6. *Hyperkinesis and other uninhibited behaviour*. From the point of view
of developmental assessment, the possibility of these sensory defects in children with cerebral palsy must be borne in mind in testing, for they may
lead to an unduly low score and to an underestimate of the child's ability.
They also lead to an unduly poor performance in the nursery school and
subsequent schools.

Reading disability (dyslexia and learning disorders

Reading disability is more a problem in the school age rather than the
preschool period, but it has its origins in prenatal and other preschool
factors. There may be indications in the preschool child that learning
disorders are likely.[13] It is an important cause of underachievement.
Suspicious early signs include poor performance in coordination, speed of
repetitive movements, motor and sensory development,[62] visuospatial
sense, matching and visual memory, tests with block patterns, geometric
forms and drawing. Delayed speech development is often a precursor of
learning disorders. Motor ability is tested by hopping, skipping, clapping
the hands or catching a ball.

Delay in learning to read is part of a wide spectrum of learning disorders, including difficulty in spelling, writing, languages and other subjects.[50,52] It occurs at any IQ level. Reading disability (dyslexia) may be defined as a reading age 2 years or more below the mental age.

Delayed reading may be merely a normal variation, commonly familial, but a major cause is mental subnormality. Mentally subnormal children are usually more retarded in learning to read than in other parts of the school curriculum. Commonly associated are features of the attention deficit disorder — overactivity, defective concentration, clumsiness, impulsiveness and aggressiveness.

Various prenatal, perinatal and postnatal factors place the child at risk of learning disorders. Prenatal and perinatal factors include chromosome abnormalities,[58] placental insufficiency, intrauterine growth retardation, virus infection, toxaemia, prenatal or perinatal hypoxia, prematurity or postmaturity, the fetal alcohol syndrome or smoking in pregnancy, malnutrition in utero and neonatal hyperbilirubinaemia.

Postnatal factors include adverse socioeconomic conditions, malnutrition, the age of the parents, poverty and unemployment, lack of suitable pre-reading play material, lack of to-and-fro conversation with the child, domestic friction, child abuse and sexual abuse, one-parent family or any cause of insecurity. Other factors include the effect of drugs (e.g. for epilepsy), cannabis, passive smoking and possibly food additives. School factors include poor teaching, lack of motivation and school absences.

At school the child may become so convinced that he cannot read that he stops trying. Teachers are liable to label him a poor reader, and he is: this is partly a self-fulfilling prophecy, the child fulfilling the expectations.[48]

Many chronic handicaps may be relevant: they include defects in vision and hearing, diabetes mellitus, haemophilia, chronic otitis media, hydrocephalus, cerebral palsy, epilepsy, phenylketonuria and Duchenne muscular dystrophy.

In our book about the childhood of famous men and women,[29] we noted the problem of dyslexia and allied learning disorders in several children destined for fame. They included Thomas Edison, Harvey Cushing, Yeats and many others. Dr John Hunter, famous British physician, could not read till he was 17, despite all efforts to teach him, and this caused great distress to his family. Auguste Rodin, as a result of his difficulty in reading and writing, was described as 'the worst pupil in school'. His father said 'I have an idiot for a son', and his uncle said that 'he is ineducable'. Spelling baffled him throughout his life. Others who had difficulty in spelling throughout their life included General Patton, Woodrow Wilson, William James, Paul Ehrlich, Hans Christian Andersen and Gertrude Bell.

It is remarkable, if true, that dyslexia is ten times more common in Western Countries than in the Far East. (It is said that in China 10 000 letters are in common use, out of a total of about 50 000.) Makita[40] wrote 'that theories which ascribe the aetiology of reading disability to local cerebral abnormalities, to lateral conflict, or to emotional pressure may be valid for some instances, but the specificity of used language, the very object of reading behaviour, is the most contributing factor in the formation of reading disability. Reading disability is more of a philological than a neuro-psychiatric problem.' 'It is unthinkable that the Americans and the Europeans have ten times the population with maldevelopment or malformation of cerebral gyri than do the Japanese. It is hardly believable that the prevalence of hemispheral dominance conflict or split laterality is ten times less in the Japanese than in Westerners. It is equally absurd to suspect that children with emotional distress are ten times less frequent in Japan.' 'The impression I myself gathered in Europe was that the largest numbers of reading disabilities were from English speaking countries, next from German speaking countries and least from Latin speaking countries such as Italy or Spain.'

The so-called 'specific reading disability', or 'specific dyslexia' is a diagnosis which should be made only with the help of expert psychological advice. There is almost invariably a family history of the same complaint, or at least of part of the syndrome. It is four times more common in boys — while other types of reading delay are evenly divided between the sexes. If specific dyslexia occurs in one of uniovular twins, it occurs in the other too: the incidence in both of binovular twins is less. There are problems of laterality — left or mixed handedness, a tendency to read from right to left, to reverse letters as the younger normal child does (interpreting a p as q), or to reverse symbols (interpreting ; as ?). Words are often reversed, so that 'was' is interpreted as 'saw'. Letters are often omitted or inserted in the wrong place. There may be poor auditory discrimination of speech sounds, so that common sounds are forgotten, or a failure to synthesise into their correct word letters sounded correctly individually (e.g. CLOCK pronounced as COCK). There is often mirror reading.

Boder[9] wrote that the diagnosis must be made:

1. By exclusion — of mental deficiency, visual or auditory defects, emotional causes, dyslalia, emotional deprivation and poor teaching.
2. By positive signs – crossed laterality, right–left disorientation, clumsiness, overactivity, WISC and Bender Gestalt tests and the Goodenough test.
3. By specific signs — analysis of reading and spelling for reversals, extraneous letters, omissions of letters and errors of letter order.

The prognosis is uncertain. Many children grow out of their difficulty without special help, though often with some residual spelling difficulty: in fact Holt,[26] referring to normal children, without any special disability, wrote: 'I quite firmly believe that with the possible exception of children in a very remote rural environment, most children would learn to read if nothing were done about it at all.' Methods of treatment for specific dyslexia include efforts to combine the visual, auditory and kinaesthetic senses at the same time — reading a word slowly, displaying the word in large letters, and getting the child to feel cut-out plastic letters. But various studies[5,21,22] found that remedial teaching had little permanent effect. Gittleman[21] wrote that 'No teaching program has been shown to induce significant improvement in the reading ability of children with learning disorders'. It is now suggested[22] that concentration on the language disorders is more likely to be effective than concentration on perceptual and sensory difficulties.

Whatever method of remedial teaching is used, it is essential that the teachers and parents should be fully aware of the nature of the problem, so that they know that the child cannot help it, and is not just being naughty and stupid. It should help them to know that many eminent persons have experienced the problem.

Advanced reading ability may be a feature of an unusually high level of intelligence in a child with a good home where the parents have read to him from an early age, shown him pictures, given him pre-reading toys, such as picture matching, jigsaws, picture dominoes, and cardboard or plastic shapes and forms; and where he is given the opportunity to practise visuospatial development.

Multiple factors affecting development

One often sees a combination of retarding factors which make a developmental assessment extremely difficult. I found it almost impossible to determine the level of intelligence in an athetoid child who was blind and deaf. Retardation of walking in children with cerebral palsy is usually due to at least two factors — the mechanical disability due to the hypertonia and the mental retardation. Institutional care and emotional deprivation is often a third factor.

The following case record illustrates the difficulty which multiple factors cause in development assessment:

Case record.   This girl was referred at the age of 28 months on account of lateness in walking. She was born at term, weighing 3630 g. The history of many of the previous milestones could not be obtained. It seemed that she had learnt to sit at 16 months, to play patacake, to hold her arms out for clothes, and to wave bye-bye at 22 months. She was only saying one word with meaning. She could only just manage a cup, and she had no sphincter control.

On examination she was a bright girl, interested in her surroundings, with moderate concentration, and co-operated well in developmental tests, in which her performance lay between that of an 18 and 24 months old child. The DQ was about 60. She has a mild degree of spastic diplegia. She was a very long way off learning to walk. Her siblings, who were otherwise normal, had only begun to speak at 3 and 3½ years respectively.

In this case the spastic diplegia and mental retardation retarded the walking, and the mental retardation and probably the familial trait retarded the speech. One could not use the development of speech to assess the IQ because of the family history of late speech development. Owing to the alertness and good concentration, I gave a guarded prognosis, saying that she would be educable, and that she might well fare better than appeared likely from her present level of development.

Summary and conclusions

1. All children are different. They differ in the rate of development as a whole, and in the rate and pattern of development within each field.

2. Motor development may be advanced. In certain ethnic groups of negroes, children may show notable motor advancement. Gross motor development (sitting and walking) may be considerably delayed without any discoverable cause, some normal children being unable to walk until 2 to 4 years of age.

Known causes of delayed motor development are:

Familial factors
Environmental factors; emotional deprivation, lack of opportunity to practise
Personality — excessive timidity
Mental subnormality
Hypotonia or hypertonia; gross spinal defects
Neuromuscular disorder
Shuffling
Blindness.

It is almost certainly *not* due to congenital dislocation of the hip.

3. There is much less variation in fine motor development (manipulation), except in association with mental retardation and cerebral palsy.

4. Delayed visual and auditory maturation may occur.

5. There is little variation in the age of chewing, except in association with mental retardation.

6. The age at which children learn to feed and dress themselves is affected by their intelligence, aptitudes, opportunities given to them to learn, and by mechanical difficulties.

7. Acquisition of sphincter control is delayed by:

Mental subnormality
Familial factors
Psychological factors: stress, laziness
Overenthusiastic or neglectful training
The ego and personality of the child; the personality of the mother
Polyuria, frequency, organic disease.

8. Speech is delayed by:

Low intelligence
Genetic factors
Hearing defects

Delayed maturation and familial factors
Poor environment
Twinning
Psychoses
Disturbance of lateral dominance
Cerebral palsy
Problems related to dyslexia and aphasia.

It is *not* delayed by tongue-tie, by jealousy, or 'everything being done for him'. The frequency of lulls in the development of speech is emphasised.

Stuttering is discussed briefly. The main known factors are:

(a) Parental efforts to make the child speak distinctly, together with their failure to recognise that the child's apparently hesitant speech is normal
(b) Familial factors, including imitation
(c) Problems of laterality
(d) Insecurity
(e) Constitutional factors
(f) The personality of the child.

It is probable that stuttering develops when there is a combination of these factors in operation during the early months of speech development.

Known causes of indistinctness of speech include cleft palate, submucous cleft, malocclusion, adenoids, and cerebral palsy.

9. The ability to read is delayed by:

Low intelligence
Emotional factors
Environmental factors
Delayed maturation
Poor teaching
Visual, auditory and spatial difficulties.
Genetic factors ('specific dyslexia') or specific learning disorders.

10. The frequency with which there is a combination of retarding factors is emphasised.

REFERENCES

1. Abercrombie, M. L. J. Perceptual and visuomotor disorders in cerebral palsy. Clinics in Developmental Medicine. No. 11. London. Heinemann. 1964.
2. Ainsworth, M. Infancy in Uganda. Baltimore. Johns Hopkins Press. 1967.
3. Andrews, G., Harris, M. The syndrome of stuttering. Clinics in Developmental Medicine. No. 17. London. Heinemann. 1964.
4. Bakwin, H., Bakwin, R. M. Clinical management of behavior disorders in children. Philadelphia: Saunders. 1966.
5. Belmont, I. & Birch, H. G. The effect of supplemental intervention on children with low reading readiness scores. J. Spec. Educ. 1974.8.81.

6. Berg, I. Day-wetting in children. J. Child Psychol Psychiatry. 1979.20.167.
7. Biescheuvel, S. Symposium on current problems in the behavioural sciences in South Africa. S. Af. J. Sci. 1963. August, 375.
8. Boberg,E., Shea, R. Stuttering — recent developments in theory and therapy. Can. Med. Assoc. J. 1978.119.357.
9. Boder, E. Developmental dyslexia: prevailing diagnostic concepts and a new diagnostic approach. In Myklebust, H. R. Progress in learning disabilities. New York. Grune and Stratton. 1971.
10. Cole, G. F., Hungerford, J., Jones, R. B. Delayed visual maturation. Arch.Dis. Child. 1984.59.107.
11. Crisp, D. E., Ziter, F. A., Bray, P. F. Diagnostic delay in Duchenne's muscular dystrophy. J. Am. Med. Assoc. 1982.247.478.
12. Curlee, R. F., Perkins, W. H. Nature and treatment of stuttering, Philadelphia. University of South California, 1985.
13. Denhoff, E., Hainsworth, P. K., Hainsworth, M. S. The child at risk for learning disorders. Clin. Pediatr. (Phila.) 1972.11.164.
14. Essen, J., Peckham, C. Nocturnal enuresis in childhood. Dev. Med. Child Neurol. 1976.18.577.
15. Foley, J., Gordon, N. Recovery from cortical blindness. Dev. Med. Child Neurol. 1985.27.383.
16. Fransella, F.Stuttering. Some facts and treatment. Br. J.Hosp.Med. 1976.16.70.
17. Freedman, D. G. Smiling in blind infants and the issue of innate VS acquired. J. Child Psychol. 1964.5.171.
18. Fung, K. P., Lau, S. P. Denver developmental screening test. Cultural variables. J. Pediatr. 1985.106.343.
19. Gardner-Medwin, D., Bundey, S., Green, S. Early diagnosis of Duchenne muscular dystrophy. Lancet. 1978.1.1102.
20. Geber, M., Dean, R. F.A. Le developpement psychomoteur et somatique des jeunes enfants Africains en Ouganda. Courier. 1964.14.425.
21. Gittleman, R., Feingold, I. Children with reading disorders: efficacy of reading remediation. J. Child Psychol. Psychiatry. 1983.24.193.
22. Gittleman, R. Controlled trials of remedial approaches to reading disability. J. Child Psychol. Psychiatry. 1985.26.843.
23. Gordon, N. Visual agnosia in childhood. Dev. Med. Child Neurol. 1968.10.377.
24. Harel, S., Holtzman, M., Feinsod, M. Delayed visual maturation. Arch. Dis. Child. 1983.58.298.
25. Holley, W. L., Churchill, J. A. In: Perinatal factors affecting human development. WHO Scientific publications No. 185.1969.
26. Holt, J. The underachieving school. London: Pelican. 1974.
27. Holt, K. S. Early motor development. Postural induced variations. J. Pediatr. 1960.57.571.
28. Illingworth, R. S. Birch, L. B. The intelligence of children with cleft palate. Arch. Dis. Child. 1956.31.300.
29. Illingworth, R. S., Illingworth, C. M. Lessons from childhood. Edinburgh. Livingstone. 1966.
30. Illingworth, R. S.Delayed visual maturation. Arch. Dis. Child. 1961.36.407.
31. Ingram, T. T. S. Personal Communication 1960.
32. Ingram, T. T. S. Delayed development of speech with special reference to dyslexia. Proc. Roy. Soc Med. 1963.56.199.
33. Jaffe M., Kosakov C. The motor development of fat babies. Clin. Pediatr. (Phila.). 1982.21.619.
34. Jan, J. E. Delayed visual maturation. Personal communication.
35. Kolvin, I., Fundudis, T. Elective mute children: psychological development and background factors. J. Child Psychol. Psychiatry. 1981.22.219.
36. Kolvin, I., MacKeith, R. C., Meadow, S. R. Bladder control and enuresis. Clinics in Developmental Medicine. Nos. 48 and 49. London. Heinemann. 1973.
37. Lancet. Leading article. Delayed visual maturation. 1984.1.1158.
38. Lorber, J. Recovery of vision after prolonged blindness in children with hydrocephalus or following pyogenic meningitis. Clin. Pediatr. (Phila.). 1967.6.699.

39. McMenamin, J., Becker, L. E. Murphy, E. G. Congenital muscular dystrophy. J. Pediatr. 1982.100.692.
40. Makita, K. The rarity of reading disorders in Japanese children. In: Chess, S., Thomas, A. Annual progress in child psychiatry and child development. New York. Brunner Mazel. 1969.
41. Mellor, D. H., Fielder, A. R. Dissociated visual development: electrodiagnostic studies on infants who are slow to see. Dev. Med. Child Neurol. 1980.22.327.
42. Miller, F. J. W., Court, S. D. m., Walton, W. S., Knox, E. G. Growing up in Newcastle-upon-Tyne. London. Oxford University Press. 1960.
43. Miller, F. J. W. Child morbidity and mortality in Newcastle upon Tyne. N. Engl. J. Med 1966.275.683.
44. Morley, M. E. The development and disorders of speech in childhood. Edinburgh. Livingstone. 1972.
45. Peckham, L. S. Speech disorders in a national sample of children aged seven years. Br. J. Dis. Commun. 1973.8.2.
46. Reitman, M. A., Casper, J., Coplan, J. et al. Motor disorders of voice and speech in Reye's syndrome survivors. Am J. Dis. Child. 1984.138.1129.
47. Renfrew, C., Murphy, K. The child who does not talk. Clinics in Developmental Medicine, No. 13. London. Heinemann. 1964.
48. Rosenthal, R., Jacobson. L. F. Teacher expectations for the disadvantaged. Scientific American. 1968.218.19.
48a. Roy, F. H. Ocular autostimulation. Am. J. Ophthalmol. 1967.63.1776.
49. Rutter, M., Martin, J. A. The child with delayed speech. Clinics in Developmental Medicine No. 43. London. Heinemann. 1972.
50. Rutter, M. (Ed.) Developmental neuropsychiatry (Symposium on learning disorders). London. Churchill Livingstone. 1984.
51. Shaffer, D., Gardner, A., Hedge, B. Behavior and bladder disturbance of enuretic children: a rational classification of a common disorder. Dev. Med. Child Neurol. 1984.26.781.
52. Shaywitz, S., Shaywitz, B., Grossman, H. J. Learning disorders. Pediatr. Clin. N. Am. 1984.31.277.
53. Smith, E. D. Diagnosis and management of the child with wetting. Austr. Paediatr. J. 1967.3.193.
54. Söderling, B. The first smile. Acta Paediatr. (Uppsala). 1959.48. Suppl. 117.78.
55. Solomons, H. C. The malleability of infant motor development. Clin Pediatr. (Phila.) 1978.17.836.
56. Super, C. M. Environmental effects on motor development. The case of African infant precocity. Dev. Med. Child Neurol. 1976.18.561.
57. Vernon, P. E. Intelligence and cultural environment. London. Methuen. 1969.
58. Walzer, S. X chromosome abnormalities and cognitive development. J. Child Psychol. Psychiatry 1985.26.177.
59. Weir, K. Night and day wetting among a population of three year olds. Dev. Med. Child Neurol. 1982.24.479.
60. White, M. A thousand consecutive cases of enuresis. Medical Officer. 1968.120.151.
61. Williams, J. R., Scott, R. B. Growth and development of Negro infants. IV. Motor development and its relationship to child rearing practices in two groups of Negro infants. Child Dev. 1953.24.103.
62. Wolff, P H., Gunnoe, C., Cohen, C. Neuromotor maturation and psychological performance: a developmental study. Dev. Med. Child Neurol. 1985.27.344.

8

The developmental history

I have already indicated that in my opinion the history is a vital part of the developmental diagnosis. Without a good history which I have taken myself, I am most reluctant to give an opinion about a child's development. It is in this matter that I disagree most strongly with those psychologists who attempt to make their developmental diagnosis and predictions purely on one objective examination. In my opinion this attempt to be really scientific by using nothing but objective methods leads to considerable inaccuracy. They ignore vital information which has a profound bearing on the child's assessment. The history must include all factors which may affect development, whether prenatal, perinatal or postnatal.

The importance of the history

The history is an essential part of the developmental diagnosis for the following reasons:

1. *A history of prenatal and perinatal factors is likely to be highly relevant to the assessment;* it is certainly likely to be relevant to the understanding of the child's development (Chs. 1 and 2). The history must include the 'risk factors' for mental and physical development, including the risk factors for handicaps — blindness, deafness, subluxation of the hip, cerebral palsy and mental subnormality. The history must include important genetic conditions, such as degenerative disease of the nervous system, and partly genetic conditions such as schizophrenia and manic depressive psychoses. Of less but nevertheless significant importance is a family history of sinistrality, ambidexterity or specific learning disorders.

2. *Preterm delivery* The baby with low birthweight appropriate for gestation must be distinguished from the baby who was small for dates, commonly after intrauterine growth retardation. The distinction is of great importance, for one has to decide whether or not to allow for the preterm delivery when relating his test performance to his age. It should be obvious that if a baby is born prematurely, he has missed a period of development in utero, and allowance must be made for it. If, for instance, he was born 3 months prematurely, and he is assessed 6 months after birth, he must be

compared not with an average 6-month-old baby but with a 3 month-old one. One must not expect a baby born 8 weeks early to begin to smile at 4 to 6 weeks, like a full-term baby, but at 4 to 6 weeks plus 8 = 12 to 18 weeks.[1] In the following Table I have shown the difference which correction to the real age makes in calculating the developmental quotient.

16 weeks after birth	Developmental level (weeks)	DQ
Full term	16	100
6 weeks premature		
(therefore real age = 10 weeks)	16	160
Full term	10	62
4 weeks postmature	16	?

It can readily be seen that if allowance is not made for prematurity, gross errors will be made in the case of the young child. Many psychologists failed to make such an allowance. I am constantly being asked up to what age one has to allow for prematurity, and 'how long does it take for a preterm baby to catch up?' These always seem to me to be particularly silly questions. As for the first question, it is surely obvious that the younger the baby the more important it is to allow for prematurity: an allowance of 2 months for development missed in utero matters a great deal in the early weeks; it would hardly be significant when he is 10 years old. As for the second question, the preterm baby does not 'catch up'. He does not develop more quickly than full-term children: he is not 'retarded' just because he missed 2 months' development in utero.

In a study which compared the motor development of full-term infants and preterm infants at 12, 15 and 18 months, using the Peabody developmental motor scales[3] it was shown that there was no difference between the two groups provided only that proper allowance was made for prematurity.

It is uncertain whether allowance should be made for postmaturity. Postmaturity is rare now, because of the risks: it is so often associated with placental insufficiency that it may perhaps be incorrect to allow for postmature delivery.

3. *The history must include environmental factors which affect development* (Ch. 3). For instance, when assessing motor development in a 6-month-old baby, the opportunity given to the child to bear weight is highly relevant. A history of child abuse, or even less serious emotional deprivation and absence of the normal desirable mother-child relationships, must be elicited before a proper assessment can be made. When assessing such skills as feeding and dressing and sphincter control, one must know about the opportunities which the mother has given the child to learn.

4. *Relevant illnesses — malnutrition.* These may be highly relevant to the

child's development — and therefore to his performance in developmental tests.

5. *The assessment of the rate of development.* This vital piece of information must be obtained from the mother at the time of the first interview. A careful history of the milestones of development gives one a good idea of the course of development. This history is particularly important in the case of those children who develop normally up to a point and then deteriorate. The history may suggest that the baby has been a slow starter, or has an illness, and is now catching up. It may indicate that there has been a sudden spurt of development, such as is common when a child is learning to speak.

6. *The familial pattern of development.* There may be a family history of early or late motor development, sphincter control or of speech. It would be silly to give a child a low score for late walking when other normal members of the family exhibited the same trait.

7. *The history of achievements to supplement and confirm one's own observations.* The observant mother may observe many skills which one cannot necessarily see in a short examination oneself, particularly if the child is being uncooperative on account of sleepiness or other factors. For instance, when showing a child a picture card, I usually ask a mother whether she thinks that her child would know the objects in question.

It is useful to determine whether the mother's account of the child's development tallies with one's own assessment. It does not always do so. One occasionally sees a child who is said by the mother to have been able to go for objects and grasp them for months, and yet who, on examination, has such an immature grasp that one does not believe the mother's story. On the other hand, one sometimes sees a child who is said to be unable to sit, yet who can sit steadily like an 8 or 9-month-old child.

The essential developmental history

The first essential is that each should understand what the other means. The details of the child's development are asked in simple language, and the questions are put in a precise manner. The choice of questions will depend on the child's age and the doctor's rough estimate of his mental age. For example, when taking the developmental history of an apparently average 10 month old baby, it would not be useful to ask about the age at which the child began to smile and to vocalise, because the mother would not remember. But if the 10-month-old baby were obviously retarded, the child may have begun to smile only recently, so that the mother's story would be more likely to be accurate.

In taking the developmental history, one asks not just *whether* he has a certain skill, but *when* he developed it and *how often*, and with what degree of maturity.

I suggest that the following questions should be asked, where relevant.

1. *Has he begun to smile at you when you talk to him? You mean when you*

talk to him? or — *when did he begin to smile when you were talking to him? You mean when you were talking to him?*

It is not enough to ask 'When did he first smile?' Mothers may interpret as a smile any facial movement in sleep, or a wince of pain from wind, or facial movement as a result of tickling the face with the finger. The early smile must be the result of social overture. If the mother says that he has not begun to smile, one asks *Does he watch you carefully when you talk to him?* A baby watches his mother intently as she speaks to him, opening and closing the mouth, bobbing the head up and down, long before the smile begins. The average full-term baby begins to smile at 4 to 6 weeks.

2. *Does he make little noises as well as smiling when you talk to him?* or *When did he begin to make little noises as well as smiling when you talked to him?* Vocalisation usually begins a week or two after the smile.

3. *Does he smile much? Is it only an occasional smile?* This question is relevant in the case of mentally subnormal children. Whereas a normal child who begins to smile at 4 weeks smiles a great deal by the age of 8 to 10 weeks, a defective child who begins to smile at 3 months may smile only occasionally by 6 months.

4. *Does he hold a rattle or toy when you put it into his hand, and does he play with it?* or *When did he begin to . . .?* The average full-term baby will hold a rattle placed in the hand and play with it by about 3 months of age. It is not enough to ask when he first began to grasp. She may be confused by the grasp reflex, which has to disappear before voluntary grasping can begin.

5. *Does he turn his head when he hears things? When did he begin?* (Average age 3 to 4 months.)

6. *Will he go for a toy and get it without it being put into the hand? You mean without your putting it into the hand?* or *When did he begin to . . .? You mean'. . .?* The average age is 5 months. It is essential to be sure that she is not referring to the age at which he will play with a rattle or toy only when it is put into his hand.

7. *Does he pass a toy from one hand to the other?* or *When did he begin to.'.?* The average age is 6 months. (It may be argued that it is unnecessary to ask the mother whether he transfers objects, because the examiner can observe this himself. As with several of the other questions, it is useful to compare the mother's version with one's own objective findings.)

8. *When did he first sit without support on the floor for a few seconds without rolling over?* (Average age 6 to 7 months.) It is useless to ask 'when did he sit?' A newborn baby can be held in the sitting position. An average baby can sit propped up in a pram at any age after 2 or 3 months. He can sit 'unsupported' in the pram — with support, however, around the buttocks — several weeks before he can sit on a firm surface without support.

9. *Does he chew things like a biscuit? I don't mean does he suck things but does he really chew, moving his jaws? When did he begin. . .?* Mothers inevitably think of teeth when this question is asked.

10. *Does he creep on hands and knees? When did he begin to. . .?* The mother has to distinguish the crawl, whereby he pulls himself forward by his hands when lying flat, the legs trailing behind (average 9 months), from the true creep on hands and knees (average 10 months).

11. *Does he say any words meaning something?* (Average age 1 year.) *What does he say?* It is useless merely to ask when he began to talk. Mothers are likely to interpret the 6-months-old baby's mum-mum in crying as a word of meaning. When the 7-month-old baby begins to combine syllables such as 'dada' or 'dadada' these sounds are interpreted as words. In the case of 'dada', one wants to know whether the word is spoken only in the father's presence, or when he is not there. It is difficult to know when a 'word' is a word. A child may say 'g' for 'dog' or 'og' before he can say the full word, but he is given the benefit of the doubt when he has obviously attempted to say the word.

12. *How much does he understand of what you say to him? Can he point out objects in books? For instance when you show him a picture book, can he point out the dog, horse, house etc?*

13. *Does he imitate anything which you do — making little noises, laughing or putting the tongue out for instance? When did he. . .?* (Average age 7 or 8 months.)

14. *Does he help when you are dressing him? When did he begin? How does he help you?* The average 10-month-old baby holds an arm out for a coat, a foot out for a shoe, or transfers a toy from one hand to another to allow the hand to go through a sleeve.

15. *Does he play patacake (clap hands)? When did he begin? Does he wave bye bye? When did he begin?* (Average age 10 months.)

16. *Does he join any words together to make little sentences? When did he begin. . .?* This is different from imitating phrases like 'oh dear'. One needs to know when the child spontaneously began to join words together. (Average age 21 to 24 months.)

17. *Does he walk holding on to furniture? When did he begin?* (Average age 10 months.)

18. *Does he walk without any help at all? When did he begin?* (Average age 13 months.) A child of 9 months or so can walk with hands held.

19. *Does he tell you when he wants to use the pot? When did he begin?* (Average age 18 months.)

20. *Is he reasonably dry by day if you catch him? When was he reasonably reliable in the day?* (Average 2 years.)

21. *Is he normally dry at night? When did he become dry at night?* (Average 3 years.)

It is essential to distinguish conditioning the child to use the pot, any time from 3 to 4 weeks of age, from voluntary control, which only begins at about 18 months, when the child tells the mother that he has wet himself, then that he is just about to, and later tells her in time.

22. *Can he manage a cup, picking it up, drinking from it and putting it down without much spilling? When did he begin?* (Average age 15 months, but there is much variation depending on how much chance he has been given to learn. One must be sure that the mother is referring to an ordinary cup, and not a special closed one with a hole in it.)

23. *Does he imitate you doing things about the house like sweeping, dusting or washing up? When did he begin?* (Average age 15 months.)

24. *Can he dress himself fully, apart from back buttons? When was he able to do that?* (Average age 3 years if he has been given a chance to learn to do it: otherwise it is greatly delayed.)

25. *How long does he play with any one toy?* This is an estimate of the child's powers of concentration, but it must be distinguished from the obsessional play of the defective child with one particular toy, or the refusal of a psychotic child to part with a favourite toy.

26. When mental subnormality is suspected —

How does he compare in general understanding with his brothers (or sisters) when they were his age, apart from his speech (if he is backward in speech)? What are the others like? If at school — *how are they doing at school?* It is obvious that in asking this question one must determine whether the siblings are apparently normal.

A particularly useless question is — When did he first begin to hold his head up? Any answer means nothing. A baby can hold his head up momentarily in the sitting position when a few days old. He can spontaneously lift his head off the couch in the supine position when he is about 5 to 6 months old.

Less important questions are the following:

Is he interested when he sees a feed being prepared?

How much does he sleep? This is relevant in mentally retarded infants who often sleep excessively.

Can he roll completely over from his tummy to his back — not from his back to his tummy? You mean completely over? A clear distinction must be made between rolling from the prone to the supine (average five months) and from supine to prone (average six months). It is even more important to be sure that the mother refers to rolling completely over — not merely on the side, an arm getting in the way and preventing the full movement.

When did he begin to hand you a toy and give it to you (as distinct from handing it to you but not letting it go)?

Can he pull himself to the standing position? When did he begin? (Average age about 8 to 9 months.) It depends partly on how much chance he has been given to do this.

In taking a history about a child who is suspected of having defective hearing, one asks:

Can he hear? Why do you think that he can hear?

Does he like being sung to?

Does he respond to music?

Has he favourite nursery rhymes?
Does he hear the telephone, aeroplane, father's footsteps?
Will he come from another room when you call him without his seeing you?

I do not think that other questions are relevant or important except in a particularly difficult exceptional case.

The reliability of the history

I disagree with those who consider that a mother's developmental history is totally unreliable.[2] It is obvious that the further back one goes, the less reliable a history will be, but one does not usually need to go a long way back. A London study concluded that 'routine developmental history taking is likely to be inaccurate and clinically misleading': but the study was based on replies to questions about milestones reached months or years previously; it excluded children with mental or physical handicaps (in whom deviations from the average development are most marked), and it asked questions to which precise replies could not be expected (the age at which persons were named, or the age at which the first words were spoken.) When faced with a mentally subnormal boy of 10 years, minutiae of developmental history are irrelevant. One does want to know details, however, in a baby.

It is always the doctor's task to assess the reliability of a story about anything, whether an illness or otherwise. One has to form one's own opinion about a mother's memory. One has to form one's own conclusion as to whether she is fabricating a reply, as to whether she is trying to make one believe that the child was 'normal' when he was not, and as to whether she is merely basing her replies on the age at which she thinks a child should achieve the skills in question.

In order to check a doubtful reply one comes round to the question in a different way after an interval in order to see if the answers tally.

One checks the answer about one milestone by that about another. For instance, one can readily check the likelihood that a mother's reply about the age of smiling is correct by asking when he began to vocalise as well. If she said that the baby began to smile at 3 weeks, but did not begin to vocalise until 3 months, one will know that one or other answer is almost certainly incorrect. Babies usually begin to vocalise 1 or 2 weeks after they have begun to smile. One constantly checks one milestone against another, and one will also check the mother's story against one's own findings on objective examination.

Summary

A detailed history is an essential part of developmental diagnosis.

Common mistakes must be avoided, especially imprecise history taking (for instance, with regard to such features as 'smiling', 'talking', 'walking', etc.), and imprecise record making (e.g. 'holding the head up', bearing weight on the legs').

REFERENCES

1. Crow, B. M., Gowers, J. I. The smiling age of preterm babies. Dev. Med. Child Neurol. 1979.21.174.
2. Hart, H., Bax, M., Jenkins, S. The value of a developmental history. Dev. Med. Child Neurol. 1978.20.442.
3. Palisano, R. J. Use of chronological and adjusted ages to compare motor development of healthy preterm and full term infants. Dev. Med. Child Neurol. 1986.28.180.

9

Head circumference

The measurement of the maximum head circumference is an essential part of the examination of a baby. The growth of the head depends on the growth of the cranial contents. If the brain does not grow normally to its full extent, the head will be small, and so an unusually small head circumference is a pointer to mental subnormality. On the other hand an obstruction in the cerebrospinal fluid pathways will increase the volume of the cranial contents, and an unusually large head circumference may be the first pointer to hydrocephalus. There have been several studies of the relationship of head size in infancy to subsequent intelligence.[8] It was found in a study of 334 school boys[13] that all physical measurements correlated with at least 273 psychometric scores. Within individual social classes the head circumference was the best physical predictor of WISC IQ and was significantly correlated with it in classes one to four. In a study of the outlook for 127 low birthweight infants,[5] in relation to later Bayley scores, it was found that the head circumferene at birth was 'the single most important variable for subsequent neurobehavioral outcome'.

Tables 3a, b, and c show the head circumference measurements against birthweight and gestational age[10] based on 300 neonates, and Table 4 shows our Sheffield figures for head circumference and weight in full-term babies.

Figures 74 and 75 are graphs from the paper by Nellhaus[7] obtained from 14 reports in the World literature published after 1948: there were no significant racial, national or geographical differences in the figures for head circumference.

It is said that there is a tendency to secular variations in head size,[9] but it is not clear whether these changes are related to changes in the overall size of children.

The head circumference must be related to the size of the baby. A large baby is likely to have a larger head than a small baby, and a small baby a smaller head than a large baby. It is surprising that so many papers on the relation between head size and intelligence fail to take the size of the baby into account: unless they do so the studies are meaningless. In Sheffield we measured the head circumference in relation to the weight in 670 babies[2,4] (Table 4) and determined the best measurement to which to relate the head

181

Table 3a Measurements against birthweight. From Usher, R., McLean, F.[11]

Weight (g)	Head (cm)	S.D.
501–1000	23.2	1.63
1001–1500	26.6	1.0
1501–2000	30.0	1.14
2001–2500	32.0	0.94
2501–3000	33.7	0.72
3001–3500	34.7	0.78
3501–4000	35.4	0.89
4001–4500	36.2	0.70

Table 3b Measurements against gestational age. From Usher, R., McLean, F.[11]

Gestation (weeks)	Wt. (g)	Head (cm)
24–26	853	23.2
27–28	1115	25.8
29–30	1261	26.7
31–32	1632	29.2
33	1943	31.3
34	2095	31.8
35	2382	32.3
36	2482	32.8
37	2961	33.6
38	3231	34.7
39	3310	34.7
40	3477	34.7

Table 3c Smoothed curve measurement data against gestational age. From Usher, R., McLean, F.[11]

Gestation (weeks)	Mean head circumference (cm)	Mean birthweight (g)
26	24.0	933
28	25.6	1113
30	27.6	1373
32	29.6	1727
34	31.4	2113
36	33.0	2589
38	34.3	3133
40	35.1	3480

circumference. We related the head circumference to the weight, chest circumference, spine length and crown rump length at birth, 6 weeks, 3 months and 6 months, in 50 boys and 56 girls. We found that the head circumference was highly correlated with the body weight and that it also correlated well with the chest circumference.

Table 4 Sheffield figures for head circumference and weight (full-term)

	Males (Total approximately 360)				Females (Total approximately 310)			
	Head circumference		Weight		Head circumference		Weight	
	(in)	(cm)	(lb oz)	(g)	(in)	(cm)	(lb oz)	(g)
Birth	13.7	34.8	7.5	3180	13.8	35.0	7.5	3180
6 weeks	15.3	38.9	10.13	4860	14.9	37.8	10.0	4500
6 months	17.5	44.4	18.12	8520	17.0	43.2	17.7	7840
10 months	18.4	46.7	22.2	10,460	17.9	45.5	20.1	9380

The placings of the head circumference and the weight on their respective charts should more or less correspond with each other, though familial factors may be relevant. There may be a familial tendency for its members to have an unusually small or unusually large head, though normal. A

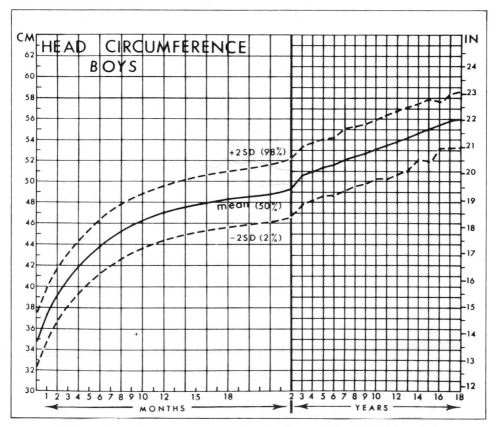

Fig. 74 Composite graph for males from birth through 18 years. (Courtesy G. Nellhaus, Pediatrics.[7] 1968.41.106–114. Copyright American Academy of Pediatrics 1968.)

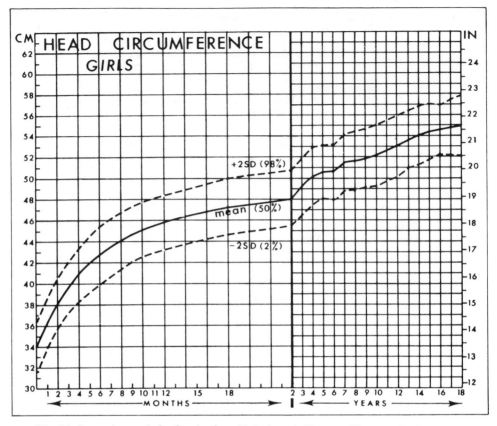

Fig. 75 Composite graph for females from birth through 18 years. (Courtesy G. Nellhaus, Pediatrics. 1968.41.106–114. Copyright American Academy of Pediatrics 1968.)

sudden spurt of physical growth (Figs 79 and 80) is likely to be associated with a spurt in the head size. An erroneous diagnosis of hydrocephalus could be made. An exactly average head circumference may signify mental subnormality if the weight, on the centile chart, is excessive (Figs 81 and 82).

When there is doubt, serial measurements are essential. Even though a head is somewhat small in relation to weight, serial placements on the chart may indicate that the growth of the head size is normal. There is certainly no need for anxiety if the head size, being unusually small, corresponds with the weight (Fig. 76), and the rate of growth of the head size is normal. But when serial measurements show that the growth of the head size is slowing down (Fig. 77), serious mental subnormality is almost certain.

The examination of the head is not confined to the measurement of the head circumference. One automatically palpates the fontanelle and the degree of separation of the sutures.

The shape of the head is important, but one must beware of giving an

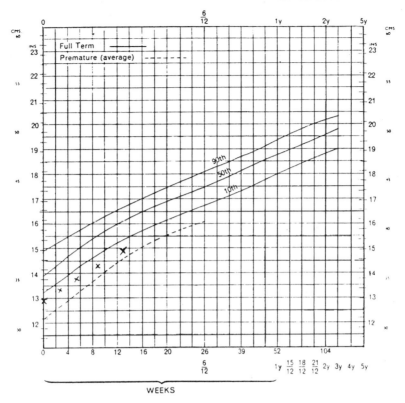

Fig. 76 Normal small child with small head.

unfavourable prognosis based only on the shape. Napoleon, on account of the ugly shape of his head, was thought to be the least likely member of his family to achieve much. Mirabeau was regarded as the ugly duckling of his family because of his disproportionately large head.[3]

Some degree of asymmetry of the head is common and normal. Many babies commonly chose to lie on one particular side, and the head becomes flattened on that side and bulges out at the other side. The asymmetry disappears as the infant gets older. Severe degrees of asymmetry due to craniostenosis, hypertelorism and other conditions, are another matter. The head of a microcephalic child tapers off towards the vertex, and so there is often a sloping forehead. Some children have what can only be called a badly shaped head — the sort of head which one knows from experience is likely to be associated with poor mental development. This includes the flat occiput — but this is sometimes a racial feature.

A skull may be broad in the lateral direction, and narrow from back to front. In such a case the maximum circumference is greater than one would guess. I suspect that a head of this shape is more likely than others to be associated with mental subnormality.

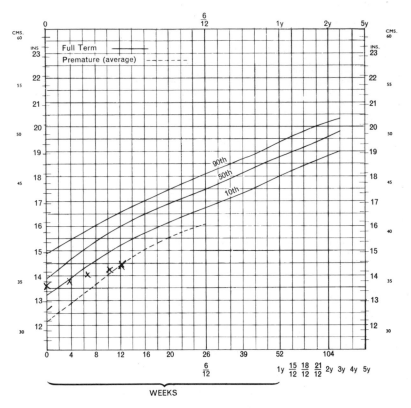

Fig. 77 The measurements of a child with microcephaly; the growth of the head size is defective.

Changes in the newborn period

In small infants there may be some degree of shrinkage in the head size in the newborn period due probably to shifts of sodium and water outwards from the intracranial cavity with loss of weight[14] Japanese workers[10] found that the head size of normal full-term infants increased in the first week, as did that for infants who were small-for-dates, but there was a decrease in the case of small infants whose weight was appropriate for dates. There was an increase in those born by breech or Caesarian section, with a marked increase in those born by vacuum extraction.

A small head

The usual causes can be summarised as follows:

Normal variation
Small baby
Familial feature

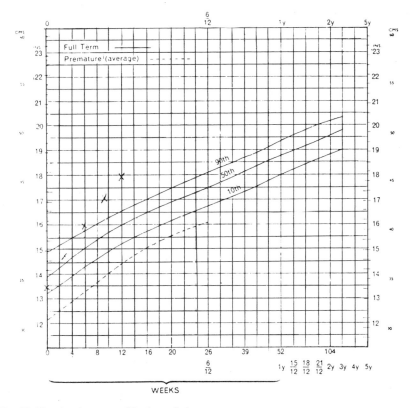

Fig. 78 The development of hydrocephalus.

Mental subnormality
Craniostenosis.

The term 'microcephaly' commonly refers to a head size below the 10th centile in relation to gestational age in the newborn period, or two or more standard deviations below the mean for age for older children.

Children with fairly severe or severe mental subnormality usually have microcephaly if the defect dates from birth or before birth. When a child develops normally for the first few months, and then develops mental subnormality as a result of some postnatal factor, the circumference of the head depends on the age of onset of the mental subnormality. The brain reaches half the adult size by the age of 9 months and three-quarters by the age of 2 years. If severe mental subnormality develops any time in the first year, the head is likely to be small. If it develops after that, the head size is likely to remain normal. This is an interesting differential feature between mental subnormality of early onset and that of later onset.

An unusually small head circumference by no means necessarily signifies mental subnormality. It may be a genetic trait.

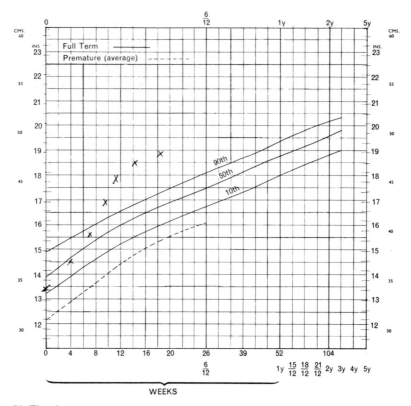

Fig. 79 The chart at one stage suggested the development of hydrocephalus. In fact the rapid increase in the size of the head coincided with a rapid spurt in the growth of the baby as a whole (same child as Fig. 80).

A large head

The usual causes can be summarised as follows:

Normal variation
Large baby
Familial feature
Hydrocephalus
Megalencephaly
Hydranencephaly
Cerebral tumour
Subdural effusion.
Storage disease
Canavan's disease

A large head may be due to hydrocephalus, hydranencephaly, subdural effusion, a cerebral tumour or megalencephaly (a large brain of poor

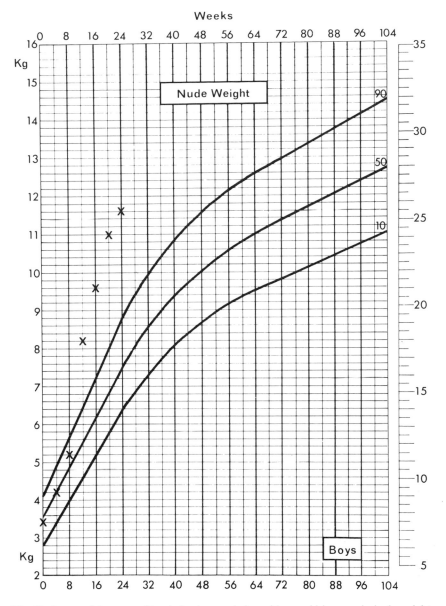

Fig. 80 A normal increase of head size in association with a rapid increase in body weight (same child as Fig. 79).

quality).[6] Children with achondroplasia have a large head, largely due to mcgalencephaly, but partly due to slight ventricular dilatation. When a child has an unusually large head transillumination in a dark room is a useful diagnostic procedure prior to further investigation such as air studies

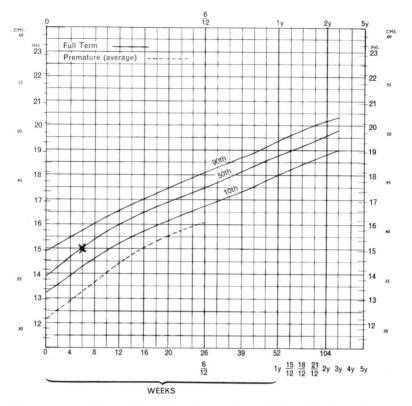

Fig. 81 An apparently 'normal' head circumference in association with advanced growth in weight: the child was a microcephalic.

or subdural taps. Figure 78 shows the typical chart of a baby with hydrocephalus.

When an older baby is malnourished ('failure to thrive') the brain suffers less than the rest of the body, and the head seems to be relatively large. I have seen several mistaken diagnoses of hydrocephalus made in such babies. Dean[1] found that the relationship between the circumference of the head and that of the chest was useful for assessing children with severe malnutrition. Normally the circumference of the head is greater than that of the chest until the age of 6 months, and smaller thereafter. Dean[1] found that in malnutrition the measurement least affected was the head circumference, and that the head is nearly always larger than usual in relation to the size of the infant as a whole. A word of warning was sounded by Swedish workers.[12] They examined the size of the cerebral ventricles of Ethiopian children by encephalography, and found a moderate but significant increase in ventricular size in those suffering from Kwashiorkor, but not other forms of marasmus. The head circumference in these children would be deceptive.

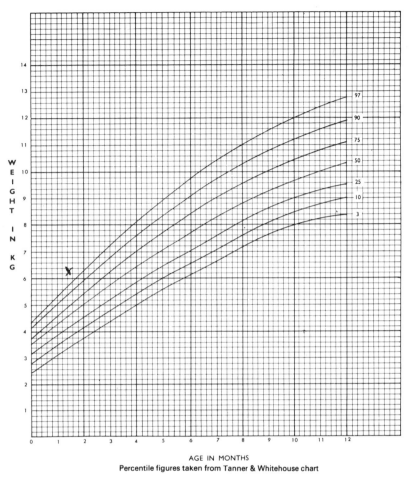

AGE IN MONTHS
Percentile figures taken from Tanner & Whitehouse chart

Fig. 82 Weight chart, same child as Fig. 81. Child well above average weight. Head circumference small in relation to weight.

The prematurely born baby has a relatively large head, and I have seen incorrect diagnoses of hydrocephalus made in such babies.

For an analysis of the causes of a large head in 557 children, see the paper by Lorber and Priestley.[4]

Summary

The measurement of the maximum head circumference in relation to weight is an essential part of the developmental examination of an infant in the first year or two.

I have discussed the diagnosis of the unusually large or small head, noting especially the familial factor.

REFERENCES

1. Dean, R. F. A. Effects of malnutrition, especially of slight degree, on the growth of young children. Courrier de Centre de l'enfance, 1965.15.73.
2. Illingworth, R. S., Eid, E. E. The head circumference in infants and other measurements to which it may be related. Acta Paediatr. Scand. 1971.60.333.
3. Illingworth, R. S., Illingworth, C. M. Lessons from childhood: some aspects of the early life of unusual men and women. Edinburgh Livingstone. 1966.
4. Illingworth, R. S., Lutz, W. Measurement of the infant's head circumference and its significance. Arch. Dis. Child. 1965.40.672.
5. Lipper, E., Lee, K., Gartner, L. M., Grellong, B. Determinants of neurobehavioral outcome in low birth weight infants. Pediatrics. 1981.67.502.
6. Lorber, J., Priestley, B. L. Children with large heads: a practical approach to diagnosis in 557 children, with special reference to 109 children with megalencephaly. Dev. Med. Child Neurol. 1981.23.494.
7. Nellhaus, G. Head circumference from birth to 18 years. Pediatrics, 1968.41.106.
8. Nelson, K. B., Deutschberger, J. Head size at one year as a predictor of four-year. I.Q. Dev. Med. Child Neurol. 1970.12.487.
9. Ounsted, M., Moar, V. A., Scott,A. Head circumference charts updated. Arch. Dis. Child. 1985.60.936.
10. Tamaru, M., Kurosawa, K., Yoshino, S. The fronto-occipital circumference, fronto-occipital diameters, biparietal diameters and head volume of newborn infants during the first week of life. Acta Paediatr. Japonica. 1979.21.30.
11. Usher, R., McLean, F. Intrauterine growth of live born Caucasian infants at sea level. J. Pediatr. 1969.74.901.
12. Vahlquist, B., Engsner,G., Sjögren, I. Malnutrition and size of cerebral ventricles. Acta. Paediatr. Scand. 1971.60.533.
13. Weinberg, W. A., Dietz, S. G., Penick, E. C., McAlister, W. H. Intelligence, reading achievement, physical size and social class. J.Pediatr. 1976.85.482.
14. Williams, J., Hirsch, N., Corbet,A., Rudolph, A. Postnatal head shrinkage in small infants. Pediatrics 1977.59.619.

10

Assessment of maturity

In the past, the term 'premature baby' was taken to include all babies who weighed 5½ lb or less at birth (2500 g), irrespective of the duration of gestation. This definition is no longer acceptable, because many babies weigh less than 2500 g at birth though born at term. Others, though born before term, are smaller than the average for the duration of gestation. It is usual now to refer to those born before 37 weeks of gestation as 'preterm' babies, and to those weighing 2500 g or less as 'low birthweight' babies. The small-for-dates baby has a weight two standard deviations (approximately 5th centile) below the average. Low birthweight in relation to the duration of gestation may be due to malnutrition, abnormalities of the placenta, hereditary or other factors. The behaviour of the 'small-for-dates' baby is different at birth from the truly preterm baby of the same birthweight, and because the prognosis with regard to subsequent mental and physical development is different, it is of importance to recognise the distinguishing physical and neurological features.

A baby may be 'small-for-dates' and also born prematurely. For instance, a baby of 36 weeks gestation may weigh only 3 lb 8 oz (1590 g). The average weight at birth in relation to the duration of gestation in England and Wales is as follows:[12]

Gestation	Mean birthweight (g)	
(weeks)	Boys	Girls
28	1360	1330
32	1950	1880
36	2940	2840
40	3460	3330

The mean birthweight of babies born before 30 weeks gestation was found to be as follows.[4]

Gestation	24	25	26	27	28	29	30
Number	17	12	37	32	44	33	47
Mean birth weight (g)	634	845	891	1008	1062	1212	1394

In Finland the mean weights are considerably higher than in England and Wales.[18]

The distinction between the 'small-for-dates' and 'preterm' baby is of more than academic interest. A mother's dates may not be accurate, and it is useful to be able to check her dates by an objective examination. It may be important for assessment for adoption or for medicolegal reasons to be able to assess a baby's development. If one carries out an examination at 17 weeks, and one does not know whether the 1590 g baby was 8 weeks premature or born at term, one cannot assess his development. One does not know whether to compare him with an average 17-week-old-baby, or with a baby of 17–8 = 9-week-old infant. The following are the main differences between a preterm baby and a full term one (see Table 5, for summary). Wherever possible I have included illustrations of the points described, but have not referred to the figure numbers in the text.

1. *The preterm baby sleeps for the most part of the day and night.* The full-term baby may also sleep for a large part of the 24 hours, but not as much as the average preterm baby.

2. *The cry.* The preterm baby cries infrequently; the cry is feeble and not prolonged. The cry of the full-term baby is more prolonged and vigorous.

3. *Movements.* The preterm baby shows faster, wilder and more bizarre movement of the limbs, with writhing of the trunk. The full-term baby shows more frequent movements, which are more coordinated than those of the preterm baby. The 28 to 32 week preterm infant does not move one limb at a time, movement being generalised; the full- term baby commonly moves one limb.

4. *Feeding behaviour.* The preterm baby cannot be relied upon to demand feeds, while the normal full-term baby can. The preterm baby may be unable to suck or swallow. He is liable to regurgitate and to inhale feeds, with resultant cyanotic attacks when being fed. Mouthing reflexes are difficult to elicit in the infant born before about 34 weeks of gestation: they are easily obtained in the full-term baby.

5. *Muscle tone.* The muscle tone of the preterm baby is less than that of the full-term infant. Muscle tone increases first in the legs (by about $7\frac{1}{2}$ months of gestation) and later in the arms.

6. *Posture.* In the prone position the preterm baby characteristically lies flat on the couch, with the pelvis low and the knees at the side of the abdomen, the hips being acutely flexed. The full-term baby lies with the pelvis high and the knees drawn up under the abdomen.

In the supine position the 28 week preterm baby lies with the lower limbs extended and the hips abducted, so that the limbs are flat on the couch, in a 'froglike' attitude. The upper limbs lie in a similar position. The 32 week preterm baby lies with the arms extended, but with the lower limbs flexed at the knee and abducted at the hip. The 36 week preterm baby lies less frog-like, mainly flexed. The full-term infant lies with the limbs

Table 5 Scoring system for external criteria. From Dubowitz, Lilly M. S., Dubowitz, V., Goldberg, Cissie. Clinical assessment of gestational age in the newborn infant. J. Pediatr. 1970.77.1–10, adapted from Farr and associates. Dev. Med. Child Neurol. 1966.8.507.

External sign	Score 0	1	2	3	4
Oedema	Obvious oedema of hands and feet; pitting over tibia	No obvious oedema of hands and feet; pitting over tibia	No oedema		
Skin texture	Very thin, gelatinous	Thin and smooth	Smooth; medium thickness. Rash or superficial peeling	Slight thickening. Superficial cracking and peeling especially of hands and feet	Thick and parchment-like; superficial or deep cracking
Skin colour	Dark red	Uniformly pink	Pale pink; variable over body	Pale; only pink over ears, lips, palms, or soles	
Skin opacity (trunk)	Numerous veins and venules clearly seen, especially over abdomen	Veins and tributaries seen	A few large vessels clearly seen over abdomen	A few large vessels seen indistinctly over abdomen	No blood vessels seen
Lanugo (over back)	No lanugo	Abundant; long and thick over whole back	Hair thinning especially over lower back	Small amount of lanugo and bald areas	At least half of back devoid of lanugo
Plantar creases	No skin creases	Faint red marks over anterior half of sole	Definite red marks over anterior half; indentations over anterior third	Indentations over anterior third	Definite deep indentations over anterior third
Nipple formation	Nipple barely visible. No areola	Nipple well defined; areola smooth and flat, diameter 0.75 cm	Areola stippled, edge not raised, diameter 0.75 cm	Areola stippled, edge raised, diameter 0.75 cm	
Breast size	No breast tissue palpable	Breast tissue on one or both sides, 0.5 cm diameter	Breast tissue both sides; one or both 0.5–1.0 cm	Breast tissue both sides; one or both 1 cm	
Ear form	Pinna flat and shapeless, little or no incurving of edge	Incurving of part of edge of pinna	Partial incurving whole of upper pinna	Well-defined incurving whole of upper pinna	
Ear firmness	Pinna soft, easily folded, no recoil	Pinna soft, easily folded, slow recoil	Cartilage to edge of pinna, but soft in places, ready recoil	Pinna firm, cartilage to edge; instant recoil	
Genitals: Male	Neither testis in scrotum	At least one testis high in scrotum	At least one testis right down		
Female (with hips half abducted)	Labia majora widely separated, labia minora protruding	Labia majora almost cover labia minora	Labia majora completely cover labia minora		

strongly flexed. The head in the 28 to 32 weeks infant is turned to one side. The full-term baby tends to keep the head aligned with the trunk.

7. *Head rotation.* In the 28 week preterm baby the head can be rotated so far that the chin is well beyond the acromion: in the full-term baby the chin can rotate only as far as the acromion.

8. *The scarf sign.* This depends on the deltoids, teres major and rhomboids. During the test the baby should be comfortable, in the supine position, with the head central. The hand is led across the chest to the opposite side of the neck. The hand of the 28 week preterm baby reaches well past the acromion: that of the full-term baby does not go beyond the acromion. In the posterior scarf sign, which depends on the pectoralis major and latissimus dorsi, the hand is led behind the neck to the opposite side. There is a similar difference in the range achieved in the preterm and full-term baby.

9. *The Moro reflex.* This is present in preterm babies, except the very small ones, but the arms tend to fall backwards on to the table during the adduction phase because the antigravity muscles are weaker than in the full-term baby.

10. *Wrist flexion.* Flexion of the wrist of the 28 week preterm baby is incomplete, so that a 'window' is formed between the hand and the

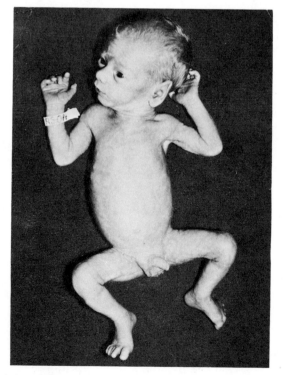

Fig. 83 Preterm baby, supine.

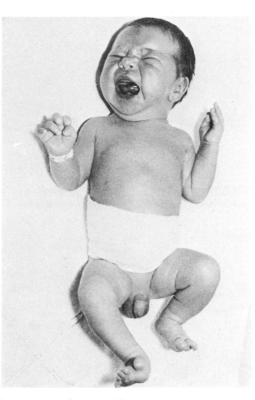

Fig. 84 Full-term baby, supine, flexed positions.

forearm; that of the full-term baby is complete, so that the hand is in contact with the forearm.

11. *The grasp reflex*. This is difficult to obtain in the 28 week preterm baby. There is no flexion of the elbow or contraction of muscles at the shoulder. In the full-term baby the elbow and shoulder take an active part in the response. The grasp reflex is at its strongest at 40 weeks.

12. *'Redressement du tronc'* — so called by the French writers. When the infant is held with his back against one's body, the young preterm baby cannot extend the trunk. At 35 weeks gestation the back begins to extend: at 37 weeks the back extends and the child extends the neck, as in the case of the full-term infant.

13. *Crossed extension reflex* (Ch. 4). The reflex is incomplete in the young preterm baby. In the case of the 28 week preterm baby there is flexion of the opposite leg without extension or adduction. In the case of a 32 week baby some extension occurs after flexion: in the 36 week baby slight adduction follows the extension.

14. *Knee extension*. When the hip is flexed so that the thigh is in contact with the side of the abdomen, the knee of the young preterm baby can be fully extended. As maturity increases from 28 weeks gestation, less and less

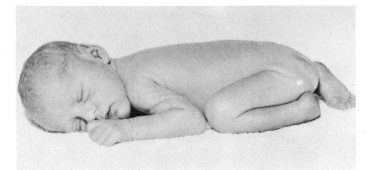

Fig. 85 For comparison with Fig. 86. Prone position in preterm baby. (At 9 weeks before term.) Hips abducted, but flexed; pelvis less high than in full-term baby.

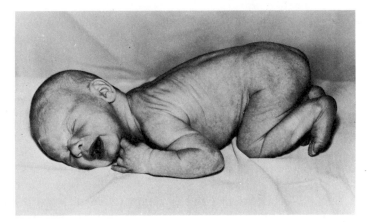

Fig. 86 Prone position, full-term baby. (Above 0–2 weeks of age.) Pelvis high, knees drawn up under abdomen.

extension is obtained. In the full-term baby extension is incomplete by about 20 °.

15. *Dorsiflexion of the foot.* In the 28 week preterm baby, dorsiflexion is incomplete, so that there is a fairly wide gap between the foot and the foreleg. In the full-term baby the foot is brought into contact with the front of the leg.

16. *The grasp reflex in the foot.* This is much weaker in the preterm baby than in the full-term one.

17. *The walking reflex.* This is very feeble in the 28 week preterm baby, but it is easily elicited in the 36 week baby and the full-term one. The 32 week preterm baby usually walks on the toes, whereas the full-term baby walks with the foot flat on the couch.

18. *Ventral suspension.* Held in ventral suspension, the young preterm baby hangs limply, with no extension of the spine or neck, and with no

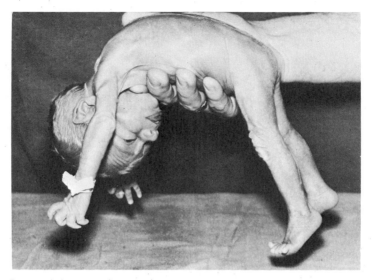

Fig. 87 Preterm baby, ventral suspension.

Fig. 88 Full-term, ventral suspension.

flexion of the elbows, hips or knees. The full-term baby has a straighter back, holds the head up a little, and flexes the elbows and knees and slightly extends the hips.

Claudine Amiel-Tison,[2] has written a brief clear account of her method of assessing the maturity of the baby, basing the method largely on the assessment of tone.

Robinson[20] carried out 219 neurological examinations on 62 infants having a gestation period varying from 25 to 42 weeks. He found that the five most useful tests of gestational age were the reactions of the pupil to light, consistently absent under 29 weeks and present after 31 weeks, the

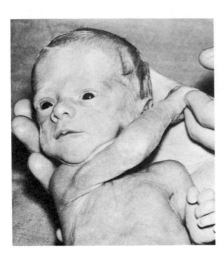

Fig. 89 Scarf sign. Preterm baby. Note position of elbow and hand.

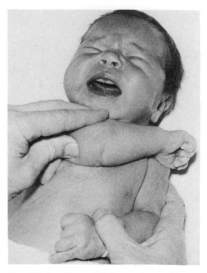

Fig. 90 Scarf sign. Full-term baby. Note position of elbow and hand.

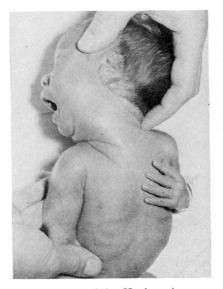

Fig. 91 Preterm baby. Head rotation. Chin beyond tip of shoulder.

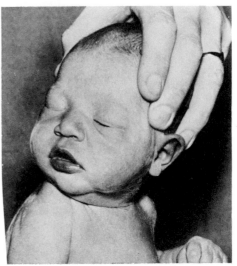

Fig. 92 Range of head rotation. Full-term baby. Chin on acromion.

glabellar tap reflex, which is absent before 32 weeks and present after 34 weeks, the traction test for head lag, which is positive after 33 weeks, the neck righting reflex, which causes the trunk to rotate when the examiner rotates the head, present by 34 to 37 weeks, and the turning of the head to light, by 32 to 36 weeks.

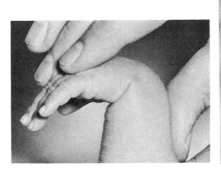

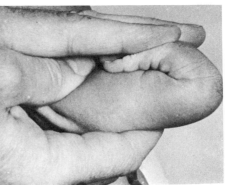

Fig. 93 Window sign, preterm baby.   **Fig. 94** Window sign, full-term baby.

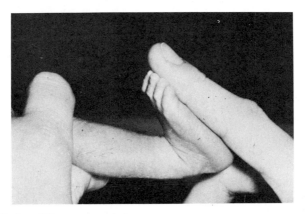

Fig. 95 Dorsiflexion of foot; preterm baby.

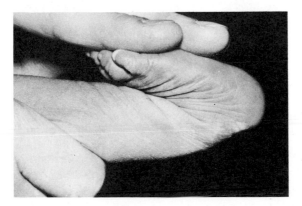

Fig. 96 Dorsiflexion of foot; full-term baby.

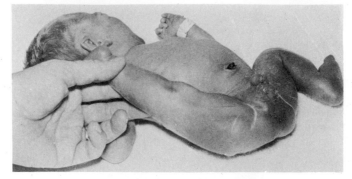

Fig. 97 Preterm baby, hip flexed, full knee extension.

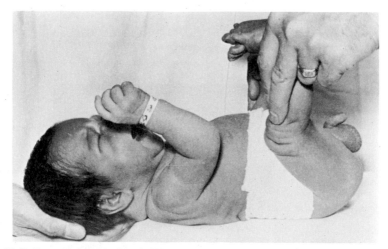

Fig. 98 Full-term baby, hip flexed, limited knee extension.

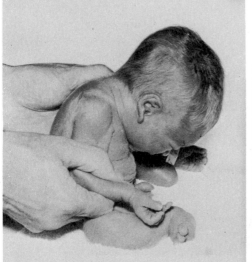

Fig. 99 Preterm baby, sitting position.

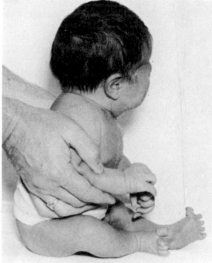

Fig. 100 Full-term baby, sitting position.

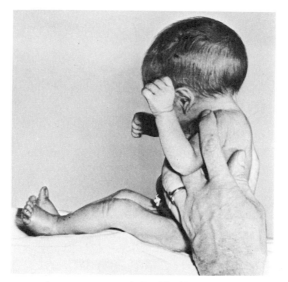

Fig. 101   Redressement du tronc, preterm baby. Unable to straighten back.

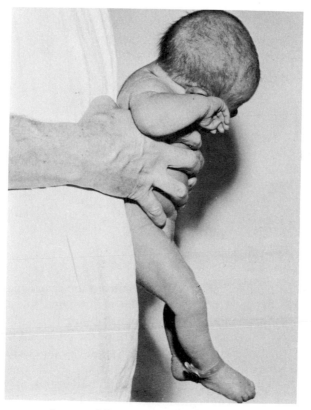

Fig. 102   Redressement du tronc, full-term baby. Straightens back.

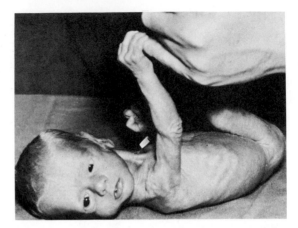

Fig. 103 Grasp reflex, preterm baby.

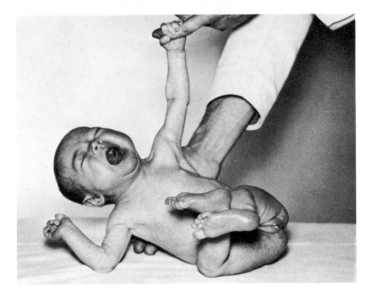

Fig. 104 Grasp reflex, full-term baby.

Farr[8] used 10 signs in her attempt to estimate the gestational age; they were the degree of motor activity, reaction of the pupil to light, rate of sucking, closure of the mouth when sucking, stripping action of the tongue, passive resistance, forearm recoil, plantar grasp, the pitch and the intensity of the cry. We found that the reaction of the pupil to light is a difficult sign to elicit in the newborn baby.

Experience has shown that there is a significant degree of variation in the age at which these neurological signs appear. In consequence it seems reasonable to advocate that an assessment should never be made on the

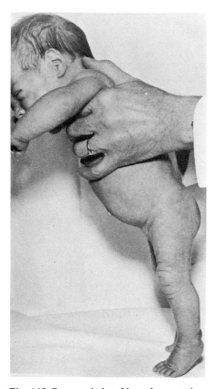

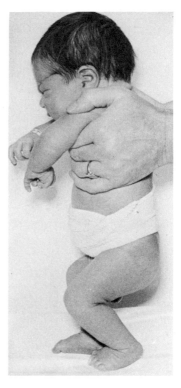

Fig. 105 Preterm baby, 30 weeks gestation, birthweight 3 lb 3 oz (1443 g) 9 weeks after birth. Standing on toes.

Fig. 106 Full-term baby, sole of foot flat on couch.

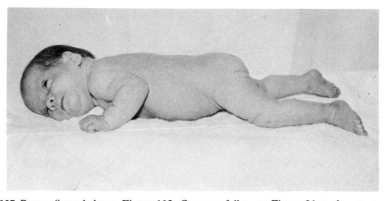

Fig. 107 Prone. Same baby as Figure 105. Compare full-term, Figure 86, and preterm baby, Figure 85, and 6 weeks baby, Figure 25.

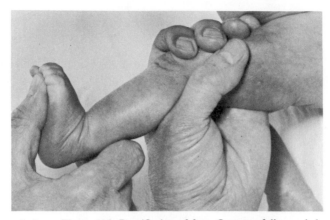

Fig. 108 Same baby as Figure 105. Dorsiflexion of foot. Compare full-term baby, Figure 96.

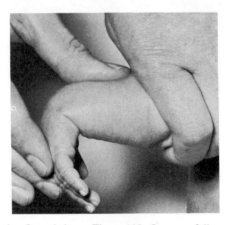

Fig. 109 Flexion of wrist. Same baby as Figure 105. Compare full-term baby, Figure 94.

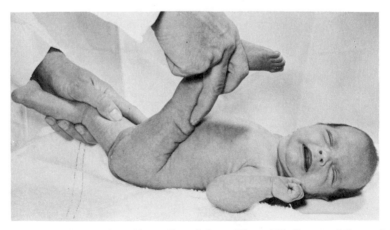

Fig. 110 Hip flexed, extension of knee. Same baby as Figure 105. Compare full-term baby, Figure 98

basis of single signs, but on a combination of signs. For instance, if 10 signs are tested for, the mean maturational age for the total of the 10 should be calculated.

Parkin[16] reviewed the various methods of assessing the maturity, including the date of the last menstrual period, quickening, the size of the uterus, vaginal cytology, the examination of the amniotic fluid for cells, sodium, creatinine and bilirubin: x-ray for ossification centres; ultrasonic fetal cephalometry, measurement of the head circumference, the length of the child, the chest circumference and the skin folds. He studied the amount of vernix, the texture of a fold of abdominal skin, the colour of the skin, oedema, lanugo, the length and texture of the nails, the firmness of the ears, breast size, the localisation of the testes, prominence of the labia minora, the hardness of the skull, and the creases on the soles of the feet. He found that if the skin was pink, the gestational age was unlikely to be less than 36 weeks; if pale, 40 weeks. If all the vernix was off, it was unlikely to be less than 39 weeks; if there were areas of baldness — no less than 37 weeks; if the testes were fully descended — not less than 36 weeks: if the breast is palpable, not less than 34 weeks. The most useful signs were the skin colour and texture, the breast size and the firmness of the ears, in combination. Parkin[16] and his colleagues, studying 205 boys and 187 girls, with a gestation period of 177 to 317 days, found that the estimation was accurate to within 15 days.

A combination of physical and neurological features seems likely to give the highest degree of accuracy. Dubowitz[6] reviewed the various tests, and eliminated tests which were difficult to elicit — such as the pupillary and righting reflexes. They gave a score of 0 to 4 for various items, as shown in Figure 111 and Table 3. The details are as follows:

Posture. Observed with infant quiet and in supine position. Score O: Arms and legs extended; 1: beginning of flexion of hips and knees, arms extended; 2: stronger flexion of legs, arms extended; 3: arms slightly flexed, legs flexed and abducted; 4: full flexion of arms and legs.

Square window. The hand is flexed on the forearm between the thumb and index finger of the examiner (Fig. 94 and 109). Enough pressure is applied to get as full a flexion as possible, and the angle between the hypothenar eminence and the ventral aspect of the forearm is measured and graded according to diagram. (Care is taken not to rotate the infant's wrist while doing this manoeuvre.)

Ankle dorsiflexion. The foot is dorsiflexed onto the anterior aspect of the leg, with the examiner's thumb on the sole of the foot and other fingers behind the leg (Fig. 96 and 108). Enough pressure in applied to get as full flexion as possible, and the angle between the dorsum of the foot and the anterior aspect of the leg is measured.

Arm recoil. With the infant in the supine position the forearms are first flexed for 5 seconds, then fully extended at the side of the trunk by pulling on the hands, and then released. The sign is fully positive if the arms return briskly to full flexion (Score 2). If the arms return to incomplete flexion or the response is sluggish it is graded as Score 1. If they remain extended or are only followed by random movements the score is 0.

Leg recoil. With the infant supine, the hips and knees are fully flexed 5 seconds, then extended by traction of the feet, and released. A maximal response is one of full flexion of the hips and knees (Score 2). A partial flexion scores 1, and minimal or no movement scores O.

Popliteal angle. With the infant supine and his pelvis flat on the examining couch, the thigh is held in the knee-chest position by the examiner's left index finger and thumb supporting

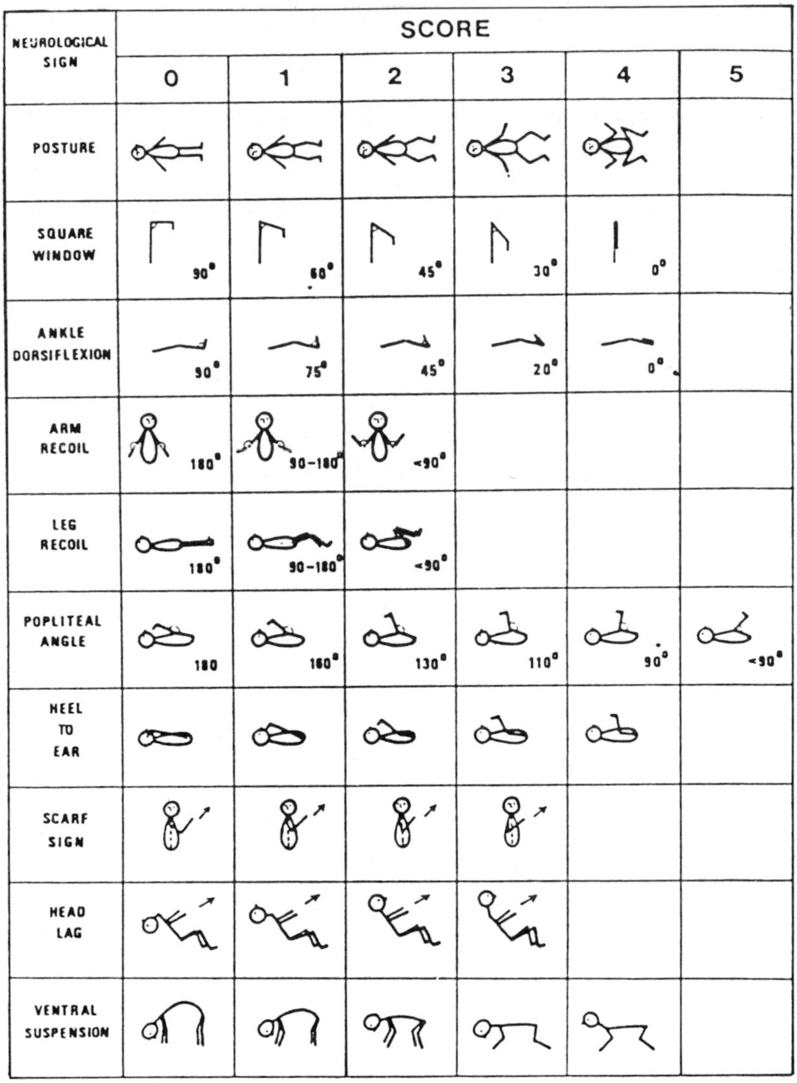

NEUROLOGICAL SIGN	SCORE					
	0	1	2	3	4	5
POSTURE						
SQUARE WINDOW	90°	60°	45°	30°	0°	
ANKLE DORSIFLEXION	90°	75°	45°	20°	0°	
ARM RECOIL	180°	90–180°	<90°			
LEG RECOIL	180°	90–180°	<90°			
POPLITEAL ANGLE	180	160°	130°	110°	90°	<90°
HEEL TO EAR						
SCARF SIGN						
HEAD LAG						
VENTRAL SUSPENSION						

Fig. 111

the knee. The leg is then extended by gentle pressure from the examiner's right index finger behind the ankle and the popliteal angle is measured.

Heel to ear manoeuvre. With the baby supine, draw the baby's foot as near to the head as it will go without forcing it. Observe the distance between the foot and the head as well as the degree of extension at the knee. Grade according to diagram. Note that the knee is left free and may draw down alongside the abdomen.

Scarf sign. With the baby supine, take the infant's hand and try to put it around the neck and as far posteriorly as possible around the opposite shoulder. Assist this manoeuvre by lifting the elbow across the body. See how far the elbow will go across and grade according to illustrations. Score O: elbow reaches opposite axillary line; 1: elbow between midline and opposite axillary line; 2: elbow reaches midline; 3: elbow will not reach midline.

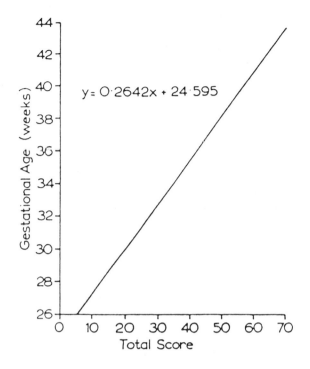

$$y = 0.2642x + 24.595$$

Fig. 112

Head lag. With the baby lying supine, grasp the hands (or the arms if a very small infant) and pull him slowly towards the sitting position. Observe the position of the head in relation to the trunk and grade accordingly. In a small infant the head may initially be supported by one hand. Score O: complete lag; 1: partial head control; 2: able to maintain head in line with body; 3: brings head anterior to body.

Ventral suspension. The infant is suspended in the prone position, with examiner's hand under the infant's chest (one hand in a small infant, two in a large infant). Observe the degree of extension of the back and the amount of flexion of the arms and legs. Also note the relation of the head to the trunk. Grade according to diagrams.

If score differs on the two sides, take the mean.

Their scoring system has proved to be a reliable technique. The paediatric residents at the Jessop Hospital for Women at Sheffield carry out the assessment as a routine on all babies born in the hospital, totalling about 3000 per year, and they find that the whole procedure occupies about 10 minutes. The test gives 95% confidence limits of 2.0 weeks.

Other workers have used different tests or combination of tests.[9,19] Finnstrom estimated skin opacity, plantar creases, nipple formation, ear firmness, breast size, scalp hair and finger nails. Another group[14] used four characteristics — anterior vascular capsule of the lens, plantar creases, breast nodule and ear firmness, claiming a 95% confidence limit of 11 days. It has been suggested[23] that Dubowitz tests are not reliable for the ill child, and[21] that the Parkin and Dubowitz tests tend to give too high a score for very small preterm babies.

Other distinguishing features

Visual and acoustic evoked responses have been used for the estimation of maturity.[7,17,22] The visual evoked responses may help to recognise abnormal babies.[17] Photic latency was found to be inversely related to conceptional age. It was interesting to note that full-term girls responded faster to light than full-term boys. Sheffield studies[5,13] showed that the motor nerve conduction time gave a good guide to gestational age as long as 6 months after birth.

Bishop and Corson[3] estimated conceptual age by cytological examination of the amniotic fluid. They wrote that the cells of the amniotic fluid are primarily composed of desquamated fetal cells, squamous and sebaceous. The percentage of lipid containing cells reflects the progressive development of sebaceous glands with increasing gestational age. After a study of 350 specimens, it was found that when the count was less than 2%, 85% were preterm; when the count was over 20%, all were over 36 weeks gestation. Several workers have studied the maturity of enzyme systems and of other biochemical features for the estimation of maturity. It is said[3] that the proportions of albumin and gamma globulin in the umbilical vein is less is preterm babies than in full-term ones.

The preterm baby who has reached term

When the preterm baby has reached term (e.g. born at 30 weeks gestation, 10 weeks after birth), he is different from the full-term baby (Figs 105–110).

1. Held in the walking position, he tends to walk on his toes, while the full-term baby walks with the foot flat on the couch. In the walking reflex, the rhythm of the stepping movements is less regular than that of a full-term baby.
2. Muscle tone is less than in the full-term baby.
3. Dorsiflexion of the foot and flexion of the wrist is less than in the full-term infant, but extension of the knee with the hip flexed is more complete.
4. In the prone position he kicks out more, holds the head up better, and tends to be more active than the full-term baby. He lies flat, like a 6-week-old full-term baby. In the supine position the preterm baby shows more varied and ample movement than the full-term one. He has a more advanced head the trunk posture than the full-term baby,[6] and the limbs tend to be more extended.

Small-for-dates babies

The behaviour of 22 full-term newborn babies who were small in relation to the duration of gestation was compared by German workers[11] with that of 25 full-term babies who were of normal birthweight. The examinations were carried out between the third and seventh day. The following differences were found:

1. The Moro reflex. In phase 1, normal birthweight infants showed only short extension and abduction of the arms, followed by marked flexion and adduction; in the small-for-dates babies, the Moro reflex was often characterised by more extension and abduction of the arms, not always followed by flexion and adduction.
2. The asymmetrical tonic neck reflex was weak or absent in the normal birthweight infants, but sustained and marked in the other group.
3. Windmill movements of the arms were weak or absent in the normal birthweight infants, but frequent in the small-for-dates babies.
4. The normal birthweight infants stood on the lateral part of the sole of the foot and showed a more marked walking reflex, while the small-for-dates infants had a weaker or absent walking reflex, and stood predominantly on the full sole.

Another group of workers[1] compared 10 low birthweight full-term babies with 10 normal weight full-term infants, using the Brazleton scale. They described the typical low birthweight baby as having 'poor tone, low activity levels, poor hand to mouth coordination, poor defensive reactions, with jerking or cogwheel-like movements of the limbs, with restricted arcs. He is floppy on pull-to-sit and does not show good crawling, walking, sucking or rooting.' In a study of 80 preterm (27–35 week, 765–2490 g) babies examined at 40 weeks gestation age, compared with 40 full-term babies, all vertex deliveries, with weight appropriate to gestation,[15] the preterm babies showed less flexion in the supine position, less arm traction, arm and leg recoil, but better visual and auditory orientation and alertness than full-term babies. In another study[10] of 118 low birthweight infants at 40 weeks gestational age compared with 76 normal full-term infants, the low birthweight infants tended to show less rooting reflex and grasp reflexes.

Summary

For many reasons it is important to be able to assess the maturity or duration of gestation of the newborn baby.

The maturity can be assessed with considerable accuracy by a combination of neurological signs, but not by single signs; by a combination of physical features, but not by single features; and by the motor nerve conduction velocity. Other methods are still experimental.

REFERENCES

1. Als, H., Tronick, E., Adamson, L., Brazleton, T. B. The behaviour of the full-term but underweight newborn infant. Dev. Med. Child Neurol. 1976.18.590.

2. Amiel-Tison, C. Neurological evaluation of the maturity of newborn infants. Arch. Dis. Child. 1968.43.89.
3. Bishop, E. H., Corson, S. Estimation of fetal maturity by cytological examination of amniotic fluid. Am. J. Obstet. Gynecol. 1968.102.654.
4. Brooke, O. G., McIntosh, N. Birth weight of infants born before 30 weeks' gestation. Arch. Dis. Child. 1984.59.1189.
5. Dubowitz, V. Nerve conduction velocity — an index of neurological maturity of the newborn infant. Dev. Med. Child Neurol. 1968.10.741.
6. Dubowitz, L., Dubowitz, V. The neurological assessment of the preterm and full-term newborn infant. Clinics in Developmental Medicine No. 79. London. Heinemann. 1981.
7. Engel, R., Benson, R. C. Estimate of conceptual age by evoked response activity. Biol. Neonat. 1968.12.201.
8. Farr, V. Estimation of gestational age by neurological assessment in first week of life. Arch. Dis. Child. 1968.43.353.
9. Finnstrom, O. Studies on maturity in newborn infants. Acta Paediatr. Scand. 1977.66.601.
10. Kurtzberg, D., Vaughan, H. G., Daum, C. et al. Neurobehavioral performance of low birthweight infants at 40 weeks conceptional age: comparison with normal full-term infants. Dev. Med. Child Neurol. 1979.21.590.
11. Michaelis, R., Schulte, F. J., Nolte, R. Motor behavior of small for gestational age newborn infants. J. Pediatr. 1970.76.208.
12. Milner, R. D. G., Richards, B. An analysis of birth weight by gestational age of infants born in England and Wales 1967–71. J. Obstet. Gynaecol. B. C. 1974.81.956.
13. Moosa, A., Dubowitz, V. Assessment of gestational age in newborn infants: nerve conduction velocity versus maturity score. Dev. Med. Child Neurol., 1972.14.290.
14. Narayanan, I., Dua, K., Gujral, V. V. et al. Assessment of gestational age in newborn infants. Pediatrics 1982.69.27.
15. Palmer, P. G., Dubowitz, L. M., Verghote, M., Dubowitz, V. Neurological and neurobehavioural differences between term and full-term newborn infants. Neuropediatrics. 1982.13.183
16. Parkin, J. M., Hey, E. N., Clowes J. S. Rapid assessment of gestational age at birth. Arch. Dis. Child. 1976.51.259.
17. Placzek, M., Mushin, J., Dubowitz, L. M. S. Maturation of the visual evoked response and its correlation with visual acuity in preterm infants. Dev. Med. Child. Neurol. 1985.27.448.
18. Rantakillio, P. Groups at risk in low birth weight infants and perinatal mortality. Acta Paediatr. Scand. 1969. Suppl. 193.
19. Robertson, A. Commentary — gestational age. J. Pediatr. 1979.95.732.
20. Robinson, R. J. Assessment of gestational age by neurological examination. Arch. Dis. Child. 1966.41.437.
21. Vogt, H., Haneberg, B., Finne, P. H., Stensberg, A. Clinical assessment of gestational age in the newborn infant. Acta Paediatr. Scand. 1981.70.669.
22. Watanabe, K., Iwase, K., Hara, K. Maturation of visual evoked responses in low birth weight infants. Dev. Med. Child Neurol. 1972.14.425.
23. White, P. L., Fomufod, A. K., Rao, M. Comparative accuracy of recent abbreviated methods of gestational age determination. Clin. Pediatr. (Phila.) 1980.19.319.

11

The neurological examination of the newborn baby

The value of the neurological examination

Hardly a day passes in a large obstetrical unit without a child being born who gives some anxiety with regard to his immediate survival, and if he survives, with regard to the ultimate developmental prognosis. Pre-eclampsia, hypertension, antepartum haemorrhage, prematurity, fetal hypoxia and difficult labours remain regrettably common, and all of them predispose to fetal abnormalities. Apnoeic attacks and convulsions are frequently seen in the newborn baby, and both these conditions are associated with a higher incidence of abnormality than that found in normal infants. Undue irritability, drowsiness, hypotonia or other variations from the normal in the newborn period may subsequently be shown to have some bearing on problems in the school child, such as overactivity, poor concentration or learning difficulties.

The neurological examination is important for the study of the effect of trauma and hypoxia on the baby and this may have a bearing on future obstetrical management.

The assessment at birth

Virginia Apgar's method of evaluating the newborn infant (Table 6) is now in standard use. It is useful to make serial Apgar scores: the longer the score remains low, the worse the prognosis with regard to mortality or neuro-

Table 6 Evaluation of the newborn infant 1 minute after birth* (Apgar)

Score	Heart rate	Respiratory effort	Reflex irritability	Muscle tone	Colour
2	100–140	Normal cry	Normal	Good	Pink
1	100	Irregular and shallow	Moderately depressed	Fair	Fair
0	No beat obtained	Apnoea for more than 60 sec	Absent	Flaccid	Cyanotic

* Each type of observation scored as indicated. Total scores: 8–10, good; 3–7; fair; 0–2, poor condition.

213

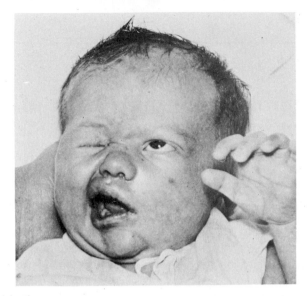

Fig. 113 Facial palsy.

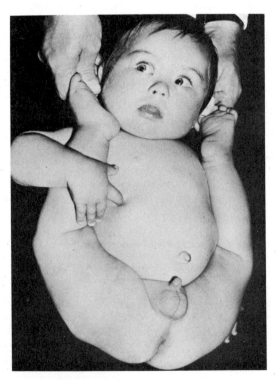

Fig. 114 Down's syndrome, showing marked hypotonia.

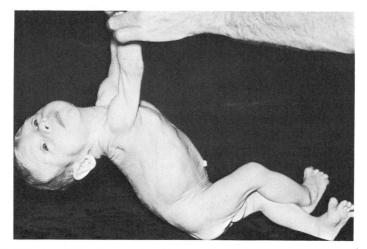

Fig. 115 Defective child with severe head lag, age 8 weeks.

logical sequelae. Some workers have found, however, that the Apgar score correlates poorly with fetal acidosis at birth and with cerebral palsy.[25]

Brazelton[4] described a complex series of observations in the examination of the newborn with 28 behavioural items, each scored on a 9-point scale, and 18 elicited responses, each scored on a 3-point scale. Each score was based on the infant's best response, not on the average response. The test included observation of the child when asleep and awake, his alertness, eye following, response to sound, irritability, social interest in the examiner, passive movement of the arms, habituation, vigour, tremulousness and

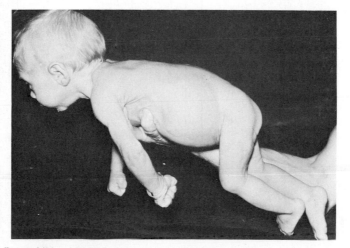

Fig. 116 Same child, with deceptive excessive extensor tone, giving impression of good head control in ventral suspension.

Table 7 Professor Dubowitz's forms for assessment

NAME   D.O.B./TIME   WEIGHT   E.D.D. L.N.M.P.   E.D.D. U/snd.

HOSP   NO.   DATE OF EXAM   HEIGHT

RACE   SEX   AGE   HEAD CIRC.

GESTATIONAL SCORE WEEKS ASSESSMENT

STATES

1. Deep sleep, no movement, regular breathing.
2. Light sleep, eyes shut, some movement.
3. Dozing, eyes opening and closing.
4. Awake, eyes open, minimal movement.
5. Wide awake, vigorous movement.
6. Crying.

					STATE	COMMENT	ASYMMETRY

HABITUATION (<state 3)

LIGHT
Repetitive flashlight stimuli (10) with 5 sec. gap.
Shutdown = 2 consecutive negative responses

- No response
- A. Blink response to first stimulus only. B. Tonic blink response. C. Variable response.
- A. Shutdown of movement but blink persists 2-5 stimuli. B. Complete shutdown 2-5 stimuli.
- A. Shutdown of movement but blink persists 6-10 stimuli. B. Complete shutdown 6-10 stimuli.
- A. Equal response to 10 stimuli. B. Infant comes to fully alert state. C. Startles + major responses throughout.

RATTLE
Repetitive stimuli (10) with 5 sec. gap.

- No response
- A. Slight movement to first stimulus. B. Variable response.
- Startle or movement 2-5 stimuli, then shutdown
- Startle or movement 6-10 stimuli, then shutdown
- A. / B. / C. Grading as above

MOVEMENT & TONE

POSTURE
(At rest — predominant) *
Undress infant

- (hips abducted)
- (hips abducted)
- (hips adducted)
- Abnormal postures: A. Opisthotonos B. Unusual leg extension C. Asymm. tonic neck reflex

ARM RECOIL
Infant supine. Take both hands, extend parallel to the body; hold approx. 2 secs. and release.

- No flexion within 5 sec.
- Partial flexion at elbow >100° within 4-5 sec.
- Arms flex at elbow to <100° within 2-3 sec.
- Sudden jerky flexion at elbow immediately after release to <60°
- Difficult to extend; arm snaps back forcefully

ARM TRACTION
Infant supine; head midline; grasp wrist, slowly pull arm to vertical. Angle of arm scored and resistance noted at moment infant is initially lifted off and watched until shoulder off mattress. Do other arm.

- Arm remains fully extended
- Weak flexion maintained only momentarily
- Arm flexed at elbow to 140° and maintained 5 sec.
- Arm flexed at approx. 100° and maintained
- Strong flexion of arm <100° and maintained

LEG RECOIL
First flex hips for 5 secs, then extend both legs of infant by traction on ankles; hold down on the bed for 2 secs. and release.

- No flexion within 5 sec.
- Incomplete flexion of hips within 5 sec.
- Complete flexion within 5 sec.
- Instantaneous complete flexion
- Legs cannot be extended; snap back forcefully

Table 7 (contd)

Test						Score
LEG TRACTION Infant supine. Grasp leg near ankle and slowly pull toward vertical until buttocks 1-2" off. Note resistance at knee and score angle. Do other leg.	No flexion	Partial flexion, rapidly lost	Knee flexion 140-160° and maintained	Knee flexion 100-140° and maintained	Strong resistance: flexion <100°	
POPLITEAL ANGLE Infant supine. Approximate knee and thigh to abdomen; extend leg by gentle pressure with index finger behind ankle.	180-160°	150-140°	130-120°	110-90°	<90°	
HEAD CONTROL (post. neck m.) Grasp infant by shoulders and raise to sitting position; allow head to fall forward; wait 30 sec.	No attempt to raise head	Unsuccessful attempt to raise head upright	Head raised smoothly to upright in 30 sec. but not maintained.	Head raised smoothly to upright in 30 sec. and maintained	Head cannot be flexed forward	
HEAD CONTROL (ant. neck m.) Allow head to fall backward as you hold shoulders; wait 30 secs.	Grading as above	Grading as above	Grading as above	Grading as above		
HEAD LAG * Pull infant toward sitting posture by traction on both wrists. Also note arm flexion.						
VENTRAL SUSPENSION * Hold infant in ventral suspension; observe curvature of back, flexion of limbs and relation of head to trunk.						
HEAD RAISING IN PRONE POSITION Infant in prone position with head in midline.	No response	Rolls head to one side	Weak effort to raise head and turns raised head to one side	Infant lifts head, nose and chin off	Strong prolonged head lifting	
ARM RELEASE IN PRONE POSITION Head in midline. Infant in prone position, arms extended alongside body with palms up.	No effort	Some effort and wriggling	Flexion effort but neither wrist brought to nipple level	One or both wrists brought at least to nipple level without excessive body movement	Strong body movement with both wrists brought to face, or 'press-ups'	
SPONTANEOUS BODY MOVEMENT during examination (supine). If no spont. movement try to induce by cutaneous stimulation.	None or minimal Induced	A. Sluggish B. Random, incoordinated C. Mainly stretching.	Smooth movements alternating with random, stretching, athetoid or jerky.	Smooth alternating movements of arms and legs with medium speed and intensity	Mainly: A. Jerky movement. B. Athetoid movement. C. Other abnormal movement.	
TREMORS Mark: Fast (>6 sec.) or Slow (<6 sec.)	No tremor	Tremors only in state 5 6	Tremors only in sleep or after Moro and startles	Some tremors in state 4	Tremulousness in all states	
STARTLES	No startles	Startles to sudden noise, Moro, bang on table only	Occasional spontaneous startle	2-5 spontaneous startles	6+ spontaneous startles	
ABNORMAL MOVEMENT OR POSTURE	No abnormal movement	A. Hands clenched but open intermittently. B. Hands do not open with Moro	A. Some mouthing movement. B. Intermittent adducted thumb	A. Persistently adducted thumb. B. Hands clenched all the time.	A. Continuous mouthing movement. B. Convulsive movements.	1 2

Table 7 (contd)

REFLEXES

Item						STATE	COMMENT	ASYMMETRY
TENDON REFLEXES Biceps jerk, Knee jerk, Ankle jerk	Absent	Present	Exaggerated	Clonus				
PALMAR GRASP Head in midline. Put index finger from ulnar side into hand and gently press palmar surface. Never touch dorsal side of hand.	Absent	Short, weak flexion	Medium strength and sustained flexion for several secs.	Strong flexion; contraction spreads to forearm	Very strong grasp. Infant easily lifts off couch			
ROOTING Infant supine, head midline. Touch each corner of the mouth in turn (stroke laterally).	No response	A. Partial weak head turn but no mouth opening. B. Mouth opening, no head turn.	Mouth opening on stimulated side with partial head turning	Full head turning, with or without mouth opening	Mouth opening with very jerky head turning			
SUCKING Infant supine; place index finger (pad towards palate) in infant's mouth; judge power of sucking movement after 5 sec.	No attempt	Weak sucking movement: A. Regular. B. Irregular.	Strong sucking movement, poor stripping: A. Regular. B. Irregular.	Strong regular sucking movement with continuing sequence of 5 movements. Good stripping.	Clenching but no regular sucking.			
WALKING (state 4, 5) Hold infant upright, feet touching bed, neck held straight with fingers.	Absent	Some effort but not continuous with both legs	At least 2 steps with both legs	A. Stork posture; no movement. B. Automatic walking.				
MORO One hand supports infant's head in midline, the other the back. Raise infant to 45° and when infant is relaxed let his head fall through 10°. Note if jerky. Repeat 3 times.	No response, or opening of hands only	Full abduction at the shoulder and extension of the arm	Full abduction but only delayed or partial adduction	Partial abduction at shoulder and extension of arms followed by smooth adduction. A. Abd>Add B. Abd=Add C. Abd<Add	A. No abduction or adduction; extension only. B. Marked adduction only.		J	S

NEUROBEHAVIOURAL ITEMS

Item						STATE	COMMENT	ASYMMETRY
EYE APPEARANCES	Sunset sign Nerve palsy	Transient nystagmus. Strabismus. Some roving eye movement.	Does not open eyes	Normal conjugate eye movement	A. Persistent nystagmus. B. Frequent roving movement C. Frequent rapid blinks.			
AUDITORY ORIENTATION (state 3, 4) To rattle. (Note presence of startle.)	A. No reaction. B. Auditory startle but no true orientation.	Brightens and stills; may turn toward stimuli with eyes closed	Alerting and shifting of eyes; head may or may not turn to source	Alerting; prolonged head turns to stimulus; search with eyes	Turning and alerting to stimulus each time on both sides		S	

Table 7 (contd)

VISUAL ORIENTATION (state 4) To red woollen ball	Does not focus or follow stimulus	Stills; focuses on stimulus; may follow 30° jerkily; does not find stimulus again spontaneously	Follows 30-60° horizontally; may lose stimulus but finds it again. Brief vertical glance	Follows with eyes and head horizontally and vertically, with frowning	Sustained fixation follows vertically, horizontally, and in circle		
ALERTNESS (state 4)	Inattentive; rarely or never responds to direct stimulation	When alert, periods rather brief; rather variable response to orientation	When alert, alertness moderately sustained; may use stimulus to come to alert state	Sustained alertness; orientation frequent, reliable to visual but not auditory stimuli	Continuous alertness, which does not seem to tire, to both auditory and visual stimuli		
DEFENSIVE REACTION A cloth or hand is placed over the infant's face to partially occlude the nasal airway.	No response	A. General quietening. B. Non-specific activity with long latency.	Rooting; lateral neck turning; possibly neck stretching.	Swipes with arm	Swipes with arm with rather violent body movement		
PEAK OF EXCITEMENT	Low level arousal to all stimuli; never > state 3	Infant reaches state 4-5 briefly but predominantly in lower states	Infant predominantly state 4 or 5; may reach state 6 after stimulation but returns spontaneously to lower state	Infant reaches state 6 but can be consoled relatively easily	A. Mainly state 6. Difficult to console, if at all. B. Mainly state 4-5 but if reaches state 6 cannot be consoled.		
IRRITABILITY (states 3, 4, 5) Aversive stimuli: Uncover Ventral susp. Undress Moro Pull to sit Walking reflex Prone	No irritable crying to any of the stimuli	Cries to 1-2 stimuli	Cries to 3-4 stimuli	Cries to 5-6 stimuli	Cries to all stimuli		
CONSOLABILITY (state 6)	Never above state 5 during examination, therefore not needed	Consoling not needed. Consoles spontaneously	Consoled by talking, hand on belly or wrapping up	Consoled by picking up and holding; may need finger in mouth	Not consolable		
CRY	No cry at all	Only whimpering cry	Cries to stimuli but normal pitch	Lusty cry to offensive stimuli; normal pitch	High-pitched cry, often continuous		

NOTES * If asymmetrical or atypical, draw in on nearest figure

Record any abnormal signs (e.g. facial palsy, contractures, etc.). Draw if possible.

Record time after feed:

EXAMINER:

Reprinted from *The Neurological Assessment of the Preterm and Full-term Newborn Infant*, by Lilly and Victor Dubowitz.
© 1981 Spastics International Medical Publications, 5A Netherhall Gardens, London NW3 5RN.

consolability, with response to 20 primitive reflexes — the examination taking 25 to 35 minutes. He suggested that one should observe the infant for 2 minutes, to assess the state of consciousness, depth of sleep, alertness if awake: apply a flashlight three to 10 times through closed lids, use the rattle and bell, test five times with light pin-prick, test for ankle clonus, the plantar grasp reflex, the plantar response, passive movement and tone, auditory and visual orientation, the palmar grasp, the response to pulling him from the supine to the sitting position, the standing and walking position, the limb placement reflex, Galant's reflex, ventral suspension and prone position, the glabellar tap reflex, response to spinning, defence response (cloth over face), tonic neck, startle and Moro reflexes, the lability of skin colour, and other elicited responses.

For research purposes such an extensive examination may be of value: but for practical purposes in a large obstetrical unit such a long examination is impossible, except in the case of selected babies. Although Brazelton has described the examination and the suggested tests in detail, he did not in his paper state the reason for selecting those tests. I am unable myself to determine the developmental significance of many of his tests, such as that for the Galant reflex. He wrote that 'at present[5] the method is a research instrument'. His method enables the neonatal status to be scored, but it does not give the significance of the score with regard to prediction of the child's future neurological status. For practical purposes, as distinct from research, it is necessary to focus down on those tests which matter because they give specific developmental or neurological information.

Another method of assessing the newborn is that of Heinz Prechtl and Touwen at Groningen, Holland.[19,27] The examination includes assessment of tone, muscle power, movement, posture, alertness, irritability, involuntary movements, resistance to passive movement and the range of movement. The examination takes about 30 minutes: a modified screening test, based on Prechtl's method, and not taking as long, has now been devised.[27] The various methods of assessment of the newborn have been reviewed by Yang[28] and Self and Horowitz.[24]

Professor Dubowitz has given me permission to reproduce his detailed assessment in toto. It overlaps to some extent with his form for assessment of maturity, but he advised me to reproduce both forms, because the forms serve a different purpose — one for the assessment of maturity, and other for the routine neurological examination and assessment of normality (Table 7).

Conduct of the examination

The conduct of the examination must be standardised because many of the signs are influenced by both internal and external factors. If only one examination is carried out this should be delayed until the third day or later because the signs are particularly variable earlier than this. One examination is insufficient, however, and Mdme Saint Anne Dargassies wrote that one looks for criteria of normality in the first 5 days, for criteria of maturity between 6 and 9 days, and for criteria of progression of development from 10 to 15 days.[22]

About 2 hours after the last feed the baby is usually sufficiently alert to be responsive to the tests and yet is not too fretful. He should be placed on a table sufficiently large to allow rolling from side to side without risk of falling. The room should be warm and reasonably draught free. There should be a good diffuse light. It is often advantageous to carry out the examination in front of the mother, who gains confidence from seeing her baby handled, and any points which arise can then be discussed at once.

For the purposes of research, or for the evaluation of minor signs, the standard practice must be adhered to, but in the busy daily care of the newborn this may not be possible, and the examiner must select the most useful parts of the examination, concentrate upon the babies at risk, and develop experience to avoid drawing conclusions from signs influenced by external factors.

The examination is carried out in the following sequence: observation; estimation of alertness; estimation of muscle tone; elicitation of special reflexes; examination of cranial nerves and special senses; and the performance of special tests.

Observation

Careful observation amply repays the time spent upon it. The examiner must train his powers of observation to be aware of the many significant signs which can be seen from the moment the baby is first approached and not just when he is placed on the examination table.

The following features in particular must be noted.

The posture

The normal full-term baby lies on his side with arms and legs flexed. Placed on his back he rolls to one side or the other. Placed prone the head is turned to one side so that his breathing is unrestricted. His limbs are flexed and the pelvis is raised from the couch with the knees drawn high up under the abdomen. When he is supported in ventral suspension gravity is stronger than the extensor tone, and the head, arms and legs hang downwards, usually with some flexion of the elbow and knee and some extension of the hip. In contrast, when held in dorsal suspension the stronger flexor tone counteracts the effects of gravity and the baby lies in a position of incomplete extension.

When the baby is placed in the supine position, and the arm is extended and then released, the arm returns to the flexed position. If the arm is flexed and then released, it extends.

When held inverted by the ankles, the hips and knees are flexed; the arms are flexed and adducted across the chest.

Full extension of the legs would suggest increased muscle tone. The frog-like appearance of the younger preterm infant in the supine position would suggest hypotonia. It must be remembered that if the infant were born as a breech with extended legs, the infant is likely to keep the legs fully extended in the newborn period.

Opisthotonos is usually abnormal: but after a face presentation the head is commonly arched back, so that the baby gives the appearance of opis-thotonos. Muscle tone, however, would be normal, whereas in true opis-thotonos one would expect to find hypertonia.

It is important to note asymmetry of posture. This may result from asymmetry of muscle tone (as in spastic hemiplegia), or from fracture of the clavicle or humerus, or from a brachial plexus injury.

The cry

A good nurse unfailingly recognises the high-pitched cry of an abnormal baby. The paediatrician readily recognises the hoarse cry of a cretin or the 'cri du chat' syndrome. The cry may be absent altogether, or excessive and continuous. The former would be abnormal and the latter may be so.

The movements

Movements are spontaneous or provoked. Spontaneous movements include tremors, twitchings and sudden shock-like movements without apparent stimulus. The Moro and startle reflexes are examples of provoked movement. It is particularly important to note symmetry or asymmetry of movement, for asymmetry of movement is more likely to be significant.

It is often difficult to distinguish normal movements in an infant from abnormal ones. A convulsion in a newborn baby rarely presents as a fit such as one sees in older children or adults. It commonly presents as mere twitching of a limb or fluttering of an eyelid. The twitching may migrate from one limb or part of the body to another. Conjugate deviation of the eyes or stiffness at the time of the movements would prove conclusively that the movements are convulsive in nature. Convulsive movements must be distinguished from the normal sudden jerks in sleep or on awakening, and from the tremulousness of a hungry baby. The normal jittery tremulous movements of a limb, but not convulsive clonic movements, can be stopped by flexing the limb. Jittery tremors can be provoked by external stimuli. They may be due to hunger, hypoglycaemia, thirst, hypocalcaemia, hypernatraemia, hypomagnesaemia, maternal thyrotoxicosis, or drug withdrawal.

Prechtl[19] described the hyperexcitable child as showing low frequency, high amplitude tremors, exaggerated reflexes, and a low threshold Moro reflex. There may be a marked startle reflex on gently tapping the sternum.

The McCarthy reflex is obtained by tapping the skull some distance from the supraorbital region. Some such babies are hyperkinetic and cry excessively. He described the apathetic baby as having a high threshold for stimulation of reflexes, some responses being absent altogether. Such infants move less than normal babies, show a decreased resistance to passive movement, and are difficult to arouse. Twitching and rapid rhythmical movements are usually abnormal, though occasional tremors of the chin are normal.

Wakefulness and sleep

Abnormal babies commonly sleep for excessively long periods.

Other features

A thumb across the palm in a clenched hand is usually abnormal.

It is useful to note the respiratory movements, because irregularity of respiration and apnoeic periods (cyanotic attacks) are often associated with cerebral damage.

The face repays careful study. The baby with kernicterus has a wide-eyed, anxious expression, and the baby with hydrocephalus has a prominent forehead, bulging fontanelle, distension of the scalp veins, and a down-turning of the eyes so that a complete superior rim of sclera can be seen, giving a 'setting sun' sign. There may be a roving incoordinated movement of the eyes. Facial palsy should be noted.

Other features which are noticed during the observation period include the presence of congenital malformations, the colour, the presence of skin pigmentation and of naevi.

Estimation of alertness

The findings on neurological examination must be compared with the general condition of the baby and his alertness and responsiveness. One notes the degree of spontaneous activity, the response to mildly noxious stimuli, such as pinching the lobe of the ear or the big toe, the quality of the attention span and the degree of ocular fixation when his mother talks to him.

Habituation

Dubowitz[9,11] and Brazelton[4] include habituation in visual and auditory tests, with repeated light and sound stimuli (at 5-second intervals).

Reflexes

The biceps jerk, knee jerk and ankle jerks should be tested: these are of great importance for the diagnosis of cerebral palsy of the spastic type.

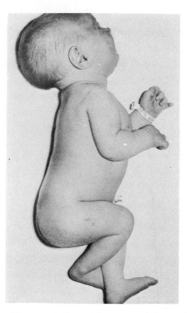

Fig. 117 Face presentation. Characteristic position, resembling opisthotonos, but muscle tone normal. Age 4 weeks.

These reflexes vary markedly in different children, and by themselves one pays little attention to them (unless there is asymmetry) (Ch. 16); but in conjunction with other signs they are of great importance in diagnosis.

I discussed the significance of primitive reflexes in Chapter 4.

Estimation of muscle tone

Muscle tone is difficult to define. It is that condition of the muscle, determined by physical, chemical, and nervous influences, which, although it is not an active contraction, determines the body posture, the range of movement at joints, and the feel of the muscle.

Muscle tone is assessed in the newborn or older infant as follows:

1. Observation of posture
2. Feeling the muscles
3. Assessing the resistance to passive movement
4. Assessing the range of movement
5. Shaking the limb
6. Indirect assessment — by tendon jerks, plantar responses and Moro reflex.

1. Observation of posture — at rest in the supine position, when held in ventral suspension and when pulled to the sitting position. The severely hypertonic child (Fig. 151) characteristically lies with the legs extended,

and with the hands tightly clenched. This is in contrast to the flexed posture of the lower limbs in a normal baby (Fig. 150) and the pithed frog position of the hypotonic infant. Any baby clenches his fists at intervals: one has to determine by observation whether this is a constant feature. By 2 or 3 months the hand is usually largely open. When there is excessive extensor tone the baby holds the head up well in ventral suspension and in the prone, but has excessive head lag when pulled to the sitting position. When pulling the child to the sitting position, one feels the resistance of the erector spinae, glutei and hamstrings — as described in more detail in Chapter 16.

2. Feeling the muscles between one's forefinger and thumb. This is of more value when there is hypotonia, as in Down's syndrome: the difference in the 'feel' of the muscles of Down's syndrome, or of a baby with the Werdnig-Hoffmann syndrome, is strikingly different from that of a normal child.

3. Assessing the resistance to passive movement — in flexing or extending the elbow or knee, or in abducting the hip. It is easy to be misled by the baby's voluntary resistance.

4. Assessing the range of movement. The most important joints to assess for this are the hip and the ankle. If further information is wanted, one rotates, flexes and extends the neck and bends it sideways. One flexes and extends the elbows and wrists, and assesses the scarf sign (conveying the hand in front of the neck towards or beyond the shoulder). The range in the hip joint should be estimated by flexing to a constant angle (90°) or full flexion, and then abducting. Normally the knees of a newborn infant touch or almost touch the examining table, but there is much less abduction at six weeks of age. Abduction of the hip is restricted in hypertonia and in certain other conditions, and is increased in hypotonia. Dorsiflexion of the ankle is reduced in hypertonia and increased in hypotonia.

5. Shaking the limb. Holding the arm below the elbow or the leg below the knee one rapidly shakes the limb, in order to observe the degree of movement of the wrist or ankle. There is excessive movement in hypotonia, and it is reduced in hypertonia. It depends largely on the stretch reflex. If properly performed the test is a sensitive one.

A corresponding test is used for testing head control when the baby is older; when he is in the sitting position the body is wobbled from side to side to assess the lateral movement of the head: it should be minimal by the age of 6 months.

6. The tendon jerks, ankle clonus, plantar responses. An exaggerated knee jerk with an extensor plantar response is invariable in the spastic form of cerebral palsy. A well sustained ankle clonus is a confirmatory sign of hypertonia, but it is not necessarily abnormal. The decreased movement in the Moro reflex of the hypertonic child has been described in Chapter 4. Dubowitz[11] adds the response to limb traction and limb recoil — there being reduced or absent recoil in hypotonia.

Whatever the method used, it is important to note the symmetry of the muscle tone. Asymmetry is more important than increased but symmetrically increased tone.

Hypotonia is important because it has a vital bearing on the assessment of motor development. For a full review of the causes of hypotonia the reader is referred to the papers by Dubowitz.[11,12] Hypotonia involving the lower limbs alone may be due to a meningomyelocele or diastematomyelia. It follows that the back of the child must be examined with these two conditions in mind. One also routinely examines the whole of the midline of the back for a congenital dermal sinus. A sinus in the cervical, dorsal or lumbar region, sometimes revealed by a tuft of hair or patch of pigmentation, may pass right through to the subarachnoid space, and cause recurrent meningitis or other neurological signs. Rarely a congenital dermal sinus at the upper end of the natal cleft tracks up to the subarachnoid space, and therefore could cause meningitis. There is a rare form of cerebral palsy in which in the early weeks there is hypotonia with signs of mental subnormality.

There are considerable variations in muscle tone in normal children. It must not be assumed that because muscle tone is greater than usual, organic disease is necessarily present.

Dubowitz[10] investigated the physical signs in infants with intraventricular haemorrhage. They were in particular hypotonia, tight popliteal angle, reduced motility and poor visual following.

The hips

Up to the age of about 2, the routine examination of a child includes examination of the hips, in order to exclude congenital dislocation. This is not strictly part of the developmental examination, but estimation of the range of abduction of the hips is part of the routine examination, and if the range is restricted, one has to distinguish the two commonest causes — hypertonia and dislocation.

Certain factors increase the risk that the child will have a dislocated hip. These are as follows:

Family history of dislocated hip.
Geographical factors. (Dislocation is particularly common in Northern Italy.)
Breech with extended legs
Severe hypotonia involving legs, e.g. meningomyelocele.
Severe spasticity. Arthrogryposis.
Oligohydramnios. Multiple pregnancy.
Bilateral talipes in a girl.
Congenital torticollis (sternomastoid tumour). Swaddling.

Many articles have been written about the diagnosis of congenital dislocation of the hip in the newborn infant. I feel confused by the description

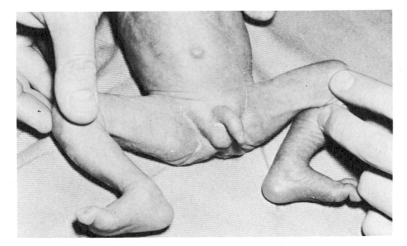

Fig. 118 Abduction of hip.

of the tests given in most of these papers, largely because of the use of the words backwards, forwards, upwards and downwards. Hence I asked my orthopaedic colleague, J. Sharrard, FRCS to describe the principal tests in simple words which I could readily understand. Below is his wording:

1. *Ortolani's test.* The child is laid on his back with the hips flexed to a right angle and the knees flexed. Starting with the knees together the hips are slowly abducted and if one is dislocated, somewhere in the 90 degrees

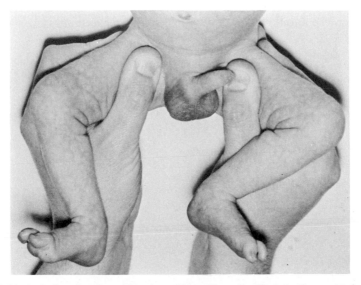

Fig. 119 Method of testing for subluxation of hips (Stage 1). The baby lies on his back with the hips and knees flexed and the middle finger of each hand is placed over each great trochanter.

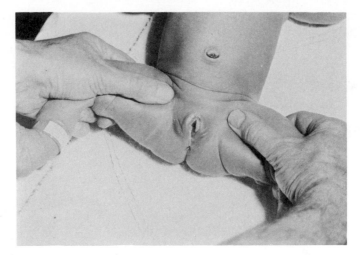

Fig. 120 The thumb of each hand is applied to the inner side of the thigh opposite the lesser trochanter.

arc of abduction the head of the femur slips back into the acetabulum with a visible and palpable jerk. A 'click' in the newborn is of no importance: a 'jerk' is unlikely to be felt in the first 3 months.

2. *Barlow's test — part 1.* The baby is laid on his back. The hips are flexed to a right angle and the knees are fully flexed. The middle finger of each hand is placed over the greater trochanter and the thumb of each hand is applied to the inner side of the thigh close to but not quite in the groin. The hips are carried into abduction. With the hips in about 70 degrees of abduction the middle finger of each hand in turn exerts pressure away from

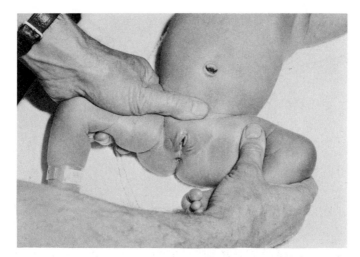

Fig. 121 In a doubtful case the pelvis may be steadied between a thumb over the pubis and fingers under the sacrum while the hip is tested with the other hand.

the examining couch as if to push the trochanter towards the symphysis pubis. In a normal child no movement occurs. If the hip is dislocated, the greater trochanter and the head of the femur with it can be felt to move in the direction in which the pressure has been applied.

3. *Part 2*. With the hips in the same position as described in the last paragraph, the thumb, which is applied over the upper and inner part of the thigh, exerts pressure towards the examination couch. In a normal child no movement occurs. In a child with a dislocatable hip the head of the femur can be felt to slip out and to come back immediately the pressure is released.

After 4 or 5 weeks, the best single sign of subluxation or dislocation of the hip is limited abduction, with the hips flexed to a right angle. If the dislocation is unilateral, there will be apparent shortening of the leg. The main causes of limited abduction of the hip are as follows:

1. Normal variation. The hips of some normal babies abduct further than those of others. In part this is due to differences in muscle tone, but it also depends on the ligaments of the hip.
2. Increased muscle tone (in the adductors). As always, it is impossible to draw the line between the normal and the abnormal and slight variations from the average may be insignificant. In all children with the spastic forms of cerebral palsy one expects to find limitation of abduction on the affected side.
3. 'Stiff adductors' or 'congenital shortening of the adductors'. These terms are used by orthopaedic surgeons to explain limited abduction without subluxation of the hip.
4. Subluxation of the hip.

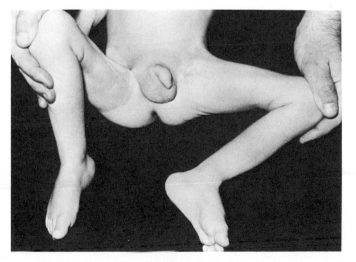

Fig. 122 Subluxated left hip, showing limited abduction.

5. Coxa vara.
6. A variety of hip diseases.
7. Ligamentous abnormalities, as in Trisomy E.
8. Muscle contracture — mainly in hypotonic babies and children who lie constantly in one position.

Forty years' experience of examining babies in child health clinics and elsewhere has left me in considerable doubt the diagnosis of subluxation of the hip. One in 20 to 50 babies at 6 weeks of age has limited abduction of one hip. Unfortunately orthopaedic experts disagree as to the significance of the signs and the action to be taken.[15,16] Some prove to have subluxation of the hip: others acquire normal abduction without treatment after a few weeks of observation. Several workers have suggested that dislocation may occur some weeks after birth. For this reason, and because of the difficulty of being certain in some children, repeated examination of the hip in the first-year is most important. It is now recognised that the common 'click' on abducting the hip is of no significance:[8,20] but the jerk or 'clunk', not found before 3 months of age, signifies a dislocatable hip requiring treatment.

A great difficulty is the finding that in up to 10% of children with a dislocated hip, there is no limitation of abduction.[3,15,20]

The diagnosis can be very difficult, and numerous papers have been written about this, and about late-diagnosed cases.[3,8,15,16,20] For instance, Bjerkreim[3] reviewed 815 'late' cases. When there is clinical doubt, the diagnosis is established by ultrasound.

Vision

For visual perception in infants,[6] see Chapter 4.

An essential part of the routine examination of the new baby is a rapid examination of the eyes, for nystagmus (which usually signifies a defect of vision), or an opacity (especially cataract, retinoblastoma or, later, retrolental fibroplasia). One should note other abnormalities, such as inequality of pupils, conjugate deviation of the eyes, or a fixed squint. It is important that a cataract should be diagnosed early, for treatment should be given by the age of 8 weeks.[21] There may be a white pupil and a small eye: but sometimes the cataract is posterior, and is found by the absence of the red reflex on ophthalmoscopy. A defect of vision would be suspected if the mother or examiner noticed absence of visual fixation or nystagmus.

The risk factors, which indicate the need for special care in the examination, are mainly the following:

Family history of blindness.
Preterm delivery, especially when extreme.
Rubella in the first 3 months of pregnancy.
Severe pre-eclampsia — risk of myopia.

Mental subnormality.
Cerebral palsy.
Hydrocephalus.
Craniostenosis.
Ophthalmia neonatorum.

André-Thomas used the following test for vision.[1] The child is held vertically, facing the dark part of the room. He is then turned on his body axis to make him face the lighted part of the room. The head and eyes turn more quickly to this part of the room. The eye which is nearer to the window opens wider. Finally the head and eyes are raised towards the sky. The child is rotated further so that he turns away from the source of light. His head and eyes do not follow the rest of the body as long as the light is perceptible. They return to their original position as soon as the light gives way to darkness. (See also Doll's Eye Response, pp 64 and 259.)

Paine used another rotation test. The baby is held facing the examiner, who rotates two or three times. The baby opens his eyes. The eyes deviate in the direction of movement as long as the rotation continues, and rotatory nystagmus in the opposite direction occurs when the movement stops. The responses are incomplete if there is weakness of the ocular muscles or defective vision. Vision can also be tested by the use of a revolving drum on which stripes have been painted; the presence of nystagmus indicates that vision is present (opticokinetic nystagmus).

A good description of the methods used to test 7-day-old babies was given by Boston workers.[4] One to two hours after a feed the infants were tested by a bright red 2 inch diameter ball suspended by a rubber band 6 to 10 inches from the face. The ball was moved slowly in different directions. One examiner handled the baby while two examiners observed the degree of horizontal and vertical deviation of the eyes, the duration of responsiveness and the associated head movements. Opticokinetic responses to a special moving drum were also recorded. The capacity to fix, follow and alert to the visual stimulus provided good evidence of an intact visual apparatus.

Newborn infants tend to keep the eyes closed when one tries to examine them, and any attempt to retract the eyelids makes the baby close the eyes more tightly. Babies may be induced to open the eyes by inducing sucking, or by swinging them round in one's hands.

More sophisticated methods of vision testing include visual evoked potential and electroretinoscopy,[18] and discrimination of vertical stripes of various width against a grey area matched for luminescence.[14] Visual acuity can be assessed by ability to distinguish black and white stripes of different widths.

For delayed visual maturation[7] see Chapter 7.

It is easy to describe in words the method of testing for a squint in a baby, but it is much more difficult to satisfy oneself, when a baby is uncooperative, that a squint is or is not present. When a light is pointed in the direction of the eye, with the head central, the light reflex should be in the same position on each eye. When one has caused the child to look at a light, and one covers one eye, there should be no movement of that eye on uncovering it. An epicanthic fold or broad bridge of the nose may lead to the erroneous diagnosis of a squint. By pinching the nose in such a way that the epicanthic folds are obliterated, one can more readily determine whether there is a squint or not. The so-called 'setting sun sign', so commonly seen in the presence of hydrocephalus, may be normal.

Hearing

All infants should be screened for their ability to hear, and a rough hearing test should be part of the routine examination in the early weeks and certainly by the age of 3 or 4 months (Ch. 12). Many feel that all infants at special risk should be screened in the newborn period. Risk factors include virus infections, such as rubella, in pregnancy, the use of ototoxic drugs in pregnancy, history of congenital deafness and severe perinatal hypoxia. (See Ch. 12 for a more comprehensive list.)

It has been suggested that brainstem electric response audiometry (the BERA test) should be performed in all infants at the time of their discharge from an intensive care unit.[23] The test was said to give a precise estimate of the threshold of responses to clicks in a few minutes, readily singling out abnormal babies.

The newborn baby may respond to a loud noise[13] by a startle reaction, a facial grimace, blinking, gross motor movements, quieting if crying, or crying if quiet, opening the eyes if they are closed, inhibiting sucking responses, or by a catch in the respirations. There may be a change in the heart rate, as demonstrated by the cardiotachometer, and changes in the EEG. It is often difficult to elicit a response to sound in the newborn period by simple clinical means. Orientation to sound is tested by a rattle held 10 inches away from the ear, on a level with the ear:[11] the movement of the eyes or head in response are noted. A Japanese paper[13] added sucking movements in response to sound — more marked in preterm than full-term neonates: by startle response audiometry it was found that auditory acuity gradually increased with development.

The interpretation: prognosis

The greater one's experience of developmental assessment, the more difficult it appears to become. This applies especially to the assessment in the newborn period.

The main difficulty is that abnormal neurological signs detected in the newborn period or in the early weeks may completely or almost completely disappear (Ch. 16). For instance, the range of muscle tone varies widely in normal babies. All that one can say is that the further away from the average a child is in any feature, the less likely is he to be normal. Excessive tone may be a temporary phenomenon, and so may hypotonia, unless it is severe. One pays more attention to asymmetry of tone, but even marked degrees of asymmetry of tone, suggestive of a spastic hemiplegia, may disappear in a few weeks. Exaggerated knee jerks and even well sustained ankle clonus by no means signify a permanent physical defect. One pays more attention to a combination of abnormal signs than to a single one. I would pay no attention to exaggerated tendon jerks in an otherwise normal baby. I would regard a well-sustained ankle clonus merely as an indication for examination at a later date, and I certainly would not even hint to the mother that there might be an abnormality. If, however, a baby in addition to displaying a well-sustained ankle clonus had a small head circumference in relation to his weight, or showed delayed motor development, or had not begun to smile at his mother by 6 weeks (if full term), then I would certainly suspect an abnormality. I would also be influenced by a history of important 'risk factors'. For instance, if a baby showed exaggerated muscle tone, and had suffered hypoglycaemic convulsions, or had been a small preterm baby, or was one of twins, I would be more suspicious that the child was abnormal. On the other hand, one must remember that babies who suffered severe hypoxia at birth are likely to be normal in later months and years.

I have seen many impressive examples of recovery after grossly abnormal physical signs in the newborn period. They include the following:

1. A baby with suprabulbar palsy whose mother had had hydramnios. He had signs of spastic quadriplegia, with well sustained ankle clonus, exaggerated tendon jerks, excessive muscle tone and tightly clenched hands. He had to be sucked out every 10 to 15 minutes for the first few weeks. By 12 weeks the sign of spasticity had largely disappeared. By 6 months the only residual sign was a slightly abnormal hand approach to an object. At 10 years he was normal, though there was a trivial tremor in the hands within normal limits. His progress at a normal school was average. In a paper on dysphagia[14] I have described other examples of the complete disappearance of dysphagia due to bulbar palsy or incoordination of the swallowing mechanism.

2. A child with typical signs of spastic hemiplegia in the first 3 months, one arm being notably stiff and relatively immobile. At the age of 12 years the only residual sign was a unilateral extensor plantar response, with no symptoms.

3. Unilateral severe hypertonia in the early weeks: at school age no sign or symptom apart from slight general clumsiness.

In a follow-up study of 79 infants who displayed abnormal neurological signs in the newborn period, only 13 were abnormal at 18 months:[2] but the absence of signs in the newborn period does not guarantee that the baby will be normal later. In this study two of the 65 control children were found to be abnormal on follow-up, without having displayed any significant abnormal signs earlier.

One can never be sure that when abnormal signs have disappeared a few weeks after birth, fine tests of manual, motor or spatial dexterity will not in later years reveal some degree of abnormality.

If the child had neonatal convulsions, the outlook depends in large part on the cause of the convulsions. If they were due to hypoglycaemia, there is much more likely to be residual abnormality than if they were due to hypocalcaemia. Hypoglycaemia may itself be a manifestation of an underlying brain defect. Severe hyperbilirubinaemia is now rare, but if it does occur, the child is at grave risk of being abnormal later.

Abnormal signs — summary[11,26]

Shrill or high-pitched cry.

Apathy, excessive somnolence; irritability, hyperalertness.

Pithed frog position in supine. Opisthotonos. Undue extension of legs. Little spontaneous movement. Asymmetrical movement.

Tremors when not crying, especially when also irritable. Apnoeic attacks. Convulsions.

Vomiting.

Head size small or large in relation to weight. Bulging fontanelle: abnormal separation of sutures.

Eyes: roving nystagmus. Conjugate deviation. Pupils pin-point or fixed dilated.

Opacity. Ocular palsy. Fixed squint. Setting sun sign. Poor orientation (eye following).

Ears: poor orientation to sound.

Reflexes: increased, absent, asymmetrical. Exaggerated startle reflex. Abnormal Moro reflex: especially without flexion or adduction. Absent oral reflexes. Poor sucking and feeding.

Later: persistent grasp, Moro and asymmetrical tonic neck reflex. Persistence of clenched hand. Absence of gag or cough reflex, pooling of saliva (bulbar palsy).

Tone: hypotonia, hypertonia, asymmetry. Excessive extensor tone.

Gross delay in development: defective in prone, ventral suspension, pulled to sitting position.

The minimum examination

It is not always possible to carry out a full examination, either because the condition of the baby will not permit this, or because there is a shortage of time.

The following is the minimum examination of the newborn baby from the neurological or developmental aspect:

Assessment of maturity.

Observation of the cry.

Observation of the face — for facial palsy, facies of disease.

Eyes — for cataract, opacity due to retinoblastoma etc., nystagmus.

Movements — for quality, quantity, symmetry.

Posture — for excessive extension, as in spasticity.

Palpation of the anterior fontanelle and cranial sutures.

Estimation of muscle tone.

Moro and grasp reflexes.

Measurement of the head circumference in relation to weight.

Examination of hips.

Knee jerks, ankle clonus.

Examination of back for congenital dermal sinus.

If possible rough test for hearing.

If there is doubt as to whether there is hydrocephalus, the skull should be transilluminated.

REFERENCES

1. Andre-Thomas, Chesni, Y., Saint-Anne Dargassies. The neurological examination of the infant. Little Club Clinics in Developmental Medicine. No. 1. London. National Spastics Society. 1960.
2. Bierman-van Endenburg, M. E. C. Predictive value of neonatal neurological examination: a follow-up study at 18 months. Dev. Med. Child Neurol. 1981.23.296.
3. Bjerkreim, I. Congenital dislocation of the hip joint in Norway. Acta Orthopaed. Scand. 1974. Suppl. 157.
4. Brazelton, T. B., Scholl, M. L., Robey, J. S. Visual responses in the newborn. Pediatrics. 1966.37.284.
5. Brazelton, T. B. Neonatal Behavioral Assessment Scale. Clinics in developmental medicine No. 88. London, Heinemann, 1984.
6. Cohen, L. B., De Loache, J. S., Strauss, M. S. Infant visual perception. In: Osofsky, J. D. (Ed.) Handbook of infant development. New York. Wiley. 1979. p. 393.
7. Cole, G. F., Hungerford, J., Jones, R. B. Delayed visual maturation. Arch. Dis. Child 1984.59.107.
8. Cyvin, K. B. Congenital dislocation of the hip joints. Acta Paediatr. Scand. 1977. Suppl. 263.
9. Dubowitz, L. M. S., Dubowitz, V., Palmer, P. G. et al. Correlation of neurologic assessment in the preterm newborn infant with outcome at one year. J. Pediatr. 1984.105.452.
10. Dubowitz, L. M. S., Levene, M. I., Morante, A., Palmer, P., Dubowitz, V. Neurologic signs in neonatal intraventricular hemorrhage: a correlation with real-time ultrasound. J. Pediatr. 1981.99.127.
11. Dubowitz, L., Dubowitz, V. The neurological assessment of the preterm and full term new infant. Clinics in Developmental Medicine No. 79. London. Heinemann. 1981.
12. Dubowitz, V. The floppy infant. Clinics in Developmental Medicine. London. Heinemann. 1969
13. Endo, I. Comparison of auditory acuities measured by startle response in full term and premature neonates. Acta Paediatr. Japonica 1979.21.31.
14. Illingworth, R. S. Sucking and swallowing difficulty in infancy. Diagnostic problems of dysphagia. Arch. Dis. Child 1969.44.655.
15. Jones, D. An Assessment of the value of the examination of the hip in the newborn. J. Bone Joint Surg. 1977.59B.318.

16. Mackenzie, I. G. Congenital dislocation of hip. J. Bone Joint Surg. 1972.54B.18.
17. Morante, A., Dubowitz, L. M. S., Dubowitz, V., Levene, M. The development of visual function in normal and neurologically abnormal preterm and full term infants. Dev. Med. Child Neurol. 1982:24:771.
18. Nelson, L. B., Rubin, S. E., Wagner, R. S., Breton, M. E. Developmental aspects in the assessment of visual function in young children. Pediatrics 1984.73:375.
19. Prechtl, H. Beintema, D. J. The neurological examination of the full term new born infant. A manual for clinical use. Little Club Clinics in Developmental Medicine No. 12. London: Heinemann. 1964.
20. Ramsey, P. L. Congenital dislocation of the hip. J. Pediatr. Surg. 1977.12.437.
21. Rice, N. S. C., Taylor D. Congenital cataract, a cause of preventable blindness. Br. Med. J. 1982.2.581.
22. Sainte-Anne Dargassies Le nouveau-né à terme. Aspect neurol. biol. neo-natal. 1962.4.174.
23. Schulman-Galambos, C. Assessment of hearing. In Field T. M. (Ed) Infants born at risk. New York. SP Medical and Scientific Books. 1979, p. 91.
24. Self, P. A., Horowitz, F. D. The behavioral assessment of the neonate: an overview. In: Osofsky, J. D. (Ed.) Handbook of infant development. New York. Wiley. 1979.
25. Sykes, G. S., Molloy, P. M., Johnson, P. Birth asphyxia. Br. Med. J. 1982.2.289.
26. Touwen, B. C. L. Newborn alarm signals. In: Rose, F. C. (Ed.) Paediatric neurology. Oxford. Blackwell. 1979.
27. Touwen, B., Eendenburg, M., Bierman, Van E., Jurgens-van der Zee, A. Neurological screening of full-term newborn infants. Dev. Med. Child Neurol. 1977.19.739.
28. Yang, R. K. Early infant assessment: an overview. In: Osofsky, J. D. (Ed.) Handbook of infant development. New York. Wiley. 1979. p. 165.

12

The examination of the older infant and child

THE PHYSICAL EXAMINATION AND INVESTIGATION

A full physical examination is essential, for one must detect any physical handicap which may have affected his development, and which will therefore affect his performance in developmental tests. Recognition of a handicap will influence one's prediction for future achievement.

Testing hearing

In Chapter 11 I discussed the testing of hearing in the newborn. The hearing should be screened as a routine in all infants, certainly by the age of 3 or 4 months.

The risk factors which increase the possibility of a hearing defect include the following:

Deafness suspected by the parents.
Delayed or defective speech.
Chronic or recurrent otitis media.
Cleft palate.
Rubella or cytomegalovirus infection in early pregnancy.
Ototoxic drugs in pregnancy.
Congenital deafness in the family
Rare syndromes — Wardenburg (white forelock, heterochromia of the iris and deafness), Pendred (goitre and deafness), Treacher Collins, Klippel-Feil, Kallman, congenital nephritis in males, deafness with cardiac arrhythmia, hyperprolinaemia, retinitis pigmentosa, multiple lentigines, albinism, pili torti.
Cystic fibrosis.
Down's syndrome.
Cerebral palsy. Kernicterus.
Preterm delivery.
Severe perinatal hypoxia, especially with acidosis, apnoeic spells, cerebral haemorrhage.
Mental subnormality.

Meningitis. Mumps.

Head injury.

Ototoxic drugs taken by the child. Use of ear drops.

Gesell and Amatruda[8] have described the early clinical signs of deafness in infants, listing the main features as follows:

1. *Hearing and comprehension of speech*
   General indifference to sound
   Lack of response to spoken word
   Response to noises as opposed to voice
2. *Vocalisation and sound production*
   Monotonal quality
   Indistinct
   Lessened laughter
   Meagre experimental sound play and squealing
   Vocal play for vibratory sensation
   Head banging, foot stamping for vibratory sensation
   Yelling, screeching to express pleasure, annoyance or need
3. *Visual attention and reciprocal comprehension*
   Augmented visual vigilance and attentiveness
   Alertness to gestures and movement
   Marked imitativeness in play
   Vehemence of gestures
4. *Social rapport and adaptations*
   Subnormal rapport in vocal nursery games
   Intensified preoccupation with things rather than persons
   Enquiring, sometimes surprised or thwarted facial expression
   Suspicious alertness, alternating with cooperation
   Marked reaction to praise and affection
5. *Emotional behaviour*
   Tantrums to call attention to self or need
   Tensions, tantrums, resistance due to lack of comprehension
   Frequent obstinacies, teasing tendencies
   Irritability at not making self understood
   Explosions due to self-vexation
   Impulsive and avalanche initiatives

Deaf babies gurgle and coo in a normal fashion, and from 9 to 18 months they appear to be developing speech, saying 'mumum', 'dadada', but no further progress in speech is then made. Congenitally deaf babies do vocalise, and their vocalisations undergo changes leading up to spontaneous and playful sounds. This indicates the importance of maturation in speech development. Tape recordings of infants of congenitally deaf parents and of normal parents showed no differences. The vocalisations, cooing and crying were identical, and were regarded as developmental.[13]

The response to sound in the first 2 or 3 months includes quietening if crying, crying if quiet, the startle reflex or a blink. After the age of 3 months the child should turn his head to sound (Fig. 148); and thereafter one notes not just whether he turns his head to sound, but the rapidity with which he does it. Sheridan[20,22] and Fisch[4] have described simple screening tests. The child is on his mother's lap. The room should be quiet, with little ambient noise.

Sheridan described the appropriate test for different ages from 6 months onwards, using the conversational or whispered voice, soft paper, rattles, squeaking dolls, a cup and spoon, toys and other common objects. The toys, used for the Stycar tests, are a chair, doll, car, plane, spoon, knife and fork. The sounds PS,PHTH are high pitched, and the sound OO low pitched. One must avoid blowing into the ear when making the sounds. Frequent repetition of the sounds leads to habituation, so that he no longer responds. He must not be tested when he is tired, hungry or preoccupied with some other interest. She emphasised the importance of the examiner not being too far from the child: he should be well to the side but outside the field of vision. When the baby is 6 months old, the sound is made 18 inches from the ear, on a level with the ear. When he is older, it may not be desirable to make the noises behind him; but if one is in his sight and covers one's mouth with the hand, one must avoid giving him clues by elevating the eyebrows or other facial expression. Sheridan found that clinical testing of the very young child is more accurate than audiometry.

When over the mental age of $2\frac{1}{2}$, the child can be tested by asking him to point to toys or appropriate pictures on a card — the examiner covering his mouth so that lip-reading cannot occur.

Fisch[4] made the following comments on hearing tests:

1. There is no single form of testing which will give a complete picture of the total hearing capacity of an individual.
2. Hearing tests are subjective tests requiring co-operation. There is no mechanical device which would enable us to test a child without gaining his confidence or cooperation. The handling of the child is decisive.
3. One should not draw far-reaching conclusions or make final decisions on the basis of observations carried out on a single occasion.
4. A test should not be of such a nature that it would be associated with unpleasant or frightening experiences.
5. The child's obvious reaction to certain sounds or his understanding of familiar speech sounds in *tête-à-tête* conversation does not mean that the child could not have a hearing loss. When deafness is suspected, only a complete test is conclusive.

For the older child the Peep-Show technique of Dix and Hallpike may be used, in association with pure tone audiometry. Fisch's method[4] depends largely on the establishment of conditioned reflexes — training the child to make a particular movement, such as putting a brick into a cup — when a sound is made.

Full audiometry can be carried out from the mental age of three. More sophisticated tests were discussed by Beagley.[2] They include impedance audiometry with tympanometry and acoustic threshold measurements, electrocochleography and brain stem evoked responses.[5] I have no experience of these, and therefore prefer not to discuss them.

When it is found that the child can hear, it is then necessary to determine whether he can understand what he hears. He may suffer from congenital auditory imperception. As Sheridan has said, hearing is the reception of sound by the ear, and involves the cochlea, eighth nerve, brain stem and primary auditory area of the cortex. Listening is paying attention to sound in order to comprehend what is heard. This may involve coding, memory, emotion and previous experiences.

Vision testing

In Chapter 11 I discussed the risk factors for a defect of vision, and the method of testing in the newborn period. After the newborn period, children should be screened for conditions which may damage vision, including strabismus, muscle imbalance, myopia, glaucoma or retinoblastoma.

In the older child the chief causes of blindness are trauma, rheumatoid arthritis, various causes of cataract formation, and the effect of drugs (such as chloroquine or corticosteroids). For a comprehensive list see my book, *Common Symptoms of Disease in Children.*[10]

The method of inspecting the eye of the newborn baby has been discussed in Chapter 11. Ophthalmoscopic examination is essential if a defect of vision is suspected, but the findings are not necessarily easy to interpret. When a baby is mentally subnormal, and therefore late in development of the usual responses, it can be extremely difficult to decide whether he can see or not. On ophthalmoscopy one sees the pale disc which is normal in the early weeks, and it is difficult to determine whether the pallor of the disc is within normal limits.

Dr Mary Sheridan has described the method of screening young or handicapped children for vision,[21,22] and reference should be made to her papers. From the age of 21 to 36 months she tested with miniature toys,* the child having one set and the examiner, having an identical set, holds up one after another at 10 feet from the child, who is asked to match the examiner's toy with his own. The Snellen letters can be used after the age of three. The Sheridan test depends on the fact that the first letters to be learnt by a child are usually the V, O, X, H and T, and later the A, U, L, and C: the child matches letters from his own set with those held up 10 feet away by

---

* STYCAR test — chair, doll, car, plane, spoon, knife, fork.

the examiner. In a review of clinical tests for visual function, Bax and colleagues[1] discussed the application of some of the Sheridan tests. The tests for infants over the age of 6 months include the use of graded balls, measuring $\frac{1}{8}$ to $2\frac{1}{2}$ inches, with the child on the mother's knee: balls of decreasing size are rolled across a dark cloth 10 feet away: the examiner first attracts the baby's attention: he then observes the child's tracking ability. The 2-year-old is shown seven or more toys — a doll, chair, car, plane, knife, fork or spoon and asked to match them with corresponding toys held by the examiner. From $2\frac{1}{2}$ years of age, the child is asked to match letters.

As Sheridan has pointed out, there is an important difference between seeing and looking. 'Seeing' is the reception of patterns of light and shade by the eyes and the transmission of this sensory information in some form of neurological activity to the occipital region of the brain. 'Looking' is paying attention to what is seen with the object of interpreting its significance. It depends upon the ability to integrate the sensory information received into meaningful messages. Everyday visual competence involves seeing and looking and presupposes previous adequate opportunity to learn from experience.

It should be noted that hypermetropia, which involves difficulty with near vision, is more common than myopia, which involves difficulty in distant vision. It is often difficult to diagnose a mild degree of strabismus, but it is of great importance to do so.

Testing for colour is a matter for the expert.[7] According to Peiper[16] colour blindness can be ruled out completely by the start of the third year. A useful screening device has been described by the Gallachers.[6] Their description is as follows: 'This simple brief evaluation employs the H.R.R. pseudoisochromatic plates which distinguish red green blindness, total colour blindness and blue yellow blindness. Graded colour symbols (triangle, circle, cross) with increasing saturation of the critical hues allow both a qualitative and quantitative evaluation of the defect; the child need only trace the symbol with a brush'.

There are several modifications of ISHIHARA tests to make the test suitable for children. About 8% of boys and 0.4% of girls have defective red green colour vision.

Speech assessment

Speech assessment is a matter for the expert who will investigate verbal comprehension, vocabulary and word structure. Those interested should consult the publications by Ingram[11] and Reynell.[18,19] The assessment of speech was discussed by Silva,[24] using the Reynell scales. The Reynell developmental language scales include verbal comprehension and verbal expression. Silva wrote that the former does not demand a verbal response, but assesses the child's understanding of language by presenting toys and getting him to point or make some non-verbal response. The verbal expression scale consists of three subscales — expressive language structure (18 items), expressive vocabulary (21 items) — naming simple objects, describing a picture, defining words: with an expressive language content (maximum score 20) in which the child is asked to talk about five pictures.

Coplan and colleagues[3] named 41 language milestones for use in the first 3 years of childhood, testing for auditory expressive ability (early vocalisation, single words, use of 'me' and 'you', naming of objects and pronouns), and audio-receptive ability (response to sound and recognition of sound, response to 'No', simple requests).

The non-expert should observe whether the child is saying single words only or is joining words together into sentences: and whether he is speaking as distinctly as usual for his age, or whether infantile substitutions are persisting beyond the usual age. For instance, the common central lisp, the substitution of 'th' for 's' as a result of protrusion of the tongue between the front teeth when pronouncing the 's', should disappear around four, and persistence thereafter should be treated by a speech therapist before he starts school. Likewise a slight stutter is acceptable at $2\frac{1}{2}$ years of age, but if it is persisting and marked, it should be treated by the age of 4.

When there is retardation in speech, it is most important to determine whether the child understands spoken language. Understanding of language precedes by a long time the ability to articulate. Language is best provoked by talking to the child (e.g. about toys), or by showing him pictures in a picture book.

Other aspects of the physical examination.

The routine physical examination includes measurement of the head size in relation to the baby's weight (Ch. 9), the palpation of the anterior fontanelle and sutures in infancy, inspection of the mouth, auscultation of the heart and chest, palpation of the abdomen and testes, and in the first 2 years, examination of the hips. The femoral pulses should be felt to exclude coarctation of the aorta.

Special investigations

No special investigations are required in routine developmental assessment, though phenylketonuria and hypothyrodism are routinely eliminated in the newborn period. But when an abnormality is found, an accurate diagnosis must be made, if possible, not only for purposes of appropriate treatment, but for genetic reasons (Ch. 2). An EEG in taken only for investigation of certain forms of epilepsy. Other commonly used special investigations include ultrasound and other methods of scanning. The finding of 'cortical atrophy' can be misleading, and have little or no correlation with the findings on developmental testing.

THE DEVELOPMENTAL EXAMINATION

In Chapter 6 I have outlined the normal development of the infant and young child. In this chapter 1 shall discuss the technique of testing.

Equipment required

The following equipment is required for developmental testing in the first 5 years:

Ten 1-inch cubes
Hand bell
Simple formboard
Goddard formboard
Coloured and uncoloured geometric forms
Picture cards
Scrap book
Cards with circle, cross, square, triangle, diamond drawn on them. These
   can be made at the time of examination out of sight of the child
Patellar hammer
Paper
Pellets (8 mm). These can be made at the time of examination from
   cotton wool or paper.
The relevant items are illustrated in figures.

The various structures made from the cubes are also illustrated (Figs 130–134).

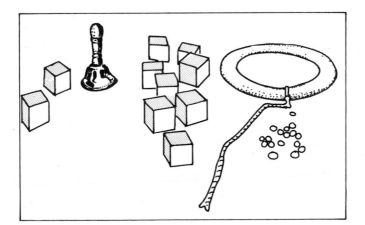

Fig. 123 Equipment for testing a baby. (The 1-inch cubes are used from 5 months to 6 years.) Pellets, dangling ring, 1-inch cubes, small bell.

Examination after the newborn period

This section is based on the work of Arnold Gesell and has been modified for use in a busy paediatric out-patient clinic. The more one digresses from the exact technique of examination for developmental tests, the less valid is the statistical basis of one's tests. I regard the modifications suggested as so small that they do not invalidate the result; and a follow-up study already discribed (Ch. 1) and many hundreds of other personally observed cases, have shown that the tests as outlined are of predictive value.

For further details of developmental tests the reader should refer to Arnold Gesell and his colleagues in *Developmental Diagnosis* and the book by Knobloch and her colleagues.[12]

One pays particular attention to the persistence of certain primitive reflexes and features of behaviour beyond the age at which they should have disappeared. For instance, the persistence of hand regard after about 20 weeks, of mouthing, drooling and casting objects after about 15 months, is a significant indication of mental subnormality.

Age of testing

The ideal age at which a developmental examination should be made, if one can choose the age, is of importance. For the purposes of adoption I would feel that the age of 6 weeks or 6 months is ideal for the purpose. In some ways I would rather give an opinion about a child when he is 6 to 8 weeks of age than I would when he is 3 or 4 months old. This has been the experience of others, including Cattell.

The age of 10 months is a good one at which to assess a baby, and if I am in doubt about the development of a baby at 6 months, I try to see

Fig. 124 Simple formboard. $14\frac{1}{2} \times 6\frac{1}{2}$ inches.

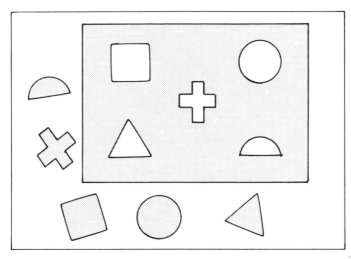

Fig. 125 Coloured geometric forms. Red card mounted on plain carboard (12 × 20 inches), with corresponding cut-out pieces.

him again at 10 months. At 10 months one has available various new milestones of development — the index finger approach to objects, the finger — thumb apposition, the child's cooperation in dressing (holding an arm out for a sleeve, a foot out for a shoe, transferring an object from a hand which is about to be put into a sleeve), the creep, the ability of the child to pull himself to the standing position, and to cruise (walking, when holding on to the furniture). There is the imitation of the mother (bye-bye, 'patacake', 'so big'), and the possibility of words with meaning. The age

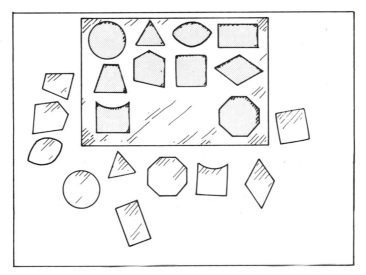

Fig. 126 Uncoloured geometric forms. Similar to above, but uncoloured and more difficult.

Fig. 127 Goddard formboard.

of 10 months is an excellent one for assessing a baby. By the age of 12 to 24 or more months, children are often coy and non-cooperative, and difficult to test.

Wherever possible I would avoid testing a child between 8 and 16 weeks of age and between 8 and 9 months of age.

Arrangements for the examination

For the purposes of the developmental examination, and to a lesser extent for the purpose of the physical examination, it is important to have the infant or small child in as good a temper as possible. In the Yale Clinic of Child Development, under Gesell, social workers visited the home in order to determine the baby's normal play time, and the developmental examination was arranged accordingly. Unfortunately the busy paediatrician cannot work under such ideal conditions, but he can at least see that the infant is not hungry at the time of examination. If he is sleepy, a note to that effect is made and he is re-examined before an opinion can be given. One would not attempt a developmental examination if the child is hungry, tired or unwell, or has had a major convulsion an hour or two ago, or who is under the influence of a sedative or antiepileptic drug.

I see no need for a special room for developmental examination. Most paediatricians will of necessity have to examine infants and young children in the course of ordinary outpatient duties, in the usual room reserved for that purpose. I have not found the presence of students or doctors a disadvantage. The child should not be within sight of a window through which he can see objects and people passing. Irrelevant toys must be out of reach and sight. I always conduct my examination of the child in the mother's presence. This seems to be the normal and natural arrangement.

Fig. 128 Pictures of common objects for picture identification.

Occasionally a mother is unable to resist trying to help a child to perform a test, but she can be asked to leave the test to the child. She is liable to tell a child that he is making a mistake (in the formboard test, for instance), but she has to be asked not to do this. Sometimes the mother may help by asking the child to carry out a test, such as building a tower of cubes, when he shows no sign of doing it for the examiner. When one is not sure whether he has really done his best, it is useful to ask the mother if she thinks that the child could do the test in question, or would be able to recognise the objects shown, so that one's findings can be confirmed.

Order of testing

The developmental examination of young children should always be performed before the physical examination, because the child may cry during the physical examination and he would then be unlikely to cooperate in developmental tests. It is often advisable to carry out the developmental examination before taking the history, for a young child, and particularly a retarded one, will soon become bored and restless and so cooperate less well.

In all tests one observes the child's interest, distractibility, degree and duration of concentration, social responsiveness, alertness and rapidity of response. The child is watched intently throughout the examination. One particularly looks for abnormalities of movement (e.g. athetosis, ataxia, spasticity or tremor). One also listens and notes the vocalisations — their nature and frequency, and later the quality of speech.

Fig. 129 Incomplete man.

All tests are carried out as quickly as possible, in case he becomes bored, or refuses to cooperate because he regards the tests as just silly. If he does not seem to be interested in a test, another is promptly substituted. As soon as a test object has been used, it should be removed from his sight. There is no need to keep to a rigid order of testing. In developmental testing of young or retarded children there is no place for long tests. I cannot agree with those who say that developmental testing in infancy is very time-consuming. It must not be.

Babies and young children readily begin to cry when undressed or when placed in the prone or supine position. Accordingly one begins by acquiring as much information as possible as soon as the child comes into the room, when he is fully dressed. After that he is completely undressed for the rest of the examination and the nappy must be removed. The child should not have a dummy in the mouth or an object in the opposite hand: I find that in either case it is less easy to secure the child's interest and cooperation.

Summary — essential observations (1–3 months)

1. Observe and watch the baby on his mother's knee. If possible observe him when his mother talks to him, to see whether he watches her, smiles, vocalises. One notices his interest in his surroundings. Note the shape and size of head. The heart is auscultated for abnormal murmurs.
2. Palpate the anterior fontanelle. If doubtful, feel the sutures of craniostenosis.
3. Hold in ventral suspension. Observe head control and limb position. In

the normal child there is some extension of the hips, with flexion of the elbows and knees. In the abnormal child the arms and legs hang down lifelessly, and there is poor head control. Inspect the eyes for opacity or nystagmus which suggests a visual defect. If the eyes are closed, he will usually open them if one swings him round.

4. Place in prone position. Note elevation of the chin off the couch. Note whether the pelvis is high off the couch or flat. Observe for congenital dermal sinus.

5. Supine position. Note if the hands are unduly tightly closed.
   The umbilicus is inspected for infection and the abdomen is palpated. Examine the hips: estimate hip abduction.
   Assess dorsiflexion of the ankles — for tone. Test for ankle clonus. Shake the limbs and assess resistance to passive movement for tone. Test the knee jerks. Pull to the sitting position — to compare head control with that in ventral suspension and prone: and note resistance to pulling to sit position — all to eliminate excessive extensor tone.
   Measure the head circumference. Relate it to the weight. Check his response to sound by crinkling paper etc., on a level with the ear but out of sight: note cry, startle, quietening, blink.

The whole of the above together with inspection of the mouth (e.g. for thrush), auscultation of the heart, inspection of the umbilicus, and palpation of the abdomen and testes, takes not longer than 2 minutes. It will take longer if doubt about normality arises. It is assumed that the screening tests have been performed to eliminate phenylketonuria and hypothyroidism.

Three to 6 months

The mother sits at the side of the desk, holding the baby on her knees.

1. Observe the size of the baby's head in relation to his weight, and the shape of the head. Note the facial expression and vocalisations. Note if both hands are largely open. (The hand is likely to be closed more if the child is spastic.)

2. Test the hearing by crumpling paper etc., (out of sight, on a level with the ear, about 18 inches from it). Look at the eyes for opacity, nystagmus or strabismus.

3. If he is three to four months old, place a rattle in his hand: observe whether he plays with it.

4. Place a one-inch cube on the desk in front of him. Note whether he gets it, and how long he tries to get it.
   If he gets it, note whether he transfers it to the other hand. Note how soon he drops it — as a sign of maturity of the grasp. Put a date to his manipulative development. If for instance, he cannot get hold of a rattle but will hold it when it is placed in the hand and play with it, his manipulative development is not less than 3 months, but not that

of a 5-month baby. This gap is narrowed by observing whether he merely shows a desire to get it, without reaching for it, like a 3- or 4-month baby, or whether he reaches for it without actually getting it, like a 4-month baby. If he can get it without it being placed in the hand, his development is not less than 5 months. If he transfers it, he cannot be less than the level of a 6-month baby. One confirms this by watching the maturity of the grasp — the younger baby holding the cube in an insecure palmar grasp, dropping it promptly, the older one by a more secure grasp, using the fingers more.

5. Place him without clothes in the supine position. If he spontaneously lifts his head off the couch, his motor development cannot be less than that of a 6-month baby. He may not have reached that point: he may merely lift his head up when he sees that he is about to be pulled up.

6. Examine the hips for the degree of abduction, in order to eliminate subluxation or abnormality of muscle tone. Test the knee jerks, ankle dorsiflexion and test for ankle clonus.

7. Watch for hand regard — a developmental trait seen in a narrow period of 12 to 20 weeks. It should not continue after that in a full term baby.

8. Pull him to the sitting position, to determine the amount of head lag, if any. If there is head lag, one can say immediately that his motor development is less than that of a 4–5-month baby. Note whether there is a feeling of resistance when he is pulled up as in cerebral palsy, and with the hand in the popliteal space as he is pulled up note whether there is spasm of the hamstrings. When he is leaned forward, note whether he persistently falls back, as in the spastic form of cerebral palsy. When he is in the sitting position, his body is swayed from side to side. There should be little head wobble by the age of 5 months. (This test corresponds to the test for 'passivité' when one shakes the limbs in order to assess muscle tone.)

9. Pull him to the standing position to assess weight-bearing, but remember that success in this depends largely on the opportunity which his mother has given him to stand.

10. If the baby is 3 to 5 months old, assess him in the prone position.

11. Measure the head circumference and relate it to his weight.

12. Throughout note responsiveness, interest, alertness and concentration. Always be sure that you have elicited the maximum performance. It is not enough to determine whether he can reach out and get an object: one has to determine the maturity of the grasp — how far he has developed in that skill. It is assumed that phenylketonuria and hypothyroidism have been eliminated.

Seven to 12 months

The baby sits on his mother's knee at the side of the desk.

1. Observe his face, skull size and shape, interest, alertness, and the quality

of vocalisations. Observe the eye for opacity, nystagmus or strabismus.
2. Offer a cube and observe the maturity of the grasp.

    Observe particularly the index finger approach. If this is seen, his manipulative development cannot be less than 9 to 10 months. In the case of the younger baby in this age group, note transfer from hand to hand.

    As soon as he takes one cube, offer another. The younger child drops the first but the older one retains it.

    Note 'matching' — the baby bringing one cube to the other as if to compare the two (average age 9 to 10 months). If he is around 9 months or more, offer a small pellet of paper. Note the index finger approach which dates his level of development immediately.
3. Note whether he can pick up the pellet between the tip of the thumb and the tip of the forefinger. (Finger–thumb apposition: average age 9 to 10 months. If he has the index finger approach he will almost certainly show finger–thumb apposition.) If he cannot get the pellet between the finger and thumb he will probably 'rake' with his whole hand.
4. Test for hearing by crumpling paper out of sight, on a level with the ear, about 18 inches away. Try other sounds. ('oo', 'ps'). Note particularly the rapidity of the response on each side. The retarded or deaf child is likely to be slow in responding.
5. Place him in the sitting position to assess his motor development: observe whether he needs his hands forward as props or whether he can sit steadily. See whether he can pivot round for a toy when sitting.
6. Place in the prone in order to see whether he goes into the creep position (9 to 10 months), or places the sole of the foot on the couch when in the creep position (average age 11 to 12 months).
7. Pull to the standing position and assess weight bearing.
8. Place in the supine position. Examine the hips, assess the range of ankle dorsiflexion, the briskness of the knee jerks, and test for ankle clonus.
9. Measure the head circumference and relate it to his weight. Possibly — ask him to hand a toy to you to determine whether he will release it into your hand (11 to 12 months).

One to 2 years

1. If he is walking, which his gait as he walks into the room and assess its maturity.
2. When he is on his mother's knee, offer him the ten 1-inch cubes. If necessary, show him how to place one on top of another to build a tower. Note how accurately he places one on top of another and record the number forming the tower. Note tremor or ataxia. Observe his interest, alertness, concentration, speech, cooperativeness.
3. Make a train of nine cubes and place one on top of the first to make a train. Ask him to imitate the process. Observe whether he adds the

chimney. If he makes a train, show him how to make a bridge of three cubes and ask him to imitate the process. If you build the bridge when he is watching, he 'imitates': if you build a bridge out of his sight (shielded by a card or hand), he 'copies'. The two are scored differently. Note particularly whether he takes a cube to his mouth (he should have stopped this by 13 to 15 months), or whether he 'casts' one brick after another to the floor (he should have got out of this by 15 to 18 months), and whether he is slobbering.

4. Give him the simple formboard. Decide on a rough guess about his maturity whether to give him the round block only or all three. If he gets the round block in, take it out, say 'watch me carefully' and rotate the board slowly. See if he gets the round one in with or without error. If he can get the round one in, offer all three: if he can get them in,

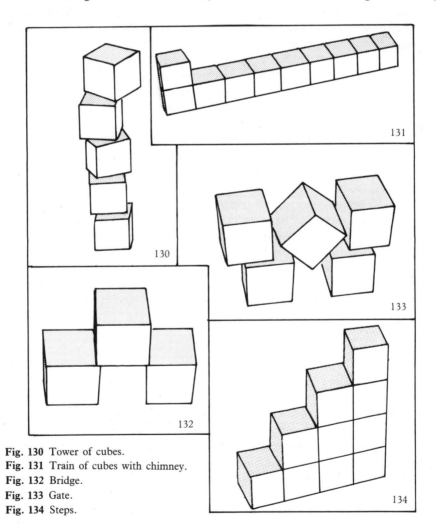

Fig. 130 Tower of cubes.
Fig. 131 Train of cubes with chimney.
Fig. 132 Bridge.
Fig. 133 Gate.
Fig. 134 Steps.

rotate as above. If necessary, as it commonly is, repeat the process two or three times, so that one can be sure that one has elicited the maximum performance.

5. Show him the picture card. Ask him 'where is the cat?' or 'show me the cat, basket, clock' etc. This is picture identification. If you ask him 'what is that?', pointing to the cat, this is termed 'picture naming', which is more difficult.

6. In the latter part of the period give him a pencil and paper. Ask him to 'imitate' the drawing of a vertical stroke, horizontal stroke or circle, according to maturity. If he is more mature, ask him to 'copy' these strokes (which were made out of his sight behind a hand or card).

   Note — all tests of drawing depend largely on the opportunity which he has been given to learn. If he has never been shown how to hold a pencil, he is unlikely to do well in the tests. All test objects must be given rapidly, one after the other, before interest flags.

7. Test his hearing.

Age 2 to 5 years

Note his gait as he enters the room and his head shape, interest in surroundings and responsiveness.

In the case of the younger child in this age group, or of a retarded older child, it is important to carry out the developmental tests as soon as the child comes into the consulting room, before he becomes bored with waiting while a long history is being taken.

There can be no rule as to the order in which tests are given. The essential thing is to maintain the child's interest and to carry out each test quickly, changing to another if signs of boredom appear. If there is a complaint of clumsiness, or if a neurological abnormality is noticed, and he is over 3 years of age, he is asked to stand on one foot — without holding on to anything. (Normal age for standing for seconds on one foot — 3 years.) This is a sensitive test for a neurological abnormality such as hemiplegia.

It is often convenient to begin with the cubes. Usually the child in this age group spontaneously begins to build a tower. One watches the hand movements for tremor or ataxia and tries to persuade the child to grasp with each hand, so that one can be sure that cerebral palsy is not present. One notes the accuracy of release, assessed by the accuracy with which one cube is placed on another. The child is then asked to build a train, bridge, gate or steps, according to one's rough assessment of the level he has reached, so that one can determine his maximum ability. In the case of the bridge, gate and steps, these are constructed behind a card or paper, so that the child cannot see the process of construction. He is then asked to copy the structure.

The child may then be given a pencil and paper. He is asked to imitate a vertical stroke, horizontal stroke, circle, cross, square, triangle or diamond, according to the level he is likely to have reached, being asked to draw these after the examiner, or he is asked to copy them.

Show him the picture card and ask him to identify or name objects, according to his maturity.

In the early part of the period he will be shown the simple formboard (as described above) and after about the third birthday, or before in a highly intelligent child, he is timed in his performance on the Goddard formboard, the score being based on the best of three trials. If he can place the blocks correctly in the simple formboard, he should be tried with the coloured geometric forms, and if he is successful with these he is tried with the uncoloured forms. In each case he is asked where the shapes fit, being handed one after the other. On no account is he told that he has made a mistake. It is always my practice to give the child another chance with those which he has placed wrongly.

The child is then asked to repeat digits. For intance, he is asked, 'Say after me nine, seven, eight', and he is given three trials. If he can repeat these, one tries four digits, and if he can repeat these, five digits, in each case giving three trials of different numbers. He is also asked to identify colours in a picture. One must separate the digits equidistantly, i.e. one will not separate digits as one may do when dictating a telephone number (265–421).

By the age of 3 or 4 years he is given a Goodenough 'draw a man' test. One gives the child pencil and paper, and asks him to draw a man. The scoring is described on page 261.

In each case one must obtain the maximum achievement for each test. For instance, one must determine how many digits he can repeat.

Throughout the test one observes his powers of concentration, distractibility, interest, and alertness, and listens to and assesses his speech. One notes and records his degree of cooperativeness in tests.

In the section to follow I have named the test recorded with the average age at which success is achieved.

SUMMARY OF TEST MATERIALS

One-inch cubes (Total needed — 10)

16 weeks	Tries to reach cube, but overshoots and misses.
20 weeks	Able to grasp voluntarily. Bidextrous approach.
24 weeks	More mature grasp. Drops one cube when another is given.
28 weeks	Unidextrous approach. Bangs cube on table. Transfers. Retains one when another is given.
32 weeks	Reaches persistently for cube out of reach.
36 weeks	Matches cubes.
40 weeks	Index finger approach. Release beginning. Holds cube to examiner but will not release it.

Fig. 135 1 year 6 months

Fig. 136 2 years 3 months.

Fig. 137 2 years 11 months

Fig. 138 3 years 4 months.

44 weeks   Begins to put cubes in and out of container.
52 weeks   Beginning to cast objects on to floor.
15 months   Tower of two holds two cubes in one hand.
18 months   Tower of three or four.

A eirl

Fig. 139 4 years 3 months.

Fig. 140 4 years 3 months. (Girl with toy cupboard.)

Fig. 141 5 years 3 months. (In colour.)

Fig. 142 6 years 0 months.

2 years	Tower of six or seven.
	Imitates train; no chimney.
2½ years	Tower of eight
	Imitates train, adding chimney.
3 years	Tower of nine. Imitates bridge.
3½ years	Copies bridge.
4 years	Imitates gate.
4½ years	Copies gate.
5 years	Cannot make steps.
6 years	May make steps.

Additional information is given by the cubes — the detection of mechanical disability in the hands, such as spasticity, athetosis, ataxia, tremor or rigidity.

Simple orders. (Take ball to mother, put it on chair, bring it to me, put in on table.)

18 months	two
2 years	four

Common objects. (Penny, shoe, pencil, knife, ball.)

18 months	Names one.
2 years	Names two to five
2½ years	Names five

Picture card

18 months	Points to one ('Where is the . . .?')
2 years	Points to five. Names three ('What is this?')
2½ years	Points to seven. Names five.
3 years	Names eight
3½ years	Names 10.

Fig. 143 7 years 5 months.

Fig. 144 8 years 11 months. (In colour.)

Fig. 145 9 years 9 months. (In colour.)

Colours
3 years	Names one.
4 years	Names two or three
5 years	Names four.

Drawing
15 months	Imitates scribble or scribbles spontaneously.
18 months	Makes stroke imitatively.

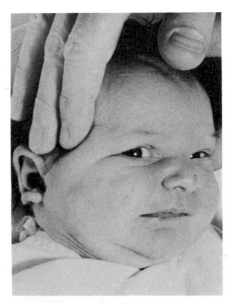

Fig. 146 The doll's eye phenomenon (see Ch. 11).

Fig. 147 Fixation and following with the eyes (see Ch. 5).

2 years	Imitates vertical and circular stroke.
2½ years	Two or more strokes for cross. Imitates horizontal stroke.
3 years	Copies circle. Imitates cross. Draws a man.
4 years	Copies cross.
4½ years	Copies square.
5 years	Copies triangle.
6 years	Copies diamond.

The Goodenough 'draw-a-man' test[17]

The examiner asks the child to draw a man. He is urged to draw it carefully, in the best way he knows how and to take his time. The test is reasonably reliable, correlating well with the Binet tests. The test is most suitable for children between 3 and 10 years of age.

The child receives one point for each of the items which is present in his drawing. For each four points 1 year is added to the basal age which is 3 years . Thus if the child's drawing shows that nine items are present in his drawing he scores nine points and his mental age score is 5¼ years.

Method of scoring the Goodenough* Draw-a-Man' Test:[17]
1. Head present
2. Legs present
3. Arms present

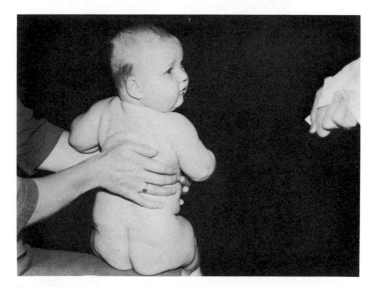

Fig. 148 Testing hearing: paper crinkled behind baby, on a level with his ear. Four month old baby turning his head to the sound.

---

* From Goodenough, F. L. Measurement of intelligence by drawings. New York. World Book Company.

4. Trunk present
5. Length of trunk greater than breadth
6. Shoulders indicated
7. Both arms and legs attached to trunk
8. Legs attached to trunk; arms attached to trunk at correct point
9. Neck present
10. Neck outline continuous with head, trunk or both
11. Eyes present
12. Nose present
13. Mouth present
14. Nose and mouth in two dimensions; two lips shown
15. Nostrils indicated
16. Hair shown
17. Hair non-transparent, over more than circumference
18. Clothing present
19. Two articles of clothing non-transparent
20. No transparencies, both sleeves and trousers shown
21. Four or more articles of clothing definitely indicated
22. Costume complete, without incongruities
23. Fingers shown
24. Correct number of fingers shown
25. Fingers in two dimensions, length greater than breadth, angle less than 180 degrees
26. Opposition of thumb shown
27. Hand shown distinct from fingers or arms
28. Arm joint shown, elbow, shoulder or both
29. Leg joint shown, knee, hip, or both
30. Head in proportion
31. Arms in proportion
32. Legs in proportion
33. Feet in proportion
34. Both arms and legs in two dimensions
35. Heel shown
36. Firm lines without overlapping at junctions
37. Firm lines with correct joining
38. Head outline more than circle
39. Trunk outline more than circle
40. Outline of arms and legs without narrowing at junction with body
41. Features symmetrical and in correct position
42. Ears present
43. Ears in correct position and proportion
44. Eyebrows or lashes
45. Pupil of eye
46. Eye length greater than height
47. Eye glance directed to front in profile

48. Both chin and forehead shown
49. Projection of chin shown
50. Profile with not more than one error
51. Correct profile.

It is said that the score tends to be unduly low in children who suffered hypoxia in utero and to be unduly high in children with schizophrenia.

Gesell 'incomplete man' test

3 years	One or two parts
4 years	Three parts
4½ years	Six parts
5 years	Six or seven parts
6 years	Eight parts

Simple formboard

15 months	Inserts round block without being shown
18 months	Piles three blocks, one on top of another
2 years	Places all three. Adapts after four errors
2½ years	Inserts all three, adapting after errors
3 years	Adapts, no error, or immediate correction

Goddard formboard. (Best of three trials)

3½ years	56 seconds
4 years	46 seconds
4½ years	40 seconds
5 years	35 seconds
6 years	27 seconds
7 years	23 seconds
8 years	20 seconds

Coloured geometric forms

2½ years	Places one
3 years	Places three
4 years	Places all

Uncoloured geometric forms

3 years	Places four
4½ years	Places six
4 years	Places eight
4½ years	Places nine
5 years	Places all

Digits

2½ years	Repeats two, one of three trials

3 years	Repeats three, one of three trials
3½ years	Repeats three, two of three trials
4 years	Repeats three, three of three trials
4½ years	Repeats four, one of three trials
5 years	Repeats four, two of three trials
6 years	Repeats five
7 years	Repeats three backwards: ('Say these figures backwards')
8 years	Repeats six digits, one of three trials

Simple orders. (Put the ball under the chair, at the side of the chair, behind the chair, on the chair.)

3 years	Obeys two
3½ years	Obeys three
4 years	Obeys four

Book

15 months	Interested
18 months	Turns pages two or three at a time
	Points to picture of cat or dog
2 years	Turns pages singly

The Oseretsky tests

I have no personal experience of the Oseretsky tests of motor function, but thought that a brief note might be useful for research purposes. They were devised in Russia in 1923, and provided the only standardised motor proficiency tests to include coordination, motor speed, voluntary and involuntary movements. The tests take over an hour per child, but an abbreviated practical modification was devised in Northern Ireland.[14] The tests can be applied after the age of about 4; they include instructions to the child to remain standing with the eyes closed for 15 seconds, touching the nose alternately with the right and left index finger with the eyes closed, hopping with feet together seven or eight times in 5 seconds, putting 20 coins in a box within 15 seconds; describing circles in the air with the right and left index finger with the arms extended for 10 seconds, and clasping the examiner's hand with each hand separately, then together.

The developmental assessment of handicapped children

The assessment of the developmental potential of handicapped children can be a matter of great difficulty, but it is also a matter of great importance because of the necessity of selecting the right form of education for them. A comprehensive account of the method of testing children with cerebral palsy was given by Hauessermann.[9] The book by Edith Taylor[25] provides further valuable information. Parmelee *et al.*[15] found that Gesell tests were suitable for testing blind infants. Reynell[18], Reynell and Zinkin[19] and Sheridan[23] have described a satisfactory procedure for the developmental assessment of young children with a severe visual handicap.

Tests have to be modified for children with mechanical and other handicaps, and any departure from the exact method described by the authors of the tests must inevitably to some extent invalidate the results. This problem is covered in Hauessermann's book. That it was possible to form a reasonably reliable assessment of developmental potential in infants with cerebral palsy was shown by a study in Sheffield, to which reference has already been made (Ch. 1). In that study we followed children with cerebral palsy who had been thought to be mentally retarded in infancy, and assessed the IQ at 5 years or later. Of 35 children in whom mental retardation was diagnosed in the first 6 months of life, 20 survived, and 19 proved to be mentally retarded later. Of 40 considered to be mentally retarded when seen at 6 to 12 months of age, 29 survived, and 26 were found on follow-up examination to be retarded; and of 59 considered to be retarded when seen between 12 and 24 months, 52 survived, and the diagnosis of retardation was confirmed in 51.

Allowance must be made for the particular difficulty which the handicapped child has to face. Tests depending on vision, for instance, cannot be used for the blind child, and tests depending on hearing or speech cannot be used for the deaf child. Tests of manipulative development cannot be used for the child with severe spastic quadriplegia. In this case, however, one presents the test toy and observes the child's interest and desire to get hold of it. For instance, a 9-month-old athetoid or spastic child with good intelligence will try really hard for a prolonged period to get hold of a brick or bell, and although he may fail to grasp it, he can be given a rough score for his determination to try to get it. In contrast a mentally subnormal child with cerebral palsy would show little or no interest in the object. One has to confine one's tests to those which are applicable to the child in question.

When examining children with cerebral palsy it is particularly important to remember the sensory and perceptual difficulties which some of these children experience. It should also be remembered that late maturation is more common in these children than in those with uncomplicated mental retardation, so that they may fare better in the future than one would dare to expect when examining them in infancy. The difficulty of prediction, especially in the case of athetoid children, is considerable, but our findings have shown that only occasional mistakes will be made, and one must be constantly aware that these mistakes *may* be made.

Developmental assessment must include the full physical and developmental examination, including the head measurement in relation to the weight, and the testing of vision and hearing.

One must be satisfied that the child's performance in developmental tests is the optimum which he can achieve.

Normal physical variants such as a widely open fontanelle, late teething, epicanthus, or a single palmar crease, should not lead to a diagnosis of mental subnormality.

It is essential to note not just *whether* a child achieves a certain skill, but *how* he does it, and with what degree of maturity.

One must note the quality of vocalisation, the unscorable items such as responsiveness, alertness and other insurance factors.

Of great importance is the observation of the persistence of hand regard, casting, mouthing, and slobbering after the normal age at which these should have ceased.

REFERENCES

1. Bax, M., Hart, H., Jenkins, S. Clinical testing of visual function of the young child. Dev. Med. Child Neurol. 1981.23.92.
2. Beagley, H. A. Audiology and audiological medicine. Oxford. Oxford University. Press. 1981.
3. Coplan, J., Gleason, J. R., Ryan, R., Burke, M. G., Williams, M. L. Validation of an early language milestone scale in a high risk population. Pediatrics. 1982.70.677.
4. Fisch, L. (Ed.) Research in deafness in children. London. Blackwell. 1964.
5. Galambos, R., Despland, P. The auditory brain stem response evaluates risk factors for hearing loss in the newborn. Pediatr. Res. 1980.14.159.
6. Gallacher, J. R., Gallacher, C. D. Colour vision screening of preschool and first grade children. Arch. Ophthalmol. 1964.72.200.
7. Gardiner, P. A colour vision test for young children and the handicapped. Dev. Med. Child Neurol. 1973.15.437.
8. Gesell, A., Amatruda, C. S. In: Knobloch, H., Pasamanick, B. (Eds) Developmental diagnosis. New York. Hoeber. 1974.
9. Hauesserman, E. Developmental potential of preschool children. London. Grune and Stratton. 1958.
10. Illingworth, R. S. Common symptoms of disease in children. 9th Edn. Oxford. Blackwell Scientific Publications. 1987.
11. Ingram, T. T. S., Anthony, N., Bogle, D., McIsaac, M. W. Edinburgh articulation test. Edinburgh. Churchill Livingstone. 1971.
12. Knobloch, H., Stevens, F., Malone, A. Manual of child development. Hagerstown. Harper and Row. 1980.
13. Lenneberg, E. H., Rebelsky, F. G., Nichols, I. A. The vocalisations of infants born deaf. Human Dev. 1965.8.23.
14. McMahon, N. Oseretsky tests of motor proficiency. M. Phil. Thesis. University of Coleraine, Ulster. 1978.
15. Parmelee, A. H., Fiske, C. E., Wright, R. H. The development of ten children with blindness as a result of retrolental fibroplasia. Am. J. Dis. Child. 1959.98.198.
16. Peiper, A. Cerebral function in infancy and childhood. London. Pitman. 1963.
17. Phillips, C. J., Smith, B., Broadhurst, A. The draw-a-man test: a study in scoring methods, validity and norms with English children at 5 and 11 years. Clinics in Developmental Medicine. No. 46.1973.
18. Reynell, J. Developmental Language Scales. Slough: National Foundation for Educational Research. 1969.
19. Reynell, J., Zinkin, P. New procedures for the developmental assessment of young children with severe visual handicaps. Child. 1975.1.61.
20. Sheridan, M. D. Simple clinical hearing tests for very young or mentally retarded children. Br. Med. J. 1958.2.999.
21. Sheridan, M. D. Vision screening of very young or handicapped children. Br. Med. J. 1960.2.453.

22. Sheridan, M. D. The development of vision, hearing and communication in babies and young children. Proc. Roy. Soc. Med. 1969.62.999.
23. Sheridan, M. The Stycar Panda test for children with severe visual handicap. Dev. Med. Child Neurol. 1973.15.738.
24. Silva, P. A. The prevalence, stability and significance of developmental language delay in preschool children. Dev. Med. Child Neurol. 1980.22.768.
25. Taylor, E. M. Psychological appraisal of children with cerebral defects. Cambridge Mass. Harvard University Press. 1959.

13

Interpretation

General remarks

One's assessment of a child will depend in large part on the accuracy of the history, and on one's interpretation of the physical and developmental findings on examination.

One must know the reasons for variations in development. For instance, in assessing the 6 week old infant in the prone position, one must know that infants when asleep revert to the fetal position and so are likely to lie with the pelvis high and the knees drawn up under the abdomen, like a newborn baby.

It is useful in an assessment of a baby whose development is doubtful to make a rough score in one's mind for various fields of development. For instance, if one sees a baby transfer an object from one hand to another, one may say 'his manipulative development cannot be worse than the 6 months' level'; if one sees a baby go for an object with the index finger, one can say that he must be at least at the 10 month level; if a child is talking in sentences by 21–24 months, his overall level of intelligence must be normal. Often when assessing a baby I ask myself 'Is there any aspect of development in which he is better than, say, the 13 month level?'

It is often useful, having formed one's conclusion, to ask the parents what level they think he has reached in comparison with an average child: in my experience the parents are nearly always remarkably accurate in their assessment.

RELATIVE IMPORTANCE OF DIFFERENT FIELDS OF DEVELOPMENT

Some fields of development are more important for assessment purposes than other fields. Below is a summary of my opinions on this.

Gross motor development

It is unfortunate that the aspect of development which is the most easily scored is the least valuable for the overall assessment of a child's development and capability. It would be wrong to suggest that gross motor development is useless as part of the developmental examination. It is of great value, but its limitations have to be recognised. Defective motor development, as determined by head control in ventral suspension and the prone position, is commonly the first sign of abnormality in a child who is mentally subnormal from birth or before birth. The majority of mentally subnormal children are late in learning to sit and walk, but the exceptions are so frequent that the age of sitting and walking is of only limited value in assessing intelligence. A mentally subnormal child may learn to walk at the average age, but his aimless overactivity, apart from other features, should enable one to avoid a mistake in the assessment.

In Table 8 I have analysed the age at which mentally retarded children, seen by me at the Children's Hospital, Sheffield, learnt to sit for a few seconds without support. None had cerebral palsy or other mechanical disability. None had a degenerative disease, so that there was no deterioration. Children with Down's syndrome are kept separate from the others. The gradings 'educationally subnormal' (severe) and 'educationally subnormal' (moderate) were based on IQ tests at school age.

It will be seen that the age at which unsupported sitting began was average (6 to 7 months) in 8.3% of the seriously subnormal children, in 6.7% of Down's syndrome, and in 10.7% of those who were moderately

Table 8   Age of sitting unsupported

Age (months)	Educationally subnormal (S) Total 48 Percentage	Educationally subnormal (M) Total 28 Percentage	Down's syndrome Total 45 Percentage
6 to 7	8.3	10.7	6.7
8 to 9	14.5	39.3	31.1
10 to 11	2.1	7.2	26.6
12 to 17	35.4	39.3	22.0
18 to 23	15.0	3.6	
24+	22.9	0	13.4

Age of walking unsupported

Age (months)	Educationally subnormal (S) Total 59 Percentage	Educationally subnormal (M) Total 42 Percentage	Down's syndrome Total 37 Percentage
Under 12 months	0	4.7	0
12 to 14	5.1	9.5	0
15 to 17	10.1	14.3	0
18 to 23	18.6	19.0	24.3
24 to 35	37.2	40.5	51.4
36 to 47	13.5	4.7	10.7
48 to 59	10.1	2.4	
60+	5.1	4.7	13.5

subnormal. On the other hand the skill was not acquired until after the first birthday in 73.3% of the seriously subnormal children other than those with Down's syndrome, in 35.4% of those with Down's syndrome, and 42.9% of the moderately subnormal children. The age of walking without support was average (12 to 17 months) in 15.2% of the seriously subnormal children other than those with Down's syndrome, and in 29.5% of the moderately subnormal ones. No child with Down's syndrome walked as soon as this. On the other hand the skill was not acquired until the second birthday or after in 65.9% of the seriously subnormal children, 75.6% of those with Down's syndrome and 52.3% of the moderately subnormal ones.

There are great variations in the age of sitting and walking in normal children, some learning to walk without support by the age of 8 months, and some not until the age of 2 or 3 year or even later. Early locomotion does not indicate a high level of intelligence.

The main clinical importance of delayed locomotion lies in the fact that it should make one careful to look for signs of cerebral palsy, hypotonia, or muscular dystrophy, though delayed locomotion may occur without discoverable cause. The main importance of unusually early locomotion is that it almost excludes significant mental subnormality or cerebral palsy.

Fine motor development (manipulation)

The development of manipulation is a better guide to the level of intelligence than is gross motor development. I have not seen delay in manipulative development in normal children. If I saw a baby reach out and get an object at 5 months without it being put into the hand, or if I saw a baby of 6 months rapidly transfer an object from one hand to another, or if I saw a 9-or 10-month-old baby promptly go for objects with the index finger, and pick up a pellet between the tip of the forefinger and the tip of the thumb — in any of these three circumstances I would say that that baby was mentally normal. I have never yet seen an exception to this at those age periods. I have never seen a mentally subnormal baby with normal manipulation for his age. Advanced manipulative development would suggest to me a high level of intelligence — though admittedly some have special aptitudes and are unusually good with their hands without being particularly intelligent.

As for the child after infancy, if I had to choose a single set of equipment with which to assess a small child's intelligence, I would want a set of ten 1-inch cubes. I have never seen a mentally subnormal child perform the various tests with cubes, building a tower, making a train, bridge, gate or steps at the 'normal' ages which I have listed. As I was writing this section, I was asked to see a 24-month child with late speech: when I saw him build a tower of eight cubes, concentrating well, I knew that his speech delay was not due to mental subnormality. Dubowitz and her colleagues[3] recently showed that these various tests with cubes correlated well with more detailed psychometric tests. Obviously the above does not apply if there is a physical disability, such as cerebral palsy.

Speech

The words speech and language are often used as synonyms, whereas they should be distinguished from each other. By speech one denotes the use of words, but by language one means the expression of thought in words. The assessment of language from the developmental point of view is difficult, but the use of 'speech' as an indication of developmental level is relatively easy, the two chief milestones being the age at which words are first used with meaning, and the age at which words are first joined together spontaneously.

It is the experience of many workers that the early development of speech is a most important sign of a good level of intelligence. Terman wrote that 'Earliness of onset of speech is one of the most striking developmental characteristics of intellectually gifted children'. Ausubel wrote that 'intelligence is perhaps the most important determinant of precocity in speech, since it affects both the ability to mimic and to understand the meaning of verbal symbols'. In one study[1] it was found that 'language presents the highest infant predictive correlation of all child behaviour to later intelligence'. Catalano and McCarthy[2] described work by Fisichelli, who made a phonemic analysis of tape recordings of the vocalisations of 23 infants in an institution at the mean age of 13.3 months. They followed these children up and conducted Stanford-Binet tests on them at the mean age of 44.8 months. There was a strongly positive correlation between the infant sounds and the subsequent Standford-Binet tests, especially with regard to consonant types, the frequency of consonant sounds, the number of different kinds of consonant sounds, and the consonant–vowel frequency and type ratio.

In my opinion the greatest importance should be attached to speech development as an index of intelligence; but the development of speech may be delayed in children of average or superior intelligence, so that it follows that delayed speech in itself can never be used as an indication of mental subnormality. Advanced speech, however, is in my experience always an indication of superior intelligence. I should be most surprised if I heard a child speaking well in sentences at 15 months and subsequently found that his IQ was 100 (unless there was subsequent emotional deprivation or other retarding factor).

The understanding of words far outstrips the ability to articulate them. I should be just as impressed with a child who was able to point to a large number of objects in a picture book as an indication that he understood the meaning of words.

Just as advanced speech can be regarded as a sign of superior intelligence, average speech can be regarded as a sign of at least average intelligence, though a child of 12 to 24 months with average speech may also prove to be of superior intelligence. This is important, because one sees children with delayed motor development, with or without some mechanical disability, in whom an assessment of intelligence is required. The presence of average speech immediately tells one that his intelligence is normal, even though he is also retarded another field in such as sphincter control.

Speech is important in the assessment of retarded children, and especially those with a physical handicap such as cerebral palsy. If, for instance, a child were severely retarded in all fields but speech, in which retardation was only slight, I should give a good prognosis with regard to his intelligence, because I would think that his IQ would be only slightly below the average. I have only once seen a possible exception to this.

At with all other fields of development, one must understand the normal variations and the reasons for those variations. For example, lateness in speech is *not* due to laziness, 'everything being done for him', or jealousy (Ch. 7).

Smiling and social behaviour

The age at which a baby begins to smile is of considerable importance in the assessment of a child. The mentally subnormal child almost invariably begins to smile long after the age of 4 to 6 weeks, the average age. The mean age of smiling in a consecutive series of 62 children with Down's syndrome seen by me was 4.1 months. It is vital to make due allowance for prematurity in these early milestones. I do not know whether unusually early smiling presages superior intelligence, or whether it is affected by the child's personality. I suspect that it usually presages superior intelligence.

There is some disagreement as to what the baby's early smiles signify. Bowlby regarded the smile as a 'built-in species specific pattern' — a view with which I agree. Bowlby implied that the smile is not merely a learned conditioned response, as has been suggested by some. It has been shown that the essential stimulus for the early smile is the face.

Whatever the psychological explanation of the smile, the age at which the baby begins to smile at his mother in response to her overtures is an important and valuable milestone of development, in that this is bound up with the child's maturity and therefore with his mental development. Smiling is in some way dependent on maturation, though environment must play a part. If I saw a baby smiling at his mother in response to social overtures at 4 or 5 weeks, and better still, vocalising as well as smiling, I would know that the child was mentally normal.

It is important to note the age at which babies begin to laugh, to play games, to imitate, to draw the attention of their parents (e.g. by a cough), and their general social responsiveness.

Sphincter control

This is of relatively little value for the assessment of a child. Mentally subnormal children are usually late in acquiring control of the bladder, but not always, while many children of superior intelligence are late in it. Apart from constitutional and anatomical factors, the parental management has considerable bearing on the age at which control is learnt, and this is irrelevant in the assessment of a child's intelligence.

Chewing

I find that the age at which a child begins to chew is of considerable value is assessing a child. Mentally subnormal children are always late in learning to chew. It is my impression that babies who begin to chew unusually early (the earliest being about 4 months), are bright children, but I have no figures to support this.

It has already been said that an extraneous factor has to be considered (and eliminated by the history) and that is failure of the parents to give the child solid foods to chew. This would delay the development of chewing — or at least the age at which it is observed.

Other features

If I saw a child turn his head promptly to sound at 3 or 4 months, I would think that it would be exceedingly unlikely that he would be mentally subnormal; but I would view with concern the persistence of hand regard, casting and mouthing at an age when they should have stopped.

The relationship of one field of development to another: dissociation

In assesssing the value of the history for diagnosis and prediction, it is important to balance one field of development against another. The development in one field normally approximates fairly closely to the development in another. For instance, most children at the age of 6 to 7 months are nearly able to sit on the floor without support: they are able to grasp objects easily and they have recently learnt to transfer them from hand to hand: they have recently learnt to chew: they have just begun to imitate: they are making certain characterisitc sounds when vocalising. In assessing a child one automatically assesses his development in each field. Gesell remarked that the developmental quotient can be specifically ascertained for each separate field of behaviour and for individual behaviour traits.

The development in one field is sometimes out of step with that in other fields. It has been explained that there are great individual variations in various fields of development, children learning some skills sooner or later than others, though they are average in other fields. For instance, some children are late in single fields, such as speech or walking, and yet are average in other aspects of development. I have termed this 'Dissociation'.[9] It is important for enabling one to determine the likelihood that the mother's story is correct, and it draws one's attention to variations in development, such as lateness in one field, which required investigation. The following case history may be cited as an example:

Case report.   This girl, born at term, reached important stages of development at the times below:

6 weeks	Smile.
5 months	Grasp objects voluntarily.
6 months	Chew.
1 years	Casting. Saying three words. Good concentration and interest. Very defective weight bearing, equivalent to that of average 3-month-old baby. Knee jerks normal. Marked general hypotonia with normal intelligence.
Diagnosis	Benign congenital hypotonia.

She walked without help at 5 years. Her IQ was 100.

Whenever one finds that a child is notably retarded in one field as compared with his development in others, a search should be made for the cause. Often no cause will be found, but the cause will be found in others. Below is an example of dissociation.

Case record.   Diplegia in an infant with minimal neurological signs.

This boy was referred to me at the age of $5\frac{1}{2}$ months for assessment of suitability for adoption. He had been a full-term baby. He began to smile at 7 weeks and to vocalise 2 weeks later. It was uncertain when he had begun to grasp objects. He had not begun to chew. It was said that he was very interested when his feed was being prepared.

On examination he did not grasp an object. The head control was not full, being that of a 4-month-old baby. He bore very little weight on his legs — being no better than an average 2-months-old baby, though it was said that he had been given a chance to do so. I thought that the knee jerks were normal. The baby seemed alert. I advised the foster parents to let me see the boy in 3 months, and not to clinch the adoption until I had done so.

I saw him at $9\frac{1}{2}$ months. He had begun to chew and to sit without support at 6 months. At that age he had begun to cough to attract attention, and to shake his head when his mother said 'No'. He could not nearly grasp the pellet between finger and thumb, but his grasp of a cube (with each hand) was average for the age. He was alert, vocalising well and sitting securely. He had begun to play patacake. Yet his weight bearing was seriously defective. I now realised that both knee jerks were definitely exaggerated and there was bilateral ankle clonus. The knee jerk was more brisk on the left than on the right. When I discussed this with the foster parents they remarked that he had always kicked more with the right leg than the left. The diagnosis was spastic diplegia, with a normal level of intelligence. The full implications were explained to the parents, who unhesitatingly decided to adopt him in spite of his physical handicap.

This case was interesting because of the minimal signs of spastic diplegia, discovered on routine developmental examination. There were no suggestive symptoms and the only developmental sign pointing to the diagnosis was defective weight bearing. It may be that the inability to grasp the pellet was the only sign of minimal involvement of the upper limbs, for judging from his developmental level in other fields he should have acquired finger–thumb apposition.

Below is another case report which illustrates the importance of balancing one field of development against another.

Case report. Mental subnormality with anomalous features.

This girl was referred to me at the age of 14 months because the parents were unable to accept the gloomy prognosis given to them by a paediatrician in another city.

She was born a month after term by Caesarean section as a result of signs of fetal distress. The birth weight was 4340 g. Pregnancy had been normal throughout. There were no other children. She was asphyxiated at birth and had several convulsions in the first 3 weeks. She was kept in an oxygen tent for 5 days. The condition in the newborn period was such that the parents were given a bad prognosis with regard to her future development.

The subsequent history was somewhat confusing. She had never picked any object up. Both parents were uncertain whether she could see. She had been examined on that account by an ophthalmologist when she was under an anaesthetic, and no abnormality was found in the eyes. She was said to turn her head to sound at 3 months. She had begun to smile at 4 or 5 months, and to vocalise at 6 or 7 months. She was said to laugh heartily now. At 6 months she had begun to hold a rattle in her hand. She had begun to imitate sounds (a laugh, a song) at 8 months and to imitate the rhythm of songs. She had said 'dadada' from 8 months. She had just begun to play with her hands, watching them in front of her face (hand regard). She had begun to chew at 11 to 12 months, and at that age would eat a biscuit.

On examination she was a microcephalic girl with a head circumference of 42.8 cm, which was very small when her weight at birth was considered. The fontanelle was closed. She was obese, weighing 14.5 kg and tall for her age. She showed no interest in test toys, but was seen to smile at her mother when she talked to her. She was heard to make vocalisations (complex sounds with 'ch' and 'dada') such as one would expect to hear at 10 months. The grasp of a cube placed in the hands was immature. Her head control was that of a 3-month-old baby. In the prone position her face was held at an angle of 45 degrees to the couch. There was head lag when she was pulled to the sitting position, with considerable head wobble when she was swayed from side to side. There were asymmetrical creases in the thighs. She played for a prolonged period with a rattle placed in the hand, but would not go for an object. She bore virtually no weight on her legs. It was difficult to assess muscle tone owing to the obesity, but the impression was one of hypotonia rather than hypertonia; and abduction of the hips was greater than usual. The knee jerks were normal, but there was bilateral unsustained ankle clonus. The optic fundi were normal. The x-ray of the hips was normal, and the x-ray of the skull showed normal sutures. The urine did not contain phenylpyruvic acid.

There were difficulties about giving a confident prognosis here, and these difficulties were explained to the parents, who were intelligent. The developmental history and examination indicated dissociation. She was severely retarded in manipulation and motor development, and there was no evidence that she could see — though is is difficult to be sure whether a severely retarded baby can see or not until he is old enough. On the other hand, in chewing, imitation, and vocalisation she was only moderately retarded and her IQ in these respects would indicate that she should fall into the educable range later. This strongly suggested a mechanical disability, and the unsustained ankle clonus suggested that she might prove to have the spastic form of cerebral palsy. Subsequent athetosis, however, could not be excluded. The relatively good development in speech and imitation suggested that the IQ would not be as bad as it appeared on the surface.

The second difficulty was the question of blindness. I was unable to say whether the child could see or not. Blindness would explain some of the features of the history and examination, and in particular the complete lack of interest in surroundings was out of keeping with the fact that the girl turned her head to sound from about 3 months.

The third difficulty was the history of convulsions. There was a considerable possibility that convulsions would occur later, possibly with mental deterioration.

I gave my opinion that the prognosis was bad, and that she would probably prove to be seriously subnormal, but said that in view of the difficulties mentioned above she might prove better than expected — though possibly with the complication of cerebral palsy and perhaps with blindness. I arranged to see her in a year. She was then backward, but not seriously so.

The significance of the development of speech in relation to other fields has been mentioned. In general the finding that speech development is relatively more advanced than motor development would make one look particularly carefully for a mechanical disability, such as hypertonia or hypotonia, though the occasional late walker has also been discussed. Assessment can be particularly difficult when a child is retarded in more than one field of development.

Case report. Boy aged 36 months: opinion asked because he was not talking: he said mum only. Hearing was normal. His father had died in the boy's infancy, and there was no available history of the age at which his father began to talk. The boy had not begun to walk alone until 18 months — but his mother had begun to walk at the same age. He had no control of the bladder, but the bladder was distended and there was dribbling incontinence — ascribed to urethral obstruction. The boy was therefore retarded in speech, motor development and sphincter control.

With the ten 1-inch cubes he rapidly made a neat tower, a train with chimney and a bridge; with the simple formboard he made no error on 'adapting': he immediately identified all ten pictures on the card. He neatly copied the O and +. He was alert, responsive and cooperative. His overall developmental quotient was 100 to 115.

This child was retarded in three major aspects of development, and yet had an above average developmental quotient. This was confirmed on follow-up.

Below in an example of the difficulty of assessing a child when there is much scatter in various aspects of development. I saw the girl for the first time at the age of 3 years and 5 months. The following are extracts from the letter which I wrote to the family doctor.

'There are several difficulties about giving a confident prognosis here. One is that there is a family history of late walking in both mother and father, and it would not be surprising if the children were to take after them.

There was delayed motor development. She began to sit without help at 14 months and walk without help at 22 months. I have seen quite a few normal children who were unable to walk until after the second birthday. On the other hand her speech was good. She was saying single words under a year, and sentences at 18 months. I have never met a mentally subnormal child who could do that. Furthermore sphincter control began at 12 months. She has, however, been late in learning to manage a cup, and she has only just begun to do so, and she is not very good at dressing herself, but I am not sure whether the parents have given her a chance to learn these things. This is a difficult age at which to carry out developmental testing, but I have come to the conclusion that in one or two tests she was average, but in others she was retarded. There is, therefore, considerable scatter in her performance which makes a confident opinion about the future impossible. She looks normal. She concentrated well on a doll's house when I was talking to the mother. Her head is of normal size. Her gait is normal. I explained that when a child has learned to walk as late as this, you must expect her to be unsteady in walking for quite a long time afterwards.

On the whole I think that Mary will prove to be normal, and not below the average, but one cannot be sure at this stage. I shall be seeing her again in about a year in order to re-assess progress.'

I followed her progress with interest. By the age of 4 years she was reading well, and at 5 years she was assessed as having a reading age of $9\frac{1}{2}$ years. Her manipulative, creative and physical ability were described by her teacher as excellent.

Risk factors

The term 'children at risk' is applied to children who for various reasons, prenatal or postnatal, are more likely than others to have certain handicaps, emotional, sensory or physical. For instance, a girl born with bilateral congenital talipes has an approximately 40 per cent risk of having a dislocated hip. A child with a cleft palate has a considerable likelihood of later developing deafness. In developmental assessment one notes risk factors, but one must not exaggerate their importance. For instance, when assessing a child's suitability for adoption, the fact that one of the real parents was mentally subnormal is a risk factor, but it is only one factor amongst many which one has to consider in the overall assessment. In my follow-up study of babies whom I had assessed for adoption, there were 22 which I passed as normal in spite of the fact that they all had a certified mentally subnormal parent: at the age of 7 to 8 years, the mean IQ of these 22 was 100.1 (less, however, than the mean IQ of the whole series of adopted babies).

A developmental diagnosis — or a diagnosis of cerebral palsy or of mental subnormality — must be made on a combination of factors, and never on one physical sign. If one is assessing a baby at the age of 6 months, and in all respects his development is average, one would ignore the fact that the real mother had been mentally subnormal — unless she had phenyl-ketonuria, a hereditary degenerative disease of the nervous system. But if there were some doubt some feature of the development, such as poor interest in surroundings, doubtful manipulative development, a congenital anomaly of the eye, or a head circumference which was small in relation to weight, then the risk factor of maternal mental subnormality is an additional factor which increases one's doubt about the child being normal. I have often heard of babies being rejected for adoption merely because the mother or father was mentally subnormal. This is a tragic error.

Cultural and other environmental factors: physical handicaps

No one has yet devised intelligence tests which are suitable for all cultures. Certain cultural factors have a considerable relevance to developmental assessment. For instance, in various African countries the effect of cultural practices on gross motor development was discussed in Chapter 7, as was the possible effect of prone sleeping on prone development. If a child has never been given the chance of holding a pencil and drawing on paper, a Goodenough Draw-a-Man Test would hardly be relevant. Visuospatial deficiencies amongst Bantus, as a result, probably, of early deprivation of the relevant sensory experience, was described in Chapter 3. In Israel, children brought up in a Kibbutz have a higher mean IQ score than Middle Eastern Jewish children brought up at home. When the Denver developmental screening test was used in South East Asia,[12] it was found that children from Laos, Vietnam and Cambodia failed certain tests, presumably because of cultural factors, and therefore could be thought to have delayed development.

When a child has suffered emotional deprivation, or has been deliberately kept off his feet because his mother feared that weight-bearing would cause rickets or bow legs, or when he has paralysed legs as a result of a meningomyelocele, or cannot speak because he is deaf, or cannot control his bladder because he has a structural abnormality or because he has a mother who has the wrong idea of 'training' him, it seems to me to be absurd to give him a lower score on objective developmental tests — as psychologists do. Ruth Griffiths, for instance, in her tests ignored these factors — and such a highly relevant factor as prematurity — in her assessment of babies.

In some cases the difficulties of assessment are such that it is impossible to forecast the child's future without further observation. When a child who has suffered a severely adverse environment, such as prolonged institutional care, or has had a serious disease, is found to be uniformly retarded, it is impossible to predict his future development. A period of observation after correction of those adverse factors is essential before a sensible opinion can be expressed. If a child has been brought up in an institution, and is found to be below average in development, one should not return him to the institution and then see him again in order to reassess him; he would be likely then to be still more retarded: one should try to get him into a good home, where he will be loved and stimulated, and then see him again in order to determine what improvement has occured.

One must avoid the mistake of diagnosing mental subnormality when his backwardness in due to emotional deprivation. I was asked to assess the development of an ill 6-month-old baby with coeliac disease. I refused. I was asked to assess a 6-year-old with severe renal failure which was first diagnosed in the newborn period: partly because of prolonged hospital management he was rejected by his parents who did not want to take him home. He was unable to walk, partly because of his severe renal rickets. I refused to attempt to assess his intelligence.

I was asked to assess the mental development of a 21-month-old child with nephrogenic diabetes insipidus. He had not thrived, weighing only 15 lb (6.8 kg) at the time. He had had repeated admissions to hospital. His general level of development was that of a 12-months-old baby with little scatter in different fields, though he showed good interest in his surroundings and in toys — an important observation suggesting that he might prove to have a normal level of intelligence. It was impossible to assess this child's developmental potential without serial observations of his rate of development. He has been followed up since then. At the age of 6 years 4 months he is progressing normally in an ordinary school. Physically he is small, weighing 27 lb 6 oz (12.4 kg) and measuring 39¾ inches (100 cm).

The experienced paediatrician will resist the temptation to attempt to give an accurate figure for the child's developmental quotient. He is merely deceiving himself if he thinks that he can distinguish a developmental quotient of 70 from one of 71. He can and should be able to place the child into an approximate position in the developmental range. Any attempt to be more accurate will only lead to inaccuracy.

The range of normality: centile distribution

It would be convenient if one could give the range of normality in development, but it is impossible, for one can never draw the line between normal and abnormal. All children are different. The truly average child, who is exactly average in all fields of development, is rare indeed. Hence it is wrong to say that a child *should* pass a milestone at a specified age.

Some have calculated the centile distribution of various milestones.[13] The Denver Scale[5] gives the 25th, 50th, 75th and 90th centile for 105 developmental items, including gross motor, language, fine motor, adaptive, and personal social features: it was standardised on 1036 presumed normal children aged 2 weeks to 6 years. These milestones are shown in graphic form and the writers claim 'it vividly shows on the chart the normal variation. It enables the examiner to determine whether he [the child] is in the normal range'. In fact it is absolutely wrong to suggest that these centiles indicate whether a child is normal or not: I have seen scores of children who were normal, though in certain of those milestones they would fall outside the 'normal' range (see Chapters 6 and 7).

The Newcastle study[13] gave the 3rd, 10th, 25th, 50th, 75th, 90th and 97th centile for four milestones: sitting unsupported, walking, saying single words and making sentences. The figures were as follows:

Milestones	Number	3	10	25	Centiles 50	75	90	97
Sits unsupported	3831	4.6	5.2	5.8	6.4	7.2	8.1	9.3
Walks	3554	9.7	10.7	11.8	12.8	14.2	15.8	18.4
Single words		8.7						
Boys	1824		10.0	11.6	12.4	15.0	18.0	21.9
Girls	1747	8.6	9.8	11.5	12.3	14.6	17.3	20.1
Sentences								
Boys	1653	17.5	19.1	21.4	23.8	26.8	32.5	36.0
Girls	1575	16.2	18.4	20.4	22.9	25.0	30.8	36.0

The Newcastle study gave the age of 18.4 months for the 97th centile for walking without help; the Denver scale gave the age of 14.3 months for the 90th centile for the same skill. But I have seen dozens of normal children who were unable to walk without help until after 14.3 months, and a considerable number who could not walk without help until 18.4 months or later. The number of proved followed-up normal children who were unable to walk without support until after 2.0 years, seen by me personally, is now well over 20.

It is true that the further away from the average a child is in anything (haemoglobin, blood urea, age of walking etc.), the more likely he is to be abnormal: but it is totally wrong to say that figures on a chart showing the centile distribution of developmental milestones will show whether a child's performance is normal or abnormal.

It is important to distinguish studies, such as the Newcastle one in which the centiles are based on the age at which children first reached certain milestones, i.e. walking, from studies such as the Denver one, which are based on the ability of the child to pass certain tests at given ages — a very different matter: for in the latter case a child who passes a test might have been able to pass it a long time previously. It is in fact very difficult in the case of most milestones to say precisely when a certain milestone is reached. For instance, it is difficult to say accurately when a child first smiles at his mother in response to her overtures, first chews, or first says single words. As I explained elsewhere, a child trying to say the word dog is likely to say 'g' and later 'og' when he sees a picture of a dog, or hears a dog barking, or imitates a bark: it is difficult to decide at what age he should be regarded as first having said the word. Looking at the Denver figures one notes that some of the milestones would be very difficult to define accurately: e.g. sits, head steady (50th centile 2.9 months); bears some weight on legs (50th centile 4.6 months), walks well (12.1 months); stands holding on (4.8 months). A newborn baby bears some weight on the legs: and the degree of weight-bearing after the first few weeks is governed not only by the maturation of his nervous system, but by the opportunity given by his mother to bear weight. One also notes that the 50th centile given by the Denver workers is in some milestones considerably different from that of the New Haven children examined by Gesell. For instance, 'Rolls over' — Denver figure 2.8 months; turns to voice (5.6 months); the former is far earlier than the Gesell figures, and the latter much later; and the 50th centile given by the Denver study for sitting without support (5.5 months) is much earlier than that given by Gesell, and that given by the Newcastle team (6.4 months).

I am not in favour of making accurate analyses of inaccurate data. I have many times seen an IQ score given to one place of decimals, and occasionally to two places of decimals. Considering the inaccuracy of many of the data on which such a score is based, I do not favour this. In the years since the papers from Denver and Newcastle were published I have not felt the need to refer back to them except for the purpose of this book: I have certainly not needed them to help me in the assessment of some hundreds of babies. I have not yet been able to think of the circumstances in which I should want the information.

Importance of follow-up when in doubt

When there is the slightest doubt about one's assessment of a child, one must see him again. One must observe the *rate* of his development, in order to determine whether his development is steady, improving or slowing down. One may have to withhold judgment altogether until one has been able to re-examine the child at a suitable interval.

It is likely to be impossible to give a prognosis when there have been adverse environmental factors, such as child abuse: only follow-up examination will indicate whether the damage was reversible or not. The same applies to many other adverse postnatal factors, such as infections, especially meningitis or encephalitis, or the sudden development of fits.

Developmental diagnosis is fraught with difficulties, and he who is over-confident, makes 'spot diagnoses', and fails to follow up the children whom he has assessed, will inevitably make unnecessary mistakes. A careful follow-up system is essential for anyone hoping to become proficient in this field. Mistakes made must be examined in detail, the reasons for the mistakes being determined, so that they can be avoided in future.

If children are assessed for the purposes of adoption, they should be re-examined (preferably by a different person) when they are of school age, so that the accuracy and usefulness of one's asessments can be determined. If mental subnormality or cerebral palsy is diagnosed in infants, they should be followed up so that one's opinion can be confirmed or disproved. A punch card system, which enables one to determine in a moment the names of children who are due for follow-up examination, is invaluable. I found that repeated cinematographic records of infants with suspected abnormality is useful not only for self-instruction, but for the teaching of others. If one is to learn from mistakes, and become reasonably proficient in developmental assessment, a really adequate follow-up scheme is absolutely essential.

In some children, owing to the presence of confusing factors, prediction is impossible without further prolonged observation. The following is an example of a combination of difficulties of this nature.

Case report. Unusual skull, developmental retardation and difficulties in prediction.
I was asked to see this boy at 11 weeks because of suspected hydrocephalus. The circumference of the head at birth was 37.5 cm, his weight then being 3800 g. On examination at 11 weeks the circumference was 42.5 cm, but the fontanelle and sutures felt normal. There was a slight anti-mongoloid slant of the eyes, and there was a prominent forehead, but I thought that the head could be within normal limits. The head was unlike that of either parent. The boy was said to have begun to smile at 7 weeks and to vocalise at 8 weeks. The head control was that of a 6 weeks' old baby. There were no other abnormal physical signs.

He was seen at intervals. He was said to hold a rattle placed in the hands at 3 months. At 4 months the head control was that of a 3-month old baby.

At 1 year the head circumference was 49.5 cm. I thought that the clinical picture was that of megalencephaly. He showed hand regard. The head control was that of a 3½-month-old baby. He was unable to grasp objects, though he 'grasped with the eye'; he did not hold on to an object placed in the hand. I wrote that 'In no way can I see development beyond the 4 month level.' I thought that his development had slowed down.

At this stage a full investigation was carried out with a view to possible operation for hydrocephalus by insertion of a valve. Ventricular studies and an air encephalogram showed that there was no hydrocephalus, and the appearance was consistent with a diagnosis of megalencephaly. The EEG was normal. The interpupillary distance was large — 55 mm. While in hospital he was able to sit like a 7-month baby (at the age of 13 months), and he was seen to wave bye-bye. This had just begun. He bore virtually no weight on the legs. Voluntary grasping began at 14 months.

At 20 months the head measured 50.8 cm. I was immediately impressed by his incessant jargoning, and his responsiveness to his parents. He had begun to jargon at 18 months. He said eight or nine words clearly. He was unable to crawl or roll, but he could bear almost all his weight on his legs momentarily. He could not stand holding on to furniture. He was said to play only a short time with individual toys, usually merely throwing them to the ground. He would not grasp cubes or other test objects. His mother said that he would be unable to point out objects in pictures. He would not feed himself at all with a biscuit or spoon, and there was no sphincter control. He held his arms out for clothes from 18 months and played pat-a-cake at the same age. I thought that in view of the speech he had developed as far as a child of 14 or 18 months, though in all other respects he was much more retarded. I gave as my opinion that his IQ would be not less than 60 or 70, and that it might well turn out to be well up to the average.

The family developmental history was interesting. An older child had been a 'slow starter'. I had seen him at 2 years, when he had just begun to walk a few steps. He was then very advanced in speech, speaking in long mature sentences. In all respects he was a normal child of advanced intelligence. The parents thought that the youngest child (with the megalencephaly) had throughout compared well with his older sibling in speech and all other aspects of development.

I have described this case at some length to show the difficulties which are sometimes encountered. Firstly, he had a peculiar head. Secondly, his development appeared to slow down and he took less interest in his surroundings. Thirdly (at 20 months), his speech had made remarkable progress, and was far in advance of all other fields of development. (No physical disability, such as spasticity, had ever been found.) One rarely sees a child with uniform retardation except in speech, in which retardation was only slight. Fourthly, there was the family history of severe motor retardation in a sibling, who was now normal and of superior intelligence.

In such a case a prognosis must be guarded, and only prolonged observation could give one a clear picture of the developmental potential. The parents, who were highly intelligent, were given a full explanation of my difficulties in assessment, and I gave them hope that the child would be normal. I promised that he would not be severely subnormal (unless he developed some unforeseen complication like encephalitis).

One must always be prepared to withhold a prognosis altogether, sometimes even for 2 or 3 years in particularly difficult cases.

Long-term prediction

In developmental assessment we can say something about a child's talents and potential, but we cannot say what he will do with them. We cannot say how much he will succeed in life, nor can we define success. A person may be highly successful in his work, but not at all successful in domestic and other personal relationships, or with his upbringing of the children. A person may be clever, but not nice: and the nicer person may achieve more in life than the more clever person.

Personal factors

Personal factors which are relevant to his future include his level of intelligence, aptitudes, learning ability, personality and health, Liam Hudson[7] suggested that an IQ of above 115–125 has little bearing on later intellectual achievement — creativity being more important. Ogilvie,[14] referring to primary school children, pointed out that a gifted child may excel in any of numerous aspects of life — mathematics, music, art, drawing, wit, literature, drama, gymnastics, mechanical skills, finance, personality or leadership. Some children, like Sibelius, or Charles Darwin, only show their aptitudes in later years. Some are 'slow starters'. Gardner[6] referred to different types of intelligence — linguistic, musical, spatial, personal, kinaesthetic and logical.

Some children experience special learning problems — in reading, spelling, languages, spatial appreciation or mathematics — and may as a result be thought to be generally backward and to have poor prospects. We discussed those in our book about the childhood of famous men and women.[10]

Many features of the personality have a vital bearing on future prospects. They include the ability to get on well with people, to concentrate, to profit from mistakes. willingness to work hard, powers of observation, thoroughness, creativity, an inquiring mind, determination and ambition. Some are kept back by laziness, daydreaming, slowness of thought, difficulty in expressing themselves or by overactivity and defective concentration, even though highly intelligent.

The choice of subject at school and choice of career are important factors for achievement.

Physical factors affecting a child's prospects include physical handicap, malnutrition and poor health.

Factors in the home, neighbourhood and influence of friends

In Chapter 3 I discussed the factors in the home which help a child to achieve his best. They included wise management, security, opportunities for the child to learn, interest in education, ambition and expectations. Good socioeconomic circumstances were by no means an essential.[11] Extreme poverty was experienced by many children destined for fame — for example Keir Hardie, Aneurin Bevan, Ernest Bevin, Michael Faraday, Henry Ford and George Stephenson.

Factors in the school

These include the quality of teaching, the motivation of pupils, the expectations for them, and the relationship between pupil and teacher. They include the teacher's ability to bring the best out of children, whatever the level of IQ, including th encouragement of pupils' special interests and aptitudes, and the recognition of ability. In our book about the childhood of famous men and women, we discussed numerous example of teachers' failure to recognise pupils' ability: a long list included Joshua Reynolds, Gaugin, Manet, Rossini, Delius, Edison, Einstein, John Hunter, Jean de la Fontaine, Hans Andersen, Emile Zola, G. K. Chesterton, Wordsworth, Sheridan, Byron, Leo Tolstoy, Rommel, Jung and Froebel. In many cases pupils were regarded merely as mediocre, when special aptitude and abilities should have led to different assessments: examples included Toulouse Lautrec, Auguste Rodin, Epstein, Cezanne, James Watt, Isaac Newton and Pasteur. In an interesting study Herbert Birch found that only 45% of children with an IQ of 136 or more were thought by the teachers to be gifted, whereas 31% of children were thought to be gifted and of high intelligence, when in fact tests showed that they were only average.

Mental superiority

The classic long-term follow-up of mentally superior children was that of Terman and Oden[15] in their unique study of 1528 Californian children with an IQ of 135 or more, who were followed up to an average age of 35. Compared with controls the children had tended to walk and talk earlier: they had a better physique and fewer illnesses: they had been less boastful and more honest, and they were more stable emotionally: and they tended to have earlier puberty. They had a wide range of interests and they showed curiosity, sustained attention and creative ability. Nearly half had learned to read before going to school. (The age of starting school is later in America than that in England.) Their greatest superiority was in reading, language usage, arithmetical reasoning and information in science, literature and the arts. They were less good in arithmetical computation, spelling and factual information about history. Their main interests were reading and collecting. There was no difference from controls in play interests. The early indications of superior intelligence most often noted by parents were quicker understanding, insatiable curiosity, extensive information, retentive memory, large vocabulary and unusual interest in number relations, atlases and encyclopedias. When these children were followed up it was found that they suffered less insanity and alcoholism than the controls: the suicide rate and incidence of juvenile delinquency was less. The marriage rate was higher and they tended to marry earlier. They had fewer children than the controls. They tended to choose a partner in marriage of higher intelligence than did the controls. The divorce rate was lower. Their income was greater. Six per cent became minor clerical workers, policemen, firemen or semi-skilled craftsmen. One became a truck driver. Six per cent became doctors. The mean IQ of the 384 offspring was 127.7 and the proportion of children with an IQ of 150 or more was 28 times that of the general population.

Any long-term prediction of a child's achievement is apt to be bedevilled by unexpected deterioration (Ch. 6) — or, conversely, by a person's totally unexpected change of aptitude with maturation, or late development of a skill. I once wrote[8] that

> 'Parents and teachers who despair of their young charges should beware. The rude, uncouth, bad mannered teenager who slouches about, refuses to work, and seems to be against everyone but himself may soon become a delightful, well mannered, popular business or professional man. The adololescent who smells, walks badly, dresses eccentrically, behaves abominably and rebels against authority may (perhaps) be the genius of tomorrow.'

Mental subnormality

The unexpected improvement seen in some mentally subnormal children has already been described. I think that this improvement is chiefly confined to the first years of life. I have not seen a mentally subnormal child of 5 years improve rapidly and reach a near-normal level of intelligence.

In attempting to give a prognosis we must remember not only the possibility of unexpected improvement, but the possibility of deterioration, especially if epilepsy develops.

Much depends not just on the level of intelligence, but on the child's behaviour and on the presence of other handicaps. Life expectancy is reduced in mental subnormality, especially when it is severe. Underachievement is as common, perhaps more common, than it is in normal children, so that the quality of education, as far as it is possible, is important. If he is a hyperkinetic, destructive type he is likely to achieve less than a quiet, easily managed child of the same level of intelligence. He is likely to achieve more if brought up at home than if he is placed in an institution.

A child may have to be graded seriously subnormal even though his IQ is well over 50. I saw one child with an IQ of 77 who was so intensely hyperkinetic that he could not be managed in a special school and he had to be certified as seriously subnormal. A child with cerebral palsy may have to be certified as seriously subnormal on account of his physical handicap, even though his IQ score is well over 50.

As for the ultimate prognosis in mentally retarded children, it is roughly true to say that a child with an IQ of over 50 is likely to be able to earn his living, unless there are associated handicaps, or a high level of unemployment. In Fairbank's well-known study 122 subnormal chidren were followed up for 17 years; 95 were self-supporting, two-thirds of them in manual labour. Compared with normal controls there was more juvenile delinquency, a higher marriage rate, more children and more divorces.

Ferguson and Kerr[4] followed 400 boys and girls from special schools in Glasgow for mentally handicapped children and re-examined them in their early 20s. Seventy-five per cent of the girls with an IQ of over 50 had at least 5 years' continuous employment. Only eight boys were unemployed. Thirteen of the 162 boys were skilled craftsmen. Half the girls and a fifth of the boys were in semi-skilled jobs. By the age of 22, 30% had one or more convictions in law. In a follow-up study of 1000 boys for a 10-year period, 75.8% of those with an IQ score of more than 60 were self-supporting.

Some mentally subnormal adults have acquired remarkable facility in certain skills, such as arithmetic. Others have shown remarkable talents in music and feats of memory.

Conclusions

1. Some fields of development are much more important than others for developmental assessment. The least important is gross motor development. Early speech is a good sign of high intelligence, but speech is often retarded despite mental superiority.
2. The range of normality is discussed. It is impossible to draw the line between normal and abnormal. If one field of development is significantly retarded in comparison with other fields, it is important to look for a possible cause.
3. No child should be penalised, in his overall assessment, for difficulties arising from his speech, sensory or other handicap. Allowance must be made for those. Understanding of words is far more important for assessment than the ability to articulate them. One must avoid the common mistake of arguing that a child's delayed speech is due to laziness, jealousy, 'everything done for him so that he does not need to speak', or tongue-tie.
4. One must avoid being misled by a child's ugliness, facial expression, charm, behaviour or facile conversation (as in hydrocephalus).
5. Long-term prediction of future prospects for children, especially with mental superiority or inferiority, is fraught with difficulties because of the innumerable variables which will influence it.

After taking a full history and conducting a full physical and developmental examination, the paediatrician allows for prematurity, considers the head circumference in relation to the baby's weight, considers the risk factors, familial rate of development, the previous rate of development, illnesses, physical factors including sensory and all other handicaps, the mother's management of the child, emotional deprivation, cultural factors, the relative importance of different fields of development, giving more weight to some than to others, puts all this into his cerebral computer, and emerges with the most likely answer concerning the child's potential. He then follows the child up in order to learn, and is prepared for surprises.

All this for psychologists is distressingly unscientific: but a good paediatrician considers the whole child in relation to his environment and all possible relevant factors. It is a good thing then, when faced with a difficult case, to ask oneself, 'Can I be wrong? Is there anything which can alter my assessment — anything which can cause deterioration, including drugs for epilespy or epilepsy itself, psychoses, or undesirable home circumstances, or anything that may be associated with unexpected improvement — such as Gesell's insurance factors (the child's alertness, responsiveness, concentration and interest in surroundings)?'

REFERENCES

1. Capute, A. J., Accardo, P. J. Linguistic and auditory milestones during the first two years of life. Clin. Pediatr. (Phila). 1978.17.847.
2. Catalano, F. L., McCarthy, D. Infant speech as a possible predictor of later intelligence. J. Psychol. 1954.38.203.
3. Dubowitz, L. M., Leibowitz, D., Goldberg, C. A clinical screening test for assessment of intellectual development in 4 or 5 year old children. Dev. Med. Child Neurol. 1977.19.776.
4. Ferguson, T. Kerr, A. W. After-histories of boys educated in special schools for mentally handicapped children. Scot. Med. J. 1958.3.31.
5. Frankenburg, D. K., Dodds, J. B. The Denver developmental screening test. J. Pediatr. 1967.71.181.
6. Gardner, H. Frames of mind. The theory and nature of intelligence. London. Heinemann. 1983.
7. Hudson, L. The ecology of human intelligence. London. Penguin. 1970.
8. Illingworth, R. S. Destined for fame, but one would not think it. Pediatrics. 1974.54.133.
9. Illingworth, R. S. Dissociation as a guide to developmental assessment. Arch. Dis. Child. 1958.33.118.
10. Illingworth, R. S., Illingworth, C. M. Lessons from childhood. Some aspects of the early life of unusual men a women. Edinburgh. Livingstone. 1966.
11. Illingworth, R. S. How to help a child to achieve his best. J. Pediatr. 1968.73.61.
12. Miller, V., Onatera, R. T., Deinard, A. S. Denver developmental screening test. Cultural variations in South East Asian children. J. Pediatr. 1984.104.481.
13. Neligan, G., Prudham, D. Norms for four standard developmental milestones by sex, social class and place in family. Dev. Med. Child Neurol. 1969.11.413.
14. Ogilvie, E. Gifted children in primary schools. London. Macmillan. 1973.
15. Terman, L. M., Oden, M. H. The gifted child grows up. Stanford. Stanford University Press. 1974.

14

The diagnosis of mental subnormality

This is only a brief chapter, because the diagnosis of mental subnormality has been mentioned directly or indirectly in almost every preceding chapter.

In the sections below I shall bring together the main points about the early diagnosis of mental subnormality. The term 'mental subnormality' is loosely used. By the term I denote an IQ score of less than 70.

The child at risk

As implied in previous chapters, the following conditions place a child at greater risk of being mentally subnormal than others:

Prenatal family history — mental subnormality, degenerative diseases of the nervous system, maternal phenylkenoturia

Previous relative infertility.

Placental insufficiency; toxaemia; intrauterine growth retardation: antepartum haemorrhage; hypertension.

Infections — especially rubella, AIDS.

Drugs — irradiation, alcohol in pregnancy.

Socioeconomic factors: malnutrition: stress.

Low birthweight, especially small-for-dates.

Multiple pregnancy.

Chromosome abnormalities.

Severe congenital anomalies.

Hypothyroidism.

Cerebral palsy, hydrocephalus, craniostenosis.

Perinatal hypoxia, hypoglycaemia, hyponatraemia, hypernatraemia, acidosis, hyperbilirubinaemia, cerebral haemorrhage.

Postnatal meningitis, encephalitis, cerebral tumour or abscess.

Severe hypoglycaemia, hypernatraemia.

Head injury.

Epilepsy and drugs used for its treatment.

Drugs and poisons.

Malnutrition.

Emotional deprivation: socioeconomic problems.

Various metabolic diseases.

Clinical features

The essential principle in the early diagnosis of mental subnormality is the fact that the mentally subnormal child who is retarded from birth or before birth is backward in all fields of development, except occasionally in gross motor development and rarely in sphincter control. He is relatively less retarded in gross motor development than in other fields unless there is a superimposed mechanical difficulty, such as cerebral palsy; he is relatively more retarded in speech, and in the amount of interest which he shows in his surroundings, in concentration, alertness and promptness of response.

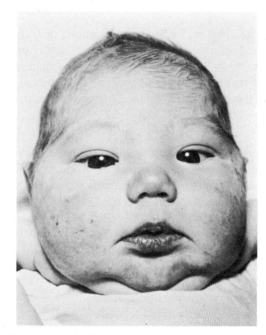

Fig. 149 Child with severe microcephaly.

The situation is different in the case of a child who develops normally for a time, and then develops a degenerative disease, or infantile spasms with mental subnormality. In the case of the latter condition one may see a child of 7 months who has learnt to grasp and to sit and who therefore appears to be up to the average in motor development, but who is totally disinterested in his surroundings and has stopped smiling, and who, in fact, has a grave degree of mental subnormality.

As in any developmental assessment, one takes the history of all relevant prenatal, perinatal and postnatal factors which may have affected his development.

The early weeks

As the mentally subnormal child is retarded in all fields except occasionally gross motor development, it follows that the mentally subnormal child at birth is in many ways in a similar position to the preterm baby who has a normal level of intelligence. He is likely to sleep excessively, and to have feeding difficulties such as failure to demand feeds, drowsiness, difficulty in sucking and easy regurgitation. The excessive tendency to sleep may persist for several months. Below are some comments by mothers about their severely subnormal children in the early weeks:

1. He didn't move much when a baby. He didn't seem to live until he was 8 months old.
2. She was a good baby. She never cried.
3. She seemed to live in a world of her own.
4. She was good all the time. She never cried. She just lay.
5. He was a marvellous baby. He was very good. He lay without crying
6. He just lay in his pram. We didn't know we had him.
7. He just lay in his pram without moving for 6 months. He used to sleep nearly all the time.
8. He was like a cabbage for the first 2 years. He would just sit in his pram.
9. He was a very good baby, and no trouble at all; his brother was a lot more trouble. (The older brother was normal.)

The developmental history after birth is nearly always one of lateness in everything, except occasionally in learning to sit and to walk. There is no need to recapitulate the various milestones here except to mention certain special points.

1. The first obvious sign of mental subnormality is likely to be lateness in smiling and taking notice, with delayed motor development, as seen in the ventral suspension, supine and prone position. One can detect many cases of mental subnormality in the first 6 to 8 weeks if one is in the habit of performing rough developmental tests on all babies in a child health clinic.

2. The lateness in following with the eyes often leads to an erroneous diagnosis of blindness. The child appears to take no notice of his surroundings, so that blindness can be suspected.

3. The lateness in responding to sound often leads to a mistaken diagnosis of deafness.

4. The lateness in learning to chew leads to feeding difficulties. If the retarded child is given solid foods (as distinct from thickened feeds) before he can chew, he may vomit, and if he is not given solids when he has recently become able to chew, he may pass the critical period and refuse solids or vomit them.

5. The reciprocal kick, which disappears normally when a child is

beginning to walk, persists in a retarded child until he can walk. One may see it in a retarded child at 2 or 3 years of age.

6. The persistence of hand regard. The normal baby between 12 and 20 weeks of age can frequently be seen lying on his back watching the movements of his hands. This can frequently be seen in retarded children much older than 20 weeks of age.

7. Mouthing — the taking of all objects to the mouth, characteristic of the 6- to 12-month-old child, persists in retarded children. It normally stops when the child has become proficient in manipulation. One sees, therefore, a 2- or 3-year-old retarded child taking cubes and toys to the mouth.

8. Casting — the deliberate throwing of one object after another on to the floor — normally stops by 15 or 16 months. It continues long after that in subnormal children.

9. Sloberring normally stops by the age of about a year, but it persists in subnormal children.

10. Toothgrinding (Bruxism). Toothgrinding when awake is almost (but not entirely) confined to mentally subnormal children.

11. Altered vocalisations. By means of spectographic analysis[5,6] the Finnish workers showed that the cry of mentally subnormal children is different from that of normal ones. In the abnormal child there was a much longer latent period between the application of the stimulus and the cry. He needed repeated or almost constant stimulation to elicit the cry. The voice quality was different in the abnormal child, and was often guttural, in some it was piercing and shriek-like, and in some high pitched, weak or thin. The normal increasing variety of sounds found in the developing normal infant was greatly delayed in the abnormal one.

12. Lack of interest and concentration. Of all features of the subnormal child, these are the most important. There is a notable lack of interest in surroundings. There is a fleeting interest in toys, or else he does not seem to notice them at all. If given a toy, he will not do anything constructive with it. It does not hold his attention. If he drops it he makes no effort to recover it. If it is out of reach he makes little or no effort to obtain it. He lacks an alert expression and is easily distracted. He is usually less responsive than a normal child. He is slower at responding to test situations.

I have repeatedly seen children who were average in motor development, but whose defective interest and concentration indicated marked subnormality. For instance, a full-term child learnt to sit without support at 8 months and to walk without support at 17 months. She was dry by day at 18 months and dry by night at 2 years. At 1 year her interest and concentration were defective. She began to say single words at 3 years and sentences at 5 years. At the age of 9 years her IQ was 20. There had been no deterioration.

13. Aimless over-activity. Many children who were sleeping excessively and 'so good' as babies undergo a remarkable transition as they grow older, to aimless over-activity, with defective concentration.

Physical findings

These include in particular the presence of major congenital abnormalities, cerebral palsy, abnormalities in the size or shape of the skull or facial features of disease. Any significant congenital abnormality carries an increased risk of mental subnormality. In Chapter 9 I emphasised the extreme importance of the measurement of the head circumference in relation to the child's weight, adding that certain important features of the shape of the skull are commonly found in mental subnormality. I emphasised the importance of serial measurements of the skull circumference: the outlook is particularly bad when the placing of the head circumference on the chart falls away from the earlier centile position (see Fig. 77, Ch. 9).

Features which do *not* help in the diagnosis of mental subnormality are an epicanthus, open fontanelle, late teething, or a central palmar crease — because they can all occur in normal children. The frequency with which cerebral palsy is associated with mental subnormality is noted in Chapter 16.

Differential diagnosis

It is a tragedy to diagnose mental subnormality when the child is normal, for the mistake will cause untold anxiety and suffering. On the other hand it is important for many reasons not to miss the diagnosis.

Many of the sources of confusion in the diagnosis have been discussed by writers under the heading of pseudofeeblemindedness.

The following are the main conditions which have to be distinguished from mental subnormality.

1. *Delayed maturation.* This has been discussed in Chapters 6 and 7. An occasional child is backward in the first weeks and subsequently catches up and becomes normal. If there is microcephaly, such a course of events is unlikely to occur: but if the head circumference is of normal size, one should be particularly cautious in giving a definite prognosis without follow-up study.

2. *Cerebral palsy.* It is easy to confuse some forms of cerebral palsy with mental subnormality. The two conditions are commonly combined. A child with athetosis, particularly before the athetoid movements become obvious, can be thought to have simple mental subnormality, whereas in fact his IQ level is normal.

3. *Neuromuscular diseases.* Failure to diagnose muscular dystrophy, hypotonia, or spinal muscular atrophy may lead to an incorrect diagnosis of mental subnormality. But the somewhat low mean IQ of boys with Duchenne muscular dystrophy (mean score around 80) confuses the picture.

4. *Sensory defects.* Failure to recognise a visual defect or a defect of hearing may well lead to an erroneous diagnosis of mental subnormality.

A visual defect may affect the age of smiling, eye following and manipulation.

Sensory defects, such as visual or auditory impairment, may lead to emotional deprivation and reduced manipulative or other experiences: one defect may lead to another, so that development is retarded by a combination of factors. A sensory defect, especially that of hearing, may lead to a poor performance in some developmental tests, with consequent underestimation of the intelligence. In an older child, the specific problems of dysphasia, dyslexia, difficulties of spatial appreciation and allied conditions, are important pitfalls.

5. *The effect of drugs.* Drugs, especially those used in the treatment of epilepsy when the blood levels are not being estimated, so that they are too high, can confuse the diagnosis. Barbiturates are common offenders.

6. *The effects of emotional deprivation.* The subnormality which can result from severe emotional deprivation was described in Chapter 3. It is especially important to remember in assessing children for suitability for adoption when they have been in an institution, or have been moved from one foster home to another. I pointed out that when retardation in such a child is found, one must never suggest that there should be a further period of institutional care, in order that his progress can be assessed, for a further period would retard his development still further. The correct procedure is to place him in a good foster home, and then observe his development after a period of say 3 months in that home. Sometimes a retarded child has had such an unfavourable environment that it is unwise to express an opinion about his potentialities at all. One must always be prepared to postpone judgment if in doubt, or to withhold one altogether.

7. *Schizophrenia and infantile autism.* There is disagreement about the diagnosis of autism. I prefer to adhere to the original description by Leo Kanner of Baltimore, but others have extended the original description to include large numbers of mentally subnormal children. It is found that many seriously subnormal children show some features of autism: but I have seen many children who have been termed by some autistic, and whom I considered to be typical mentally subnormal. Many feel that the condition is frequently overdiagnosed. Owing to differences of opinion, it is difficult to assess research which has indicated association with immunological factors,[9] William's syndrome,[7] Rett's syndrome[3] and the fragile X syndrome.[2,4] Around 40% have been found to have a high blood serotonin level.[1]

The symptoms and signs of autism are present before the age of 30 months.[8] As a baby, he probably shows no interest in being picked up and cuddled. He may cry only rarely, or scream continually without apparent reason. Later there is profound delay in language development, commonly leading to a wrong diagnosis of severe deafness. There are stereotyped mannerisms, gaze aversion, minimal facial expression, ritualistic behaviour, such as flicking his fingers in front of his eyes, rocking, or whirling objects.

He prefers toys to persons. Most autistic children have a normal-shaped head and often an intelligent appearance, so that they look normal — but they may function as mental subnormality. A quarter develop epilepsy in adolescence.

I was asked to see a boy of 4 with a diagnosis of mental subnormality. My immediate impression when he walked into the room was that the diagnosis was correct, for he took no notice of anyone in the room. I gave him a Goddard formboard to keep him occupied for a few minutes, and was immediately impressed by the way in which he rapidly fitted the blocks in their correct places. I knew immediately that he was a case of autism.

Autism has to be distinguished from schizophrenia. Autism manifests itself in early infancy, or at least within the first 2 years, while schizophrenia rarely manifests itself before the age of 4. There is only a small genetic factor in autism, but there is a family history of schizophrenia in 12% of cases. Hallucinations occur in schizophrenia but not in autism.

The symptoms of schizophrenia[8,11] are severe impairment of emotional relationships, solitariness, remoteness, lack of feeling for people, abnormal postures, striking immobility, or aimless overactivity, ritualistic mannerisms (e.g. rocking and spinning), pathological preoccupation with a particular toy, resistance to change, abnormal response to stimuli, hallucinations and irrelevance of speech. A book by professional parents[10] gave a vivid description of their own schizophrenic son.

Summary

1. The diagnosis of mental subnormality may be made wrongly, when the true diagnosis is emotional deprivation, mere temporary slow maturation ('slow starter'), a sensory defect (hearing or vision), neuromuscular disease, cerebral palsy, the effect of drugs, or infantile autism.
2. The normal variations must be remembered. Mental subnormality is never diagnosed on a single feature, such as isolated retardation in some field of development, but always on a combination of abnormalities.

REFERENCES

1. Ciaranello, R. D. Hyperserotonaemia and early infantile autism. N. Engl. J Med. 1982.307.181.
2. Gillberg, C. Identical triplets with infantile autism and the fragile X syndrome. Br. J. Psychiatry 1983.143.256.
3. Gillberg, C., Wahlström, J., Hagberg, B. Infantile autism and Rett's syndrome: common chromosomal denominator. Lancet. 1984.2.1094.
4. Gillberg, C., Wahlström, J. Chromosome abnormalities in infantile autism and other childhood psychoses: a population study of 66 cases. Dev. Med. Child Neurol. 1985.27.293.
5. Michelsson, K., Wasz-Hockert, O. The value of cry analysis in neonatology and early infancy. In: Murry, T., Murry, J. (Eds.) Infant communication: cry and early speech. Houston. College Hill. 1980.

6. Michelsson, M., Tuppurainen, A., Aulaa, P. Cry analysis of infants with karyotype abnormality. Neuropediatrics 1980.11.365.
7. Reiss, A. L., Feinstein, C., Rosenbaum, K. N. et al. Autism associated with William's syndrome. J. Pediatr. 1985.106.247.
8. Rutter, M. The treatment of autistic children. J. Child Psychol. Psychiatry. 1985.26.193.
9. Stubbs, E. G., Ritvo, E. R., Mason-Brothers, A. Autism and shared parental HLA antigens. J. Am. Acad. Child Psychiatry. 1985.24.182.
10. Wilson, L. This stranger my son. London. Murray. 1968.
11. Wolff, S., Barlow, A. Schizoid personality in childhood: a comparative study of schizoid, autistic and normal children. J. Child Psychol. Psychiatry. 1979.20.29.

15

The association of mental subnormality with physical defects and disease

It would be impossible in one chapter to discuss all the many diseases and congenital abnormalities associated with mental subnormality because the number of relevant conditions is so vast. But it is a good general rule that any major congenital abnormality, such as cleft palate, congenital heart disease, polydactyly, syndactyly and especially congenital abnormalities of the eye, are indications that the child is 'at risk' of mental subnormality — that is, he is more likely than children without those abnormalities to have a lower than average level of intelligence. Most chromosomal defects are associated with mental subnormality — as are many examples of abnormal aminoaciduria.

In a series of 1068 personally observed mentally subnormal children at Sheffield, excluding Down's syndrome, hypothyroidism, hydrocephalus and cerebral palsy, 312 had major congenital anomalies (29.3%). They included 89 children with serious eye disease, of which 23 had optic atrophy, and the remainder had cataracts, colobomata, retinal changes, buphthalmos or anophthalmos: 43 children had congenital heart disease, and 13 had a cleft palate. This study was based on children seen in hospital, to which many children with severe congenital anomalies are sent, and it is not therefore completely unselected.

It is interesting to note that in a series of 702 personally observed children with cerebral palsy, only 53 had congenital anomalies (7.5%).

It would not be profitable to discuss each of the numerous congenital defects separately: but I have picked out a few of the more important conditions associated with mental subnormality; including certain features of physical growth.

Physical growth and other features

Mentally subnormal children tend to be small in stature. Sexual development is often delayed and hypogenitalism in boys is common. It some cases the stunting of growth is extreme. A child under my care weighed 11.8 kg at the age of 11 years and was 94 cm in height, but no cause could be found after the fullest investigation. I would say that when an infant fails to thrive and remains unusually small, when the food intake is adequate and the fullest investigation has failed to reveal a cause, the diagnosis of severe mental subnormality should be considered and examined for by means of developmental testing.

Approximately 20% of the mentally subnormal children seen by me were low birthweight babies, whereas the incidence of low birthweight in Britain is between 6% and 7%. Many of these were 'small-for-dates'. It seemed that defective physical and defective mental growth had commenced in utero.

The age at which the *anterior fontanelle* closes is of little importance in the study of mental subnormality. Though it may remain open unduly long in some mentally subnormal children without hydrocephalus, the intelligence is normal in the majority of children in whom it has remained open longer than usual. In microcephalic infants the anterior fontanelle closes unusually early, but it often closes unusually early in normal infants.

The teeth in mentally subnormal children are more liable to be carious than those of normal children. This may be due to poor nutrition, defective chewing or other factors. In a study of 319 mentally subnormal children significant structural alterations were found in the teeth of 84. It was thought that the abnormalities were of prenatal origin.

Many workers have studied the *skin markings* on the hands of mentally subnormal children. The frequency of whorls in the palms of seriously subnormal children is said to be less than that in the general population. A single palmar crease in common in Down's syndrome and other mentally subnormal children[8] but it also occurs in normal children. A single palmar crease was found in 3.7% of 6299 newborn babies. It was more common in boys than girls, in preterm babies, and in infants with congenital anomalies. It is a useful pointer to a prenatal cause of a defect, such as mental subnormality or cerebral palsy. An incurving little finger is not confined to Down's syndrome, being common in normal children: it is often familial: it may occur in other chromosomal anomalies.

Some pay much attention to low-set ears. It is difficult to define these. Robinow and Roche[44] noted that ears appear to be low-set when the neck is extended or short, or when the cranial vault or the mandibular ramus is high. There is a high cranial vault in hydrocephalus and the Treacher-Collins syndrome; a short mandibular ramus in the Cornelia de Lange syndrome, the bird-headed dwarf, the cri du chat syndrome, the Pierre Robin syndrome, trisomy 13–15 or trisomy 18, and in renal agenesis. There is a short neck in the Klippel Feil syndrome and in certain mucopolysaccharidoses. Abnormality of the shape and structure of the ear is a feature of some mentally subnormal children.

Down's syndrome

Children with Down's syndrome are developmentally at their best in the first few months of life. I have seen several who were able to sit without support on the floor at 7 or 8 months, though the average age at which these children learn to sit is 1 year. Development then seems to slow down, so that they become seriously mentally subnormal. I saw a fullterm child who began to smile at 4 months, to grasp objects voluntarily at 7 months, to roll from prone to supine at 7 months, and to sit without support at $7\frac{1}{2}$ months. When he was 8 months old, however, I was interested to note his defective concentration and the persistence of hand regard — a sure sign of retardation. He walked without help at 34 months, and joined words to form sentences at 69 months. His IQ test score at 6 years was 28. After the early weeks there is a steady slowing down in development, the decline reaching a maximum at 52 weeks.[11] Development slows down more when the child is reared in a foster home than in an ordinary home. Relatively advanced development in early months should not lead one to suppose that the intelligence is unusually high. In one study Gesell tests in the first year did not correlate with subsequent development, but tests in the second year did. According to Gesell, the average child with Down's syndrome learns to sit at 1 year, to walk at 2 years, to say single words at 3 years, to feed himself at 4 years, to acquire clean habits at 5 years and to join words to make sentences at 6 years. In a study of 612 cases brought up at home, it was shown[40] that the average age at which they passed certain milestones was as follows:

	Boys	Girls
	(months)	
Sit unsupported	12.5	11.1
Walk	26.1	22.7
Toilet trained	34.8	34.8
First word	26.6	21.8
Sentences	41.8	52.1

I feel unable myself to predict whether one affected child will prove to have a lower or higher IQ than other affected children. I do not think that the relatively advanced motor development which one occasionally sees is indicative of a better than usual level of intelligence. I fell that one's estimate of the home environment, with the amount of love and stimulation which is likely to be given to the child, provides the only clue as to the possibility that an individual child will fare somewhat better than others. Conversely, placement in an institution would suggest that he will fare less well than others more fortunately placed. I know of no study in which the head circumference of these children has been related to their eventual level of intelligence. The degree of facial stigmata provide no clue as to future IQ.

There are numerous papers concerning the IQ scores of children with Down's syndrome. The mean IQ is around 28. Opinions differ as to the number who achieve an IQ of over 50: Engler in his study of 100 cases gave a figure of 2% and Brousseau in a study of 206 gave a figure of 1%. Wunsch found that 13% of 77 cases had a score over 50, and Quaytman found the same figure in 75 cases. I feel that the lower figure of 1 to 2% corresponds with my own experience. The highest IQ found by Oster in 526 cases was 74. Oster found that practically all over 10 understand when spoken to, and that most adult cases speak intelligibly. Speech, however, is retarded, with a husky voice and poor articulation. One or two had been known to learn to read and write, but probably without understanding it. No child with Down's syndrome, he said, had been found to be able to add sums. I have seen a 12-year-old child who, as a result of prolonged and probably misguided teaching, could read simple books (at the 5–6-year-old level) and make simple additions. On investigation, however, it was found that she had no idea what she had read, and the figures meant nothing to her. Her IQ test score was about 30. In a study of 293 cases[22] the mean IQ of 18 mosaics was the lowest, of 254 trisomies was intermediate, and of 21 translocation cases the highest. The stigmata were the same in all groups, but the translocation ones were the most active and aggressive. Yet another study[14] of 25 mosaics and 25 trisomies found the opposite — that the mosaics had a significantly higher intellectual potential, better verbal ability, and less visuo-spatial difficulties, but no difference in behaviour. It is said that children with Down's syndrom are more clumsy than other subnormal children of the same IQ.[15] Deafness is common, and may further lower a child's performance in IQ tests. Significant hearing loss was found in two-thirds of 107 child cases,[3] and in 51–74% of 51 affected adults.

Although one still hears or reads the comment that children with Down's syndrome are docile, easy to manage and musical, there is no evidence to that effect.[4] Convulsions are extremely rare; I have not yet seen a case with cerebral palsy.

The mortality continues to be high, about half dying by the fifth year.

Other chromosomal variants

The mean IQ of children with chromosome abnormalities is below the average. In an Edinburgh survey[43] the mean IQ of children with Klinefelter's syndrome was 94.3, compared with a score of 104.7 for controls. The figure for Turner's syndrome is similar.[27]

Walzer[58] reviewed the cognitive and verbal difficulties of children with certain chromosome abnormalities. The specific difficulties of children with the XO karyotype lies in non-verbal congnitive functioning, with regard to visuospatial appreciation, directional and constructional abilities: the children score worse on performance tests than on verbal tests. Children with the XXY karyotype have a worse performance on verbal than on performance tests; they have special difficulties with speech, reading and spelling.

There have been numerous papers on the 'fragile X' syndrome.[55,56] Features commonly found are a large head, large testes, large nose and lower jaw, with a large birthweight and moderate mental retardation. There is a unique language deficit, in which expressive language is worse than receptive language.[58]

Convulsions and epilepsy

There is a strong association between epilepsy and mental subnormality, due to the frequent association between epilepsy and underlying brain disease. In an institution for mental subnormality, convulsions are likely to be common. Kirman wrote that of 777 in the Fountain Hospital in 1953, 185 (25%) had fits while in hospital. Of 218 with Down's syndrome, only two had fits.

In my series of 444 mentally subnormal children without cerebral palsy, and excluding Down's syndrome, the overall incidence of convulsions was 31.3%. In those slightly to moderately subnormal the incidence was 16.3%: in those severely subnormal the incidence was 46.8%. None of 87 with Down's syndrome had fits. In 285 mentally retarded children with cerebral palsy, the incidence of fits was 37.5%. In the slightly or moderately subnormal ones the incidence was 22.8% as compared with a figure of 53.7% in the severely retarded ones. In all groups, cases of postnatal origin were excluded.

The prognosis of neonatal convulsions depends on the cause. A follow-up study of 137 infants[45] indicated that 86% of those who had neonatal convulsions with a normal EEG were likely to develop normally, irrespective of the cause. Those with a flat, periodic or multifocal EEG had a 7% chance of normal development, and those with a unifocal lesion were uncertain. Rose and Lombroso[45] analysed the result in relation to the cause, those with hypocalcaemia having the best outlook. In another study of 151 infants with hypoglycaemia[25] those who had symptoms and fits had a poor prognosis: asymptomatic cases showed no brain damage.

There is a strong relationship between the type of epilepsy and the level of intelligence. The so-called infantile spasms (akinetic seizures, 'salaam spasms', 'myoclonic jerks'), with the EEG picture of hypsarrhythmia are usually associated with severe mental subnormality. This kind of epilepsy is associated with a wide variety of diseases, including serious brain defects, phenylketonuria, neurodermatoses, sequelae of severe hypoglycaemia, toxoplasmosis and pyridoxin dependency. Jeavons and Bower in their review[21] found that 3% of their cases became mentally normal. A Japanese study[39] of 200 cases claimed that 9.5% made a complete recovery: but the prognosis was not related by the authors to the cause of the infantile spasms. There have been many studies of the outcome of infantile spasms after treatment with corticotrophin or corticosteroids; but they have not related the outcome to the cause. It is obvious that if the cause is a degenerative disease of the nervous system (in its broadest sense) the outcome will be bad whatever the treatment. I have emphasised the striking fact that those children who appear to develop normally until 5 or 6 months and then develop infantile spasms, become mentally subnormal immediately the fits begin, but do not undergo progressive deterioration. After a period of some weeks they commonly improve and may occasionally become normal. In view of the multiplicity of causes of infantile spasms, it is hardly likely that any particular treatment is likely to have a significantly beneficial effect on the intelligence.

Petit mal does not lead to mental impairment, though frequent attacks during school lessons may cause a child's performance to fall off. Temporal lobe epilepsy is liable to lead to mental impairment.

Mental deterioration in epileptics may be due to the underlying brain defect: hypoxia or multiple petechial haemorrhages: repeated head injuries: psychological factors — exclusion from school: learning difficulties, and the effect of medication, especially of barbiturates.

When assessing the mental development of a child with epilepsy, the mere measurement of the IQ score is inadequate. Epileptic children may have a variety of cognitive difficulties. Stores[53] reviewed their problems. Children with damage to the left hemisphere if dominant for speech tended to have defective verbal abilities: those with damage to the right hemisphere had visuospatial or perceptual-motor defects. Epilepsy in the dominant temporal lobe was apt to be associated with defects of memory or learning. Centrencephalic epilepsy was associated with impairment of sustained attention. Phenobarbitone overdosage may cause drowsiness and defective concentration. Stores wrote that 'the assessment of the intellectual capabilities of a child with epilepsy in terms of IQ alone can be most misleading, for hidden in this global assessment may be specific defects which if unrecognised might adversely affect learning in various spheres of life'.

The psychological difficulties of epileptic children are important. Ounsted described a syndrome of epilespy with hyperkinesis, usually but not necessarily associated with a low IQ. It was common in boys, and made them intolerable at school.

In an outstanding long-term study of 100 children with temporal lobe epilepsy[32] followed into adult life, five died in childhood; 33% were found to be seizure-free and independent, 32% socially and economically independent but not necessarily seizure free, and 30% were dependent: 5% died before the age of 15. Adverse prognostic factors were an IQ below 90, onset of fits before 28 months, five or more grand mal attacks, temporal lobe fit frequency of one per day or more, a left-sided focus, hyperkinetic syndrome, catastrophic rage and special schooling.

Hydrocephalus and spina bifida

Now that operative procedures are commonly carried out in these children, it has become more important to know the natural history of untreated cases, in order that one can assess the results achieved by various surgical procedures. Hydrocephalus is not necessarily incompatible with a good level of intelligence. In the first place, it may be arrested at birth. I well remember seeing a seriously disturbed mother who had been told that her baby had hydrocephalus and would be spastic and mentally defective. The diagnosis was undoubtedly correct, but I told the mother that the prediction given, though likely, was by no means necessarily correct. Within a month it was obvious that the hydrocephalus was arrested, and the child proved to be normal.

Bakwin described the dreadful tragedy which resulted from a wrong diagnosis of mental subnormality in a child with hydrocephalus and spina bifida. The father was given a bad prognosis and was given the extraordinary advice that he should tell his wife that the baby had died. The girl was then transferred to an institution, but as she grew older it became clear that her intelligence was within normal limits. The father was then advised to tell his wife that the girl was in fact alive, but he would not do os. The mother was then told by another person.

Hydrocephalus may cause difficulty in two ways. In the first place, the process may become arrested at any stage, so that development may be normal. In the second place, it is difficult to assess head control, when the sheer weight of a large head may cause undue head lag.

In an Australian study of 45 children of primary school age who had had surgical treatment for hydrocephalus in infancy, there was at least a four times greater incidence if psychiatric disorders than in controls.[7] They may have been due to a combination of factors, such as brain damage, physical handicap and difficulties with the shunt.

Laurence followed up 179 of 182 unoperated cases seen in London. Eighty-nine (49%) had died. Nine remained progressive, and three were not traced. Eighty-one (47%) had become arrested, and of these 75% were in the educable range, 33 of them having an IQ of 85 or more, and 26 having an IQ of 50 to 84. Twenty-seven of the 81 had little or no physical disability. There was little relationship between the IQ and the circumference of the head or the thickness of the cortex as measured in the air encephalogram. A child with a cortical thickness of 0.5 cm was found to have an IQ of 85, and another child with a similar measurement had an IQ of 100. Laurence's figures may be too optimistic. His case material consisted of children who were referred to a neurosurgeon who did not operate on children with hydrocephalus and therefore the patients referred were already to some extent selected. Even so, only about one-third of the survivors had an IQ of 85 or over at the time of the survey. Results indicate that with a ventriculocaval shunt, the outcome is likely to be much better. Children with hydrocephalus are commonly facile in behaviour, and exccssively talkative, a feature which often leads to an overestimate of their IQ. They are pleasant, but with a tendency to clumsiness and slight ataxia. Poor concentration is a prominent feature.[2]

In a prospective study of an unselected series of 475 newborn babies born with spina bifida or hydrocephalus,[35] and assessed by a psychologist at the age of 5 to 9 years, the following were the IQ scores:

		Hydro-cephalus with spina bifida	Spina bifida without hydrocephalus	Hydrocephalus without spina bifida	Total	%
Superior	120+	3	5	4	12	2.5
High average	110–119	13	19	7	39	8.2
Average	90–109	73	54	35	162	34.1
Low average	80–89	47	18	25	90	18.9
ESN	51–79	83	14	18	115	24.2
Below 50		21	3	33	57	1.2
		240	113	122	475	

Table 9 shows the IQ scores in a study of 136 children with meningomyelocele and hydrocephalus followed to the age of 6 to 11 years, of whom 68, the milder cases, had no shunt, and 68 had a ventriculocaval shunt — usually the more severe ones.

Table 9   IQ scores in hydrocephalus

IQ	68 unoperated	68 operated
120–129	5	—
100–119	19	8
80–99	32	29
50–79	9	26
below 50	1	4
unknown	2	1

Table 10 shows the IQ scores in a later study of 31 children of school age who had no hydrocephalus, 28 with hydrocephalus of slight degree not requiring a shunt and 75 children who had hydrocephalus and a shunt.

Table 10   IQ of children with spina bifida, with or without hydrocephalus

IQ	No hydrocephalus (31) and hydrocephalus with no shunt (28) $n = 59$	Hydrocephalus and shunt $n = 75$
Average	87	79
	%	%
100+	31	10
80–99	52	33
60–79	12	30
Below 60	5	18

Table 11 shows the relationship between the prognosis with regard to mental development and the preoperative thickness of the cerebral mantle, as determined by air studies.

Owing to the frequent association of hydrocephalus with meningomyelocele, one would expect that the mean IQ level of children with meningomyelocele would be rather low. In the absence of hydrocephalus, however, the mean IQ would probably be little below the average.

Table 11 Relationship between thickness of cerebral mantle and IQ scores

Preoperative mantle	Number	Survivors	IQ over 80	%
10 mm or less	32	16	5	31
11–35 mm	235	125	79	63
(a) Unoperated	177	91	53	58
(b) Operated	58	34	26	76

Out of 19 children who suffered from neonatal meningitis and survived with gross residual hydrocephalus, treatment by ventriculocaval shunt resulted in prolonged survival in 14 children. Seven of these were of normal intelligence, but seven others were retarded.[33]

The prognosis of hydrocephalus following subdural effusion and other intracranial haemorrhage was described by Lorber[34] Of 32 survivors who were assessed at 18 months to 16 years of age, following intracranial haemorrhage in the newborn period, 16 had a normal intelligence (IQ 80 to 114), nine of them with no physical sequelae; 16 were retarded, 12 grossly so.

Megalencephaly

For megalencephaly see chapter 9.

Craniostenosis

The level of intelligence found in children with craniostenosis depends in part on the extent of the premature fusion of the sutures. In some of the mildest forms children appear to develop normally at first, but drop behind when it becomes impossible for the brain to enlarge further owing to the fusion of the sutures. In more severe ones, in which the skull is already severely deformed at birth, mental development seems to have been subnormal before operation was possible.

I have the impression that the level of intelligence is lower when there are other associated congenital anomalies (as in Apert's syndrome).

Hypertelorism

Anomalies associated with hypertelorism include shortening of the digits, amyotonia and congenital heart disease. The intelligence may be normal, but it is usually below average.

Cleft palate

As there was little literature on the level of intelligence found in children with cleft palate, we studied 112 consecutive cases of cleft palate with or without hare lip, taken from an alphabetical and entirely representative list. The mean IQ of 80 children on whom we were able to carry out Stanford-Binet tests was 95.4; 47 had an IQ test score of less than 100, and 33 had an IQ over 100. School reports obtained on a further 17 gave comparable results. It appeared that the mean IQ was slightly lower than that of the population as a whole.

Achondroplasia

The mean IQ of affected children is somewhat below average. There is usually head enlargement, due to megalencephaly or to slight hydrocephalus: the larger the head the lower is the likely IQ.

Neuromuscular conditions

The mean IQ of boys with Duchenne muscular dystrophy is around 80 to 85.[30] In a study of 129 boys, the IQ range was 30 to 127 with a mean figure of 79: 20.4% had an IQ score of under 68. Of the 93 who had an EEG done, the tracing was abnormal in 82.2%. Progressive deterioration in unusual, but there is commonly poor verbal performance, with a high incidence of emotional problems. Intellectual impairment is common before signs of muscular involvement develop but it is not progressive and is not related to the stage of the disease. The reason for the intellectual impairment is unknown. Affected children are more likely than others to have difficulty in reading and arithmetic.

Dystrophia myotonica is often associated with mental subnormality.

Cerebral palsy

I have reviewed the literature concerning the intelligence level in children with cerebral palsy elsewhere and will summarise it below. Putting together six important papers on the subject, I calculated that the IQ of 55% of 2480 children was less than 70. Twenty per cent of the normal population have an IQ of 110 or more, as compared with 3% of 1768 affected children described by four workers. It seems to be the general opinion that the intelligence level of children with athetosis is little different from that of children with the spastic form of cerebral palsy. The mean IQ of 1000 children with cerebral palsy in Long Island was 52:85% had a score below 85.[13]

For a variety of reasons the assessment of a child with cerebral palsy is fraught with difficulties. Cerebral palsy causes mechanical difficulties which interfere with the use of the hands and with gross motor development; it is frequently associated with visual and auditory defects, with mental subnormality, with poor attention span even in the absence of mental subnormality, with emotional problems and with perceptional difficulties such as defects of body image, space appreciation and form perception, so that tests with formboards are misleading; and there may be other defects arising from cortical damage. Speech is usually defective. The child's environment has not been conducive to a good level of achievement in tests commonly employed, he may have been kept indoors, and had little contact with other children, and be unable to speak. Haeussermann[17] emphasised the fact that brain lesions 'penalise' a child. She wrote that: 'While the actual ability to comprehend and reason may be well within the normal range, in some cases the level of adaptation may be disproportionately lower'. 'Children with cerebral palsy will be more readily understood and their attempts to communicate more alertly observed and accepted by an examiner to whom it has become evident that while a child may be non-speaking, he may be far from non-communicating.'

Of all forms of cerebral palsy in which mistakes can be made in the assessment of intelligence, I would think that athetosis has the pride of place. Perlstein has made the same comment, when referring to kernicterus. I have myself made such a mistake. The following is a brief case history:

Case report. This boy was born at term, by a difficult forceps delivery, weighing 3860 g. There was a severe degree of asphyxia, but he was well in the neonatal period. I saw him at 1 year because of lateness in sitting and walking. The milestones were confusing. He had learnt to chew at 8½ months, and to roll from supine to prone at 6½ months. He had begun to say single words just before I saw him. He was interested, and laughing at the antics of his sibling. There was no sign of the spastic form of cerebral palsy. The grasp was a little ataxic, like that of a 5 month old baby. There were no abnormal movements. In my letter to the consultant who referred him to me, I wrote, 'I find it difficult to reconcile the fact that in the development of speech and chewing he is at the level of an 8 month old child, while in the use of hands and of sitting he is only at the level of a 5 month old child. This would suggest a mechanical difficulty. There is no doubt at all that he is quite considerably mentally retarded, apart altogether from his mechanical difficulty. Further observation is essential over a period of some months, in order to see how he develops.' (In retrospect, the diagnosis of mental retardation was obviously wrong, because of the normal speech development.)

At 18 months I wrote: 'There is a mechanical difficulty, which is not spasticity. The point I made before about the lack of correlation between his locomotor development and speech is particularly obvious now, for he can say a lot of words and still cannot sit. This must represent a mechanical difficulty, and not mere mental retardation, for no child who is unable to sit on account of severe mental retardation is nevertheless able to talk.'

He began to put words together and to walk a few steps at 2 years. At 4 years athetoid movements became obvious. His IQ at 5 years was 100.

Another difficulty in the assessment of infants with cerebral palsy is the delayed maturation which is sometimes seen, and to which reference has already been made.

With regard to the relation of the IQ to the distribution of spasticity in the spastic form, the IQ of those with spastic quadriplegia is likely to be the lowest, and of those with spastic diplegia to be the highest. The mean IQ of those with hemiplegia is about 77. There is probably no difference in the IQ of those with left and right hemiplegia, though there is a difference of opinion on this point.

The IQ of children with the rigid form of cerebral palsy in almost invariably extremely low. They are all in the seriously subnormal class. The same applies to the IQ of those with the rare 'atonic' form of cerebral palsy.

I have no figures for the IQ of children with congenital ataxia. My clinical impression is that the mean IQ of these children would be below 100.

It is generally agreed that the more severe the cerebral palsy, the lower is the IQ likely to be, though this does not necessarily apply to athetoid children. It is usually the case that the IQ tends to be less in children who have convulsions.

Neurodermatoses

The mean IQ of children with the various forms of neurodermatoses is considerably below the average. This applies particularly to the Sturge Weber syndrome and tuberous sclerosis, but to a less extent to neurofibromatosis.

Blindness

The intellectual level of blind children depends on the cause. All major congenital anomalies, particularly those involving the eye, carry an increased risk of mental subnormality. In my series of 1068 mentally subnormal children seen by me in Sheffield, excluding hydrocephalus, Down's syndrome, hypothyroidism and post-natal cases, 89 (8.3%) had major eye defects, such as optic atrophy, cataract or chorioido-retinitis.

The mean IQ of children with retrolental fibroplasia is considerably below the average. This may be largely due to the factors commonly associated with retrolental fibroplasia — extreme prematurity, apnoeic attacks, or cerebral haemorrhage.

The overall IQ level in blindness was reviewed by Steward-brown and colleagues.[52] The mean IQ in myopia is above average; that in amblyopia is slightly decreased. The majority of visual defects did not affect learning, with the exception of hypermetropia, which made reading difficult.

Blind children are likely to be late in learning to sit and walk; but their development depends greatly on parental management. Failure to give the child normal sensory stimulation, with overprotection against possible injury, causes pseudo-retardation.

Deafness

There are so many conditions which are associated with deafness that figures for the mean IQ of deaf children are meaningless. Unilateral hearing loss probably causes few if any educational problems.

Phenylketonuria

When assessing studies of the IQ scores achieved by children with phenylketonuria, one must know that the diagnosis was correct, the age at which treatment commenced and the quality of the management with the level of serum phenylalanine maintained, for the brain is damaged by too low or too high a serum phenylalanine. A further difficulty in assessing the many papers on the prognosis lies in the fact that phenylketonuria is not a single condition: there are at least nine types of phenylalaninaemia: up to 3% are deficient in either dihydropteridine reductase or dihydrobiopterin synthetase rather than the usual phenylalanine hydroxylase: the response to treatment is much better in the last of these;[28] that with dihydropteridine reductase deficiency deteriorates despite treatment.

About one in seven untreated cases has an IQ over 70;[51] there have been several reports of untreated cases with an average or above average IQ. There is a wide range of IQ varying from severe mental subnormality to normality. Nearly all workers emphasise that the earlier treatment is commenced, the better are the results. Menkes reported on the IQ scores of 43 children treated from birth. They were as follows:

Number	IQ
1	53–67
5	68–82
17	83–97
14	98–112
6	113–127

In a comprehensive review by Dobson et al,[12] relating the IQ score achieved to the age of onset of treatment, the following were the findings:

Age of starting treatment (months)	Number	IQ
Birth-1	11	89
1–4	9	77
5–10	11	68
11–17	19	67
18–24	21	73
25–36	13	65
37–47	16	63
48–72	14	57

In a British Paediatric Association study the IQ score at 8 years was related to the age at which the diet started. The findings were as follows:

Age at which diet started (days)	Total	Mean IQ
0–9	14	104
10–19	76	101
20–29	35	97
30–39	16	94
40–49	16	92
50–59	12	88
60–69	7	87
70–79	2	83

Hsia wrote that all that one could expect to achieve by treatment was a maintenance of the status quo, so preventing deterioration: but early treatment improves behaviour and reduces irritability. The mean IQ of children starting treatment in the first 3 months is probably around 85. In another study[12] the mean IQ of 111 4-year-old early treated children was 93. Sibinga[48] followed 89 children; the mean final IQ of those treated from birth was 95.6; for those starting treatment at 1 to 6 months of age, the mean final IQ was 79.1

There is still disagreement as to when it is safe to discontinue treatment. Some[24,47,50] reported a significant impairment of performance when the diet was stopped. It has been said that those who respond less well to the diet are particularly likely to deteriorate when placed on a normal diet. In an American collaborative study[24] to assess the effect of discontinuing the diet at 6 years or persisting with it, there was little difference in the IQ scores or arithmetic tests in the two groups, but significant changes in reading and spelling.

Attention is now being focused on the management of mothers with phenylketonuria in pregnancy.[54] In an international survey of the outcome of 524 treated and untreated pregnancies, the offspring of homozygotes had a high incidence of cardiac anomalies, intrauterine growth retardation and mental subnormality; those of heterozygote women (who had only minimal phenylalanine elevation), had an increased incidence of pyloric stenosis but not of mental subnormality or other anomalies.[31] In pregnancy, a test for phenylketonuria should be routine.

Several studies have shown that however well the treatment has been controlled children with phenylketonuria have school difficulties such as overactivity, defective concentration, clumsiness, visuospatial and learning problems, more than unaffected children of the same level of IQ.[49]

Tyrosinaemia. A study of six children with transient neonatal tyrosinaemia of high degree showed normal development at 25 months.[38]

Others have shown that infants who had a high tyrosin level in the blood in the newborn period subsequently scored significantly less well in verbal and cognitive abilities and fine motor skill.

Congenital heart disease

Ross described the association of congenital heart disease with mental subnormality in 21 cases at the Johns Hopkins Hospital, Baltimore. She suggested that the intelligence quotient in congenital heart disease tends to be lower than the average. This corresponds with the findings of Bret and Kohler in their study of 88 cases. Between 25 and 35 per cent of children with Down's syndrome have congenital heart disease.

Children with cyanotic congenital heart disease tend to score less well than those with acyanotic types; but even so the overall IQ level is probably less than the mean for the population as a whole. The low mean figure may be partly explained by the association of congenital heart disease with other conditions, such as the fetal alcohol syndrome, or Down's syndrome. The incidence of congenital heart disease in institutions for mental subnormality is much higher than that in the population as a whole. In my own series of 1068 mentally subnormal children, excluding Down's syndrome, cerebral palsy, hypothyroidism or hydrocephalus, the incidence of congenital heart disease was 4%.

Postponement of operation for the repair of cyanotic congenital heart disease, such as transposition of the great vessels, causes progressive impairment of cognitive function.[42]

There have been several studies of possible brain damage following the use of deep hypothermia and circulatory arrest for operations on congenital heart disease,[16,19,29] possibly related to extracorporeal circulation. But a Canadian study[18] of 17 children, found no neurological, cognitive, verbal or social deficit after operation. New Zealand workers[6] investigated 72 children who had been operated on at 11 days to 24 months (two-thirds of them in the first year). The mean IQ on the Stanford Binet and Peabody tests at 3 to 4 years was 92.9. The duration of arrest seemed to be irrelevant.

In another study of 38 children 22 months to 6 years after operation, the mean IQ was 99.2.[10]

Chromosome examination before and after cardiac catheterisation and angiocardiography of 20 children revealed chromosome damage in all.[1]

Ireland et al. found that the incidence of congenital heart disease in 723 mental defectives in institutions was 2.4%. This is seven times higher than that found in comparable ages in the general population. When Down's syndrome was excluded the figure was still much higher than in normal people. In my series of 1068 mentally subnormal children (excluding Down's syndrome as before), 43 had congenital heart disease (4.0%).

Thalidomide babies

In a detailed study of 22 'thalidomide' babies it was found that the mean

DQ was 90.[9] The effect of institutional care was duly considered. In view of the known association between congenital anomalies and a lower than usual level of intelligence, this result was to be expected.

McFie and Robertson[37] studied 56 affected children: four were mentally subnormal. They emphasised the difficulties of assessment if there were upper limb deformities and dependence on others. When the upper limbs were normal there was a tendency to a higher performance on verbal tests — perhaps because of stimulation by the parents. In another study of 33 Canadian children, a third had a DQ below 90.

Galactosaemia

Komrower and Lee[26] reviewed as many cases of galactosaemia as they could find in Great Britain, in order to assess their clinical, psychological and emotional state. They traced 22 boys and 38 girls, all treated cases. Eight had cataracts, one had portal hypertension, but the others were healthy. The mean IQ was 80, with a scatter from 30 to 118. The IQ decreased with age: the mean IQ for 0 to 5 years was 90, at 5 to 10 years 79, and over 10 years it was 70. They tended to show depression, timidity, withdrawn behaviour and hostility.

Diabetes mellitus

Any chronic handicap may indirectly lead to learning disorders at school — perhaps largely for psychological reasons. Repeated hypoglycaemic episodes may cause brain damage.[46] In a study of 125 adolescents with insulin-dependent diabetes, compared with 83 non-diabetic controls, it was found that the early onset of diabetes was associated with a poor performance in intelligence and visuospatial tests, school attainment, memory, motor and eye–hand coordination.

Hypothyroidism

It is often said that the younger the child when treatment is insituted, the better are the results to be expected. This is not altogether true because if hypothyroidism is diagnosed in early infancy, there is the possibility that there has been damage to the brain in utero. Control of treatment is not always satisfactory, and so it is not easy to determine from several studies whether the IQ score achieved could have been better with improved medical care. Nevertheless one's conclusion from one's own experience, and from reading the literature, is that the mean IQ of children treated early would be around 90. The figure given in a London study of 141 children was 79.5.[20] The IQ was in the normal range when treatment started in the first month,[57] but if it begins later there is a progressive irreversible fall in intelligence. Now that screening of the newborn for hypothyroidism is routine, one would expect that the mean IQ would be around 100. Relevant factors are the adequacy of therapy, family IQ, socioeconomic circumstances, and the nature and severity of the thyroid defect.[20,57]

Ataxia and clumsiness are a common finding in long term follow-up.[36]

A long-term American follow-up for 16 to 26 years following IQ testing at 5 or 6 years showed that there was a mean full scale IQ increase of 21 points, sometimes with sudden and unpredictable timing.[41]

Summary and conclusions

1. A wide variety of diseases and malformations, especially those involving the skull, eyes and skin, are associated with varying degrees of mental subnormality. Though certain anomalies, such as deformities of the ears, are often associated with mental subnormality, these so-called stigmata of degeneration should not be used as an aid to diagnosis because they are often found in normal children. Nevertheless, the finding of severe deformities of any kind should make one look particularly carefully at the level of mental development which the child has reached and follow his developmental progress.

   The anterior fontanelle is of little value for the assessment of a child's development. Physical growth is commonly defective in retarded children.

   More and more metabolic defects and abnormalities are being found in association with mental subnormality.

2. Though between a quarter and a third of all mentally subnormal children have or have had convulsions, epilepsy *per se* is not usually associated with mental subnormality. Mental subnormality in epileptics is due to the underlying brain disease, or to the effect of frequent convulsions, to psychological causes in relation to epilepsy, or to the drugs used for treatment.

   Infantile spasms are usually associated with severe mental subnormality.

3. Although mental subnormality is found in varying degrees of frequency in the above conditions, each child has to be assessed individually and never assumed to be mentally subnormal without a full developmental examination being performed. Nevertheless, the final assessment will be made against the background of the known facts concerning the intellectual level likely to be found in the various conditions described.

REFERENCES

1. Adams, F. H., Norman, A., Bass, D., Oku, G. Chromosomal damage to infants and children after cardiac catheterisation and angiocardiography. Pediatrics. 1978.62.312.
2. Anderson, E. M. Spain, B. The child with spina bifida. London. Methuen 1977.
3. Balkany, T. J., Downs, M. P., Jafek, B. W., Krajicek, M. J. Hearing loss in Down's syndrome. Clin. Pediatr. (Phila.). 1979.18.116.

4. Baron, J. Temperament profile of children with Down's syndrome. Dev. Med. Child Neurol. 1972.14.640.
5. Bess, F. H., Tharpe, A. M. Unilateral hearing loss. Pediatrics. 1984.74.206.
6. Clarkson, P. M., MacArthur, B. A., Barratt Boyes, B. J., Neutze, J. M. Developmental progress following cardiac surgery in infancy using profound hypothermic and circulatory arrest. Austr. Paediatr. J. 1978.14.298.
7. Connell, H. M., McConnel, T. S. Psychiatric sequelae in children treated operatively for hydrocephalus in infancy. Dev. Med. Child Neurol. 1981.23.505.
8. Davies, P. A. Sex and the single transverse palmar crease in newborn singletons. Dev. Med. Child. Neurol. 1966.8.729.
9. Décarie, T. G. A study of the mental and emotional development of the thalidomide child. In Foss, B. M. Determinants of Infant Behaviour. Vol. IV. London. Methuen. 1969.
10. Dickinson, D. F., Sambrooks, J. E. Intellectual performance in children after circulatory arrest with profound hypothermia in infancy. Arch. Dis. Child. 1979.54.1.
11. Dicks-Mireaux, M. J. Mental development of infants with Down's syndrome. Am. J. Ment. Def. 1972.77.26.
12. Dobson, J. C.,Williamson, M. L., Azen, C., Koch, R. Intellectual assessment of 111 four year old children with PKU. Pediatrics. 1977.60.822.
13. Fisch, C. B. Yang, D. C., Yang, D. C., Yuin, C., Fisch, M. L., Lamm, S. S. Intellectual development of children with cerebral palsy. Dev. Med. Child Neurol. 1979.21.114..
14. Fishler, K., Koch, R., Donnell, G. N. Comparison of mental development in individuals with mosaic and trisomy 21 Down's syndrome. Pediatrics. 1976.58.744.
15. Frith, V. & Frith, C. D. Specific motor disabilities in Down's syndrome. J. Child Psychol. Psychiatry. 1974.15.293.
16. Gonzalez, E. R. Deep hypothermia for infant heart surgery. J. Am. Med. Assoc. 1979.241.2585.
17. Haeusserman, E. Developmental potential of preschool children. London. Grune and Stratton. 1958.
18. Haka-Ikse, K., Blackwood, M. J. A., Steward, D. J. Psychomotor development of infants and children after profound hypothermia during surgery for congenital heart disease. Dev. Med. Child Neurol. 1978.20.62.
19. Henriksen, L. Evidence suggestive of diffuse brain damage following cardiac operation. Lancet. 1984.1.817.
20. Hulse, J. A. Outcome for congenital hypothyroidism. Arch. Dis. Child. 1984.59.23.
21. Jeavons, P. M., Bower, B. D. Infantile spasms. Clinics in Develop. Med. No. 15. London. Heinemann. 1965.
22. Johnson, R. C., Abelson, R. B. Intellectual behavior and physical characteristics associated with trisomy, translocation and mosaic types of Down's syndrome. Am. J. Ment. Def. 1969.73.852.
23. Keiser, H., Montague, J., Wold, D., Maune, S., Pattison, D. Hearing loss in Down's syndrome adults. Am. J. Ment. Def. 1981.85.467.
24. Koch, R., Azen, C. G., Friedman, E. G., Williamson, M. L., Preliminary report on the effects of diet discontinuation in PKU. J. Pediatr. 1982.100.870.
25. Koivisto, M., Blanco-Sequeiros, M., Krause, U. Neonatal symptomatic and asymptomatic hypoglycaemia: a follow-up study of 151 children. Dev. Med. Child Neurol. 1972.14.603.
26. Komrower, G. M., Lee, D. H. Longterm follow up of galactosaemia. Arch. Dis. Child. 1970.45.367.
27. Lancet, Long term outlook for children with sex chromosome abnormalities. Leading article. 1982.2.27.
28. Lancet. The growing problem of phenylketonuria. Leading article. 1979.1.1381.
29. Lancet. Brain damage after open heart surgery. Leading article. 1982.1.1161.
30. Leibowitz, D., Dubowitz, V. Intellect and behaviour in Duchenne muscluar dystrophy. Dev. Med. Child Neurol. 1981.23.577.
31. Lenke, R. R., Levy, J. L. Maternal phenylketonuria and hyperphenylalaninemia. An international survey of the outcome of treated and untreated pregnancies. N. Engl. J. Med. 1980.303.1202.

32. Lindsay, J., Ounsted, C., Richards. P. Long term outcome in children with temporal lobe seizures. Marriage, parenthood and sexual indifference. Dev. Med. Child Neurol. 1979.21.285, 433.
33. Lober, J. Neonatal bacterial meningitis. Medicine 1974.27.1579.
34. Lorber, J. Post-haemorrhagic hydrocephalus. Arch. Dis. Child. 1974.49.751.
35. Lorber, J. Results of treatment of myelomeningocele. Dev. Med. Child. Neurol. 1971.13.279.
36. Macfaul, R., Dorner, S., Brett, E. M., Grant, D. B. Neurological abnormalities in patients treated for hypothyroidism from early life. Arch. Dis. Child. 1978.53.611.
37. McFie, J., Robertson, J. Psychological test-results of children with thalidomide deformities. Dev. Med. Child Neurol. 1973.15.719.
38. Martin, H. P., Fischer, H. L., Martin, D. S., Chase, H. P. The development of children with transient neonatal tyrosinemia. J. Pediatr. 1974.84.212.
39. Matsumoto, A., Watanabe, K., Negoro, T. et al. Long term prognosis after infantile spasms; a statistical study of prognostic factors in 200 cases. Dev. Med. Child Neurol. 1981.23.51.
40. Melyn, M. A., White., D. T. Mental and developmental milestones of non-institutionalised Down's syndrome. Pediatrics. 1973.52.542.
41. Meney, M. A., White, D. T. Mental and developmental milestones of non-institutionalised Down's syndrome. Pediatrics. 1973.52.542.
41. Money, J., Clarke, F. C., Beck, J. Congenital hypothyroidism and IQ increase; a quarter century follow up. J. Pediatr. 1978.93.432.
42. Newburger, J. W., Silbert, A. R., Buckley, L. P., Fyler, D. C. Cognitive function and age at repair of transposition of the great arteries in children. N. Engl. J. Med. 1984.310.1495 (Annotation 1527).
43. Ratcliffe, S. G. Speech and learning disorders in children with sex chromosome abnormalities. Dev. Med. Child Neurol. 1982.24.80.
44. Robinow, M., Roche. A. F. Low set ears, J. Am. Med. Assoc. 1973.125.482.
45. Rose, A. L., Lombroso, C. T. Neonatal seizure states. Pediatrics 1970.45.404.
46. Ryan, C., Vega, A., Drash, A. Cognitive deficits in adolescents who developed diabetes early in life. Pediatrics. 1985.75.921.
47. Seashore, M. R., Friedman, E., Novelly, R. A., Bapat, V. Loss of intellectual function in children with phenylketonuria after relaxation of dietary phenylalanine restriction. Pediatrics. 1985.75.226.
48. Sibinga, M. S., Friedman, C. J. Diet therapy and other sources of influence on the outcome of children with phenylketonuria. Dev. Med. Child Neurol. 1972.14.445.
49. Siegel, F. S., Balow, B., Fisch, R. O., Anderson, V. E. School behavior profile ratings of P.K.U. children. Am. J. Ment. Def. 1968.72.937.
50. Smith I., Lobascher, M. E., Stevenson, J. E., Wolff. O. H., Schmidt, H., Gruber-Kaiser, S., Bichel, H. Effect of stopping low phenylalanine diet on intellectual progress of children with phenylketonuria. Br. Med. J. 1978.2.723.
51. Smith, I., Wolff, O. H. Natural history of phenylketonuria and influence of early treatment. Lancet. 1974.2.540.
52. Stewart-Brown, S., Haslum, M. N., Butler, N. Educational attainment of 10 year old children with treated and untreated visual defects. Dev. Med. Child Neurol. 1985.27.504.
53. Stores, G. Cognitive function in epilepsy. Br. J. Hosp. Med. 1971.6.207.
54. Tenbrink, M. S., Stroud, H. W. Normal infant born to a mother with phenylketonuria. J. Am. Med. Assoc. 1982.247.2139.
55. Thake, A., Todd, J., Bundey, S., Webb, T. Is it possible to make a clinical diagnosis of the fragile X syndrome in a boy? Arch. Dis. Child. 1985.60.1001.
56. Townes, P. L. Fragile x syndrome. Am. J. Dis. Child. 1982.136.389.
57. Virtanen, M., Mäenapaá, J., Santavuori, P. Congenital hypothyroidism: age at start of treatment versus outcome. Acta Paediatr. Scand. 1983.72.197.
58. Walzer, S. X chromosome abnormalities and cognitive development. Implications for understanding normal human development. J. Child Psychol. Psychiatry. 1985.26.177.

16

The diagnosis of cerebral palsy

The difficulties

The diagnosis of cerebral palsy in the first year is regarded by some as a matter of great difficulty. For instance, Scherzer[9] wrote that 'the spastic type of cerebral palsy is not apparent usually before 1 year to 18 months of age'. In fact cerebral palsy of the spastic type, except in mild cases, can be readily diagnosed in the first few days of life. I have seen an obvious case on the second day of life, and filmed and followed up cases diagnosed on the fourth and fifth day of life. The rigid form can be readily diagnosed in the earliest infancy. The athetoid form cannot usually be diagnosed early, because one cannot be sure of the diagnosis until athetoid movements develop, which may not be for 1 or 2 years after birth. Congenital ataxia cannot be diagnosed until about 6 months, because it is dependent on certain purposive movements not found before then: but tremor can be diagnosed early, certainly by the time the baby is able to sit.

It would be profitable to begin by enumerating the main difficulties in early diagnosis.

1. There are all grades of severity of cerebral palsy, from the severe form diagnosed readily in the newborn period, to the mildest form, which is first brought to the doctor's attention at 9 or 10 years, on account of clumsiness.

It can be extremely difficult to diagnose mild degrees of spasticity in early infancy. Signs may be equivocal for several months before it finally becomes clear that disease is present. Brisk knee jerks may be thought to be within normal limits, but with the passage of time it becomes clear that they are pathological. It is impossible to draw the line between normal and abnormal, and to say, for instance, whether brisk tendon jerks or slight hypertonia are normal or otherwise. Sometimes one has to be prepared to wait and see — in order to determine whether a child is affected or not. In the majority of cases, the diagnosis is obvious in the early days or weeks of life.

2. There are several types of cerebral palsy, each with its own features. Using the American Academy of Cerebral Palsy classification these are the spastic form, athetosis, rigidity, ataxia, tremor, atonic form and mixed types.

3. The diagnosis is greatly complicated by the wide range of levels of intelligence, and particularly by the frequency with which mental subnormality is found. Mental subnormality alone has a profound effect on the developmental pattern.

4. The delayed appearance of signs of cerebral palsy, particularly signs of athetosis. As babies grow older, certain signs become more obvious.

5. The occasional disappearance of signs of cerebral palsy. One sometimes detects signs of the spastic form of cerebral palsy in early infancy and finds that these signs gradually disappear. A colleague saw a boy who was born after precipitate delivery at term, weighing 3175 g, and who was well in the newborn period. He began to smile and to watch his mother at 2

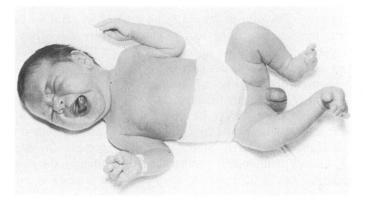

Fig. 150 Full-term normal newborn baby, flexed position.

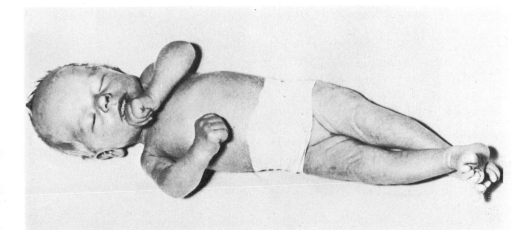

Fig. 151 Abnormal appearance of child aged 8 days. Hands tightly closed. The legs tend to cross and they are unusually extended. Knee jerks normal. Cerebral haemorrhage. Severe convulsions age 3 days.

weeks. The mother noticed right-sided ankle clonus at the age of 2 weeks, and an experienced doctor confirmed its presence. It could be triggered by just touching the feet in the direction of dorsiflexion. When the boy was 5 weeks of age clonus disappeared, and the baby walked alone without help at $8\frac{1}{2}$ months, being normal. I have many times seen considerably exaggerated tendon jerks and even persistent well-marked ankle clonus in the early weeks disappear as children grew older, so that on follow-up they were normal. But it is true to say that though well-marked signs may completely disappear, the more marked they are, and the longer they persist in the early weeks, the less the likelihood that recovery will be complete.

I have been able to follow an example from birth to the age of 14 years. In the newborn period and subsequently in the first year of life the boy had an obvious left hemiplegia. The left upper limb was not used at all for the first few months. The arm improved as he grew older, and by the age of 5 or 6 years the sole remaining sign of cerebral palsy was a left extensor plantar response. There was no spasticity of the leg. The hand was normal. There were no other abnormal signs.

André-Thomas[1] described several examples of the disappearance of signs of cortical injury, especially hemiplegia, and emphasised that on that account prognosis must always be guarded and that examinations must always be repeated. Minkowski,[7] using the André-Thomas method of examination, divided 74 newborn babies into three groups, (*a*) normal (25 infants), (*b*) minor neurological abnormalities (43 infants), (*c*) gross neurological abnormalities (6 infants). On re-examination 2 years or more later,

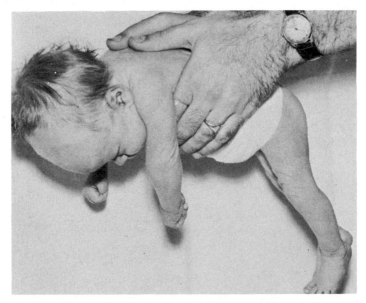

Fig. 152 Cerebral palsy. Head held up quite well, but arms and legs not flexed.

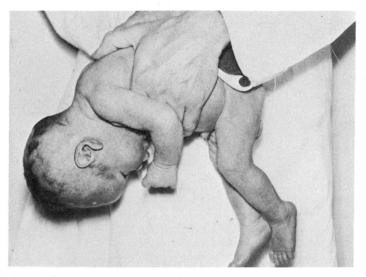

Fig. 153 A case of proved cerebral palsy at six weeks.

of the 25 who were normal in the newborn period, 19 were normal subsequently and six had minor but temporary problems (such as ocular defects and delayed walking): of 43 in Group B (showing minor neurological signs in the newborn period), 22 were normal subsequently: 18 had minor neurological handicaps, but three had serious sequelae. Of six who showed serious neurological signs in the newborn period, three continued to show severe sequelae on follow-up, while the remainder showed trivial and temporary neurological signs.

Solomons, Holden and Denhoff[10] described 12 infants who showed abnormal neurological signs in the first year, and who had been followed for a period of 1–3 years, during which time all abnormal signs disappeared.

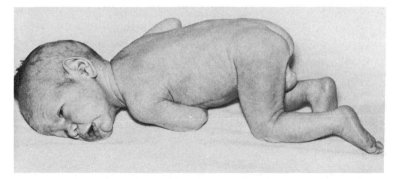

Fig. 154 Defective head control. Inadequate extension of hips and flexion of knees. Same boy as Figure 153. Pelvis rather high for the age.

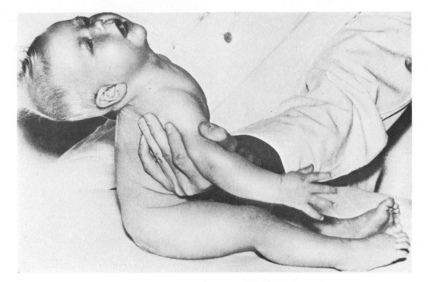

Fig. 155 Severely mentally subnormal child with spastic quadriplegia, aged 6 months, showing severe head lag on being pulled to the sitting position.

One pays much less attention to single signs than to a combination of signs. For instance, one would pay little attention to some degree of hypertonia alone, but one would pay much more attention to a combination of hypertonia and delayed motor development, or an unusually small head circumference. One pays much less attention to delayed motor development alone than one does to delayed motor development combined with delayed social responsiveness (late smiling), or a small head circumference. Cerebral palsy is not diagnosed merely on the basis of exaggerated knee jerks, or ankle clonus or hypertonia without other abnormal signs.

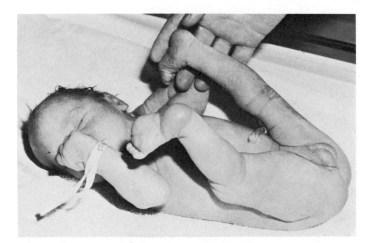

Fig. 156 Breech with extended legs. Age 10 days. Note the posture.

The difficulties in the early diagnosis, the impossibility of drawing the line between normal and abnormal in some cases (with particular reference to the knee jerks and abduction of the hip), and especially the occasional disappearance of signs of cerebral palsy, make it essential not to tell the mother about one's suspicions until one is certain about the diagnosis and the permanence of the condition. Continued observation is essential in all but the severe cases.

The child at risk

Certain prenatal and natal conditions place a child 'at risk' of cerebral palsy. They include:

Family history of cerebral palsy
Prematurity, especially extreme
Multiple pregnancy
Low birthweight in relation to the duration of gestation
Mental subnormality
Severe hypoxia, convulsions, hyperbilirubinaemia or cerebral haemorrhage in the newborn period.

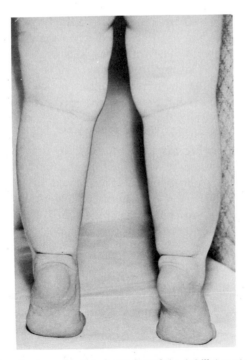

Fig. 157 Toe walking due to congenital shortening of the Achilles tendon. There is also a constriction band.

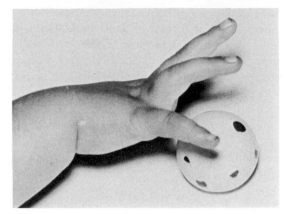

Fig. 158 Typical spastic approach to object.

Diagnosis of any form of cerebral palsy

The diagnosis must be made, as always, on the basis of the history, the examination, and the interpretation of one's findings.

The history includes the 'risk factors'. There are several genetic forms of cerebral palsy, spastic or athetoid;[8] I have seen many examples of it, and enquiry should always be made about the family history.

The mother may herself have noticed that the baby feels stiff, or is stiff on one side, or keeps one hand clenched when the other is open, or does not kick the legs properly. The baby may kick both legs together, instead of reciprocal kicking. The mother may have noticed that when the baby creeps, one leg trails after the other. She may notice that the child consistently refuses to use one hand. She may give a clear history of 'dissociation' — meaning in this context that there is severe retardation in gross motor development, such as sitting, while the baby is more advanced in other fields of development. For instance, she may say that the child can readily pick up a currant between the tip of the forefinger and the tip of the thumb, but cannot nearly sit unsupported. This would immediately suggest an abnormality of muscle tone — hypotonia or hypertonia. There is likely to be a history of delay in reaching other milestones of development, because of the commonly associated mental subnormality.

Spastic form

After taking the history, the diagnosis is made on the *developmental examination*. In summary, the following are the essential points:

First 3 months

1. If newborn, note the quantity of his movement, for the spastic child

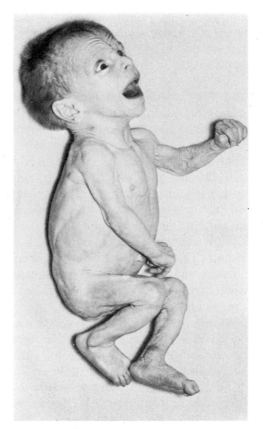

Fig. 159 Kernicterus, aged 2 weeks.

tends to be relatively immobile. If he has spastic quadriplegia he may lie with his limbs unduly extended, and his hands unusually tightly closed. After about 3 months the hands should be predominantly loosely open. A hemiplegic child would be likely to have one hand tightly closed and the other open, and there will be asymmetry of movement.

2. Observe the child, his head size and shape, his facial expression, his alertness and interest in his surroundings. A small head circumference in relation to the weight is common because of the frequency of associated mental subnormality. Because of the frequent mental subnormality, there is often a lack of normal alertness and responsiveness.

3. Hold the child up with your hands in his axilla. There may be abnormal extension of the hip and knees (or asymmetry), and the legs may cross.

4. Hold in ventral suspension. There is usually delayed motor development and so there will be excessive head lag. The arms and legs commonly hang down lifelessly without the flexion of the elbows and knees and slight hip extension seen in the normal child.

Some infants show apparently good or even advanced head control in ventral suspension and in the prone position, due to excessive extensor tone, and so give the wrong impression of having advanced motor development: but on pulling the child to the sitting position from the supine, the gross head lag is obvious. It is incorrect to term the head lag 'hypotonia'.

5. Place him in the prone position, in order to assess maturation. The spastic infant commonly assumes an immature position owing to the mental subnormality, but may show excessive extensor tone, as above.

6. Place him in the supine position. Note the symmetry or asymmetry of the kick. Note whether the hands are equally open or closed. Assess muscle tone by feeling the muscles, assessing the resistance to passive movement, assessing the range of movement, and shaking the limbs (for passivité), when holding the arm below the elbow and leg below the knee. Assess the range of movement especially in the hips (after flexing them to a right angle) and in dorsiflexion of the ankle. When doing this, test for ankle clonus. Test the knee jerks — beginning to tap over the dorsum of the ankle, and the bicep jerks, beginning to tap over the shoulder: for when they are exaggerated, the area over which the reflex is obtained is greatly increased.

8. Pull him to the sitting position in order to assess head lag. Sway him gently from side to side in order to determine the degree of head control (passitivé). When he is being pulled up into the sitting position, have the hand in the popliteal space in order to detect spasm of the hamstrings. When a child is spastic one feels a resistance to pulling him up to the sitting position and the knees may flex: one can see this and feel the

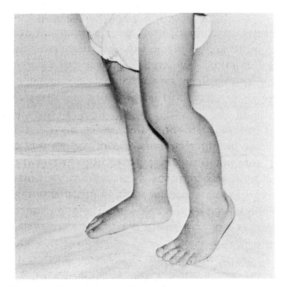

Fig. 160 Child with mild left hemiplegia. Toe walking.

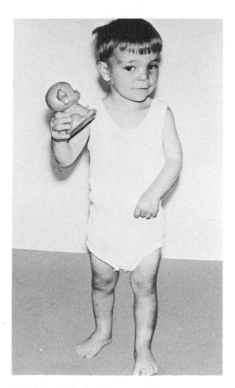

Fig. 161 Child with mild left hemiplegia. Characteristic arm posture.

spasm of the hamstrings. When leaned forward he repeatedly falls back, because of spasm of the erector spinae, glutei and hamstrings. When he is pulled up to the sitting position, he may rise to his feet, because of excessive extensor tone, and give the wrong impression of advanced weight bearing. The true diagnosis is revealed by the other signs of excessive tone, mentioned above, the exaggerated knee jerks, the ankle clonus, and reduced abduction of the hip and ankle dorsiflexion, with head lag when he is pulled up.

9. Measure his head circumference and relate this to his weight.
   At the end of this period, persistence of the Moro reflex, grasp reflex and asymmetrical tonic reflex, point to the diagnosis. They should have disappeared by 2 to 3 months.

Four to 8 months

1. Observe the child, as in the case of the younger infant, noting the quality, quantity and symmetry of movement.
2. Give the child a 1-inch cube to go for. This may reveal the typical spastic approach, unilateral if he has hemiplegia, with the slow characteristic

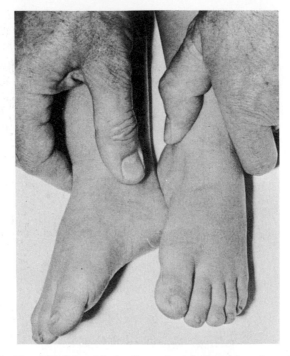

Fig. 162 Child with mild left hemiplegia. Shortening of affected leg, shown by position of left internal malleolus in relation to the right, when the child is lying on his back with the legs fully extended. Thumbs on internal malleoli.

dorsiflexion of the wrist with splaying out of the fingers as he approaches the object, often with ataxia and tremor. In a mild case this may be missed, but careful observation of the two hands shows the difference in the two sides in a hemiplegic child. It is different from the ataxic approach of the athetoid child, who does not show the wrist dorsiflexion and splaying out of the fingers. One can usually make the diagnosis of spastic hemiplegia at a glance when the child reaches for an object and grasps it: but one confirms the diagnosis by the other tests enumerated.

3. Hold the child up with your hands in his axilla, in order to determine whether there is excessive extension of the legs. Test in ventral suspension and the prone position, as above.

4. Place him in the supine position. Note undue closure of one hand (as in hemiplegia). Note the symmetry of the kick. Test the knee jerks, the degree of hip abduction and ankle dorsiflexion, and test for ankle clonus. Elicit the plantar response which in a normal child (or in an athetoid or ataxic child) is flexor. The most sensitive area for it is the distal half of the outer side of the foot. One tests with the thumb, and *never* with a pin or key, which hurt. Do not convey the stimulus across the sole of the foot, for this confuses by introducing the plantar grasp reflex, which is flexor. When in doubt squeeze the calf muscles (Gordon's sign)

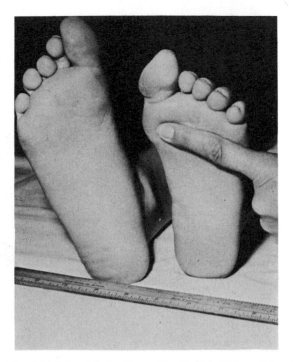

Fig. 163 Child with mild left hemiplegia. Shortening of affected leg as shown by relative position of the heels when the legs are fully extended.

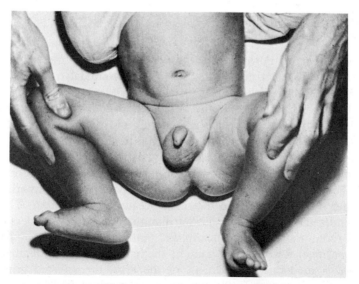

Fig. 164 Child with mild left hemiplegia. Limited abduction of left hip, owing to hypertonia.

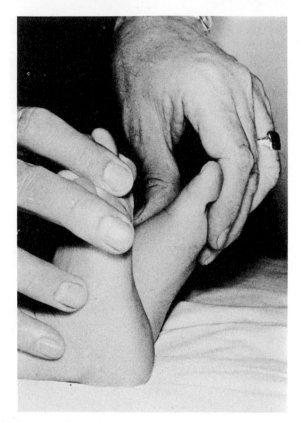

Fig. 165 Child with mild left hemiplegia. Limited dorsiflexion of left foot, owing to hypertonia and perhaps some shortening of the Achilles tendon.

or stroke firmly down the tibia (Oppenheim's sign): these signs depend merely on the fact that in disease of the pyramidal tract the area over which the reflex is obtained is increased. Pull him to the sitting position, as before. As before, note the resistance to pulling him up (because of spasm of the erector spinae and glutei) and the repeated falling back when placed sitting forward. Note shortening of the limb if there is hemiplegia. See that the child is lying flat and straight on the couch, and bring the malleoli together, to see if one leg is shortened. From the end of the couch note whether the heels are parallel — or whether one is higher up the couch than the other because of shortening. The foot of a hemiplegic limb may be smaller than the normal foot. Unless the child and room are warm, the hemiplegic limb is cold as compared with the normal one: feel with the palm of the hand. If there is hemiplegia and there is moderate involvement of the arm, the affected arm will be shorter, and except in a warm room, relatively cold as compared with the normal side.

5. Note signs of general retardation.
6. Measure the head circumference.
7. Check the hearing.

Nine months onwards

1. Observe for the same signs.
2. Offer the child a pellet of paper and 1-inch cubes and if he is old enough, get him to build a tower. In trivial cases the ataxia or tremor may be slight and readily missed: there may be merely slight clumsiness in building the tower. Give him beads to thread: a timed bead threading test may reveal slight neurological involvement. One can frequently make the diagnosis at a glance as he tries to pick up a pellet of paper; if he has a hemiplegia the difference in the use of the two hands is immediately obvious. One then confirms the diagnosis by the other tests, such as the estimation of muscle tone by shaking the limb, the tendon jerks and the range of movement in the hip and ankle. As before, pull him up to the sitting position to feel for the resistance when he is pulled up, and to feel the spasm of the hamstrings.
3. If the child is standing or walking, note toe walking and note the gait. Note shoe wear.
4. If old enough (over 3) get him to stand on one foot. This is a sensitive

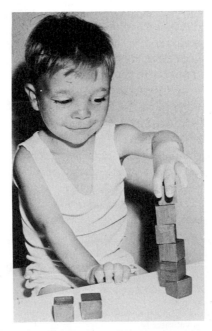

Fig. 166 Child with mild left hemiplegia. Typical splaying out of affected hand when building a tower of bricks.

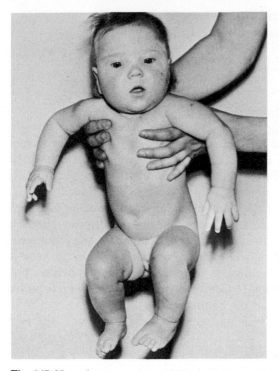

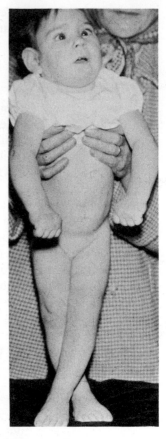

Fig. 167 Normal posture when child is held by hands in the axilla.

Fig. 168 Spastic child, hands holding child in the axilla — legs cross owing to adductor spasm, hands clenched.

test, in the case of hemiplegia immediately showing the difference in the two sides.

5. Note signs of general retardation. Measure the head circumference.

These are the basic signs of the spastic form of cerebral palsy. In a busy clinic, it would take perhaps 2 or 3 minutes to carry out the tests described.

The following is a typical case history of a mentally retarded child with cerebral palsy of the spastic type:

Case report.
This boy was born at term by normal delivery and was well in the newborn period. The subsequent course can be summarised as follows:

4 weeks	I wrote, 'Note the immature prone position. Suggestion of spasticity in lower limbs, but hands loosely open.'
6 weeks	'Very primitive in prone position. Poor head control.'
9 weeks	Smiles.
14 weeks	Vocalising. Following with eyes.
6 months	Grasping voluntarily.
15 months	Sitting, no support.
18 months	Single words beginning.

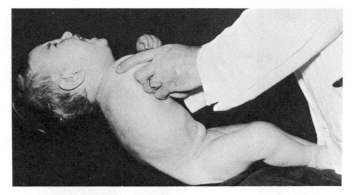

Fig. 169 Spastic child being pulled to sitting position — knees flex because of muscle spasm.

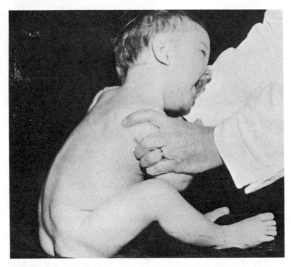

Fig. 170 Spastic child pulled further to sitting position — spasm of hamstrings causing marked flexion of knee. If his support is removed when in this position, he repeatedly falls back because of extensor tone.

2 years	Walk, no help — no sphincter control. Cannot feed self. Concentration defective. Would do nothing with cubes.
3 years	Words together.
5½ years	IQ 47.
	Very mild right hemiplegia, with mental subnormality.

Athetosis

It is virtually impossible to make a definite diagnosis of athetosis until the athetoid movements are seen, and these may be delayed for some years, though I have seen them in the first week. The condition may be suspected

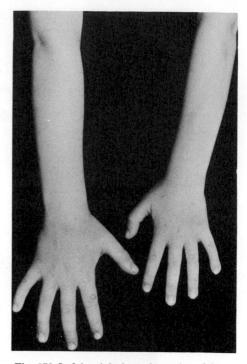

Fig. 171 Spastic child who has risen to standing position while being pulled to sit, due to excessive extensor tone.

Fig. 172 Left hemiplegia — shortening of the left arm.

because of one of the conditions known to place the child at risk of athetosis — particularly severe hypoxia or hyperbilirubinaemia. When those 'risk' conditions occurred, it is easy to imagine that the child has athetoid movements, when the movements are the normal arm and leg movements.

The signs of kernicterus appear not later than the sixth day in a full-term baby, or the tenth day in a preterm baby; the signs are a high pitched cry, rolling of the eyes, opisthotonos, refusal of feeds, hypertonia, tightly-clenched fists, loss of the Moro reflex and possibly fits or apnoeic attacks. The infant may characteristically extend the elbows and pronate the wrists. There may be excessive extensor tone, so that there is severe head lag when the child is pulled from the supine to the sitting position, while there is apparently good head control in the prone or ventral suspension. Rhythmical tongue thrusting is often an early feature, and sucking and swallowing difficulties are common. In the early weeks there are usually signs of delayed motor development (and often other signs of more general retardation), sometimes with attacks of opisthotonos. Athetoid movements may be observed anytime after the first 6 months (and possibly sooner), but more often after the first year. As they are difficult to be certain about, opinions as to when they first appeared are open to doubt. My view is that

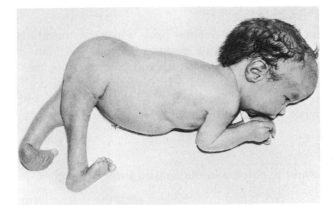

Fig. 173 Arthrogryposis — somewhat resembling spasticity.

the earliest suspicious sign of the development of athetosis is ataxia on reaching out for objects — a movement quite different from the splaying out of the hands when a spastic child is reaching for a toy. After the first year there is usually difficulty in vertical gaze, enamel hypoplasia of the deciduous teeth and high tone deafness. The plantar responses and knee jerks are normal in athetosis, because the pyramidal tract is not involved.

It would be wrong and irrational to suppose that kernicterus is clinically an all or none condition. Often, after neonatal hyperbilirubinaemia, the only sequela is slight developmental retardation and possibly high tone deafness. Even if a child proves to have an IQ of 100 after neonatal hyperbilirubinaemia, no one can say whether his IQ would have been much higher if severe jaundice had been prevented.

Not all athetoids had previous hyperbilirubinaemia. The signs after the newborn period are mainly developmental delay (though this is not always present), followed by ataxia on reaching out for objects, followed by the development of athetoid movements.

Though many will disagree with me, I regard the diagnosis of mixed forms of cerebral palsy as usually incorrect. The characteristic awkwardness of the hands of a spastic child are commonly thought to be 'athetoid'.

Rigidity

The rigid form is diagnosed by the extreme rigidity of all limbs, in the absence of signs of disease of the pyramidal tract, such as increased tendon jerks, ankle clonus, positive stretch reflex, and extensor plantar response. It is almost always associated with a severe degree of mental subnormality.

Ataxia

The ataxic form is diagnosed by the ataxia in the child's approach to an object, and ataxia in sitting and walking.

Hypotonic form of cerebral palsy

This is a very rare form of cerebral palsy which can readily be confused with the hypotonias. Almost all infants with this condition are mentally subnormal.[6] The circumference of the skull is likely to be small. There is an increased range of movement. Fits occur in a third. The plantar responses are extensor and the knee jerks are exaggerated, so that benign congenital hypotonia and the Werdnig-Hoffmann syndrome can be readily excluded.

Confusion about hypotonia in the spastic form of cerebral palsy

One frequently hears it said that children with the spastic form of cerebral palsy are commonly or even usually 'hypotonic' in the early months. I disagree with this. I understand why the excessive head lag usually seen in spastic infants in the early weeks (as in Fig. 155) is thought by some to indicate hypotonia: but examination of the rest of the child (e.g. for the range of hip abduction or ankle dorsiflexion) readily demonstrates the hypertonicity.

The clumsy child

There are all gradations between the normal and the abnormal, and it is impossible to draw the line between the two. Not all clumsy children should be included in the section on cerebral palsy, but it is likely that many clumsy children are examples of that condition. The intelligence of the clumsy child may be average or superior but it is more often below average. Gubbay[3] found that 56 of 1000 Australian school children were 'clumsy'. In another study[4] he wrote that 5% of normal school children have significant problems owing to clumsiness.

Clumsy children are usually regarded as normal for several years, and then they begin to get into trouble at school or worry their parents because of their awkwardness. Mothers commonly say that the child 'falls a lot', 'always has bruises on his legs', is 'awkward with his hands', 'cannot pedal a cycle', and say that the teacher complains that 'his writing is bad', or that 'he doesn't seem to hold his pencil properly'.

The child is accused of being lazy, careless, or badly behaved. He is poor at sport, and as a result often unpopular: he is ridiculed because of his poor performance in physical exercise; he is often unhappy and insecure as a result. He is described by some as a 'motor moron', or as having 'congenital maladroitness', or 'minimal birth injury'. He tends to misjudge distances, as when passing through a doorway, and to break objects more than others.

Clumsiness is often associated with poor concentration, distractibility, overactivity, visuospatial difficulties, difficulty in right-left discrimination and later in learning disorders, and the attention deficit disorder.

Clumsiness may be a mere normal variation. It may be a familial feature. It may be due to delayed maturation: all normal babies are clumsy in the early days of the development of motor skills, but they lose their clumsiness as they mature. Mentally subnormal children are later than normal ones in losing this clumsiness; and otherwise normal children may be later than others in losing it, presumably because of slow maturation. Emotional factors, such as ridicule or unjustified criticism at home or school increase the clumsiness; he is expected to be clumsy, and he is.

Malnutrition in utero or in the early months after delivery may lead to clumsiness (Ch. 2). In a Swedish study,[2] 65 children aged 5 to 6, born to mothers of a mean age of 39.4 years, fared significantly less well in attentiveness, fine motor coordination and visuoperceptual function than 55 children of the same age born to younger mothers whose mean age was 27.9 years. Other causes include the following:

Abnormalities of muscle tone: hypotonia, hypertonia
Hyperextensible joints
Muscular dystrophy
Hypothyroidism
Visual defects
Side effects of drugs: alcohol, amitriptyline, antihistamines, anti-epileptic drugs, chlordiazepoxide, colistin, cyclopentolate, diazepam, diphenoxylate, indomethacin, meprobamate, niclosamide, nitrazepam, piperazine, polymyxin, streptomycin, vincristine
Poisons — lead, mercury, solvent sniffing
Postraumatic, postencephalitis, cerebral tumour etc.
Rare diseases and syndromes: degenerative diseases of the nervous system, lipoidoses, chorea, leucodystrophies, ataxia-telangiectasia, Klippel-Feil syndrome, agenesis of the corpus callosum, platybasia, cerebral gigantism, familial dysautonomia, a-beta-lipoproteinaemia, phenylketonuria, Hartnup disease, argininosuccinicacidaemia.

Clumsiness is detected by asking the child to build a tower of 1-inch cubes, so that one can note tremor or ataxia as he builds. He may be asked to hop, skip, stand on one foot (if old enough — after the third birthday), to walk on a ledge, button his clothes, to clap his hands and then catch or throw a ball, to roll a ball with a foot, to fasten a shoe lace, thread beads, do the Goodenough Draw-a-man test or the Goddard Formboard test; he may be asked to screw a bolt, copy a square, triangle or diamond. He achieves a better score on the Wechsler verbal scale than on the performance scale. His overall IQ score may be above average; perhaps more often it is slightly below average. In some there are minimal signs of athetosis or of disease of the pyramidal tracts (in the form of an extensor plantar response).

In an Australian study,[5] 24 children were re-examined 8 years after the original diagnosis. Those originally with mild or moderate clumsiness were normal on follow-up, but the more severely affected initially were still clumsy.

From the point of view of developmental assessment, the condition is important because of the frequency with which these children are wrongly thought to be mentally subnormal. As always, one has to assess a child not on the question of whether he can do a given test, but on the way in which he does it.

Differential diagnosis

1. *Mental subnormality*. By far the greatest difficulty in diagnosis lies in the differentiation of cerebral palsy in association with mental subnormality from mental subnormality alone. The two conditions are frequently associated. It follows that when signs of mental subnormality are found, a thorough search for signs of cerebral palsy should always be made.

2. *Isolated motor retardation*. It is easy to confuse mild diplegia with isolated motor retardation. I have myself made this mistake.

> *Case report.* I was asked, by a paediatrician, Dr R. Gordon, to see a child of 10 months of age on account of defective head control and suspected cerebral palsy. There was no retardation in other fields. Diplegia was suspected, but although the knee jerks were brisk, I mistakenly decided that they were within normal limits. There was no adductor spasm in the thigh muscles. He learned to sit without support at 14 months, to feed himself with a cup at 18 months, and to join words together at 23 months. I saw him at intervals, but it was not until he was over 3 years old that it became obvious that the plantar responses were extensor. He had no deformity.

3. *Voluntary resistance to passive movement*. The child may be thought to be spastic, whereas in fact he is merely resisting passive movement. This applies particularly to abduction of the hip.

4. *Abnormality of joints*. Limited abduction of hips may be due to congenital dislocation. I have myself made the mistake of diagnosing spasticity in a newborn baby who had notable limitation of movements of the joints due to punctate epiphyseal dysplasia. The limited movement of joints in arthrogryposis multiplex congenita might be confused with spasticity. A mentally subnormal or severely hypotonic child who constantly lies in one position may develop a muscle contracture which limits the abduction of the hips and may suggest spasticity.

5. *Unsteadiness of gait*. Children who are late in learning to walk are usually later than others in learning to walk steadily: many such children are referred to me as cases of cerebral palsy.

6. *Normal movements*. It is easy to confuse the normal movements of the arms and legs of a baby with those of athetosis, if he has had some condition such as severe neonatal jaundice, which leads one to look carefully for athetoid movements.

7. *Causes of toe-walking*. Most children with cerebral palsy of the spastic type sooner or later tend to walk on their toes: but toe-walking may be normal, for some children when learning to walk develop this habit. One

eliminates the diagnosis of cerebral palsy by determining that there are no other features of cerebral palsy; for instance, the muscle tone, tendon jerks and plantar responses are normal. When one holds the preterm baby in the standing position at the equivalent of term, he tends to stand on his toes. It occurs with congenital shortening of the Achilles tendon, muscular dystrophy, unilateral hip dislocation, autism and dystonia musculorum deformans. When a toe-walker is found to have limited dorsiflexion of the ankle, one flexes his knee; dorsiflexion will be normal if the cause is spasticity, but unchanged if the cause is congenital shortening of the Achilles tendon. Furthermore, if the cause is congenital shortening of this tendon, the range of abduction of the hip will be normal, the knee jerks will be normal, and the plantar responses will be flexor. There is little excuse for confusing the two, but I have often seen the mistake made.

8. *Congenital shortening of the gluteus maximus, gastrocnemius or of the hamstrings.* This makes it difficult for the child to sit, and delays sitting. The tendon jerks in these conditions are normal, thus eliminating the spastic form of cerebral palsy.

9. *Weakness of muscles due to myopathy, hypotonia or Erb's palsy.* In all these cases, weakness rather than stiffness would be detected. Erb's palsy rarely persists, and in the older child the characteristic grasp of the spastic hand, with the slow splaying out of the fingers, is different from the grasp of the child with Erb's palsy. The muscle tone elsewhere is normal. The knee jerks, hip abduction and ankle dorsiflexion are normal. It must be noted that a true monoplegia is exceedingly rare; hence if the child had a spastic hand, there will almost certainly be some involvement of the lower limb — but that involvement may be only trivial.

10. *Other causes of involuntary movements.* These include tremor, torsion spasm, spasmus nutans, chorea and tics. It is easy to confuse athetosis with ataxia, particularly in the infant, in whom the first sign of athetosis is ataxia, before the characteristic involuntary movements begin.

In torsion spasm the first sign is often hypertonicity of the calf muscles, leading to plantar flexion and inversion with adduction of the foot. Later torticollis develops, followed later by the typical torsion spasm.

Spasmus nutans can be confused with tremor, but the characteristic head nodding or twitching, with the peculiar habit of looking out of the corner of the eyes, should establish the diagnosis, and the movements are inhibited by looking fixedly at an object.

Athetosis should not be confused with the more irregular movements of Sydenham's or Huntington's chorea.

11. *Degenerative conditions of the nervous system.* It is easy to diagnose these on the grounds that no abnormality had been previously noted, when in fact there were neurological abnormalities which had not been looked for or recognised. The conditions at issue include the lipoidoses and leucoencephalopathies. Schilder's disease (encephalitis periaxalis) and multiple sclerosis may be confused with cerebral palsy of prenatal origin. Toxoplasmosis

may cause convulsions and spasticity, the real cause being missed. Phenyl-ketonuria rarely but occasionally causes spasticity.

12. *Abnormalities of the spinal cord.* These include diastematomyelia, syringomyelia and spinal dysraphism. Diastematomyelia is a congenital anomaly in which a spicule of bone transfixes the spinal cord, and leads to progressive paresis of the lower limbs. In about half of all cases a tuft of hair or congenital dermal sinus reveals the condition.

Syringomyelia may occur in later childhood. There is likely to be muscular atrophy, arthropathy, weakness or spasticity and dissociated anaesthesia.

Congenital absence of the sacrum causes weakness of the legs with absence of sphincter control.

Spastic paraplegia is rare; nearly always careful inspection of the use of the hands (e.g. in building a tower of cubes), or careful testing for exaggeration of the upper limb tendon jerks, reveals minimal upper limb involvement, so that the true diagnosis is spastic diplegia. If one is fully satisfied that the arms are normal, so that one is sure that the correct diagnosis is spastic paraplegia, one must be certain that the child has cerebral palsy and not a spinal lesion.

Spastic monoplegia is extremely rare: on careful examination one almost always finds abnormal signs in the other ipsilateral limb. In my own series of over 750 personally observed cases of cerebral palsy, I saw one possible case of spastic monoplegia.

13. *Other syndromes.* Cleidocranial dysostosis is characterised by absence of the middle third of the clavicle, allowing the shoulders to approximate anteriorly in the midline; it is sometimes associated with spasticity and mental subnormality.

Platybasia and other anomalies of the base of the skull may be associated with shortness of the neck, ataxia or hypotonia[11]

A final word about the spastic child

Though I have said it before, it is essential in developmental assessment to know what matters most and what matters least. For example, if one is asked to eliminate cerebral palsy of the spastic type in a 6-months old baby, and one saw that his hand movements were normal on reaching for and getting a 1 inch cube, and if there is no resistance on pulling him up to the sitting position, with no repeated falling back, and with the knees fully extended on the couch as he sat, and if there were full normal abduction of the hip, and normal dorsiflexion of the ankle, with plantar flexor responses, I would eliminate the spastic form of cerebral palsy. If I saw an older child, say 24 months old, building a tower of eight 1 inch cubes, with no unusual ataxia or tremor, and with a normal approach to each cube, I would know that his upper limbs were not spastic. In the same way if I saw a 9 or 10-months-old baby go for objects with the index finger, I would know, after a single glance, that he was mentally normal for the age. As for cerebral palsy of the spastic type, if it is so slight that one cannot be sure, then it will do no harm to wait and see again: one would say nothing to the mother, but see the child again at a suitable interval: he will not develop a deformity, such as dislocation of the hip. No treatment in such a mild case would make the slightest difference.

Summary

The diagnosis of cerebral palsy is never made on the basis of a single abnormality, but only on a combination of signs. The diagnosis is therefore not made on such a variant as isolated motor retardation, toe walking, brisk tendon jerks or ankle clonus.

Abnormal signs in the early weeks, such as marked ankle clonus, may disappear.

Excessive extensor tone is readily missed, but it is of great importance.

Spastic paraplegia is rare, and one has to be satisfied that spasticity confined to the lower limbs is not due to a spinal lesion. Spastic monoplegia is very rare.

The common confusion about plantar responses in infancy should be avoided. The plantar response in normal infants is flexor, as it is in athetosis.

One must not make the mistake of interpreting restricted joint movement as spasticity: there are other important causes (e.g. dislocation of a hip, muscle contracture).

A common mistake is the diagnosis of cerebral palsy when the apparent ataxia on walking is merely due to late motor development.

REFERENCES

1. André-Thomas, Dargassies Saint-Anne. Etudes neurologiques sur le neuveau-né et le jeune nourrisson. Paris. Masson and Perrin. 1952.
2. Gillberg, C., Rasmussen, P., Wahlström, J. Minor neurodevelopmental disorders in children born to older mothers. Dev. Med. Child Neurol. 1982.24.437.
3. Gubbay, S. S. The clumsy child. Philadelphia. Saunders. 1975.
4. Gubbay, S. S. The clumsy child. In: Rose, F. C. (Ed.) Paediatric neurology. Oxford. Blackwell. 1979.
5. Knuckey, N. W., Gubbay, S. S. Clumsy children: a prognostic study. Austr. Paed. J. 1983.19.9.
6. Lesny, I. The hypotonic forms of cerebral palsy. Cerebral Palsy Bull. 1960.2.158.
7. Minkowski, A. Personal communication. 1960.
8. Monreal, F. J. Consideration of genetic factors in cerebral palsy. Dev. Med. Child Neurol. 1985.27.325.
9. Scherzer, A. L. Current concepts and classification of cerebral palsy. Clinic. Proc. Children's Hosp. Nat. Med. Center. 1973.29.143.
10. Solomons, G., Holden, R. H., Denhoff, E. The changing pattern of cerebral dysfunction in early childhood. J. Pediatr. 1963.63.113.
11. Spillane, J. D., Pallis, C., Jones, A. M. Developmental anomalies in the region of the foramen magnum. Brain. 1957.80.11.

17

Assessment of suitability for adoption

I feel strongly that children should be assessed for adoption only by someone who is especially interested and experienced in the matter. This may be a child health clinic doctor who has specialised in the subject, or a paediatrician who is specially interested in it. It is a tragedy for both child and adopting parents if a mistake is made. No child should be rejected as being unsuitable for adoption without an expert seeing the child and agreeing with the diagnosis. It is a disaster for a child to be rejected for adoption on the basis of an incorrect diagnosis that the child is mentally subnormal or spastic.

When assessing a child's suitability for adoption it must be constantly remembered that the interests of the child are the primary consideration. Nevertheless, the interests of the adopting parents have to be considered, for they have a considerable bearing on those of the child. One has to try to prevent a mentally subnormal child being unwittingly adopted, in order to protect the adopting parents from a tragic disappointment, and to protect the adopted child from possible rejection. An important aim of the doctor is therefore the detection of a severe mental or physical handicap. It may be argued that one should attempt to match the child's developmental potential with that of the intelligence and social status of the adopting parents, as was done in Arnold Gesell's clinic in New Haven. This is a debatable aim, but it is difficult to deny that a child who is thought to be of slightly below average developmental potential would fit in better in the home of a manual labourer than in the home of professional parents.

A child a little below the average at 6-months might well prove to be above average if placed in a good loving stimulating home; if placed in a less good home, he may become further retarded. In the same way a mentally superior baby might not be expected to achieve his best if placed in a poor home. Admittedly, it is not the function of the paediatrician to choose the home for a baby; but in deciding whether a baby is suitable for adoption, he may be influenced in his decision by observing the sort of foster parent who wants to adopt. Gould[2] in his book on Stress in Children wrote that ideally it would be most desirable to match the abilities and temperament of the child to those of the adoptive parents. I am not sure that it would. I am not sure that it would be better for a neurotic mother to adopt a neurotic child. Knowing the importance of environmental factors in schizophrenia, it might well be better to try to place a child of a schizophrenic parent in a particularly calm and stable home.

The assessment is made, as always, on the basis of the history, the examination and the interpretation.

The history

The importance of a full history, prior to developmental examination, has already been described. It would be wrong to agree to any child being adopted without a proper history concerning the real parents, the pregnancy, birth-weight, duration of gestation, the delivery and the condition of the child in the newborn period. One must know whether there is a family history of hereditary diseases, such as AIDS, and particularly of degenerative diseases of the nervous system or of psychosis. One must know whether there is a history of illnesses during pregnancy, such as pre-eclampsia or antepartum haemorrhage, which increase the risk of abnormality in the child. One must know about any factor making the child 'at risk', or more likely than others, to be abnormal. The greatest 'risk' factor of all is probably extreme prematurity or a marked discrepancy between the birthweight and gestational age ('small for dates'), but it is essential that none of these factors should be given an exaggerated importance. For instance, a history of mental subnormality in a parent should certainly not be regarded as contraindicating the adoption of the child. A history of epilepsy in a mother should not prevent a child being adopted, for the genetic risk is only a small one. That risk would have to be fully understood by the adopting parents. I find a constant tendency to exaggerate the importance of these factors. The doctor who assesses the baby should note the factors carefully and keep them in proper perspective. He should then concentrate on assessing the child, and except in the case of degenerative diseases of the nervous system and psychoses he should be careful not to give the 'risk' factors more importance than they merit (Ch. 13), but if there is doubt, he will ask to see the child again say at 10 months, prior to clinching the adoption, in order that he can assess the rate of development.

The paediatrician may be asked for advice as to whether a normal child can be adopted into a home containing a mentally or physically handicapped child. There is no easy answer to this. If he is adopted it is likely that he will suffer in various ways. He may grow up to be embarrassed by his handicapped 'sibling': the mother may suffer physical, emotional and financial stress as a result of having a severely handicapped child, and so the adopted child may suffer: and there is likely to be favouritism for the handicapped child. The normal child may be held responsible for the handicapped child after the death of the parents. The decision must depend on the severity of the handicap and other family circumstances. Some adoption societies will now allow a child to be adopted into a home containing a handicapped child.

The examination and its timing

The age at which the assessment is made is of the greatest importance. Presumably grossly defective infants, such as those with microcephaly or Down's syndrome, will have been sifted out, and will therefore be unlikely to reach the doctor who is assessing babies for adoption.

There is much to be said for a doctor assessing all adoption babies at roughly the same age, so that he becomes thoroughly conversant with the developmental features of that age. There is not usually much difficulty in arranging this.

It is a serious mistake, which I have seen on several occasions, to attempt to assess a baby say at 6 weeks of age when he was born 6 or more weeks prematurely.

In my opinion the earliest age at which one should attempt to assess a full-term baby is 6 weeks. This is because it is relatively easy to assess the motor development at this age, and normal full-term babies have begun to smile at the mother's overtures and probably to vocalise. They will watch her intently as she speaks to them. It is the normal practice in Britain to place an infant at the age of 1 or 2 weeks in a foster home in which the foster parents are likely to adopt; and the age of 6 weeks would be a convenient one for assessment, giving the foster parents a little time in which to become acquainted with the baby. If one is doubtful about the development at this age, he should be reassessed at 6 months, but not sooner.

I have no doubt that it is much easier and safer to assess a baby at the age of 6 months, if this can be arranged. The difficulty lies in the foster parents' natural desire to clinch the adoption, and the fear that the real mother may change her mind and demand the return of the baby. At the age of 6 months one can readily assess the gross motor development, particularly in the sitting position; the child has begun (at 4 or 5 months) to reach out and grasp objects without their being put into the hand, and the maturity of the grasp can be assessed at 6 months. He begins to transfer objects from one hand to the other at this age. He begins to chew. He may have begun to imitate (e.g. a cough or other noise). His interest in his surroundings and determination can be observed. The maturity of his response to sound can be determined. For instance, he should immediately turn his head to sound.

If one is doubtful about the baby's development at 6 months, the best time to see him again is at 10 months. By this age he should be able to stand holding on to the furniture, and perhaps to walk, holding on to it; he may be able to creep; but much more important than this is the index finger approach to objects and finger thumb apposition. He should be able to wave bye bye and play patacake, and he should be helping his mother to dress him by holding his arm out for a coat or his foot out for a shoe.

In the first year the most difficult age for assessment is 2 to 4 months, and the next most difficult age is 8 to 9 months. This is because there are so few significant new milestones at these times. It is easy to make a mistake at 2 to 4 months in the assessment of motor development, and there are no useful new developments in manipulation or social behaviour. The same applies to some extent to the age of 8 to 9 months.

It is normal practice to place the child at 1 or 2 weeks in a foster home in which adoption is desired. It is wrong to place him in an institution from birth and retain him there for some weeks, because he is likely to suffer emotional deprivation and to be retarded as a result.

The possibly backward child

Would-be adopting parents have a right to know about the health history of the real parents, as far as it is known.[1] In the same way, if one is uncertain whether a baby is normal or not, the adopting parents must be told. They will then understand why one decides to see the baby again at usually a short interval in order to assess progress.

If the final verdict is that the child is backward, one has to try to assess the degree of backwardness. It is important to try to predict whether he will be educable in an ordinary school or a school for educationally subnormal children, and still more important to predict that he will not be suitable for education at school. Such predictions are fraught with great difficulties, and one must take all possible factors into account, including the head circumference in relation to his weight. The additional finding of cerebral palsy may simplify matters, if it is severe, or make it more difficult, if it is less severe. In all cases one has to state the position to the parents, making it clear, if one thinks it to be the case, that the child may make an unexpected improvement and even turn out to be normal. This will depend in large part on the head size.

Many foster parents, on being told that the child is thought to be backward, state unhesitatingly that they will adopt in any case. In one way this is desirable, because it would be a tragedy for the child if he were not adopted. In that case prolonged stay in the foster home is the best substitute for adoption. On the other hand, it is impossible for parents who have never had a mentally subnormal child to know all the implications of adopting such a child. They cannot know all that it involves. They cannot know what it is like to have a mentally subnormal child in the home, and have to watch him all the time for his own safety. They cannot really know the physical, social, emotional and financial stresses to which they will be exposed. At least they will not feel the guilt, disappointment and other attitudes which real parents feel when they find that their own child is subnormal. They will have little sense of shame when their neighbours and relatives see the child. They may be respected for their courage for knowingly adopting such a child. They will not expect too much of him, and yet they may always hope for some improvement. It is reasonable to suppose that a couple would not deliberately adopt a subnormal child unless they were the sort of people who would be likely to be able to cope with him.

If a child is of normal intelligence, and yet is found to be handicapped, there is no objection to the child being adopted, provided that the parents understand the implications as far as possible. Again, it would be a tragedy for the child if he were not adopted.

Current adopting practices now raise new problems — that of religion, that of the coloured child, and that of a child with mental or physical handicap.[3-6]

Genetic advice

The doctor who assesses the suitability of a baby for adoption frequently has to give genetic advice. Only an expert should do this. The common problems are as follows:

1. Incest. The overall risk of abnormalities in incestuous unions is probably somewhere between 30 and 60% (see Ch. 2).

2. Schizophrenia. The genetic factor probably acts by predisposing to schizophrenia under the influence of additional environmental factors. There is probably a 10% risk of the child developing it if a parent had it. The risk is much greater if both parents have schizophrenia. The difficulty is that if the grandparent had schizophrenia, the mother may not be old enough for one to know whether she has developed it. I have met a similar problem in the case of Huntington's chorea.

3. Manic depressive psychoses. The risk of the child developing it is about 12%. Again, the mother may not develop it until the age of 40 or 50.

4. Epilepsy. The genetic factor is only a small one. The risk of the child being affected is about 2.5%. The risk is much greater if both parents have epilepsy.

5. Degenerative diseases of the nervous system. If a sibling has a degenerative disease of the nervous system, or has had infantile spasms (which can be due to a wide variety of causes), the risk for the child who is being assessed for adoption is greatly increased. If a parent has a degenerative disease of the nervous system, again the risk to the child is considerable. The opinion to be given must depend on the exact diagnosis.

6. Mental subnormality. It is impossible to give sound genetic advice concerning a child being assessed for adoption who has a defective sibling unless a full investigation has been carried out on the defective child: one has to do one's best to eliminate the recessive and dominant conditions, because of the high risk to siblings.

7. Neurosis or alcoholism. These are probably in the main environmental in origin, and so there is no added risk of the child developing it.

It is the practice in Britain for adopting parents to be informed of the background of the real mother and father. Discretion must be shown in this matter. It is certain that the adopting parents must not hear for the first time in court about diseases such as syphilis or AIDS in the real mother or father.

Conclusion

Assessment of suitability for adoption is difficult, and a matter for the expert. If there is doubt as to whether a child is in all ways normal or not, the adopting parents must be fully informed. There will always be some risk in adoption. Parents having their own children have no certainty that their children will be normal, and cannot even choose the sex. But unless adopting parents are willing to take some risk, they should not adopt at all.

REFERENCES

1. Committee on adoption and dependent care. The rôle of the paediatrician in adoption with reference to 'the right to know'. Pediatrics. 1977.60.378.
2. Gould, F. Stress in children. London. Churchill. 1968.
3. Kornitzer, M. Adoption. London. Putnam. 1976.
4. Rowe, J. Parents, children and adoption. London. Routledge and Kegan Paul. 1966.
5. Tizard, B. Adoption: a second chance. London. Open Books. 1977
6. Wolkind, S. Medical aspects of adoption and foster care. Clinics in developmental medicine No. 74. London. Heinemann.

Summary and conclusions

1. All paediatricians and anyone else concerned with the care, examination and assessment of infants and children must know the normal variations which do not amount to disease, and must try to ascertain and understand the reasons for those variations.

2. They need to know the 'normal', better termed the 'average', for comparison with the child's development up to the time of the examination.

3. They need to know the normal variations in all aspects of development. They must know that these variations are so wide that they can never draw an absolute line between the normal and abnormal. It follows that centile distributions of milestones of development have little value — except only that the further away from the average a child is, the less likely is he to be 'normal'.

4. They should try to understand the reasons for variations in development — either in overall development or development in individual fields.

Development is a complex end result of genetic, prenatal and perinatal risk factors, especially preterm delivery, and postnatal factors.

It follows that like all clinical diagnoses, the developmental assessment and diagnosis must be based on the history, the examination, physical and neurological, special investigations where necessary, and the interpretation.

The history must include genetic factors (including familial patterns of development), prenatal factors such as infections and illnesses in pregnancy, drug taking, nutrition, haemorrhage and especially preterm delivery; it must include perinatal risk factors, and postnatal factors, depending on the age of the child: his development will be profoundly affected by his health, nutrition, personality, the quality of his home, friends and teaching, and the opportunities which he receives. All these factors must be considered in the overall assessment: if preterm delivery is not taken into account when assessing a baby, a gross error will be inevitable.

A full physical and neurological examination, including screening for hearing and vision, is essential in order that allowance can be made for factors which are unrelated to his innate level of intelligence. For instance, it would be absurd to include a score for weight-bearing by a 6 month old baby if he had paralysed legs with spina bifida, or if his speech was given a score, as part of his overall score, when he is deaf. If the physical examination does not include measurement of the head circumference in relation to his weight, a most important fact is omitted from the overall assessment.

The developmental examination in a busy clinic should be confined to those tests which matter: for purposes of research a fuller examination is likely to be used.

Special investigatons (in the case of the newborn), may include EEG, computerised axial tomography and ultrasound.

In order to reach an overall assessment, all the relevant facts obtained from the history and the examination have to be taken into consideration. It is essential to know that some fields of development are far more important for assessing the child's potential than others; and that some of the most important aspects of development are unscorable, while for some fields of development there are no norms: all that the experienced observer can do is to form a clinical impression from them. The examiner considers the many different patterns of development: slow progress at one stage of development may be followed by rapid progress in another, and vice versa. He does his best to guess the degree of reversibility of damage done by an unsatisfactory home, or illness such as meningitis, or head injury — and usually, when faced with such difficult problems, he sees the child again in order to determine progress.

The observer tries to understand the reasons for the variations in development: he knows not to ascribe a child's retardation or cerebral palsy to obvious perinatal factors, such as preterm or breech delivery, or asphyxia, but to look for the prenatal causes for the prematurity, abnormal presentation or the asphyxia.

The doctor, or anyone else who assesses development, needs to know the reasons for developmental assessment, the harm which can be done by it, and its limitations. As the child matures new fields of development become available for study; he knows not to expect high correlation between tests in infancy and subsequent IQ scores, because he knows that innumerable factors will affect the child's eventual achievements. One can determine quite a lot about a child's talents, but one cannot say what he will do with them.

In conclusion, it is not sensible to try to make a scientific assessment of an infant or child on a purely objective examination, without taking into full consideration all the features of the history and examination which have profound influence on a child's development but which are not directly related to his innate potential: and it is not enough merely to assess a child on purely objective tests without trying to understand the reasons for one's findings.

No doctor will become proficient in developmental assessment of children unless he follows them up in order to determine what mistakes he has made.

Index

Page numbers in italic indicate the principal references